4c Common Words	**4d** Super-latives	**4e** Present Tense	**4f** Triteness	**4g**	
4r Capital-izing	**4s** Abbrevi-ating	**4t** Titles	**4u** Figur		
4j Identify Persons	**4k** Authority Needed	**4l** Authority Techniques	**4m** Rambl Stor		
5b Foul Language	**5c** Exagger-ation	**5d** Facts Distorted	**5e** Fair	Party Politics	Abusing Law & Order
5j Disrespect for Others	**5k** Encouraging Gambling	**5l** Offensive Details	**5m** Libel	**5n** Invasion of Privacy	**13a** Newscasts, Preparing Copy
6c Tie-backs	**6d** Playing Up a **W**	**6e** Crowding Lead	**6f** Interpret-ing **W**'s	**7a** Several Fea-ture Summary	**7b** Salient Feature
7e Crucible Lead	**7f** Identifying Features	**7g** Summarizing Features	**8a** Variety in Rhetoric	**8b** Time-liness	**8c** Local Angle (Proximity)
11a Rewrites, No Additions	**11b** Rewrites, Additions	**11c** Follow-ups	**11d** Developing Story		
9a Logical Order	**9b** Single Feature Development	**9c** Several Feature Development	**9d** Lead Feature Abandoned	**9e** Summarize Minor Features	**9f** Summary Development
9i Multiple Casualty Story	**9j** Chronological Order	**9k** Direct Quotations	**9l** Transitional Devices	**9m** Repetitious Phrases	**9n** Block Paragraphs
10b Feature Article	**10c** Human Interest Story	**10d** Surprise Climax Story	**11a** Rewrites, No Additions	**11b** Rewrites, Additions	**11c** Follow-ups
12a Cutlines, No Story	**12b** Cutlines, Story	**12c** Cutlines, Features	**13b** Newscast Sentences	**13c** Newscast Language	**13d** Newscast Devices
15c Eliminate Puffs	**15d** Writing Brevities	**15e** Better Story Overlooked	**16a** Describe Speaker	**16b** Describe Audience	**16c** Emphasize Speech
16f Quote-Summary-Quote Form	**16g** Authority Omitted	**16h** Reporting Publications	**16i** Personal Interviews	**16j** Planning Questions	**16k** Describe Interviewee
17c Meeting Story Features	**17d** Convention Features	**17e** Special Occa-sion Features			

The Complete Reporter

THE
COMPLETE
REPORTER

A General Text in Journalistic Writing
and Editing, Complete with Exercises

JULIAN HARRISS and
STANLEY JOHNSON

The University of Tennessee

Second Edition

THE MACMILLAN COMPANY, NEW YORK
COLLIER—MACMILLAN LIMITED, LONDON

DEDICATED

TO THE MEMORY OF

STANLEY JOHNSON

(1892–1946)

A giant intellectual and a gentle idealist and philosopher who took the weight of the world on his shoulders and strove to push civilization forward with his immense writing talents. A charter member of the "Fugitive Group," whose works are highly regarded in the literary world. Author of two books on citizenship and editor of a third. Author of *Professor* and co-author of *The Complete Reporter*. A journalist, professor, and public relations director as well as a creative writer.

Preface

The revised and enlarged edition of *The Complete Reporter* retains the features which brought success for more than two decades to the first edition by the late Stanley Johnson and myself. However, this new edition is far better organized and substantially more complete than its predecessor, enhancing the book's test-proven value as the text for an institution offering only one year or one semester of journalism or as the first-year or beginning text for an institution offering more than one year.

The Complete Reporter has distinctively different qualities which appear in a practical approach to learning the basic principles and general techniques of journalistic writing. These principles and techniques are the essentials that must be mastered by the beginning newspaper reporter and that also apply to writers for all media of communications.

The learning approach employed by *The Complete Reporter* involves the content and organization of chapters in the text and the use of exercises which correlate theory and practice. The chapters carry the student gradually from the basic principles of journalism to the organizational patterns of journalistic stories, then to the gathering and writing of general, simple, complex, and special types of stories, and finally to those fundamentals of editing which even the beginning reporter should know. Based on the premise that journalism cannot be learned effectively in a lecture course, this approach puts emphasis on practice, and for that reason many exercises follow each chapter. Because practice is emphasized, a "Correction Key" is an integral part of the text to simplify and speed the work of teachers in correcting papers and to guide students in reviewing rules which they failed to observe.

Revisions and expansions in this new edition include three new chapters, a complete rewriting of four other chapters, a reorganization of chapters to introduce subject matter in proper sequence, a revision of exercises in all chapters, and an updating and polishing of the entire book. New chapters deal with the writing of newscasts for radio and television, with stories in the fields of education, research, and science, and stories on religion, philanthropy, and promotion. Chapters heavily rewritten and expanded are those dealing with journalistic vocations, with stories on business, industry, agriculture, and labor, critical reviews of literature and the arts, and with editorials and editorial columns. All other chapters were also revised and improved.

Exercises with each chapter have been not only heavily revised but also carefully designed to make greater use of materials presented in earlier chapters. Assignments on newscasts and pictures are added throughout the book, for example, and exercises that can be treated as features or human interest stories are also included. Written in a telegraphic English which requires the student to compose the sentences, these exercises also contain libel, unethical statements, and trivia which will constitute errors if used. Most important, many "think exercises" are included to require the student to use extra thought and effort in writing interpretative stories—the ultimate objective of complete reporting.

Acknowledgments

For assistance in revising *The Complete Reporter,* I owe a great debt to my friend and colleague, Professor W. C. Tucker, Director of The University of Tennessee School of Journalism. Any of Professor Tucker's students will bear witness that a paper he checks cannot undergo a more thorough correction, and he was kind enough to give my manuscript that degree of scrutiny.

Others who assisted materially were Neal O'Steen, Publications Editor of The University of Tennessee, who prepared some of the exercises; my son, Robert J., a young lawyer, who reviewed the legal sections; Mrs. Ruth Thomas, who typed the final manuscript; Mrs. Evelyn Brann, who typed some of the rough manuscript; my sons, David, who helped in proofreading, and Jerry, who duplicated pages; and my wife, Virginia, who assisted in researching, typing, and proofreading, and who also endured me for the year and a half while I was devoting most of my free time to this endeavor.

Julian Harriss
Knoxville, Tennessee

Contents

THE COMPLETE REPORTER

PART ONE

BECOMING ACQUAINTED WITH REPORTING

Before attempting the ultimate objective of gathering, writing, and editing the news, the reporter should acquaint himself with the fundamentals of his undertaking. He should learn the characteristics of journalism as a vocation, the newspaper as an organization, the news product, and the basic rules governing journalistic writing.

Both personnel and mechanical equipment are engaged in processing the news story from event to reader. Both have been shaped for this special purpose, and in turn they shape the news product. To attempt news writing without reference to these matters would deprive the exercise of its proper background and desirable realism.

A Fascinating Question

"What is news?" is a fascinating question that deserves consideration prior to the effort to write news. That no wholly satisfactory definition can be established need not discourage the reporter in this investigation. An electrical engineer must explore the nature of electricity while he achieves no more than working formulas. So the reporter should ground himself in theory to acquire a sense of direction and a facility in handling his subject matter. To attempt to write news with no conception of what news is would be something of an anomaly.

Developing News Style

The news style also deserves attention before the reporter commits himself to the actual task of writing—for the reason that he is to apply a facility already in his possession to slightly novel and slightly technical problems. A runner needs to know the rules of the track before he starts his race. The reporter will develop a news style to its perfection only through long practice, but even in the beginning he should fix his eyes upon certain ideals and objectives.

Restrictions

Also influencing the reporter when he sits down to write are the restrictions on what he may include in his story. Some of these restrictions are voluntary, recognized in journalism as codes of ethics observed for the welfare of both the press and society. Other restrictions are imposed by law, and violation of these may cost the reporter a fine or a term in prison. Observance of journalistic ethics and of laws pertaining to the written word are requisites of good reporting.

Chapter 1

So You Want To Be a Journalist?

IF you have had notions of becoming a journalist and living a life of glamour, excitement, and unlimited expense accounts as you outdo the Federal Bureau of Investigation in tracking down a hidden criminal, do not let anyone deprive you of this happy illusion. A journalist's fare can be glamorous and exciting, and he will spend hours on end tracking down hidden facts (probably without benefit of expense accounts). Of course, on some days his work will be so routine and exacting that it might be boring, but that is the calm before the storm. Those very interesting "news breaks" from time to time, when fast and furious work is required to meet publishing deadlines, will make up for any boredom. Journalists will not replace the FBI nor even the local police in "making the news"—but what other vocation can more closely share the exciting moments not only of the FBI and the police but also of the fire department, the Weather Bureau, the local and state governmental offices, the schools, the churches, the business houses and industries, and other groups that constitute a community?

A Writer on Current Events. A journalist is a writer whose stock in trade consists of current events. As contrasted with other types of writers who may employ imagination in their quest for reader appeal, the reporter must deal with facts. He records and sometimes interprets what has happened or will happen, and under certain circumstances he is permitted to give his own opinions on the events he reports. Hence, the two things basic to the journalist's work are facts and writing, and his two distinctive functions are gathering information and composing stories which present this information accurately and interestingly.

The foregoing definition of a journalist is also the description of a newspaper reporter, as indeed it should be. Reporting the news is fundamental to virtually all journalistic occupations, and the newspaper is the oldest and the principal channel through which news is widely disseminated. This does not imply, however, that careers in journalism are limited to the editorial staffs of newspapers. Other communications media offer as many or more different journalistic opportunities. But an analysis of the vocational aspects of journalism should begin with newspaper reporting—which historically pro-created all other species of modern journalistic careers and which has appeals and demands common to them all.

Reporting, Doorway to Many Vocations

The beginning or "cub" reporter may launch his career with the comforting thought that opportunities in many different vocations will be open to him in the future. Newspaper reporting offers a variety of experience, particularly in the practice of interviewing and writing, which will equip a person for success in a number of journalistic offshoots and also in many nonjournalistic enterprises.

Intangible Benefits. The common reward of all newspaper men and women is the close contact with what is usually called "life." The reporter has a front seat at a very great number of public events. He is an ex-officio member of public organizations and committees. He observes events in the making. He is on the "inside" of things in general. The motives, the ambitions, the cross-currents and cross-purposes of society at large are the plots of his narratives. The pattern of the news may need to be reported as a smooth woof upon a seamy warp, but if not all is to be reported, nevertheless all must be observed.

Exposure to reality ripens character as perhaps no other schooling can. The true reporter acquires both perspective and insight. He acquires breadth of vision and at the same time a scrupulous regard for detailed fact. His critical faculties are sharpened and his sense of moral values tempered by daily exercise in judging men and evaluating events. Recurring to the words of Solomon to the effect that "wisdom is the principal thing; therefore get wisdom; and with all thy getting get understanding," one can easily recommend re-porting as the surest professional road to this end. The social pres-sures and taboos which safeguard and at the same time cramp personality and character are notable by their absence in newspaper work.

At the same time, the perils and pitfalls of the intangibles should be equally plain to those entering the vocation of reporting. The motion-picture version of the reporter as an ill-clothed sot, lacking manners and morals, is certainly possible within this profession, as in others. Reality is not always an inspiring spectacle. Nor does the profession which examines reality at close quarters afford any safeguards in the form of gloves or colored glasses to prevent injury. The reporter must be his own monitor and must achieve his own philosophy.

Opportunities on Newspapers. Beyond the period of his apprenticeship, the reporter may find a satisfying future as a seasoned member of the newspaper staff. To the extent of his talents and efforts, he can become a "big name" newswriter whose byline is readily recognized and respected. Or he may become a columnist or commentator who analyzes current events. These newswriting opportunities are available either with an individual newspaper or with the wire services (Associated Press or United Press International) or the syndicated newspaper services.

Another newspaper career open to the reporter is the field of editing. In general, editors supervise the newsgathering activities of reporters, review and copyread their stories, write headlines, and arrange placement of stories and pictures in the newspaper. These responsibilities eliminate the gathering and writing phases, but some newspapermen who carry the title of editor may have fewer or more duties than those listed under the editing functions. The science editor, sports editor, education editor, and other such staff members are generally byline reporters who specialize in one area of journalism, but some of these editors may also perform copyreading and headlining duties. The editor of a small daily or weekly newspaper usually combines newswriting and editing duties. The principal editor (editor-in-chief) of a metropolitan daily commonly limits his duties to the writing of editorials and the general supervision of the entire staff.

The editor is sometimes (but not necessarily) the owner or part owner of the newspaper, and as such he is in the vocational category recognized as publisher—another newspaper opportunity open to the reporter. The publisher is the chief officer of the newspaper, responsible for its entire operation—editorial, business, and mechanical. Obviously, to become a newspaper publisher requires management ability, a knowledge of printing processes, and a capital investment to purchase or lease either an existing newspaper or the plant and equipment needed to start one. There are approximately ten thousand weekly, semiweekly, and small daily newspapers in the United States, and several of them generally are listed in the "For Sale" columns of publications serving the newspaper industry. Often they may be bought "on the installment plan," with a reasonable down payment and the balance in periodic installments.

Opportunities in Other Fields. Although the editorial departments do not advertise their employment opportunities as training grounds for other vocations, the truth is that some reporters leave after several years of experience to take positions both related and unrelated to newspaper work. Reporting is an invaluable introduction to life at many points. In orienting the young man or woman to opportunities afforded by the community, it has no equal. The reporter can cultivate contacts and friendships which may enable him to find any type of position that interests him—in retailing, wholesaling, insurance, transportation, public service, and other areas—and the skills that he has developed in interviewing and writing will increase his chances of success in any of these fields. In other words, the young person who wants to give newspaper work a "try," being uncertain whether he would like to spend his life in journalism, can easily transfer to another field—and with decided advantages.

But by far most of the reporters leaving newspaper work find employment in related journalistic areas—press associations, magazines of general circulation, trade journals and industrial publications, radio and television stations, publicity and public relations services, and other publications of business firms, industries, institutions, and associations. Nor should the broad field of advertising be omitted, for journalistic techniques are applied in the various communications efforts of this large industry.

Finally, the newspaper is a splendid breeding ground for creative writers. Many of the successful authors of today and yesterday acquired their basic training as newspaper writers. The varied experience itself, as well as the constant use of succinct language is an excellent basis for literary achievement.

Qualifications of a Reporter

Some persons are better fitted than others to become reporters, but this does not mean that reporters are "born and not made." Most of the attributes of a successful reporter are acquired instead of inherited. Perhaps the best qualifications for a reporter—aside from a desire and an ability to write for print—are an insatiable curiosity (which surely will express itself in part through a strong habit of reading), a flexible and sociable personality, a nature that relishes a variety of experience, a temperament to work under pressure of deadlines, and a tolerance permitting objective observations of people and events.

Attributes Desired for Success in Reporting. Obviously no one should consider a career as a reporter unless he has experienced an urge to write—an urge so strong that he has learned the fundamentals of English composition and has done some writing either for outlets available to him or for his own amusement and satisfaction. Without an aggressively inquiring mind the reporter would be of little benefit to his newspaper and his own work would be without savor. Unless he is a "mixer," the reporter can scarcely enjoy or profit by the multitudinous personal contacts which constitute his news sources. While much of the reporter's work is rather routine, it is applied to a daily kaleidoscope of events and therefore requires shifting attention. The necessity of working against the clock to meet deadlines, day after day, is a frustrating and ulcer-producing situation for one who does not have the temperament to work calmly under pressure. Even with all other qualifications, the reporter cannot fulfill the responsibilities of his vocation unless he can detach his personal life from his work, taking a position as an unbiased witness in reporting the news with an accurate interpretation of the facts.

Educational Needs of a Reporter. The best possible general college education plus training in journalism should be the academic equipment of a neophyte reporter. One who plans to specialize in a small area of journalism (politics, science, foreign relations, home economics, agriculture, and other fields) should bolster a general education with extra studies relating to that specialty.

The general education of a reporter should include college studies in English composition and literature, history, political science, economics, sociology, psychology, one or more of the sciences, and one or more of the foreign languages. The use of a typewriter, whether learned in a classroom or independently, is a skill required of all reporters. Shorthand is not essential but can be very helpful in taking notes on talks or fast-moving events.

The value of a college education has grown in the field of journalism as it has in other specialized vocations down through the years. The history of all professions points up the continual increase in the educational needs of practitioners. So it has been with journalism.

Some years ago newspaper executives hiring new reporters were content to employ high school graduates and to "bring 'em up" in the editorial department. After having employed college graduates and after comparing their rate of progress and height of achievement with those of high school graduates, most employers began to look for college-trained recruits. The reason is very clear. While one possibly could acquire the equivalent of a college education through independent reading and study, not many persons can discipline themselves to perform this feat without the assistance of teachers and the incentive of meeting day-by-day demands of college classes. Employers observed that, in comparison with high school graduates, college-trained reporters generally have a greater capacity for success and thus are worth considerably more to the newspaper.

Advantages of Journalistic Training. Journalistic training is another phase of college education which at first was ridiculed by some newspaper employers but is today widely recognized as valuable for the beginning reporter. Here again the editors who had "come up the hard way" argued that there was no better introduction to reporting than practical experience in the newsroom. Here again the employers discovered that college training—this time in journalism—not only afforded a short cut to learning the basic journalistic techniques and skills but also gave the beginning reporter a broader understanding of his work. In other words, city editors and other staff supervisors have not been as successful in teaching journalistic fundamentals with the trial-and-error method as have instructors with the formal classroom procedure. Hour for hour, the student in the classroom learns these fundamentals in less than one-third the time spent by the beginning reporter taught by the trial-and-error process.

A Craft or a Profession?

After a discussion of the educational needs of a reporter, the occupational status of journalists is an appropriate subject to consider. Are journalists members of a craft or a profession? Have newswriters and commentators the right to place themselves among the professions with such time-honored groups as lawyers, physicians, teachers, ministers, and engineers? Is journalism worthy of this distinction? To examine these questions requires a penetrating look at the role of the press as well as the work of journalists.

The Press and Society. The press, including the spoken and the written word of journalists, is an important institution in modern society. It is recognized as the principal medium of mass communication, which has become increasingly important because scientific and technological advancements make it more essential to keep the people apprised of day-by-day developments.

In a democracy, particularly, the role of the press is of vital importance. The success of a democratic government depends upon the wise decisions of an informed citizenry, for a democracy is ruled by the people at the polls. Therefore, the press must be utilized to give the people the information they should have in casting votes on candidates and issues. In this respect the press is a great educational institution.

The press as an institution serving the people of a democracy was identified when journalists were designated as the "Fourth Estate." This unofficial title was given to members of the press near the turn of the nineteenth century by the British Parliament in recognition of the fact that the press represents the people and has strong influence upon public opinion. The other three recognized "estates" or classes representing the British people were the clergy, the nobility, and the commons.

Just as it is used to enlighten the people, the press under the thumb of dictatorial control can also be used to enslave a nation. The medium of mass communication can be employed to disseminate either truths or falsehoods. Hitler and other dictators before and after him have given the world tragic lessons of a controlled press. Fortunately, the freedom of the press in the United States is protected by constitutional law, and the government therefore cannot dictate what must or must not be printed in newspapers. Moreover, the people of America, the ones who elect their representatives in government, have a rather direct control over their press, for they are the ones who keep the press in business. They are the readers or subscribers, the life blood of the press. As a member of a free-enterprise system which is open to anyone who cares to venture into competition, a newspaper must maintain the confidence of its readers or its competitors will take over.

Hence the press can be described as a quasi-public agency. It has responsibilities of keeping the public informed, and it is given freedom to do so by the law of the land. But the press operates under the system of private enterprise, which divorces it from governmental control and places its fate directly in the hands of the people.

Journalism and the Professions. While the press is accorded an honored place in a democratic society, whether this warrants professional status for journalists is another question. Many of the attributes of journalists give them strong claim to this distinction. On the other hand, there are some basic requirements for professional status which journalists do not meet.

Compared with the accepted professions, journalists have great responsibilities of public service which demand high respect. The journalist is, to a large degree, an educator. He is an architect of public opinion who can influence the enactment or repeal of laws. He is an evangelist who, by factual statements, preaches the virtues of high morality. He is guardian for the people of the efficient operation of public offices and institutions. He is entrusted with the power to bring credit or discredit to the names and reputations of his fellow men. What other vocation carries so many and such tremendous public services and responsibilities?

On the other hand, journalism is unlike all of the accepted professions in that it is not—and should never be—a licensed profession. Physicians, lawyers, teachers, and others must be licensed to practice, and to obtain a license they must complete specified educational programs and in some cases must pass examinations. Further, some of these professional people can lose their licenses if they are found guilty of unethical practices. Such requirements help to maintain desired standards and thus to protect the public from the damage that could be done by unqualified persons engaging in the professions.

The licensing of journalists, however, would be a form of government control of the press. Through license laws, a dictatorial or spiteful government, by handpicking those permitted to write for newspapers and other media, could nullify the constitutional guarantee of a free press.

Professional status for journalism cannot be attained by imposing high standards through license laws, but it can be achieved through the voluntary efforts of journalists. While no law should require beginning journalists to have a college education, this is a prerequisite which more and more employers are finding much to their advantage in establishing as a general policy. While no law can require that journalists abide by a professional code of ethics, the journalists themselves have established a voluntary code which all who have a genuine respect for their responsibilities will readily agree to observe. Nevertheless, even with the widespread acceptance of voluntary professional standards, there are and will be those in the field of journalism who will violate these standards for personal gain without fear of prosecution. But medicine has its "quacks," law its "shysters," education its tenure-protected, inept teachers. Those who faithfully serve the profession of journalism, like those serving other professions, can only hope that the unethical encroachments upon their privileged vocation can be kept at a minimum and prosecuted so far as possible through regular legal channels.

Exercises

I. Write a paper on the subject "Why I Enrolled for Journalism." The paper should include a discussion of the life work you have chosen, your complete course of study, any experience you have had in journalistic writing, what you believe are your personal qualifications in the field of journalism, what you expect to learn in this course, and how this course will be of practical value to you.

II. Write a paper, of a length to be specified by your instructor, presenting highlights in the life and achievements of one of the great American journalists of the past. You may be called upon to make a brief report on your paper to the class. Among the journalists you may write about are Benjamin Franklin, Adolph S. Ochs, William Randolph Hearst, Joseph Pulitzer, James Gordon Bennett, Charles A. Dana, Horace Greeley, Henry J. Raymond, Edward W. Scripps, William Allen White, Henry W. Grady, Frank Gannett, William Rockhill Nelson, or Henry Watterson.

Chapter 2

The Reporter in the Newspaper Organization

REPORTERS are the most essential members of the newspaper organization. They are the ones who gather and refine the commodity which is the *raison d'être* of the newspaper—the news. All others who serve the publication are there for the purpose of making it possible for the reporter's stories to get into print, accurately and attractively presented, for distribution to waiting readers. All this is true, but reporters cannot afford to be arrogant about it because they would have no newspaper to carry their stories without the contributions of other members of the organization.

The editors and other staff members who supervise or collaborate with reporters do have an important function, for without them the newspaper would lack organized coverage of all events and would lose much of its reader appeal. Too, the price that a reader pays for his newspaper does not begin to cover the publication's cost, and the newspaper must have employees who can sell part of its space as advertising to make up the difference and to assure the reporters their periodic salary checks. Other employees are needed to sell thousands of copies of the newspaper and to see that delivery is made to waiting readers. Moreover, those readers would have to wait a very long time to receive their newspapers if efficient mechanical workers were not available to convert typewritten material into printed pages. Thus, reporters fit into one of the three different functions involved in the process of publishing a newspaper —writing, printing, and selling. These are the duties of the editorial, mechanical, and business departments, respectively.

Editorial Department. News must be gathered from various sources as it occurs and must be written into readable, interesting form, then edited and displayed in the newspaper. This is the function of the newspaper's editorial department. Secondary functions of the newspaper are to instruct or influence the public through editorials and special articles, and to entertain by means of comics, fiction, and other features. All these materials are processed by the editorial department.

Mechanical Department. News must also be transferred from the typewritten sheet of the reporter into metal type (or slugs and, for large dailies, into stereotyped plates) in the composing room and thereafter be printed upon thousands of pages of newsprint in the pressroom. This is a complicated, technical, mechanical process. Hence, every newspaper has a mechanical department.

Business Department. To finance these two operations, advertising space must be sold, subscriptions must be obtained, and the news commodity must be delivered—hence the advertising and circulation divisions. A third division comprises problems of management and business administration. In the smaller newspaper, advertising, circulation, and management may be combined as one business department. In the larger newspapers they may be greatly expanded and sharply differentiated.

Details of Organization

A typical organization of a newspaper in a city of 100,000 to 200,000 population is shown in the accompanying diagram. The numbers in parentheses following titles of staff members refer to numbers in the diagram.

The publisher (1) is usually the owner, or chief owner, of the newspaper. He may be more or less closely associated with its actual operation. If closely associated, he may be also general manager (2) or editor (19). He has the power (if he chooses to exercise it) to dictate all policies, editorial or otherwise. Under the publisher, the general manager is supervisor and coordinator of all departments.

The business manager (3) is shown with authority over the advertising (4), circulation (6), and office manager (8). In many instances, however, he assumes merely the rank and position of office manager. In this event the advertising, circulation, and business managers report directly to the general manager or publisher.

In the mechanical process of printing a newspaper the metal type is set on typesetting machines (large headlines sometimes set by hand) in the composing room (11) and assembled in page *forms*. (See newspaper terminology in Appendix for further explanation of italicized terms in this section of the text.) From these forms a *matrix* is made by impressing the forms against newspaper mats of

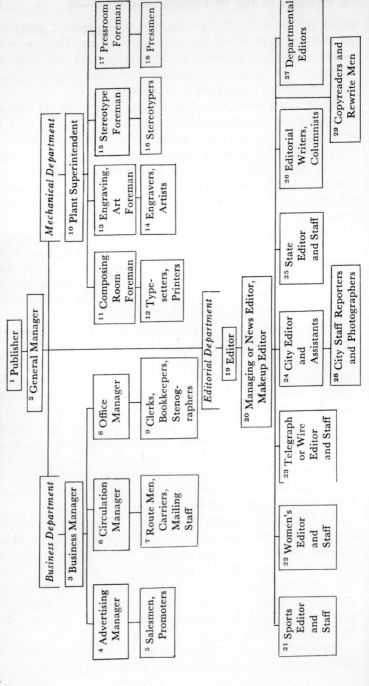

SAMPLE NEWSPAPER ORGANIZATION

1 Publisher

2 General Manager

Business Department

3 Business Manager

4 Advertising Manager
5 Salesmen, Promoters

6 Circulation Manager
7 Route Men, Carriers, Mailing Staff

8 Office Manager
9 Clerks, Bookkeepers, Stenographers

Mechanical Department

10 Plant Superintendent

11 Composing Room Foreman
12 Typesetters, Printers

13 Engraving, Art Foreman
14 Engravers, Artists

15 Stereotype Foreman
16 Stereotypers

17 Pressroom Foreman
18 Pressmen

Editorial Department

19 Editor

20 Managing or News Editor, Makeup Editor

21 Sports Editor and Staff

22 Women's Editor and Staff

23 Telegraph or Wire Editor and Staff

24 City Editor and Assistants

25 State Editor and Staff

26 Editorial Writers, Columnists

27 Departmental Editors

28 City Staff Reporters and Photographers

29 Copyreaders and Rewrite Men

special cardboard. From these matrices semicylindrical plates are cast in metal to be bolted upon the rotary presses. The process of making these plates is known as *stereotyping* (15) and is usually carried on in a special room shown between the composing room and pressroom (17) organizations in the chart.

The foregoing description of the mechanical process (11 through 16) applies to *letterpress printing*, which is commonly used by newspapers. In recent years another printing process, known as *offset printing*, has been developed and improved, and it is being used by an increasing number of newspapers. It replaces stereotyping by a negative and platemaking process, and it requires a different kind of press. Type for offset may be set by letterpress procedure or by machines which set words on film or tape.

From the editorial department the copy for the day's newspaper is sent [by all of the editors (21–29) indicated in the chart] to the composing room, to be set in type. A makeup editor (20) must plan where the various stories are to be placed in the newspaper. In other words, he makes up the newspaper. He determines where each story and picture will be placed on each page as the *galleys* of type are *locked up* in the page forms. On many newspapers the makeup editor is also the managing or news editor (20).

Most of the news that appears in the newspaper is provided by staff reporters (28) through the city editor (24), by national news agencies through the telegraph editor (23), and by correspondents (out-of-city reporters) through the state news editor (25). The women's editor (22) and sports editor (21) and their various assistants or reporters are allied with, and sometimes subordinate to, the city editor.

The editorials which appear in newspapers are written by the editor and editorial writers (26). Editors having administrative duties may write few editorials.

The *copy* (news manuscript) written by the staff reporters is carefully corrected and improved by *copyreaders* (29). Stories received by telephone from reporters or others, and stories not already in proper form for publication, are prepared by *rewrite* men (usually staff reporters on office duty). On metropolitan newspapers most headlines are written by copyreaders. (On the average-sized daily most of the copyreading and headline writing is done by the city, telegraph, and state editors.)

Photographers (28) serve under the city editor and usually are allied with reporters on assignments. Pictures must be converted into engravings (or metal *cuts*) in order to be reproduced in print. Larger newspaper have their own photoengraving plants (13). Smaller newspapers send their pictures to commercial photoengravers. Both cuts and *mats* (the matrix reproduction of a cut) are received from various other sources—press bureaus, publicity organizations, and the like. For newspapers using the offset process of printing, metal engravings and mats are not needed.

Departmental editors (27) are in charge of special features and columns or full-page departments, such as radio and television, motion pictures, the special Sunday sections (Sunday editor) and business and finance. On the smaller newspapers these special departments are allotted to various staff reporters. The departmental editors are usually under the managing editor.

The staff organization described above (and the diagram) is by no means uniform for all newspapers. The method of operation and the titles of staff members will vary among newspapers, but the essential functions as revealed above must nevertheless be performed, and this is a typical organization which can do the job.

The Morgue

Not shown in the chart but accessible to all reporters and editors is the newspaper's "morgue"—its reference files. The purpose of the morgue is to supplement current news stories (and editorials) with previously gathered information and story aids. Pictures, cuts, and mats are of primary importance. "See if we have a picture" is the first suggestion of the city editor concerning many stories. The morgue should also contain the biographies of prominent persons, ready for instant use in obituaries and stories of achievements. Clippings of stories used in the past, economic and social data, historical sketches, and "background" in general for a great variety of stories will be found in the morgue. The city directory, *Who's Who,* unabridged dictionaries, encyclopedias, and various reference books will supplement these materials. Depending on the size of the newspaper, the morgue may vary from a few files to a large reference library.

News Channels

News enters the editorial department of the newspaper through several channels and from many sources:

1. From local sources through the newspaper's own staff of reporters, who gather the news from regular beats, background it with information from the morgue, and do most of their writing in the newspaper office under the city editor.

2. From national and foreign sources through the news agencies (services, bureaus, syndicates)—Associated Press (AP), United Press International (UPI), and others. In addition many commercial syndicates furnish much feature material. Most of this material is received by telegraph or teletype and is, except for copyreading and headlining, already properly written for publication. The telegraph or wire editor is in charge, but he gives credit (by use of name or initials) to the press service for every such story used. Usually initials of a press service are in the *dateline,* which is the line at the beginning of an out-of-city story giving both date and place of origin. A local story needs no dateline.

3. From state and regional sources through correspondents. Much of this material is properly written and ready for publication. If not, it must be rewritten or heavily edited. Such stories often have "Special to the (name of newspaper)" preceding or in the datelines. The state news editor is in charge.

4. From various individuals and organizations, such as chambers of commerce, lecturers, and promotion agencies, through the mail, telephone, and personal calls. Most of this material is rewritten by the city staff under the city editor.

Through whatever channel it may subsequently pass, all news must be gathered and written at its source by reporters, and most news is, at its source, local news. An exception is news at state capitals and at the national capital affecting distant communities. In gathering and writing news a reporter faces substantially similar problems whether he is a staff reporter, a press-service reporter, or a correspondent.

Beats

A city editor would expect the following sources to yield perhaps 90 per cent of the local news and would instruct reporters to gather news from the various daily assignments, or *beats,* as indicated:

1. The city police station, county jail, fire department, and hospitals.

2. The city hall (headquarters for city legislative and executive officials).

3. The county courthouse (headquarters for county officials and state courts).

4. The state capitol or state offices (headquarters for state officials).

5. The federal building or offices (headquarters for the post office, federal law-enforcement and other offices and federal courts), and the Weather Bureau.

6. Schools, colleges, and associated organizations.

7. The chamber of commerce, business houses, industries, labor organizations.

8. Civic, fraternal, and professional organizations.

9. Churches and associated organizations.

10. Youth organizations and welfare agencies associated with the local Community Chest or United Fund, and also "health associations" (such as heart, tuberculosis, cancer) which are financed independently.

11. Motion-picture houses, radio and television stations, and organizations offering theatrical productions, athletic events, and other forms of entertainment.

12. Funeral homes.

13. Convention centers, hotels, airlines, railroads, and other firms engaged in accommodating meetings and visitors.

14. Varying local news sources, such as ships and shipping, mines and mining, oil, lumber.

It is apparent from this list of beats that the reporter has a regular and routine job. He does not stroll about the streets looking for stray news. Every day he is responsible for covering definite offices and organizations where most news emanates. Even news of murders, fires, and accidents is to be encountered at regular sources—the police and fire departments, and hospitals.

The fourteen beats listed will be altered and determined by physical locations and other conditions. If a chamber of commerce is situated near the police station, the police reporter perhaps will be required to cover the chamber of commerce also. If the city jail (police station) and the county jail are widely separated, a single reporter may not be able to cover both. Just how the beats are set up, and the number of reporters assigned to each, will be determined on a time-saving and step-saving basis adjusted to the number and ability of reporters on the payroll. In a city of 100,000 to 200,000 population, six to a dozen reporters may constitute the staff.

The Story Process

To clarify and relate the various factors of the newspaper organization, the steps in the story process from news event to reader may be listed as follows:

1. Upon the occurrence of a newsworthy event the reporter compiles the facts by interview and investigation and makes rough notes for his story.

2. He writes the story, usually returning to the office for this purpose. In critical circumstances he may write the story on the spot and send it to the city editor by messenger. Or he may telephone the facts, in which case the story is written by a reporter on rewrite duty in the newspaper office.

3. The typewritten story is delivered to the city editor (and copyreaders) for copyreading and headlining. The copyreader corrects any mistakes and attempts to polish or improve the story if necessary.

4. The city editor or news editor (or both) makes a record of the story, sometimes indicating its preferred position (for example, "page 1 must" to specify placement on the first page), and sends it to the composing room.

5. The foreman of the composing room gives the copy to a typesetting machine operator to be converted into metal type. If it is a long story or a rush order, he cuts the copy into numbered *takes* and distributes them to several operators. Large headlines are set on a special machine or perhaps by hand. The takes of type are reassembled in galleys, and a galley proof (printed impression) is made. *Proofreaders* indicate typographical errors in the galley proof, and the necessary corrections are then made in type by resetting the lines and replacing them in the galley trays.

6. The galleys of type are assembled on a *stone* (table) under direction of the makeup editor and are locked up in page forms.

7. From these forms a matrix of each page is made, and from it the semicylindrical metal page is cast (in the stereotyping room). The metal type of the original flat page forms is now melted down and returned to the typesetting machines.

8. The semicylindrical page forms are locked upon the rotary

presses in the pressroom, and the newspaper is printed, cut, and folded in one mechanical operation.

9. The printed newspapers are delivered to the circulation department for mailing, for delivery by routes, and for street sales.

This entire process of producing a newspaper can be achieved within a matter of hours. Small dailies and weeklies not possessing rotary presses print directly from the page forms. Steps 7 and 8 would therefore be omitted and other operations altered to fit the requirements of personnel and equipment. Also, steps 6 through 8 would differ as hereinbefore explained if the offset process of printing were used.

Exercises

I. Study several newspapers and select for analysis a typical edition of the local, or the most convenient daily newspaper, whose plant you may visit later. Make the following analysis:
   A. Count the number of pages, number of columns per page, length and width of columns, inches per column excluding and including headlines, number of words per column inch, and number of words per column.
   B. Estimate the proportion of advertising, news, and special features not strictly news by counting the columns devoted to each.
   C. Estimate the proportion of local news and news received by telegraph and the amount and proportion of sports, society, theater, radio and television, financial, and other special departmental news and editorials.
   D. Indicate the number, proportion, and kinds of pictures.
   E. For every item in the newspaper determine whether it was (1) prepared locally, (2) partly prepared locally, or (3) received from outside sources in the form of mats, cuts, copy, or pictures. Summarize your findings.
II. Visit a newspaper plant and acquire a complete understanding of its operations. Prior to your visit, study the newspaper terminology in the Appendix, the typical organization chart in this chapter, and the various steps in the story process from news source to reader. Identify each in your actual inspection.
   A. In the editorial department, note especially the number of reporters and the beats covered; rewrite men; copyreaders; editors —city, telegraph, state, sports, society, Sunday, special; story processes—headline writing, teletype machines, photographic and other divisions.

B. In the mechanical department, note in the composing room the cutting of copy into takes, typesetting, galley proof, proofreading, headlining, makeup, matrix, engraving process. Follow through to the pressroom, final printing, and delivery to the circulation department.

C. In the business department, note in the circulation room the amount of circulation, methods of circulation promotion, methods of delivery of newspapers; in the advertising department note the want ads and other advertising methods and processes.

D. In all departments, identify the source of all material that is printed in the newspaper and the actual steps and processes the material must go through before reaching the public.

III. Write a detailed report of your newspaper inspection tour.

IV. Clip from a newspaper a story, headline, or illustration that represents part of the work of each of the editorial staff members named in the chart. Paste these clippings on sheets of blank paper, and caption each properly.

V. Examine the local stories in two or three consecutive editions of a daily newspaper, determining the source or sources of each story.

A. What sources (beats) named in this chapter are represented, and how many stories were gathered from each source?

B. What sources do you find that are not named? Are they peculiar to the city in which the newspaper is published?

VI. Outline the beats that would be necessary to cover the city or the county in which you live.

Chapter 3

What Is News?

Up to now the word *news* has been used as though any reporter, regardless of his callowness, would readily recognize what he should gather and write. Apparently a discussion of the definition of news is unnecessary. However, on the other hand, a few problems on this subject deserve exploring.

Why is it that when Jane Hourglass, the actress, falls down two steps and sprains her shapely ankle, the mishap is considered news, but if the same thing had happened to Jane's gardener the newspapers would pay no attention to it? The difference is prominence, you say? Well, suppose sprained ankles were suffered on the same day by the local college's second-string fullback and the head of the college English department. What would the newspaper do with these two news events? From your answer, perhaps you can glean a definition of news as newspapermen view it.

Nature of News

To recognize news is easier than to define it. The following definitions, selected at random, reveal a variety of opinions of what news is:

News is an account of an event, or a fact, or an opinion which interests people.

Anything that enough people want to read is news, provided it does not violate the canons of good taste and the laws of libel.

News is anything that people will talk about. The more it will excite comment, the greater its value.

News is accurate and timely intelligence of happenings, discoveries, opinions, and matters of any sort which affect or interest the readers.

News is everything that happens, the inspiration of happenings, and the result of such happenings.

News comprises all current activities which are of general human interest, and the best news is that which interests the most readers.

There would seem to be no way to cull the common elements in these definitions to reach a general and wholly satisfactory short description of news. Nor from psychology or the social sciences has any formula been devised to detect and weigh this important commodity. Perhaps news is an account of the changing relationships between man and man and between man and his environment, but neither man nor his environment nor the various relationships can be easily fixed in definitions.

Intuition in News Judgment. To some extent the newspaper reporter depends upon his intuition in recognizing news, in distinguishing between news and non-news, and in estimating the importance of news. The "nose for news" is considered the equipment of primary importance. Whether reporters are, in this sense, "born and not made" may be debated. Certainly newspapermen make important decisions daily that are based on their intuitive news judgment. Nevertheless, practical newspapermen do recognize and apply certain news measurements and definitions when necessary, and a knowledge of these generally accepted rough principles and rules of thumb is essential for the beginning reporter. A serious effort to define news will strengthen his intuitive judgment.

The following discussion is an effort not so much to produce a profound definition of news as to clear the atmosphere for intuitive news perception. It is couched in arbitrary terms to avoid tedious reservations and exceptions. It cuts many corners and begs many questions. It invites criticism and resistance on the part of the reporter who should improve upon it at all possible points and who ultimately should achieve, if not a generally acceptable definition, at least a reasonably clear perception of news. The generally accepted news values are included in the discussion.

Many commodities obviously are not news, and the newspaper does not deal in them. Hardware, clothing, and automobiles are valuable, interesting, and merchantable commodities, but they are not news.

It is obvious, too, that certain other commodities are not news, but the newspaper does deal in them. Advertisements, editorials, cartoons, comics, fiction, book reviews, columns of philosophy and science—all appear from time to time in the newspaper. All of them may be interesting items, but they are not news.

News cannot, therefore, be defined as "whatever appears in the newspaper," nor as "whatever is interesting to people," nor as "interesting items which appear in the newspaper," nor as "interesting written or printed materials."

What, then, is the essential characteristic of the newspaper items which we recognize instantly and generally as news? The first suggestion might be that news is "an account of something that has happened"—something that, to distinguish it from fiction, has "actually happened." The non-news items mentioned above are thus excluded. The definition, however, immediately encounters difficulty. What should be said of history? Obviously, history is such an account. And, more troublesome still, most things that have actually happened, that do happen every day, are not considered to be newsworthy. An account of routine daily acts—arising, dressing, eating, working—is not news under normal circumstances, though the most trivial event can under certain conditions become newsworthy.

What are these conditions? What is the alchemy of circumstance or the intrinsic nature of the event that lifts "something that actually happens" into the newsworthy realm where an "account" of it will be interesting to readers?

To state the answer categorically: The newsworthy event is one that affects or changes social, economic, political, physical, or other relationships. Or, news is an account of man's changing relationships with his environment. Or, to be even more specific, the newsworthy development is one that disrupts or alters—or shows promise of altering—the status quo, and news is an account of such a development.

Change Essential. These, like many other definitions, suggest change, or potential change, as the essential element in news. Indeed the same quality is suggested even more directly by the word *news*. At least it is change that has a vital significance for newspaper readers, sometimes affecting them with fear over the loss of jobs, or the promise of prosperity with the opening of the new factory; sometimes stirring their hope over the new mayor, the new manager, the newlyweds, or even the new baby in the house next door. So long as conditions remain the same from day to day, there is nothing to change the pulse of vicarious reader experience on either the up or the down grades of human experience. Let an event disrupt the status quo, however, and its portent, large or small, motivates the hopes or fears of whole neighborhoods of readers. In actual fact, the individual careless and uninformed about the changing world has little chance to avoid its perils or to take advantage of its oppor-

tunities. Whether he is aware of it or not, the newspaper reader—
every individual—is deeply concerned and affected by the changing
circumstances in which he is so delicately fixed. Is it not for this
reason that he is always interested, and at times vitally interested
in news? And is not the news in which he is interested essentially
the account of events which do alter, or threaten to alter, the
normal arrangement of things and relationships and the accustomed
flow of events?

The objection may be raised that any and all events are disruptions of the status quo—even the act of eating breakfast—and that
the definition is so all-inclusive as to be useless as a news criterion.
The objection is scarcely valid on the common-sense level, for most
events—breakfast, for example—are easily recognized as routines
and not disruptions. For all practical purposes, most individuals are
quick to recognize at least the more obvious events which threaten
their security or alter their status. A new tax bill brings a quick
response from those who pay taxes and, incidentally, is front-page
news. The difference between routines and the disruption of routines
is not hard to detect. Nor is there much difficulty in distinguishing
between the trifling loss of a handkerchief by an individual and a
bank failure, as disruptions so different in degree that the former
could scarcely qualify as a disruption. Certainly the reporter faces
a more specific distinction between disruptions and nondisruptions
than between news and non-news.

A further objection may be that much news concerns the future
and not the past. Many stories deal with councils and conferences
and plans. And what about names of persons and places which
figure so largely in the news? It seems evident that all of these items
are of interest to the reader only if they deal with potential or
impending disruptions. Events in themselves are not to be isolated
from their context of circumstances, and therefore the circumstances
themselves are of interest. Indeed, coming events "cast their
shadows," and it is the reporter's special responsibility to warn
readers of their coming.

Community Consequence Required. The real difficulty with the
definition is that, once an event is recognized as a disruption, there
still remains the problem of whether it is sufficiently disruptive to
make an interesting story—that is, whether it constitutes news of
sufficient magnitude to be of interest to a sufficient number of
readers. If Johnny Doe, eight, is 30 minutes late for dinner, it is
news only if he has heretofore been punctual—and, then, news only

to his immediate family. It becomes worth publishing only as time elapses and his failure to appear leads to the serious conclusion that he is "missing." Immediately the fact becomes of major local importance. Why? Is it not because the security of every child in the neighborhood is threatened (actually or potentially)? The security of children in general becomes at stake in the community mind. It is a matter that everyone needs to know about in order to understand the peril that exists and to take precautionary steps. At just what point a disruptive event breaks over into community consequence is impossible to determine by formula. But to think of news as *a disruptive event of community consequence* certainly does not cloud the intuitive judgment.

There would seem to be little doubt that in and around the consequential *disruption of the status quo* and, by the same token, the *potential disruption of the status quo* will be found the essential nature of news. Certain it is that if everything should be tomorrow precisely as it is today, the next morning's newspaper would be dull reading. "What's happened?" "What's going on?" "Anything new?" "Anything stirring?" "Anything going to break?" These are the questions constantly in the reporter's mind. And if among the myriad of activities and comings and goings of a busy office, or of the county jail, or of the state capitol, there is no event, or potential in which events may be brewing to disrupt the status quo of routine circumstances, there would seem to be no news that day.

So much for a tentative definition of news. If the definition is sound, disruption (change) or potential disruption is the intrinsic quality of all news events. Disruption differentiates news events from non-news events. The extent of disruption (community consequence) measures the magnitude of events and determines their importance or reader appeal.

News Values

This conception of the news essence lays a common foundation for the news values. These qualifications or characteristics of the news as commonly recognized are in reality special types of disruption of the status quo. In other words, any event which is newsworthy will not only disrupt the status quo but will also disrupt it in one of the following ways:

Conflict. Most conflicts are newsworthy. Actual conflict is a visible disruption of the status quo. In its physical form it presages injury

and damage. Violent in itself, it arouses the emotion of the spectators and seems (and may be) of enormous immediate importance.
Many a high school lad, however, with passions torn at a gridiron
spectacle, has doubtless been grievously surprised to find only a few,
if any, sticks of type devoted to the game in the press. Stark as the
conflict may have seemed to him, it affords in the editor's eye no
important disruption of the status quo. The whole realm of sports
has a status quo of its own, however—and within the sports pages
purely sports conflicts find their own endemic news importance.
Conflicts of a more disruptive nature—wars, strikes, political campaigns, senatorial debates—receive ample space on the front pages.
The clash of political, economic, and social theories, the debates of
scholars and scientists—if measured by the consequence of the
issues—deserve perhaps more recognition as news than they get.
But the disruption of the status quo in such conflicts may be a
distant potential and not immediately apparent in the social order.
Instead, the divorce court, the legislative bodies, the jails, and police
stations yield a steady supply of conflict stories—broken homes,
arbitrary reforms, and bloody hospital cases—to startle the reader
with visible change. Tension and suspense are corollary qualities of
conflicts and are sometimes considered news values in themselves.

Progress and Disaster. From conflict there follows usually the triumph of one party, the defeat of another. And from the routine
struggles of life, not newsworthy in themselves, emerges frequently
the shining success. From quiet laboratories come new inventions,
new remedies, new devices—progress. Fires and earthquakes may
strike suddenly. Jobs are lost. Tenants are ejected from their rented
houses. Sharecroppers become a regional problem. Sometimes these
changes are observed and reported in the making because of the
conflicts involved. In other instances only the end result stands out
as progress and disaster, emerging from a vague or unknown background. But all are changes, all are newsworthy in greater or less
degree, for all are disruptions of the status quo.

Consequence. An event which causes or is capable of causing a
great sequence of events affecting many persons is obviously newsworthy. It is, in other words, of much consequence. Certain events
are of more consequence than others, and those of more consequence
will receive more space and larger headlines—will be, naturally,
more newsworthy. Consequence is generally accepted as a news value,
and there can be no objections to it as a general measurement of
news importance. Its defect as a specific news value is that all news-

worthy events have some consequence, for whatever other reason they are newsworthy. Consequence thus tends to be a measurement of all the other news measurements rather than an intrinsic characteristic of the news event itself. For example, a football game is of little consequence, a political campaign of greater consequence, and a war perhaps of greatest consequence. Consequence thus measures conflict. Similarly, consequence may measure disaster or progress. A fire which destroys a private dwelling is of small consequence in comparison with the San Francisco earthquake. The reporter need not cavil over this point, for any measurement which leads to a better understanding of the news is valuable whether or not it is similar to other measurements.

Eminence and Prominence. It is generally agreed that names make news, and big names make big news. Granted that this is true, how is the disruption of the status quo involved in this apparently static news value? If names alone made news, no event at all would be needed to inject names into the newspaper, and the editor could turn out a fascinating sheet by copying the pages of *Who's Who*. Indeed, Mr. Eminence must do something to alter the status quo if his name is to go into the newspaper. He may do no more than "stop over" en route to a conference at the White House. But if he is eminent enough for such a conference, around him is an aura of news potentials. If he predicts war, the stock market may go down. If he smiles upon the local pastor, the congregation may increase in numbers. Politicians would know—even if reporters and editors did not—that the big name is important because of that individual's capacity for disrupting the status quo. Big names—prominence—eminence—are newsworthy for the same reason that a political conclave or a cabinet meeting or a council of war is newsworthy. All may be quiet for the moment, but the potentials are there for the significant change which makes news.

Timeliness and Proximity. Two other news values commonly recognized are timeliness and proximity, and both are serviceable in measuring certain qualifications of the news. If a city editor, however, were to describe the commodity which his reporters should go forth to harvest each day as being all events which are "timely" and in the "proximity," he would not be defining very specifically "What is news?" He would be like the farmer who might instruct his "hands" to harvest all commodities that are "fresh" and "close at hand." A reporter can rather easily detect and report all events which are matters of conflict, or evidence of progress or disaster, or those of some consequence, and be pretty sure he is collecting news. These terms, even if overlapping and defective in certain aspects, are at least rather clearly definitive. As measurements applied to all events, they do distinguish between news and non-news. Timeliness and proximity are measurements to be applied to news *after it is recognized,* to determine whether and where it is salable and whether it is worth gathering. The farmhand—after he learns to recognize the fruits, nuts, vegetables, and melons in which the farmer deals—will leave on the tree or vine those commodities which are too old (not timely) and those which would have to be consumed too far away—in distant markets—and which would not appeal to the appetites of the local community. He will collect those commodities which are fresh (timely) and of local appeal (proximity). Since news is a commodity, the reporter is governed by these same principles of selection.

Novelty. Another news value is novelty. An adage of the newspaper profession is that, if a dog bites a man, it is not news, but if a man bites a dog, it is news. Novelties in the news include two-headed calves, deformed sweet potatoes, the vine which has grown through the trunk of a tree, straws blown into brick walls by the wind. Such events are very definite disruptions of the status quo. Some of them are sufficiently novel to bring the laws of nature into question in the popular mind. Coincidences, great contrasts, novel ways of making a living, avocations, unusual habits, and superstitions appeal to many readers. The common element of the appeal appears to be novelty—a value not difficult to recognize.

Human Interest. Many stories appear in the newspapers which at first glance do not seem to be news—as measured by conflict, consequence, progress and disaster, novelty, or any other specific news value. They are called human-interest or feature stories. The blind helping the blind, the old apple woman, fisherman's luck, the loss of a life's savings hidden in a tin can, contrasts of youth and age, the inconsequential dramatic skits of the police court, the faithful dog—plainly the reader appeal (news value) of some of these stories can be explained as a combination of the appeals already mentioned—disaster, progress, conflict. Most, perhaps all, of them are novelties in the sense of being unusual groupings of events. Perhaps they could be called human novelties. Such stories are seldom if ever of importance as isolated events. Murder is an isolated event newsworthy because of conflict and disaster. An election is an isolated event newsworthy because of conflict (also triumph and defeat) and consequence. If a one-legged prisoner outruns the policeman on the beat, the event is newsworthy because of its novelty—but the single event would make a very short news story. "Make it a human-interest story," the city editor would doubtless say, and it might deserve a half-column. Thereupon the reporter would go beyond the event into the human background of the story characters. How did the prisoner lose his leg? How did he learn to run so fast? What about his family? And the policeman—what about him? Perhaps he was a champion miler in high school. Perhaps he was not half trying. Perhaps the prisoner was a local personality whom the policeman really did not want to arrest, and so on. Thus the reporter digs into the human background.

It should be noted that for material which is characterized as human interest the reporter has gone beyond the event into the human background. He has sought the type of material which the fiction writer presents—emotions, biographical facts, dramatic incidents, descriptions, motives, ambitions, yearnings, and common likes and dislikes of people. These are not events but the background of events.

Some events lend themselves more readily than others to human-interest treatment. Many an event that would not deserve publication because of its news values can suggest a sufficient quantity and quality of human background to become the "news peg" on which the human-interest story can be hung. Moreover, very important events can sometimes be so entangled in the circumstantial web of character, passions, and conflicting interests that to disentangle them as a straight news story would deprive the events of much of their significance. Such an event was the Lindbergh kidnapping. Exposed to the public by this rent in the status quo was the colorful fabric of the private lives of eminent human beings. So rich was this fabric that it outshone the mere event and yielded one of the greatest human-interest stories in history.

An event acquires significance through its context of circumstances. The loss of a pocket knife on the city streets is a trifling event. Its loss by a shipwrecked sailor on a desert isle might be of great significance. As isolated events the two are the same. Thus one cannot measure the news value of a completely isolated event except in kind. The intensity and impact and consequence of the event will be determined by its context. The fabric of circumstance may be slightly torn or hideously rent by events of equal force *per se*. For example, kidnappings occur rather frequently in the United States;

yet in disrupting the status quo they do not reveal equally brilliant fabrics of fascinating human interest nor equal social consequences.

This line of thought suggests that the human-interest story emerges from an ordinary event measurable for its newsworthiness by its disruption of the status quo and by the commonly accepted news values. Whether it shall take off in this fashion—that is, whether it shall be a human-interest rather than a straight news story—will be determined by circumstances. Sometimes the event and its consequences stand starkly alone like a cameo of cold incident and fact against no visible background. Sometimes the background is aglow with human emotions and contrasts and is more prominent that the events. The actual events become a faint intaglio. Frequently, too, the reporter presents straight news events with an occasional human-interest flare in the background.

Human interest, then, though not strictly a news value measuring an isolated event, is a useful term to characterize those materials which pour through the event to fill the news columns with story materials. Strictly speaking, human interest is a story value and not a news value. The reporter will not need to make this precise distinction. For all practical purposes, human interest can be and is generally accepted along with conflict, consequence, disaster, progress, novelty, eminence, proximity, timeliness, and so on as a news value. Any given event may suggest and require some human-interest treatment.

Sex. Sex is sometimes proffered as a news value. It would seem, offhand, to have as great a potential as eminence for disrupting the status quo. Divorce, love affairs, elopements, film stars, famous beauties have definite reader appeal in the news. Especially when sex is coupled with eminence is a great story in the making—as was the all-time love story of the Duke and Duchess of Windsor. Conflict, human interest, disaster, and perhaps other values were added to sex and eminence to step up the news potentials of this story. Stories involving sex alone do have reader appeal. Yet it may be stretching a point to call sex a news value. While sex interest is universal, food interest and clothes interest are also universal, though not so dramatic and emotional. Is sex interesting *per se?* And is sex an intrinsic quality of an event? Or is sex interesting when it involves conflict—in the "battle" of the sexes (love) ; or disaster—in the divorce court; and eminence—in the social and theatrical world; or novelty or human interest? The reporter need not pursue these questions with a view to positive answers. It is sufficient to know—

as he does by intuition and instinct—that sex is interesting and frequently is news.

Miscellaneous Values. Stories of animals are frequently interesting, but it seems improper to include this interest quality among the news values, as is sometimes done. Only when an animal disrupts the status quo does it make news. The hero dog, the prize-winning cow, the cat on the power pole, and the eagle lost in city streets are news. But these are also definite novelties.

Many other types of stories and materials used in the newspaper are interesting. Some are not news from the standpoint of current events, but they are designed to inform or entertain, and often they have elements of timeliness, eminence, sex, and so on. Human interest stories on children, old people, adventure, hobbies, television —all these make news if the events in which they are involved are newsworthy as measured by the general principle of disruption and by specific news values.

Summary: Nature of News and News Values

The newspaper deals in a commodity called news. News differs from all other commodities and may be defined as follows:

1. News is an account of man's changing relationships.
2. News is an account of actual events which disrupt the status quo or which have the potential to cause such a disruption.
3. News is a disruptive event of community consequence.

Items of news have intrinsic characteristics which are known as news values, the presence or absence of which measures the newsworthiness and reader appeal of events, thus determining their worth to the newspaper as marketable commodities.

These news values are therefore useful measurements of happenings and, properly applied, will determine whether a given event is news.

Any (newsworthy) disruption or potential disruption of the status quo will be due to events and potentials which are characterized by one or more of the following news values:

Intrinsic Characteristics of the Event

1. Conflict (tension—surprise)
2. Progress (triumph—achievement)

3. Disaster (defeat—destruction)
4. Consequence (effects upon community)
5. Eminence (prominence)
6. Novelty (the unusual and even the extremely usual)
7. Human interest (emotional background)

Desirable Qualifications

8. Timeliness (freshness and newness)
9. Proximity (local appeal)

General Interests

10. Sex
11. Animals

Measuring the Importance of News

By intuition or by applying the news values, the reporter recognizes news when he sees it. If, however, he should collect all the news that happens in a day in his locality, the newspaper would not have space for it. The news that is printed is selected from the mass. The more important is offered to the readers; the less important is left uncollected or in the wastebasket.

News must be measured for its comparative importance—as when two or more stories compete for space. It must be measured also for its intrinsic importance—to determine the length and the display it should receive.

Are there any scales upon which the news commodity can be weighed to determine its specific gravity or importance—or weight of its reader appeal? Are there any principles to guide the reporter and the editor in selecting from the mass the most important news?

The best answer is "No." Just as the news essence, so also the news magnitude is best recognized or "felt" by intuition or instinct. The "nose for news" that detects the odor must determine also whether the odor is strong or weak. The problem is, perhaps, one and the same. However, several measurements are useful:

Extensity and Intensity. An actual odor may be strong (or weak) in one neighborhood, or it may cover a whole community. The decaying carcass of a horse, for example, might disturb the neighbors for several blocks. The odor from leaking gas tanks might stifle the whole city. Both would be news. If the intensity were equal, the larger city-wide extension of the odor would make a bigger story. On the other hand, if the carcass (undiscovered) should drive a few neighbors from their homes, and the gas odor should be merely annoying, the intensity could outweigh the extensity in measuring the importance of the story. The same principle applies to non-odorous stories. Hence a principle: the importance of a story is determined by its intensity (the amount of disruption) and by its extensity (the number of persons affected).

Proximity and Timeliness. Discussed as news values, proximity and timeliness are chiefly useful in measuring not the nature of news but their importance for use in a particular newspaper. Since a news-paper sells its news commodity to a local public, local events are more important than foreign—other factors being equal. A murder is big news in the locality (proximity) where it occurs. A similar murder elsewhere will receive space in the local newspaper only in proportion to the prominence of the persons involved or to the conflict, novelty, disaster, consequence, human interest, or other news values. Otherwise equal, the most recent or seasonal events will receive most space because of their timeliness.

Consequence. Another news value, consequence, measures the importance of news rather than its essential nature. Community consequence has already been suggested as a news determinant. Other things being equal, a news event is just as important as the results which flow from it. If two men are murdered, one the father of ten children, the other unmarried—and all other values are equal—the murder of the former is the more important event and makes the more important news story. Of two large public gatherings, the one on pleasure bent, the other demanding impeach-ment of the mayor, the latter is more important because of the consequences that may flow from it.

Variety of Appeal. Though the news values themselves do not determine the importance of news but merely its nature, it is usually true that, the more news values in the event, the greater the story interest, the greater its importance. A kidnapping is big news in itself; the kidnapping of an eminent person bigger news; conflict and bloodshed make the news still bigger—and thence through human interest, novelty, and so on. The various values must be of intensity and consequence, however. A variety of mild values will yield only a mild story interest and little importance. Variety of appeal is a measurement (like the other measurements) of magni-tude only when other values are equal.

Factors of Magnitude. In summary, the following are factors which, as rationalizations, measure the importance of the news:

1. The extent of disruption of the status quo (intensity)
2. The number of persons affected by the event (extensity)
3. The nearness of the event (proximity)
4. The recency of the event (timeliness)
5. The extent of results to flow from the event (consequence or significance)
6. The variety of news values in the event (variety)

Story Types

The newspaper personnel—reporters and editors—do not generally discuss news values nor factors of news magnitude. They merely apply these values, usually intuitively, in the writing and editing of news. They do recognize and discuss stories in other terms. The makeup editor plans a front page featuring a "fire story," perhaps, or a "crime story" or a "meeting" or "a speech." "Personals" will fill the society columns. Always, too, there will be the "weather" story. Most newspaper stories fall into more or less well-defined types which the reporter can study and master without at the same time submitting himself to any regid rules or formal story outlines. Newspapers generally recognize the following types of news stories and other editorial materials:

General Types

1. Personals and Brevities
2. Speeches, Publications, Interviews
3. Meetings and Occasions

Stories that are classified by the "package" in which they are "wrapped" rather than the contents (or subject matter) of the package. These general types deserve special consideration because they are encountered time and again in covering the subject-matter types ("Simple," "Complex," and "Special") which follow.

Simple Types

4. Illness, Deaths, Funerals
5. Fires and Accidents
6. Seasons and Weather
7. Crime

Subject-matter stories which generally require little interpretative writing by the reporter.

Complex Types

8. Courts, Trials, Lawsuits
9. Government and Politics
10. Business, Industry, Agriculture, Labor
11. Education, Research, Science
12. Religion, Philanthropy, Promotion

Subject-matter stories which generally require interpretation from the reporter's background of specialized information.

Special Types

13. Society-Women's Section
14. Sports
15. Literature, Fine Arts, Criticism
16. Editorials and Editorial Columns

Stories and articles which encompass a multiplicity of subjects and which in many cases, contain a heavy portion of interpretation requiring a high degree of general and specialized knowledge on the part of the writers.

Some of these story types are more clearly defined than others. For example, obituaries (deaths and funerals) and weather stories are rather standardized in form and subject matter. On the other hand, business stories range from simple market reports to elaborate accounts of local business developments or world economic conferences. Indeed, many of the classifications overlap. Accidents may figure in weather stories. A trial may be also a political story. Nevertheless, each type has sufficiently distinct problems to be examined independently of the others. The reporter who masters each type will have no trouble with a story in which several types merge.

News Sources

Stories of the various types and containing the various news values are gathered from many sources. The main beats covered regularly by reporters were noted in the preceding chapter. They include, in substance, all available offices of the state, county, city, and federal government; the headquarters of all civic and professional organizations; churches, schools, and charities; and many individuals, public and private, who occupy key positions in commerce, industry, transportation, utilities, and other major fields of enterprise.

Many stories may be picked up from single sources. The secretary of the chamber of commerce, for example, may provide all necessary information for a story of a new industry, or a coming convention, or the year's promotion program. On the other hand, many stories will have to be pieced together from several sources. A strike may require information from strikers, strikebreakers, employers, police, the mayor, the governor, the hospitals, charities, labor union officials, and others.

Since all details of news stories are reported, not created, by the reporter, the information in every story is traceable to its source. A sample news analysis shows how the news in one story was drawn from various sources:

Sample News Analysis 3a

Source of News	*News Type: Accident*	*News Content*
Participants in rescue work	MINEVILLE, Mar. 16—Fifty-four men entombed in the explosion-torn Wilson coal mine were feared dead tonight.	Kind and cause of accident
Participants in rescue work, hospitals, police	Five men were killed trying to rescue them. Rescue crews saved 93 other miners, most of whom where affected by the death-dealing black damp which followed a noonday blast.	Casualties Escapes
Company officials and rescue workers	Officials of the Tracey Coal Company, owners of the mine, three miles south of here, declined to speculate on the miners' fate. The 54 were cut off from fresh air and entombed behind a rock barrier.	Elaboration on kind of accident, description
One of the rescued	"But they're all dead—they couldn't live through that blast," said John Smith, one of the rescued men. This view was shared by his fellow workers.	
Rescue workers	Desperate attempts to make contact with the imprisoned men failed.	
	While rescue crews battered at the rock wall—some thought it would take all night to break through—efforts were made to force fresh air to the men down a 90-foot shaft.	Rescue attempts

| Company official and workers rescued | A check by J. J. Jones, company president, showed that approximately 150 men were in the huge mine when the accident occurred. Many gained safety through the air shaft located at the end of the three-mile long "drift," or horizontal mine. | Method of escape |

News Values

The outstanding news value of this story is its conflict or tension: a desperate struggle to save the lives of 54 men. It also contains a dramatic element, which gives it human-interest characteristics. The story is not so timely as it could be, since it is a follow-up of a preceding story which reported that the explosion trapped a number of men. However, the fact that the men are "feared dead" is timely. The explosion itself and the resultant deaths afforded the major news value of the preceding story: disaster. As it is written, the story has little proximity news value; otherwise it would be much longer and more detailed.

Exercises

I. Clip one story to illustrate each of at least ten different story types and paste each clipping to a separate sheet of paper. Indicate for each type of story the news content, the news sources, and the news values. (See sample news analysis.) Select local stories only.

II. Clip four or five additional stories that you find difficult to classify under one or more of the types. Can you discover among them an additional type or do they contain merely a miscellany?

III. Following are rough notes for stories or story leads, local to your city or community. Classify these stories under one or more of the story types. Study the apparent importance of each story (from its news values—consequence, conflict, human interest, etc.) and indicate the news values of each. Indicate the additional information needed to expand each story properly and the sources from which such information would be obtained.

A. Representatives from all civic clubs met at Chamber of Commerce last night at 7:30. Discussed "most useful citizen" award. Decided upon Hal Lawrence. Award made on third ballot. Mr. Lawrence is president of First National Bank.

B. J. P. Overton was indicted six months ago. Was bookkeeper at Hood's Department Store. Trial for embezzlement of $28,000. Jury reported this morning. Verdict guilty. Sentenced by Judge

J. L. Burke in First Criminal Court. Five to ten years in state penitentiary.

C. City Council convened this morning at 10 o'clock. Meeting was held at city hall. Decided to build new elementary school. To relieve congestion at Mulberry School. New school to be at Eighth and Broad. Decided to issue $700,000 bonds for construction.

D. Charles W. Eaton struck by automobile. Accident occurred at 9 o'clock last night on Main Street. Eaton owned grocery at 601 Main Street. Had locked up the store to go home to 1201 Main. Was struck as he crossed the street in front of store. Taken to city hospital by police cruiser. Died at 10 p.m. Automobile did not stop.

IV. By applying the tests for news values to the following items, determine which items are worth publishing. Which items deserve placement on the first page? Indicate the sources from which you would expect to obtain sufficient information for each worthwhile story.

A. Local man given honorary doctor's degree by college in another city
B. Local woman club leader dies
C. Foreign governmental official to visit city
D. Police search cemetery for lost cat
E. Special prices offered by used car firm
F. Million dollar motel to be constructed in city
G. Famous pianist to give local concert
H. Purse-snatcher caught
I. City tax assessor fired
J. Manager of drug store fired
K. Hospital opens new laboratory
L. Local church damaged $12,000 in 3 a.m. fire
M. Jury awards $25,000 to accident victim
N. Number of jobless declines during month
O. Mayor tells council that tax rate must be increased
P. Scout troop holds weekly meeting
Q. Students boycott school in protest against new teacher
R. Rain expected tomorrow
S. Local civic club to sell rose bushes
T. Homecoming queen selected by local high school

Chapter 4

Writing in the News Style

EFFECTIVE writing for the newspaper does not differ essentially from effective writing in general. Though the reporter must adapt his story to prescribed newspaper forms, he must conform to the accepted rules of punctuation and grammar and the principles of rhetoric. Good newspapermen and good English teachers have no bone of contention, despite popular belief to the contrary. True, newspapers are frequently criticized because of glaring errors in English, but those errors are not usually the work of better newspapermen. Newspapers take special liberty in headline writing, and perhaps this practice has given rise to the belief that newspaper English is a language all its own. However, headline English is not newspaper English; it is not the style observed in the news stories.

4a

Headline English is merely a device used in displaying the news stories. News stories should not—indeed, they must not—be written in shoddy English.

While newspaper language follows accepted rules of English, it also strives for certain qualities of style: simplicity, conciseness, and vividness; directness, emphasis, and originality; clarity, brevity, accuracy. These qualities cannot be sharply defined. They afford no specific rules to follow in achieving excellence and distinction. Some general principles of news style, however, can be illustrated:

Newspaper English

4b   1. Eliminate Superfluous Words.

a. Unnecessary articles:

Weak: The club members attended the meeting.
Strong: Club members attended the meeting.
Weak: He returned a part of the money.
Strong: He returned part of the money.

> (However, only unnecessary articles should be eliminated. For example, the article in "Club members attended *the* meeting" cannot be eliminated.)

b. Circuitous verb forms:

Weak: The group will hold a meeting.
Strong: The group will meet.
Weak: The judge arrived at a decision.
Strong: The judge decided.

c. Adjectives, adverbs, prepositions:

Weak: Both cars were completely destroyed.
Strong: Both cars were destroyed.
Weak: A tall 18-story building.
Strong: An 18-story building.
Weak: He stepped off of the train.
Strong: He stepped off the train.
Weak: The club will meet on Friday.
Strong: The club will meet Friday.

d. Connectives:

Weak: He said that he would go.
Strong: He said he would go.

> (However, when two or more *that* clauses follow a verb, the conjunction should be used with all clauses for purposes of clarity.)

e. Well-known place names:

Weak: He came from Chicago, Ill.
Strong: He came from Chicago.

f. Phrases:

Weak: The accident occurred at the corner of Vine and Maple Streets.
Strong: The accident occurred at Vine and Maple.
Weak: The debate lasted for a period of two hours.
Strong: The debate lasted two hours.

g. Clauses:

Weak: All who are interested can vote.
Strong: All those interested can vote.
Weak: The drought which occurred last summer.
Strong: The drought last summer.

h. Redundancies:

Weak: Past experience had taught him the way.
Strong: Experience had taught him the way.

4c   **2. Use Simple, Accurate, and Vivid Words.**

a. Short, common words are usually best. The newspaper is written to be read hurriedly by persons of all levels of intellect.

Use	*Rather than*
fire	holocaust, conflagration
died	passed away, deceased
man	gentleman
woman	lady
left	departed
body	remains
buried	interred
cancer	carcinoma

4d

b. Superlatives are usually inaccurate. There are few "catastrophes," "panics," and "fiascos."

More Accurate	*Less Accurate*
a beautiful woman	the most beautiful woman
an exciting game	the most exciting game
seldom	never
frequently	always
probably true	absolutely certain
escape	miraculous escape

4e

c. Caution must be taken in the accurate use of present tense:

Wrong: The policeman grabs the prisoner and pushes him into a cell.
Right: The policeman grabbed the prisoner and pushed him into a cell.
Wrong: Mr. Smith says he favors the proposal.
Right: Mr. Smith said he favors the proposal.
Right: Mr. Smith favors the proposal.

4f

d. Tarnished word ornaments (figures of speech) are not vivid:

Avoid

charming hostess	blushing bride
tastefully decorated	host of friends
watery grave	received an ovation
busy as bees	dance divinely
view with alarm	brutally murdered
point with pride	Joe College
stormy session	Mother Earth

e. The active voice is usually more forceful than the passive: **4g**

Weak: The man was seen by the students.
Strong: Students saw the man.
Weak: The accident was witnessed by many persons.
Strong: Many persons saw the accident.
Stronger: Eleven persons saw the accident.

But in order to emphasize the proper element the passive voice must frequently be used:

Weak: The County Election Committee elected W. P. Jones chairman.
Strong: W. P. Jones was elected chairman of the County Election Committee.
Weak: An automobile killed John Brown, county attorney, today.
Strong: John Brown, country attorney, was killed in an automobile accident today.

3. The Reporter Does not Editorialize (Express His Opinion).

He does not render verdicts or pass judgment, but writes   **4h**
from an objective point of view; consequently, he does not
use *I, me, my, we, us,* or *our* in a news story except in cases when he is quoting a person who uses these pronouns. (Certain types of *byline* stories are also exceptions to the rule.) Favorable or unfavorable phrases in a news story about a person, place, or thing must be factual, not drawn from the opinion of the reporter.

Improper: He is well qualified for the position.
Proper: He is a graduate of Michigan and has had 10 years' experience.
Improper: An interesting program has been prepared.
Proper: The program follows.
            (Let the "interesting" things speak for themselves.)
Improper: The decision was unjust.
Proper: The attorney general said the decision was unjust.
Improper: The prisoner lost his temper.
Proper: The prisoner threw his hat on the floor.
Improper: The witness lied.
Proper: The witness lied, said the prosecuting attorney.
Improper: He committed suicide by jumping from the window.
Proper: He was killed in a fall from the window, and the coroner ruled it a suicide.
Improper: Little Johnny Black, six-year-old darling son of Mr. and Mrs. W. R. Black, died today.
Proper: Johnny Black, six, died today. He was the son of Mr. and Mrs. W. R. Black.

Improper: The attractive young lady will win the hearts of all visitors when she begins serving as hostess at the chamber of commerce next week.

Proper: The attractive young woman will begin serving as hostess at the chamber of commerce next week. ("Attractive young woman" is permissible in some newspapers if she *is* attractive and young, but many newspapers consider such phrases as puff.)

Improper: The judge told me (told this reporter) the case was dismissed.

Proper: The judge said the case was dismissed.

Improper: The speaker said our city was well planned.

Proper: The speaker said Blankville was well planned.

4i   **4. Sentences and Paragraphs Should Be Short.** The news paragraph seldom exceeds 50 words and may be composed of from one to about four sentences. Four lines of typewritten material—about 30 to 40 words—make a well-proportioned paragraph.

In general, the newspaper paragraph is a mechanical and arbitrary—not a logical and essential—group of words. Its chief purpose is to break up the solid column of words to permit easy reading. As fully as its brevity will permit, however, it should achieve the standard qualities of unity, coherence, and emphasis. Short, simple sentences are better than long, involved sentences, but the effort to achieve short sentences should not result in a choppy style. Variety in the length and in the opening phrasing of both sentences and paragraphs will avoid monotony.

Involved: An invitation to new industries to locate in Blankville was issued by the chamber of commerce yesterday at its annual meeting in the dining room of the Hotel Astor, and a new secretary, Henry Ijams, 221 Belmont Street, was elected to promote the industrial program, succeeding James Butler, resigned.

Better: New industries for Blankville will be a goal of the chamber of commerce, and Henry Ijams, former newspaperman, will be the promoter in this effort.

     The chamber adopted its industrial development program and elected Mr. Ijams as secretary at its annual meeting yesterday. Mr. Ijams, 221 Belmont Street, succeeds James Butler, who resigned the secretaryship.

4j   **5. Persons Named in News Stories Should Be Identified.** The "mayor" in Mayor John Jones is sufficient identification in this and similar cases, of course. If, however, a person named is not so easily pointed out, the reporter must seek other means to identify him.

Numerous types of descriptive facts are used in identifying persons named in the news. The most common include nicknames, age, home address, occupation, affiliations with social or religious organizations, public offices held, relationship to famous or infamous persons ("nephew of Congressman Jones"), achievements ("city golf champion"), and infamy ("ex-convict").

The most commonly used identification is the home address. Some newspapers use both age and home address as a general rule. But the reporter is encouraged to use others in addition to, or in lieu of, the home address if better identifications are available. "Trent Street grocer," for example, is a much better identification than the home address of Leonard M. Jones. More persons will know Mr. Jones as a Trent Street grocer than as Leonard M. Jones of 3401 Trent Street. To the extent that the purpose of the identification is to point out a particular person—to point him out as he is known by the greatest number of persons—these conventional devices serve well enough.

6. Every News Story Should Reveal or Clearly Imply Its Source or Authority. Unless the reporter is an eyewitness of an event, **4k** he gets his facts second hand. To overcome this handicap he must state the authority or source (also called the attribution) for every fact in a news story unless that authority is implied. The reporter usually has three options:

a. He may explicitly state the source of his information:

The strike will end at noon Thursday, according to Mayor Thomas.

b. Or leave the source implied

Ten men escaped from the county jail in the early hours this morning. (The implied source is the sheriff or jailer.)

c. Or purposely conceal the source to protect some individual or maintain a news advantage:

A special session of the legislature will be called within 30 days despite the governor's denial of a rumor to that effect, it was learned authoritatively last night.

But the reporter must give the source (authority) of all opinionated items:

"Mayor Thomas is not qualified for the high office he holds," declared Councilman Harkwright.

Especially is it essential for the reporter to give the source or authority for derogatory statements. In doing so he guards against publishing biased or erroneous statements as his own. As a matter of fact, in some cases he may need to quote several persons in order to avoid presenting one version as the truth. This will alleviate his embarrassment in case he finds that he has been exploited by usually reliable sources which may have ulterior motives in generating certain news stories.

4l   To state his authority throughout a story the reporter uses both indirect and direct quotations. He employs various devices to alter the "Mr. Blank said" phrase. *This authoritative expression commonly is placed in an unemphatic position, usually at the end of the sentence.* Even in that position, such synonyms as "declared," "insisted," and "pointed out" may be used to avoid monotony. Variety also is achieved in such a sentence as " 'The tax is unfair,' said Mr. Blank," by presenting the authoritative phrase within the sentence:

> Mr. Blank condemned the tax as "unfair."
> That the tax is "unfair" was Mr. Blank's contention.

Words used in the authoritative or attributive expression must be chosen with care. To write that "Mr. Blank pointed out" implies that Mr. Blank stated an indisputable fact with which the writer agrees. In some cases the use of "admitted" has an erroneous connotation of admitting guilt to a wrongdoing. "Whispered," "screamed," "thundered," "declared," "insisted," and other such descriptive words must be used for the sake of accuracy—not for the sake of variety.

7. The Story Itself Should Be Well Organized. The incidents
4m   of a story may actually occur in the greatest chaos and confusion. The written story must analyze and relate these incidents one to another and to the central story theme. A speaker may actually ramble in this fashion:

> Gentlemen, this is a bad bill and ought not to pass. I was talking to Senator Williams last night, and he said the state can't afford all these social security payments. I'm just as anxious to help the unfortunate as the next man, but I know down in my section we've got no way of knowing who's 65 years old and who isn't. You've got to go to the family Bible to find out. This state's practically bankrupt. Besides,

business conditions are going to get better, and all we're doing if we pass this bill is encourage a lot of people not to work. You wouldn't want relatives of yours on relief when they could get jobs, would you?

But the news story probably would read:

Senator Jones opposed the bill. He argued that the state is near bankruptcy and cannot afford pensions, that there is no way to determine who is eligible for pensions, and that improved business conditions will eliminate the need for pensions.

The Stylebook

Before attempting to write news stories, the reporter should study thoroughly the stylebook of the publication for which he is working. This guide, which usually is handed a new reporter on his first day, explains the newspaper's style in preparing copy, spelling, punctuating, capitalizing, abbreviating, and other such details. The common style is observed by all staff members.

The stylebook does not pretend to be an English grammar or a guide to composition and rhetoric. A reporter is expected to know common grammatical rules before he begins his newspaper career. Also, he should make constant use of a standard handbook of English composition. The stylebook is designed to clarify certain disputed or difficult points and to explain certain accepted usages. One newspaper capitalizes street and avenue when they are used in place-names (*Fourth Street*), which is called the "up style." Another newspaper uses a lowercase letter (*Fourth street*), the "down style." Some newspapers use short forms for such words as *through,* making it *thru.* Obviously, not all stylebooks are alike, but the following can be studied as typical:

4n *Preparing Copy*

1. Prepare all copy with a typewriter.
2. Begin every story on a new sheet of paper (copy paper is generally $8\frac{1}{2} \times 11$ inches in size).
3. The reporter should place his name at the upper left-hand corner of every page.
4. In the same line with his name, or in the line below, he should write the "guideline" or "slug" for the story. This line is a brief identification of the story, such as "fire" for a fire story or "city council" for a report of a city council meeting.

5. Number every page at the top, following the slug.
6. On the first page, leave ample space between the slug and first paragraph—from one-fourth to one-third of a page.
7. Leave margins of at least one inch on both sides.
8. Double space all copy.
9. Write on one side of the paper only.
10. Do not split a word at the end of a line.
11. Do not split sentences between pages, and avoid splitting paragraphs.
12. Write "more" or draw a short down-pointed arrow in the center at the end of each page when the story continues on another page.
13. Place an end mark (# or 30) in the center of the page at the end of the story.

4o   *Spelling*

Any standard dictionary is the reference for spelling. Also, a city directory, telephone directory, almanac, and Bible are useful in checking on the spelling of proper names.

4p   *Punctuating*

Use of the period:

1. Omit the periods in abbreviations of well-known governmental and other agencies:

     FBI   ROTC   AAA   FCC   ICC   PTA   USDA

2. Use three periods (. . .) to indicate quoted matter which has been omitted (four periods if at the end of a sentence and another sentence follows).
3. Use a period to indicate cents only when the figure is more than one dollar and when the dollar mark is used. Otherwise, write the word "cents."

            $1.01   43 cents   nine cents

4. Omit periods in headlines, subheadings, captions, roman numerals, and letters used in formulas.

Use of the comma:

1. Avoid superfluous use of commas, but do not violate accepted rules as set out in a standard handbook of English composition.

2. Use commas to set off the identification of a person, unless the identification is preceded by "of":

> John Smith, 1012 Towne Street
> John Smith of 1012 Towne Street

3. Use commas in listing a series (see Semicolon, 1).
4. Do not use a comma between a man's name and "Jr.," "Sr.," "II":

> John Jones Sr.   James Smith Jr.   George VI

Use of the colon:

1. Use a colon to introduce a formal series of names or statements: The following officers were elected: John Smith, president . . . (But "Officers elected are John Smith, president . . .")
2. Use a colon before minutes in writing the time of day, as "3:30 p.m." (But "3 p.m.")
3. Use a colon between chapter and verse in referring to the Bible: *Luke 1: 3-5.*

Use of the semicolon:

1. Semicolons should be used to separate a series of names and addresses or similar series containing commas:

> Those attending where John Jones, 405 Trace Street; James Smith, 910 Drew Avenue; . . .
> Points earned by Joe Jones, 893; James Smith, 745; . . .

2. Semicolons should be used instead of periods in headlines:

> Six Convicts Escape;
> Prison Guard Wounded

Use of the dash:

1. Use dashes to indicate unfinished sentences or broken sentence structure.
2. Use dashes to set off highly parenthetical elements and to enclose appositives containing commas.

> A crowd assembled in front of the building, but the sheriff—the man for whom they called—was not to be found.
> The six students selected—three seniors, two juniors, and one sophomore—will receive . . .

3. Use dashes in Q. and A. quotations, omitting quotation marks:

> Q.—How old are you? A.—Fifty-four.

4. Use dashes to indicate omitted letters.
5. Use a dash to separate a dateline from the first word of the lead.
6. Form the dash with two hyphens (--) on the typewriter.

Use of the hyphen:

1. Use the hyphen in compound adjectives:

> coal-black chimney   well-known man
> old-fashioned dress   so-called enemy
> 10-year-old girl   10-yard gain

2. Use a hyphen with prefixes to proper names:

> un-American   pre-Christian   anti-Whig

3. Use a hyphen in writing figures or fractions:

> sixty-five   two-thirds

4. Use a hyphen between two figures to indicate the inclusion of all intervening figures, as "May 1-5."
5. Use a hyphen instead of "to" in giving scores, as "13-6."

Use of parentheses:

1. Use parentheses to insert a word within a title:

> The Bridgetown (Conn.) Fire Department

2. Use parentheses in a direct quotation to insert words which are not the speaker's:

> "They (the strikebreakers) shall not pass," said the foreman.

3. Use parentheses to enclose figures or letters which indicate subject divisions within a sentence:

> The committee decided (1) to refuse permission . . .
> The board voted (a) to build a new athletic field . . .

4. Use parentheses to indicate the political party or state, or both, of a government official, in abbreviated form.

> Senator John Smith (D, Cal.)

Use of quotation marks:

1. Use quotation marks to set off direct quotations.

4q   (SPECIAL NOTE: While most sentences can be written as either direct or indirect quotations, the use of direct quotations in newspaper stories is reserved largely for statements which are best displayed within quotation marks. Examples are highly controversial statements, colorful phrasings, pointed or well-phrased statements, ironical expressions, facts rendered inaccurate by rewording, ideas rendered ineffective by paraphrasing, and unusual combinations of words.)

2. Use quotation marks to set off titles of speeches, articles, books, poems, plays, operas, paintings, television programs:

"Pride and Prejudice" "Hamlet" "Mona Lisa" "Aida"

(*Note:* Newspapers generally do not use italic body type, and quotation marks are employed as a substitute. However, quotation marks are not used in naming newspapers and magazines.)

3. Use quotation marks to set off coined words, slang, and unusual words or expressions the first time such words are used in a story. Do not use quotation marks if the same words are used again.

4. Use quotation marks to set off nicknames when the full name is used but not when the nickname is used instead of the full name:

John "Bud" Smith Bud Smith

5. In a series of quoted paragraphs, use quotation marks at the beginning of each of these paragraphs and at the end of the last paragraph only.

6. Use single marks for a quotation within a quotation.

7. In headlines use the single quotation mark.

8. Quotation marks should always *follow* adjoining periods and commas:

"Here," she said.

His style recalled "Leaves of Grass."

If the punctuation belongs to the quotation, the question mark, the exclamation point, the colon, the semicolon, and the dash also are followed by quotation marks:

"What do you want?" she asked.

Otherwise quotation marks *precede* these punctuation marks:

Have you seen the new motion picture, "May Queen"?

Use of the apostrophe:

1. Use the apostrophe to form the plural of letters but not the plural of figures, as "A's," "60s."

2. Use the apostrophe to indicate the possessive case:

New Year's Day Master's degree children's home

3. Omit the apostrophe in such names as Blank County Farmers League, City Lawyers Association.

4r   *Capitalizing*

Capitalize:

1. Religious denominations and orders:
   Protestant   Baptist   Jesuits   Franciscan

2. Nationalities, races:
   Germans   Negro   Chinese   Bostonians

3. Names of animals, as Fido or Rover (no quotation marks).

4. Names of political organizations:
   Democratic   Republican   Communist Party

5. National, state, and local subdivisions:
   North   South   West Montana   East Blankville

6. Political divisions:
   Blank County   First District   Fifth Ward

7. Words used with numerals to form a proper name:
   Operator 7   Room 32   Lot 21   Journalism 301

8. Titles preceding proper names but not "former" or "ex" preceding such titles:
   President K. L. Burns   Prof. T. M. Smith
   former President K. L. Burns

9. Nicknames, including those of states, cities, schools.

10. *Complete* titles of all public or private organizations:
    General Assembly   City High School
    City School Board   First Baptist Church
    City Council   City Department Store
    First National Bank   Jones and Company
    Southmoor Hotel   Center Country Club

11. Place-names:
    Lake Michigan   Ohio River   Vatican
    First Creek   Atlantic Ocean
    Great Smoky Mountains National Park

12. The first and all principal words in titles of speeches, plays, books, poems:
    "An Answer to Questions on War"   "The Way of the World"

13. *Complete* titles of streets, avenues, boulevards, roads, as
    "King Street,"   "Elm Lane,"   "Queen's Way"

14. Holidays:

      Fourth of July   Labor Day   Lincoln's Birthday

15. The "Union" in referring to the United States.
16. Abbreviations of college degrees, as "B.A."
17. Abbreviations of "junior" and "senior" to "Jr." and "Sr."
18. Names of legislative acts or sections of documents, as Smith Law, Title D.

    (A final reminder: If in doubt about capitalizing a word, make it lowercase.)

Do not capitalize:

1. Seasons of the year, as "spring," "summer."
2. Points of the compass, as "northeast."
3. The abbreviations "a.m." and "p.m."
4. Titles which follow proper names, as "K. L. Burns, president."
5. Names of studies, except languages, as "mathematics," "French," "literature."
6. Scientific names of plants and animals, except names derived from proper nouns (Hereford cattle).
7. "National," "government," "state," "federal," except in titles.
8. "Association," "club," "army," "navy," "society," except in titles.
9. "Alma mater."

Abbreviating   4s

Abbreviate:

1. Months of the year of more than five letters when the day of the month is given:

    Nov. 24   the last week in January   March 21

2. Times of the day, as 6 p.m.
3. Familiar college degrees, as B.A., Ph.D., M.D.
4. Names of states only when they follow names of cities or counties:

      Blankville, Ark.   a town in Arkansas

5. Mr., Mrs., Dr., the Rev., Prof., Gov., Gen., etc., when they precede the name of the person.
6. "Saint" and "mount" only when preceding names:

    St. Louis   Mt. McKinley   "Sermon on the Mount"

7. Sr., Jr., II following proper names.
8. Titles of public and private organizations that are well known by

the readers *after* such titles have been used once in spelled-out form:

FBI   SEC   CIO   YMCA   UCLA

Do not abbreviate:

1. Christmas.
2. "Percent" as "%," except in tabulation.
3. Names of persons.
4. Points of the compass.
5. Names of cities or counties.
6. Days of the week.
7. Street, avenue, boulevard, etc.
8. "Company," except when a part of the official name.
9. Association, fraternity, university.
10. "Department" or "building."
11. "And" as "&."
12. Weights or measures, as "pound," "foot."

4†   *Titles*

1. Always give a person's first name or initials with the surname the *first* time any name is used. (Use the first name, *not* initials, of unmarried women.) Thereafter, the person may be referred to as:

Miss Smith   Dr. Smith
Mrs. Smith   Prof. Smith
Mr. Smith   Gen. Smith

2. Always use "Mrs." before a married woman's name and "Miss" before an unmarried woman's name, but do not use "Mr." before a man's name when his full name is given. "John T. Smith" becomes "Mr. Smith" on further reference.
3. For most religious denominations, it is correct to refer to the minister *first* as "the Rev. John Smith," and thereafter in a story as "Mr. Smith" ("Dr. Smith" only if he has the doctor's degree). Exceptions: Roman Catholics, "the Rev. John Smith" then "Father Smith." Jewish, "Rabbi John Milton" then "Rabbi Milton." Latterday Saints (Mormons), "President John Smith" then "Mr. Smith." Christian Scientists have officials with titles of "Practitioner," "Lecturer," and "Reader" instead of "the Rev."

4. Do not use long and cumbersome titles *before* a name. Instead of "Director of Public Parks John Smith" make it "John Smith, director of public parks."

5. Do not refer to a woman as "Mrs. Dr. John Smith" or "Mrs. Prof. John Smith." A wife has no claim on her husband's title.

6. Instead of "Mesdames" or "Messrs." use titles singly.

7. Write it "Mr. and Mrs. John Smith" instead of "John Smith and wife."

8. Do not use "honorable" in a title unless quoting someone else.

9. Do not use double titles such as "President Dr. John Smith." Choose the higher title or the one of greater relevance to the story.

10. Give *exact* titles of faculty members, public officials, business executives. "Professor" and "instructor," for example, are not synonymous.

Figures   **4u**

1. Spell out numbers from one through nine, and use digits for all numbers above nine.

   Exceptions:

   a. Spell out any number which begins a sentence.
   b. Spell out numbers referring to centuries, as "tenth century."
   c. Spell out ordinal street names, as "Fourth Street" up to 21st.
   d. Instead of "thirty-fifth," "fiftieth," use "35th," "50th," except in referring to centuries.
   e. Spell out numbers in such phrases as "one in a hundred."
   f. Use figures for all sums of money: "$5," $6.01," "$23."
   g. Use figures in reporting all scores: "City High School won 13-6."
   h. Use figures for time of day, as "3 p.m.," "8 o'clock."
   i. Use figures in tabulations.
   j. Use figures for any whole and fractional number, as "9½," "4.1."

2. Spell out fractions, except after whole numbers, as "one-third."

3. Do not use "st," "nd," "rd," "th" after dates. Write "Aug. 10, 1971."

4v   *Miscellaneous*

Use the following style:

all-state	everyone	Old Glory
all right	ex-officio	Post Office
anti-Catholic	governor-elect	reelect
anybody	half dollar	somebody
anyone	half dozen	some one
attorney general	homecoming	state-wide
baseball	Joneses (plural)	text book
basketball	line up	two-thirds
cheerleader	newspaper	upstate
cooperate	nobody	
everybody	no one	

4w   *Correcting Copy*

The beginning reporter should learn a few of the copyreading marks immediately so that he may know how to make pencil corrections in his typewritten story.

In typing a story it is proper to "x" out words and sentences and to make pencil corrections, but the copy should be clean enough to be readable, and all corrections should be clear beyond a doubt when it leaves the reporter's hands.

Following are the marks used by most reporters:

Delete letters:

Two men were in the car . . .

Delete word or words:

Two men were ~~were~~ in the car ~~behind us~~ with . . .

Transpose letters or words:

Tow men in were the car with . . .

Spell out or abbreviate (same symbol in both cases) :

2 men were in the car with Mister Jones.

Insert word or words:

Two men were in the car with Mr. Jones.

Capitalize letter:

    <u>t</u>wo men were in the car with . . .

Make letter lower case:

    Two /Men were in the car . . .

Period mark (either of two symbols) :

    Two men were in the car with Mr⊙ Jones✗

Separate letters with space:

    Two men were|in the car . . .

Bring letters together:

    Two men we⌢re in the car . . .

Restore text of copy which has been marked out:

    Two men ~~were in the car~~ *stet* with Mr. Jones.

In deleting copy on more than one line, mark out all the deleted material and draw a heavy line directly from the beginning to the end of the deleted material:

    Located in the center of the little island is a
    log cabin, ~~built perhaps 100 years ago though no~~
    ~~one knows for sure and there is no way of finding~~
    ~~out,~~ and back of the cabin is the site of the old
    Indian village.

In correcting misspelled words which have only one or two letters wrong, mark out each misused letter and place the correct letter above. If a word is badly misspelled, mark out the whole word and write it correctly above:

    The b°ay walked ~~noncholontly~~ *nonchalantly* into the room.

The reporter should use the symbols whenever possible in correcting his copy because they are time-saving devices. However, if a phrase (or word) is split between two lines, the simplest procedure is to mark through all or part of the phrase and rewrite it correctly between the lines.

Exercises

I. Study the sentences in stories appearing on the front page of a daily newspaper. Copy 10 sentences which you think achieve the qualities of simplicity, conciseness, vividness, and other characteristics of good journalism. If you find examples of poor sentences, copy them also and explain what you think is wrong with them.

II. Most if not all of the following items are written in faulty newspaper language. Copy them as they are given and make corrections with the copyreader's marks.

A. Storm hits city; two persons injured.

B. The group will engage in a discussion regarding the proposal to reduce the maximum limitations placed on the speed of automobiles.

C. Mr. Johns states that he had come from Philadelphia, Penna.

D. Jury's verdict will certainly be guilty.

E. The three men sat in an automobile which was stopped at the front of the city library.

F. The pedestrian was intercepted by the cop.

G. Councilman Jones gave a most interesting speech on vicissitudes of holding public office.

H. He went on for the length of eight pages in an effort to emphasize the great need for more successful business executives to offer themselves for service to our city.

I. The abject prisoner confessingly admitted that he is involved in four mysteries now listed as unsolved crimes in the books of police records.

J. The accident which occurred there last year was the worst in the entire history of the state.

K. A meeting of local dentists will convene on Saturday.

L. The short midget stepped up on the stairway in order that he could be seen by all members of the audience.

M. He walks to the very end of the pier, at which point the boat was docked.

N. The sweet little girl with gorgeous dimpled cheeks skipped up to the widow woman and offered her heartfelt condolences.

O. The mayor is unfair when he said that there is no need for more parks in our city.

P. The School Board decided that schools will be opened for the fall session on September 6th.

Q. He accelerated the vehicle, smacked through the intersection, and rammed into the left side of truck.

R. The act was enacted by the Legislature of the State.

S. The wintry blast was so cold that we could hardly breathe when we stepped outside the front door.

T. Mr. John Jones, who is a former city commissioner, is a proud father of a seven-pound-and fourteen-ounce son today, and the bouncing baby boy will be named John, Jr.

U. An M and M taxicab driven by Joe Johns today killed P. D. Quinn.

V. Congressman Jim Jones will make a speech at the regular weekly meeting of the Civitan Club to be held in the south end of the east ballroom of the Lakeside Hotel, 2476 Lakeside Avenue, at 12 noon on the fifteenth of next month.

W. Like all embezzlers, the accused man stoutly denied that he had anything at all to do with the missing funds.

X. He munched on the desiccated peach as though he had not eaten in a week of Sundays.

III. Copy a short local news story from a daily newspaper to illustrate the correct method of preparing copy. This exercise should be about a page and a half in length.

IV. A. Prepare a list of synonyms for "said."

B. Clip a long story from a metropolitan daily, underlining all words which give the source or authority for facts in the story.

C. Examining a metropolitan daily, jot down every different device employed to alter the "said Mr. Blank" expression. (This should not include synonyms for *said*.)

V. Observing the stylebook and using copyreading marks, make corrections in the following stories. (To avoid mutilating the text these exercises should be duplicated, line for line, for student use. Otherwise, the student should list separately the proper corrections.)

A. Smith—shotgun death.

A 10-year-old mountin boy was arrested at jonville, today on charges of killing his 11-year-old Playmate with a shotgun The boy told officers his gun went off of accidently while the two were rab bit hunting.

The boy, jack Thopmson, who explained to officers that his gun went off accidently while the two were out hunting, is the son of W. A. Thompson, prosperous farmer. Lewis Jackson the slain youth was the son of a tenant far mar.

"We were crawlling under a fence, andsuddenly I saw 4 rabbits rabbits jump up, said young Thompson. "I was trying to my gun so tha I could shoot them, though it went off too soon."

The descharge h it young J ckson back of the head, him

killing enstentantely Coroner Adcock said the shooting appeared accidental. He said char ges against the Thompson boy probably would be dismissed.

B. Smith—traffic record

Traffic accidents claim 565 lives in the state during the past year, exceeding the total for the proceeding gear by twelve, according to official statistics released today by the State Safety department.

The annual report also revealed that $\frac{1}{10}$ of the automobile collisions resulted in personal injuries, and that the largest single classification of fatal accidents was pedestrans.

A total of 86362 accidents were included in the statistics, reported by the various city and county law enforcement agencies. This figure is 103 more than the preceding year's.

"Our reporting system has improved somewhat thruout the past year, so it may be that the total number has decreased instead of increasing," said Director of the Safety Department W. M. Bill Brown, junior. "Local law enforcement bodies have been very cooperative in keeping accurate records during the year."

Individual city accident records showed that Blankville, in up state, had a higher rate than any other city in the State. With an average of 10 accidents per 1000 population, Blankville ranked second in the entire section of the union.

More acci ents occurred on Sat. than on any other day, but the fourth of July was the biggest and September 10 was the second biggest accident days of the year, a further broad-down of s tatistics revealed. Also, more accidents occurred during the Spring, especially May 1 to May 21, than during any other season.

Personal injuries were received in 8,589 of the accidents, and 77,255 caused property damage, according to the report. Fatalities resulted from five hundred and three collisions.

The largest single classification of fatal accidents was 210 pedestrians. Accidents, in which two or more automobiles were involved, resulted in the death of 118. Non-collision mishaps killed 146. 60 were killed in automobile crashes with fixed objects such as telephone poles or underpasses.

Other direct causes given were, collisions between autos and railroad trains, 20, autos and street cars, 7, autos and 'buses, 8, autos and motorcycles, 6, and autos and horse trawn vehicals, 5.

The accident prevention bureau, of the Safety department, is preparing to use those statistics in an article on Fighting for safety, in a future issue of "The Daily News." This Bureau urged all motorists to co-operate with the recent act of the general assembly requiring all drivers involved in motor accidents to report to local authorities.

Under the new Law, a fine of from two dollars to fifty dollars may be imposed on any one failing to report an adcident, said Dir. Brown.

Chapter 5

Ethics and Libel

A moral problem, vaguely shaded along its edges but of definite hue at its center, constantly faces the newspaper and the reporter. The question deals with what should and what should not be printed. The newspaper is in possession of both printable and unprintable news. The distinction between black and white offers no difficulty, but somewhere in the gray shadows, where the two merge, there is considerable difficulty in knowing not only what to say but how to say it and when.

For example, one of the city's distinguished citizens has embezzled a large sum of money. Or has he? The money has disappeared, and so has he. As the reporter probes into the matter, he discovers that the distinguished citizen has been untrue to his wife at a business convention. But what has this to do with the embezzlement? The bank would prefer that nothing be said about the missing money just now. Yet the money was a campaign fund, and the election is approaching.

Without attempting to solve this particular problem (and it is not highly imaginary), one can recognize in it the moral difficulties involved in much news reporting. On the one hand is the public interest, and on the other are special private interests. Where these are clearly conceived, the newspaper's policy (discussed in another chapter) may influence its decisions and establish its course of action. Certain larger issues of ethics and policy must await the crystallization of public opinion. For example, whether the newspapers should publish more, or less, crime news—whether they should lead or follow their public—whether they should be more, or less, free in their criticism of public men and issues—these larger ethical questions must be determined ultimately by public opinion. They cannot and need not be determined by the reporter. His principal concern is his own professional code of ethics.

Relation to Public. The reporter cannot lose sight of the fact that the public welfare may be involved in much that he writes. His writing is addressed to the public, and the public is dependent directly upon him for its knowledge of affairs by means of which, individually and in the mass, it must solve its problems. Careless, slipshod, inaccurate, or biased reporting is inexcusable under this responsibility. The reporter cannot be expected to be free of mistakes in judgment. He will face situations in which he must make decisions on what, and how, and when, and how much of his information he should reveal. His own conscience must guide him. But if he has taken the trouble to develop a sufficient background of information so that his thinking is thoroughly enlightened, and if the public welfare is his object, he can rest assured that he is performing his duty.

Relation to Newspaper. Fortunate is the reporter whose newspaper is content that he should perform his duty with truth and public welfare as his objectives, and this is the case with a large majority of the newspapers. However, some publishers, in pursuit of a policy, may expect much more or much less than the plain unvarnished truth as the reporter sees it. In rare instances, too, a change in ownership may cause the newspaper to reverse a policy, political or other. The choice for the reporter will be extremely difficult if he is instructed by his editor to twist the truth in a story. Three possible courses seem to be open to him. He may refuse to alter his own principles and resign. He may accept the assignment and salvage his self-respect as best he can. Or he may attempt to work out with the employer an agreement for his own integrity and independence. There can be no doubt that the first and third choices are strictly ethical—and should be profitable in the long run.

Relation to News Sources. The reporter's access to news sources is one of his chief professional assets. These sources must be carefully cultivated, and it is obvious that they must be honorably maintained and respected. On the basis of self-interest and professional interest, to say nothing of the basis in honor, the reporter cannot divulge secrets nor betray confidences. On the other hand, he may be wise not to accept some of the so-called confidences, for the same information may come to him from other sources. The intelligent reporter should have little difficulty in managing the ethics of this situation if he will continually be aware of the problem. He should have a clear understanding with every person he deals with. When confronted with such common admonitions as "get this on the first page" or "let me check your story," he must explain that his editors, not he, must make these decisions. He can promise not to quote direct language and not to reveal where he obtained the information —but he should be very cautious, indeed, about promising not to use materials in any way. He should respect release dates. He should protect innocent persons from false inference, but he cannot promise to abandon his pursuit of news so long as that news is in the public interest.

Accuracy as a Protection. The best protection against bias in reporting is the indefatigable pursuit of fact and the careful checking of all facts. So long as the reporter presents the news as it actually occurs, without fear or favor or emotional coloring, he is on the safe highway of his professional duty, and both he and his newspaper are largely immune to resentment or attack. There are problems to be encountered, however. A large proportion of the news will be injurious, or will be thought so by the individuals involved. The more important the revelation, the more resistance there is, usually, to the reporting of it. (Certain technical problems of privileged and nonprivileged documents will be examined presently.) But, in general, a sound reputation for accurate, professional reporting will overcome resistance, solve problems, and open many doors to the source of news.

Importance of Authoritative News Sources. Perhaps of next importance as a solution of the ethical problem is the careful use of authority in the news. It is unnecessary and usually unwise for the reporter to assume responsibility for the facts of his story. Occasionally he is an eyewitness. Frequently he is an interpreter. Always he is a reporter, however, and by attributing his materials to their proper sources he refrains from assuming responsibility for the story content. Even if he must conceal the individual whom he would like to quote, he can imply, if not the authority, at least the authenticity of his data. When all is said and done, however, the reporter must occasionally face the ultimate problem of libel.

5a   *A Code of Ethics*

What are some concrete "rules of honor" for the newspaper to observe in building a stronger, cleaner press? Each newspaper will have its own "Code of Ethics," either written or unwritten. The codes of various newspapers range in flavor from ultraconservatism to extreme sensationalism (the latter being commonly called "yellow journalism"). Below are some of the rules frequently present in the codes observed by highly respected newspapers. If they were accepted as a minimum code of ethics by every newspaper, the prestige of the press truly would be enhanced.

The newspaper must stay within the bounds of decency.
Foul language and the sordid details of crimes and other oc-   **5b**
currences which should not be read by every person in the
community, particularly the young, have no place in a newspaper.

*The newspaper should report news and should not attempt
to "make" news.* Exaggeration of a minor incident "to write   **5c**
a better story" is making news. So is the "publicity stunt"
planned by the reporter or within the knowledge of the reporter
(excluding certain promotional stories, as discussed in Chapter 26).
"Rumor stories" which are conceived by the reporter himself are
also invented news.

The newspaper should print the truth and the whole truth.
To report that "The chairman of the School Board favors   **5d**
eliminating public schools" would be an obvious attempt to
smudge character with the half truth (which in this and many other
cases becomes a falsehood) if the chairman's full statement was that
public schools should be eliminated "unless the people give adequate
financial support to make them good schools."

*The newspaper does not have the privilege to invade the private
rights of an individual* unless the actions of the individual have made
his private life "public domain" and the information sought is
considered to be something the public has a right to know. However,
public curiosity should not be substituted for public rights.

*The newspaper does not have the privilege to force individuals to
speak for publication.* Freedom of the press is not a license to command news data. The reporter must not intimidate a person, in an
attempt to get a statement, with threats of writing unfavorable
comments about him. However, if a person refuses to comment on a
matter which obviously concerns him, the reporter may so state in
his story.

*The newspaper should play fair with a person against
whom derogatory charges are made.* Unless the charges are   **5e**
made in a court hearing or before a legislative body, the
newspaper should give an accused person the opportunity to answer
the accusations—in the same story which reports the charges, if
possible. (However, having a person answer derogatory charges will
not relieve the newspaper of a libel suit if the accusations are
libelous.)

*The newspaper should play fair with persons quoted in its col-
umns.* Any person interviewed by a reporter should be made to
realize that he will be quoted in print. Quotations from speeches

should not be garbled to misconstrue the ideas of the speaker nor to achieve a more readable story. A person's grammatical errors should not be quoted in an effort to ridicule him. In summary, the reporter should use only quotations which he would be *willing* to show to the person quoted—before publication—even though a reporter rarely does so.

The newspaper should keep the confidence of its news sources. Stories should not be released before the time designated by the properly authorized news source. The reporter should not violate his promises to a news source, but he must never promise to suppress news which should be printed.

The newspaper should not suppress news which should be offered to the public. However, the newspaper has a heart and does not unnecessarily nor unjustly damage the character of an individual for the sake of a story. Sometimes stories, or names in stories, are suppressed in the case of "first offenders" arrested on minor charges, if the welfare of society is not involved. Names of juveniles arrested usually are voluntarily withheld by newspapers because child offenders should not be put in the same category as adults. The reporter should refer to his superiors all requests to withhold news.

The newspaper should not "sell" its news columns for money or courtesies. Advertisers buy space, not the privilege of getting free publicity or of determining policies of the newspaper. Special courtesies to staff member is no excuse for free publicity—nor is friendship with staff members.

5f *The newspaper should refrain from allowing party politics to enter the news column.* The editorial page is the place for the opinions of the newspaper. The news columns should present unbiased news regarding political affairs.

The newspaper should serve the whole of society, not just one "class." The same consideration should be given persons in all social and economic strata of society served by the newspapers.

5g *The newspaper should fight and discourage crime.* The newspaper is a social institution; the criminal is antisocial. The newspaper should never glorify the criminal, nor protect the criminal, nor create sympathy for the criminal who should pay the penalty of his crime. The newspaper should never overplay the crime and underplay the penalty, and it should cooperate with police in withholding news which will obviously aid the criminal in escape.

The newspaper must respect and aid the law and the courts. The newspaper should not criticize or ridicule an official for faithfully enforcing the law. Disagreement with the objectives or effectiveness of certain laws is permissible, however, as editorial comment. The newspaper should never "try" a case in its columns, nor should it call an arrested person a criminal until he is convicted in a court of law.

The newspaper should seek to build its community. "Playing up" the degrading news and giving little play to news of progressive developments will not build a community.

The newspaper should not injure the relatives and friends of a wrongdoer. Parents, brothers and sisters, the wife or **5h** husband of an accused person should not be made to suffer adverse publicity for the sake of "human-interest copy."

The newspaper should recognize divorce as an unfortunate social problem, not as an excuse for a sensational, salacious story. A divorce is news and must be printed. But the newspaper is justified in shearing the story of any indecent details.

The newspaper should recognize suicide as an unfortunate social problem, not as an excuse for a sensational story. One suicide is suggestive of others. Though the suicide should be reported, it should not be played up in detail.

The newspaper should not stoop to an attack upon competitive newspapers, nor boast about a "scoop" over other **5i** newspapers in an effort to increase its own prestige. The excellence of the newspaper should speak for itself. However, the newspaper may advertise its achievements in a positive way through regular promotional channels.

The newspaper should not ridicule the insane, or the feebleminded, or the misfortunes of an individual.

The newspaper should respect churches, nationalities, and races. Slurring nicknames pertaining to race, nativity, or **5j** religion should not be printed.

The newspaper's sports page is written for everybody, not for a selected number of "fans" or participants and certainly **5k** not for petty or big-time gamblers.

The newspaper should be prompt in correcting errors which have appeared in its columns, for errors are bound to occur. Furthermore, an earnest effort to correct errors may help mitigate damages should libel have resulted.

5l
The newspaper should remember that the news is read by young boys and girls, by the mentally unstable, and by the unassimilated foreigner as well as by the normal American adult. Stories, pictures, and advertisements appearing in its columns should not be an evil influence upon any of its readers. For some of the readers, the publication of details on certain types of crimes may lead to lower morals or even the committing of similar crimes.

5m   *The Pitfalls of Libel*

In writing news the reporter handles a valuable possession—reputations. A person's reputation (his good name) is of tangible value. The reporter who damages one's reputation will damage his position in society, his means of earning a livelihood. Such damage, if done beyond the bounds of what a newspaper is legally entitled to print, is called defamation.

Defamation is divided into two categories, libel and slander, to which different modes of procedure are given by the courts. As a general rule, libel is written defamation and slander is spoken. Others have defined libel as that type of defamation which can be observed by the sense of sight, and slander as that which is conveyed by the sense of hearing. Some courts have expanded the definition of libel, making it include all defamation which offers a greater potentiality of harm than does slander. As a result, written materials, signs, cartoons, television, and even radio broadcasts which have been taped or presented from written scripts have been adjudged as libel.

Defamation Defined. Defamation has been defined as that which tends to diminish the esteem, respect, goodwill, or confidence in which a person is held or to incite adverse and derogatory feelings and opinions against him. A person may defame another either by outright expressions or by insinuation or innuendo.

The first major question involved in a defamation case is whether the written or spoken words or signs are defamatory in the eyes of the law. Mere words of abuse and a certain amount of vulgar name-calling may be tolerated, but only when understood to amount to nothing serious. Objective standards by which the court determines what is and what is not defamatory language are not available. Whether the language is defamatory usually must be determined from the circumstances surrounding the alleged violation. Generally, the judge determines whether the language is capable of bearing a defamatory meaning and the jury decides whether it was in fact defamatory, i.e., whether it was so understood.

Who Can Be Defamed. Any living person can be defamed. A dead person cannot be defamed; however, if the words reflect upon any living person (such as a survivor), he can bring an action in his own right. A corporation and a partnership can be defamed by language which casts aspersions on its honesty, credit, efficiency, and other business character.

Every person instrumental in the publication of a libelous statement is responsible. This usually includes the person making the statement, the reporter, the editors, and the newspaper itself, but the newspaper alone is made the defendant in many suits.

Interpretation of Defamatory Words. In all actions for libel and slander, the words alleged to be defamatory must be interpreted as such; they must be understood in the defamatory sense whether or not they are believed by the listeners or readers. If the defamatory meaning arises only from the facts not apparent upon the face of the publication, the plaintiff must establish the defamatory meaning with reference to such facts. If the words are defamatory upon their face (such as naming the wrong person as a convicted criminal), this is defamatory *per se* and it does not require proof of the meaning gathered from surrounding events to be adjudged libelous. Such statements as "it is alleged," "it was reported," or "according to police" do not protect a reporter in making a libelous statement.

Proof Needed. Formerly all libel was actionable without proof of some injury or harm to person or property. Today, however, libel in many jurisdictions is treated like slander in that they require proof of the damages incurred except in the following four cases:

(1) the imputation of a serious crime involving moral turpitude,
(2) the imputation that the party is infected with a contagious disease,
(3) the imputation affecting the plaintiff in his business, trade, profession, or office, and
(4) the imputation of the chastity of a woman.

However, all jurisdictions hold that words which are libelous *per se* are actionable without having to show damage, but in most libel cases damage is shown to increase the amount of the judgment.

Intent to Libel Unnecessary. Absence of intent to libel is no defense, though it may mitigate the penalty. On the other hand, malice will aggravate the penalty, whether it is "malice in fact" or "malice in law." Malice in fact is adjudged in the case of presumed effort on the part of the newspaper to defame a person, and malice in law is declared when the newspaper shows wanton and willful disregard for an individual's rights.

Television and Radio—Whether Libel or Slander. Defamation via television is generally considered libel because it is the type of defamation which can be detected by the sense of sight. The vast audience and the ensuing increase in the likelihood of harm are additional reasons given for this interpretation. Radio presents a different problem. Most courts have held that defamation through the medium of radio is slander unless the broadcast is made from a prepared script or from a tape or other recording.

Defenses of Derogatory Statements. The defenses of a newspaper in publishing a defamatory statement about a person or thing are: (1) the statement is the truth; (2) the newspaper is "privileged" to print the statement; and (3) the statement is a fair comment or criticism of the person. In a defense, it is the responsibility of the newspaper to prove the statement true, or privileged, or a fair comment.

Truth as a Defense. A newspaper's strongest defense against libel is the verified truth. Hence, a reporter cannot rely on hearsay, opinions, or rumors. A report that "Detective Smith said Tom Johns robbed the store" is libelous unless the reporter can prove Johns robbed the store or unless the report is privileged, as explained in following paragraphs. Calling a building "an alleged house of ill repute" libels every person living in that house unless the statement can be proved.

If a statement is true, a libel suit probably will not arise, for truth is generally accepted as a "complete defense." In some states, however, the newspaper's defense must also show justification in printing a derogatory statement that is true. In these states the newspaper must show a good motive for publishing the statement.

Privilege as a Defense. The reporter is privileged to make derogatory statements which are taken from public records, judicial proceedings, or legislative proceedings (such as meetings of the city council and state legislature). Since these records and meetings are open to the public, the newspaper has a right to step in and represent the public. However, all statements must be accurate, impartial, and void of unfair comment. From police records the reporter may obtain a statement that "Tom Johns was arrested on charges of robbing the store," and he is privileged to use it, no matter how badly it damages Johns' reputation. In addition, he can prove that Johns was arrested, and he also has truth as another defense. Great caution is necessary, however, in quoting from police data on matters which have not been presented in court.

Fair Comment. The newspaper also has the right of every American citizen to criticize things offered for public approval—men, measures, and institutions of public concern, provided such criticism is fair, is not actuated by malice, and is not unjustifiably extended to the private life of the persons involved. This category would include all public officials, acts, institutions, and candidates for public office and all speeches, books, shows, and the like submitted for public acceptance. The reporter's criticism may be so severe that it is undoubtedly damaging, but no libel will be adjudicated as long as the safeguards indicated above are observed. The writer should be careful, though, to criticize only the official acts of the public official, only the actual speech of the public speaker, only the substance of the author's book.

A classic example on how far a publication can go in commenting upon a matter submitted for public acceptance was illustrated by the "Cherry Sisters Case" (114 Iowa 298). The defendants had published an article in which a reviewer gave the following graphic description of a public performance by three sisters who danced and sang:

> Effie is an old jade of 50 summers, Jessie a frisky filly of 40 and Addie (the plaintiff in the case), the flower of the family, a capering monstrosity of 35. Their long skinny arms, equipped with talons at the extremities, swung mechanically, and anon waved frantically at the suffering audience. The mouths of their rancid features opened like caverns and sounds like the wailing of damned souls issued therefrom. They pranced around the stage with a motion that suggested a cross between the *danse du ventre* and fox trot—strange creatures with painted faces and hideous mien. Effie is spavined, Addie is stringhalt, and Jessie, the only one who showed her stockings, has legs with calves as classic in their outlines as the curves of a broom handle.

In this action for libel, the trial court witnessed a repeat performance and held that the statement was within the limits of fair comment. However, this does not mean that a court today would be so liberal.

While some libel suits arise from ignorance of law on the part of the reporter, far more cases are the result of careless reporting. To say that F. L. King of 1012 Drew Street is charged with larceny is libelous *per se* if the arrested person is, instead, F. L. King of 1012 Drane Street.

Criminal Libel. Most libel cases go to civil courts, with the plaintiff suing for damages, but certain cases appear also in criminal courts and may be punishable by fine and imprisonment. Many states hold that criminal prosecution is possible if the statement tends to provoke the person about whom it was printed to wrath, to expose him to public hatred, contempt, or ridicule, or to deprive him of the benefits of public confidence and social intercourse. Criminal statutes vary on these points and it is best that the reporter consult his state statutes for the exact rules followed in his state.

Retractions of Libelous Statements. Newspapers attempt to avoid libel suits by publishing retractions of statements which are unquestionably libelous. The retraction should point out and correct the newspaper's errors, without repeating the libelous statement, and the newspaper should apologize to the person or persons concerned. The retraction notice, in order to be effective, must generally be given space or time that is equivalent to the defamatory matter. For instance, if the defamatory material was printed on the first page of the newspaper, the retraction notice should be published on the first page. This does not nullify the claim for damages against the newspaper, though it satisfies many libeled persons and causes them to decide against filing suit. If a libel suit is filed, the retraction may help reduce the damages awarded by indicating lack of actual malice.

5n   *Invasion of the Right of Privacy*

In addition to the snares of libel, the journalistic must avoid other hazards which may take him and his newspaper into court. Another legally protected interest of an individual similar to that involved in defamation is his right of privacy. Cases suggest that there are four important aspects of this right: (1) the interest in seclusion, (2) the interest in self-respect and dignity, (3) the interest in sentimental attachments and associations, and (4) the interest in privacy of a name, likeness, and life history.

As concerns the journalist, the right of privacy includes freedom from publicity even though such publicity is true and no action would lie for defamation. Publicity which violates the bounds of ordinary decency, such as publication of the picture of a person's deformed child, or the details of a person's humiliating illness, or the fact that he does not pay his debts, may create a cause of action for invasion of privacy. Other cases included under this tort are those which put the plaintiff in a false but not necessarily defamatory position in the public eye, such as by using his name or picture in an article in which he has no reasonable connection or by entering him in an embarrassing "popularity" contest.

Invasion of privacy cases are subject to the right to publish news of legitimate public interest; therefore, one who intentionally puts himself before the public, such as an actor, inventor, or public officer, has no right to complain. But a public figure does not forfeit all rights of privacy, and he may recover damages in cases when a journalist oversteps reason or when unauthorized commercial use is made of his name or photograph.

The tort of invasion of the right of privacy is invoked primarily in cases in which the defendant has made unauthorized use of a person's photograph or statement for commercial ventures. These cases are generally more strict in allowing the party aggrieved damages than are cases in which a noncommercial violation is involved. In the noncommercial cases, the plaintiff must tolerate a certain amount of abusive language and improper conduct, but when the offense reaches the point of an unreasonable risk of causing emotional distress, the invasion is actionable.

Other Legal Aspects of Journalism

So far as the reporter is concerned, the laws on libel and invasion of privacy in the state where he is working are the most important legal provisions which limit his freedom. However, there are other legal aspects of journalism which curtail the newspaper and reporter alike.

Censorship. The Constitution of the United States guarantees freedom of the press as a fundamental right in a democracy, but the extraordinary power of the federal government during times of national stress (insurrection, wars, threats of war) has resulted in a measure of encroachment upon this freedom. Newspapers have been censored to the extent that they have not been permitted to publish information which would "aid and comfort an enemy" of the American government. Certainly no loyal publisher has desired to jeopardize his nation's safety, and newspapers have been willing to accede to a reasonable amount of censorship. But government officials and newspapermen has not always agreed on what should be censored, and disputes of the government's censorship rights have grown out of these disagreements. On the other hand, newspapers have at times adopted voluntary censorship without enforcement of a governmental fiat.

Copyrights. The United States Constitution provides for copyrights just as it does for the freedom of the press, and newspapers must observe the copyright holdings of others. By the same laws, the newspaper can prevent unauthorized use of original materials it publishes by obtaining copyright privileges.

Obtaining a copyright is a simple procedure. Application forms are available from the Register of Copyrights, Library of Congress, Washington, D.C. An author or publisher may secure a copyright by returning this completed application, plus a small fee and the required number of copies of the material, and by carrying a notice of copyright on all copies published.

Written materials may be protected by copyright in the form in which they appear. However, the news facts or the ideas stated in the materials cannot be copyrighted. Copyright is an interest in the way a story is organized and treated. In other words, a newspaper cannot obtain exclusive use of the facts pertaining to a murder story, for example, by copyrighting the initial news break of that story, but it may obtain a copyright to the story as organized and presented.

Even though a newspaper cannot claim exclusive rights to the facts in a news story through the copyright procedure, it can employ other legal methods to protect itself from the wholesale use of its stories by competing news media. Several state courts have ruled that such unauthorized use of news items, taken from a newspaper and not independently gathered, is unfair competition and "violation of a property right."

Reporters may quote copyrighted material verbatim without permission provided such quotations do not exceed a reasonable length and provided the material quoted is properly acknowledged. This privilege protects newspapers in using quotations in book reviews and other types of stories.

Exercises

I. Most if not all of the paragraphs below contain statements that are libelous or unethical. Rewrite those that should be rewritten. Following each rewritten paragraph, give explanatory notes on the changes, specifically pointing out the libelous and the unethical statements. Indicate paragraphs that are acceptable in editorials or byline articles but not in regular news stories.

A. Although the detective said he had no suspects, it was evident his investigation had given him leads that he would not expose. Several arrests will probably be made as soon as officers can find the persons under suspicion.

B. The salesman's blood-soaked body was found in a ditch, his tormented face a grotesque sight as he started in death toward the open sky with the back of his head imbedded in mud. He had been stripped of his clothing, brutally beaten, then stabbed again and again.

C. Actor Jimmy Willis frequently plays religious roles, but whether he goes to church regularly is in doubt. He declined to answer a question on that subject.

D. Health Officer James H. Needle has not reported all cases of contagious diseases, said Mrs. Wilson D. Fellow in a speech before the Businesswomen's Club today. Mrs. Fellow accused Mr. Needle of "using snap judgment" and of "being greatly influenced by an effort to show low statistics" in deciding whether a case should be reported. This has given the city "a false picture" of the incidence of contagious diseases, Mrs. Fellow said.

E. Mr. Wilmetz, displaying his usual characteristics of arrogance and indifference, refused to comment on the purchase of the property.

F. Charges of "partiality" were made against Tax Assessor Felix T. Ramsey in a statement issued today by W. F. Crookshank, realtor. Mr. Crookshank told the City Equilization Board that properties owned by his company are invariably "over assessed" in comparison with the assessments on neighboring properties owned by other companies.

G. James W. Kline, unemployed automobile mechanic, today was arrested on burglary charges. Police said he is the one who has broken into and looted six grocery stores in the past three weeks.

H. Not realizing that a reporter was in the group with whom he was conversing, Dr. Horace P. Quinn revealed that he may resign his post as superintendent of the Midstate Tuberculosis Hospital and enter private practice, but "not until a suitable replacement is found."

I. The handsome gangster, outnumbered nine to one, exhibited extraordinary courage and fortitude as he fought it out with city police. He was wounded three times, but for each wound he took the life of a policeman. He would have continued fighting until the end if he had not fainted from the loss of blood.

J. Reflecting the wishy-washy policies of the City "Progressive Party," Mayor Flynn Q. White today refused to take a stand on the City Library Board's proposal to triple appropriations to the city library system.

K. Worth A. Watson, manager of Hill Department Store, today was arrested for embezzling $3,000 from the store. The arrest came as a shock to his brother, Dr. Hillory Watson, local physician, and his father, Prof. J. K. Watson of Central State University.

L. Caught in the act of robbing Blake's Jewelers, the thief claimed he was in the store at 2 a.m. because he slipped into a storage room of the store to "sleep off a drunk" and was locked in when he woke up. He will find it hard to explain to the judge why his pockets were full of stolen jewelry when police caught him in the store.

M. Always a comic, he chose to commit suicide in a comical way. He put on his loudest suit, walked to the center of the busy Main Avenue and Fifth Street intersection, and hilariously dodged traffic as a confused jaywalker until he dived under the wheels of a large truck.

N. Benton T. Wilson was carried into office as mayor by a 6,500-vote majority yesterday, marking another inaccuracy in predictions by our competing newspaper, which loudly proclaimed that the incumbent, Mayor John Smith, would win "without half trying."

O. Bradford S. Turner, as dapper a criminal ever to carry a revolver, has been arrested 17 times but never convicted of a crime. He has been shrewd enough to stay just within the law or to dispose of witnesses when he accidentally was seen in acts of violation, and police have so far been unable to get evidence to send him to the penitentiary.

P. Coming to the city with his life's savings, 74-year-old Henry Taylor sought to make a fortune and give up farming. He met one of the city's most persuasive "salesmen," bought $5,400 worth of "stock" in the city-owned Metropolitan Transit Lines, and learned today that an investment which he was told would bring in $2,400 a year was absolutely worthless. Back to the farm for Mr. Taylor.

Q. The Southdale Dairy was ordered today to "stop selling milk until all tubercular cows are eliminated from its herd." The order came from Judge Wales Johnson, before whom dairy officials were arraigned by county health officers.

R. Merchandise is being sold by Hitown Drug Store about 25 percent higher than by other drug stores in the city, several prominent citizens complained today. Since that store went under new management recently, it has gained a wide reputation as a "high-price store."

S. Dr. J. B. Smartt was fired as superintendent of county schools today because of his inability to handle the job. The School Board notified him to vacate the office by Nov. 1.

T. Sitting through a showing of "Fight On, Boys," current attraction at the Blank Theatre, is a waste of time. The acting is terrible, the jokes stale, and the plot nonexistent.

II. Your paper has published a statement that Fred Q. Makres, salesman with the City Paint Company, was arrested yesterday on a charge of reckless driving. The person arrested is Fred Makres, a traveling salesman from another state. Write a retraction of the erroneous story.

III. Clip from a newspaper ten stories containing several types (arrests, criticisms, etc.) of derogatory statements. Past them on blank sheets of paper and explain in the margins the neswpaper's defense for using each statement.

IV. Search the newspaper for stories or parts of stories which you consider violations of a proper code of ethics. Hand in the clippings and your own comments on each such example.

THE COMPLETE REPORTER
PART TWO

WRITING THE
NEWS LEAD

Having sharpened his acquaintance with the newspaper, the news commodity, and the niceties of news style, the beginning reporter is ready to attack more technical problems.

By all odds the most important problem, the very heart and center of news writing, is the one the reporter encounters first—writing the lead. Upon proficiency in this matter depends his whole future excellence as a news writer. Moreover, the problem is deceptively simple. The superficial forms can be achieved very quickly. Yet it is doubtful that many of the leads capping the important stories of even the metropolitan press achieve the distinction required by complete, interpretative, penetrative reporting of the news.

The fundamental forms and principles of writing the news lead are presented in the following pages. Forms and principles are extremely helpful, but they are not substitutes for the inward strength and brilliance with which the news lead can and should reflect the vitality of the events reported.

Chapter 6

The Simple (Single-Incident) News Lead

THE essential difference between ordinary narrative prose and news writing is illustrated in the following example:

Ordinary narrative prose:

Finishing his work at 10 P.M., Leonard M. Jones, who operates the Jones Grocery Store at 2490 Trent Street, decided to walk home rather than call a taxi. He locked the store and started the 10 blocks home. As he entered the 2500 block of Trent Street he noticed two men standing in the shadow of a tree near the middle of the block. Giving them no attention, he continued on his way. But just as Mr. Jones passed the two heavyset men, one of them stepped out and held a pistol to the grocer's back, ordering him to hold up his hands. Mr. Jones obeyed, and the other man rifled his pockets, taking his watch, fountain pen, and $19.80 in cash. Then they ordered Mr. Jones to walk on down the street as though nothing had happened. He did so for a half block and, looking back, saw that the men had disappeared. He ran into the nearest house and called the police, who are still looking for the two thieves.

The news story:

Held up by two heavyset men, Leonard M. Jones, Trent Street grocer, was robbed of $19.80, a watch, and a fountain pen in the 2500 block of Trent Street late last night, Mr. Trent reported to police.

Mr. Jones had locked his store at 2490 Trent Street and started walking home at 10 p.m. In the next block, the two men stepped from the shadows, and one of them thrust a pistol to his back, he said. Soon after the robbery Mr. Jones ran to the nearest house and notified the police.

Several important differences between these two stories should be noted. The events or facts in the ordinary prose story are in chronological order. Those in the news story are arranged, from beginning to end, in the order of their newsworthiness. The climax (most newsworthy event) of the story is, of course, the hold-up. In the first story the climax is far down in the story. In the news item it is placed first.

In ordinary prose the whole story becomes clear *gradually*. In the news story the most newsworthy portion of the event is flashed before the reader in what is called the *lead*—usually a single sentence or short paragraph. Some newspapers attempt to make every lead a one-sentence paragraph, which is quite desirable if the sentence is not cumbersome and involved.

The news story omits all insignificant details. Even the second paragraph could be omitted (and in metropolitan newspapers probably would be omitted) without detracting substantially from the story.

6a **"Logical Order."** The order of newsworthiness may be considered, and will be referred to, as the *logical* order. This term is useful in distinguishing between the arrangement of events as they actually occur (chronological) and the rearrangement imposed on these events by the reporter. The term implies also that the rearrangement will be not haphazard but in rational accordance with plan and principle. The principle to be followed is the *order of importance as measured by reader appeal*. The lead is the "showcase" of all, or of the most newsworthy, materials contained in the story. And since the lead thus reveals the whole story or its most newsworthy aspects, the subsequent parts of the story are in the nature of a logical development or proof of the lead. Hence, the relationship of a lead to a news story is similar to that of a topic sentence to a paragraph.

If news is so written that the whole story is told as fully as possible in the lead, what constitutes a "whole story"? What is it that people want to know about a news event? How can one know when he has presented all of the essential information? Are there not, for example, many more essential facts in a bank robbery than in an automobile collision? Does not every story differ from every other in the kind of information presented in its lead summary? These questions may be puzzling but the fact is that, while stories differ in their contents, the story lead has a fixed and limited purpose to perform.

6b   *The Five W's*

Fortunately (for the reporter) the human mind is capable of asking only a limited number of kinds of questions, small boys to the contrary notwithstanding. Human curiosity has only six fangs or claws for biting into or tearing apart the unknown. These are the six little questions: Who? What? When? Where? Why? How?

These are, interestingly and obviously enough, the simple elements that make up rational discourse and its vehicle, the plain grammatical sentence: subject and predicate, and the qualifications (adjectives and adverbs) of time, place, manner, and cause. It follows that when these elements have been presented properly and succinctly, the lead will have performed its function of telling the whole story—be that story large or small. It follows, too, that the rest of the story can be merely the amplification of these several elements, proportioned as the particular news event requires.

These questions and the basic information they seek are known as "the five *W*'s." The complete lead (with exceptions to be noted later) will answer *all* of these questions, though the answer may sometimes be implied and not stated. In the sample news lead on page 81, the five *W*'s and the *H* (hereinafter called the 5 *W*'s) are:

The Questions	*The Lead Answers*
What happened?	a hold-up
Who was involved?	Leonard M. Jones
When did it happen?	late last night
Where did it take place?	in the 2500 block of Trent Street
How did it happen?	by force and with a weapon (further amplified in the body of the story)
Why?	(implied) for money

Three other lead elements are frequently present. In this lead, "Trent Street grocer" identifies the "who." And the authority for the story is implied as "said the police," or "according to police." Identification and authority are—like the 5 *W*'s—frequently present in the lead, sometimes explicitly stated and sometimes merely implied. If omitted from the lead, they usually will be given immediately following in the body of the story (see **4k**). A third element, the *tie back* or *tie in,* is present in those stories **6c** which "follow up" a previous story. For example:

> Two former convicts, *indicted last week for the hold-up of Leonard M. Jones, Trent Street grocer,* will go on trial in Criminal Court today.
>
> (The tie back is in italics.)

Playing up a W   6d

One of the 5 *W*'s is frequently of much more importance than the others. This element should be placed *first* in the lead sentence;

that is to say, it should be "played up" or "featured." The following examples show how one element has been featured:

The "Who" Lead. If the "who" is a person (place or thing) well known, it is usually the feature of the lead. The name alone attracts attention. Unless one of the other elements is particularly outstanding, the "big name" comes first.

> John T. King, president of King Furniture Store, was critically injured in an automobile accident at Fourth Street and Flowers Avenue this morning.

The "What" Lead. Concerning a person of less importance, a similar lead might appear as follows:

> A head-on automobile collision at Fourth Street and Flowers Avenue today ended with Walter Davis, truck driver at Southern Coal Company, in General Hospital suffering critical injuries.

The "Where" Lead. On rare occasions the "where" is significant enough to overshadow the other *W*'s. An example:

> The dangerous intersection of Fourth Street and Flowers Avenue was the scene of another collision this morning, and Walter Davis, truck driver with Southern Coal Company, was critically injured.

The "When" Lead. Rarely is the time of an event the most interesting feature. However, circumstances may make it significant. For instance:

> Just 15 minutes after police had erected a "danger" sign at Fourth Street and Flowers Avenue today, a truck driver was critically injured in an automobile accident at the intersection.

The 'Why" Lead. The motive or cause of an event sometimes is the most important feature. Failure to discover the "why" may lose an interesting lead feature.

> In haste to get to the bedside of his dying mother this morning, Walter Davis, truck driver with Southern Coal Company, was critically injured when his sedan crashed into a parked car at Fourth Street and Flowers Avenue.

The "How" Lead. The "how" also is a potential leading feature which is sometimes overlooked by beginning reporters.

> Thrown through the windshield when his sedan crashed into a parked automobile, Walter Davis, truck driver with Southern Coal

Company, was critically injured this morning at Fourth Street and Flowers Avenue.

These examples play up (by placing first) the various features which an automobile accident might reveal. Rarely would more than one of the elements be worth featuring in a story of a single accident. The reporter's choice is usually, therefore, determined by the material itself. One feature usually "cries out" its importance and demands first place in the lead.

Crowding the Lead. If, in the simple one-incident story, two or even more of the W's seem equally interesting, the reporter will have to choose arbitrarily between them. Awkward leads result from the attempt to feature several W's.

6e

> Speeding to the bedside of his dying mother, Walter Davis, Southern Coal Company employee, was thrown through the windshield and critically injured today when his sedan crashed into a parked automobile at the dangerous intersection of Fourth Street and Flowers Avenue just 15 minutes after police had erected a danger sign.

Even if a simpler combination were more successful, it would not really play up (in the sense of placing first) more than one W. In the simple news story it is usually a good practice to play up only one W in the lead sentence, but it is possible in some stories to give emphasis to two. If the W's also deserve special attention, they can be amply emphasized in the second paragraph of the story.

Crowding the lead sentence and paragraph with unnecessary details for any reason is to be avoided. The lead must include (or imply) the 5 W's, but those W's should be shorn of all nonessential details. Generally speaking, the shorter the lead, the better. Newsworthy details held out of the lead will fall properly into the body of the news story. In the following example unnecessary details clutter up the lead:

> In haste to get to the bedside of his dying mother, Mrs. K. L. Davis, 1010 Fourth Street, this morning Walter Davis, a Southern Coal Company driver who has never before had an accident, suffered a broken arm, numerous cuts and bruises, and a fractured skull when his four-door sedan crashed into a parked coupe belonging to J. T. Lewis, manager of City Glass Company, at the corner of Fourth Street and Flowers Avenue.

If no single element in the story seems to offer an interesting feature, the routine "who" lead is generally used:

Walter Davis, truck driver with Southern Coal Company, was critically injured in an automobile accident at Fourth Street and Flowers Avenue this morning.

Many stories containing no striking feature must be handled in this adequate but dull fashion. Many such stories may contain features which the reporter fails to recognize or inquire into.

It is much easier to recognize the story elements (the 5 *W*'s) and the feature after the story is written than it is from the reporter's rough notes. In fact, the reporter himself must determine who is properly "who" and what is properly "what." If John Doe, sheriff, has a row with Councilman Richard Roe, the reporter must determine who is the "who." In this example he might evade the issue and at the same time acquire a "who" feature by writing "Two public officials clashed today . . ."—but he does face a problem in determining such story elements and the order in which they should be presented.

6f   *Complete Reporting*

It is not difficult for the reporter to pick up 5 *W*'s, fling them together, and call the result a lead. Much superficial reporting results from this careless skill. The reader is frequently left to wonder what caused the automobile accident or the fire. If he wants to know whether admission is free, whether the public is invited, whether the event will be broadcast, and when, and over what stations—let him use the telephone! If the event happened at Sevastopol, any good geography plus a world history should give him all essential information about this city. If the injured John Doe lives at 916 Clinton Street, what further identification can a reader want? These seem to be the attitudes behind careless reporting. If Congress has just enacted a law, the lead might be:

The South American Trade Bill was enacted by Congress today, and the President immediately announced that he will sign it.

Or facts might justify the following lead:

Cattlemen of the Southwest will be bankrupt and Argentine beef will feed the United States, some congressmen predicted today following passage of the South American Trade Bill.

In the first lead the reader is given a minimum of information. He is left to ferret out the significance of the event. In the second lead the reporter pushed his "what" question below the surface of things and reported an action of extreme significance.

There are strict limits to the amount of material that can be crowded into a lead. There are no limits whatever on the quality of this material. Only by reporting the significance and the essentiality of events instead of their superficial forms can the reporter achieve complete reporting. Whether he achieves this essentiality in the lead or reveals it later in his story is not wholly important—so long as he does achieve it. The lead, however, is his golden opportunity to present the quality of facts demanded by complete, penetrative use of the 5 *W*'s.

Testing a Lead

While there is no one formula the reporter can use in arriving at the best way to write a lead, he can develop his own procedures or devices to test the adequacy of a lead after it is written. Following is one such device which uses the four letters from *news* as keys:

N for newsworthiness—does the lead say anything worthy of note by readers?

E for emphasis—does the lead emphasize its most interesting fact?

W for the 5 *W*'s—are all essential *W*'s included in the lead?

S for source of information—does the lead give (or imply) the source of information, if needed?

Exercises   6g

Important: In these and following exercises are presented notes written as incomplete sentences resembling telegraphic English. The notes are such as those a reporter might jot down in gathering information for his story.

Added to each set of notes, in parenthesis, is its source of information unless the notes include or imply this source. In some stories it will not be necessary to state the source, while in other stories it is essential to do so. The student must use his judgment in determining which statements require an explicit authority.

The student must also show good judgment in the use of direct quotations in completing these assignments. The telegraphic notes within quotation marks indicate direct quotations. If these are used, additional words will have to be added to make them full sentences, of course, but the student should make only the obvious additions.

Since these are reporter's notes, they are assumed to be accurate statements from the sources of information. Hence, if the instructor permits, the student may convert an unquoted note into a direct quotation. For example, *Jones refused to take part* in the notes may be written "I will not take part in the meeting," said Councilman Jones. However, in converting an indirect quotation into a direct quotation, the student should not add imaginary facts.

Students are warned that the exercises contain some notes which, if used as given (and sometimes if used at all), will constitute errors. Such notes include trivia, editorialized matter, statements violating newspaper ethics, and libel.

Some instructors may require that their students hand in all completed (and corrected) assignments at the end of a quarter or semester.

I. Write news leads on the following chronological stories that were related by the news sources.
   A. Warren Thomas, 43, an automobile salesman who lives at 237 Francisco drive, stayed up late last night reading an exciting novel. The rest of his family had already retired for the night when Mr. Thomas finished. Feeling a little hungry, he went into the kitchen and fixed himself a cheese sandwich and a bowl of soup. He noticed that the family's tomcat, Fuzzy-Wuzzy, was still in the kitchen, sleeping under the table, and he made a mental note to speak to his son, John, about not doing his nightly chore of putting the cat out. After finishing his snack, Mr. Thomas picked up Fuzzy-Wuzzy, unlocked the back door, and carried the cat to the edge of the steps. As he leaned over to put the cat down, a masked man pointing a revolver stepped from behind a bush and sternly demanded that Mr. Thomas hold up his hands. Scared speechless, Mr. Thomas obeyed, and the gunman took the salesman's wallet containing $30 and his diamond ring valued at $2,000. Meanwhile, Fuzzy-Wuzzy ran back into the house and went to sleep again under the table. The gunman forced Mr. Thomas to lie down, face to the ground, then quietly backed off and disappeared. As soon as he was sure the robber had gone, Mr. Thomas got up, went into the house, locked the door, and called the police. Then he put Fuzzy-Wuzzy out the back door again, this time opening the door slightly and pushing the cat through the crack. Policeman Wayne Smith and Fred Moore soon arrived, heard Mr. Thomas' story, and began a search for the hold-up man. (Source: Policeman Fred Moore)
   B. Three months ago the city commission elected a new city manager to succeed Herbert F. Story, who had resigned to take a position as city manager of Brightsville. Mr. Story had served here seven years, and he had done a splendid job. Every member of the

Commission expressed regrets on his leaving. Elected successor to Mr. Story was Leonardo T. Willis, 43, a graduate of the State University who has been administrator of St. Phillips, a town of about 5,000 population. Mr. Willis has established a wonderful reputation. The new manager is to take over his position here at 8:30 a.m. tomorrow. Members of the city commission and other officials will be on hand to greet him in his office and to wish him well in his work here. (Sources: various city officials)

C. Robert J. Printon, 57-year-old bachelor who is an Internal Revenue Service officer, went to his apartment at 434 Holly Street after work yesterday. He showered and dressed in preparing to attend a birthday dinner at his nephew's home, 1404 Greene Street, in honor of his nephew's wife, Mrs. David A. Brown. When Mr. Printon was ready to leave, he went to get the birthday present which he had bought previously and had tossed to the back of the shelf of his closet. Not being able to reach it, he pulled a corrugated box from the floor of the closet and stepped upon it. The box collapsed, throwing Mr. Printon backward, his head striking the edge of a dresser. Two hours later, when Mr. Printon was already an hour late to the dinner, the worried nephew went to Mr. Printon's home and found him unconscious on the bedroom floor. The nephew called his doctor. After ascertaining that Mr. Printon suffered a broken neck, the doctor had Mr. Printon taken to General Hospital. City Detective Jim Warwick was sent to investigate the accident. Mr. Printon died at the hospital at 4 A.M. today. (Source: Detective Warwick)

D. On Monday of last week the board in charge of Washington Park Zoo voted to begin an expansion program which will double the size of the zoo within the next five years. I. Rony Mann, zoo director, was given a budget for use in the acquisition of additional animals, and he was requested to begin the expansion as soon as possible. On Thursday of last week Mr. Mann had the footings poured for the installation of new cages to house the additions, and this construction is progressing. Today Mr. Mann put in an order for nine new animals. He ordered an Indian leopard, an African leopard, two lion-tailed macaques, a monkey (preferably one who looks like Mayor Sweeney, who opposed the expansion), two painted storks, and two white-tailed sea eagles. Additional orders will be made in the near future. Mr. Mann is quite happy about the whole situation because he is a man dedicated to his job. The first order is expected to arrive in about three weeks. (Source: Mr. Mann)

E. Tom Picard, 59, and Brown Wayne, 61, who live in a shack near the railroad tracks, were released from the County Workhouse yesterday morning after serving ten days on a drunkenness charge. Both have been in and out of jail many times on the same charges. They work as handymen and yardmen to earn enough to buy alcoholic beverages. After getting out of the workhouse, they borrowed money from a friend, promising to "straighten up" and to "stop drinking." At about 2 A.M. this morning the Fire Department answered a call and found the shack already burned nearly to the ground. Mr. Wayne was lying outside, suffering a few burns but passed out from drinking. The body of Tom Picard was still in the shack. After the blaze was extinguished, the body was taken to the morgue, and Mr. Wayne was treated at General Hospital, then jailed on a drunkenness charge. Detective Wylie Farmer is investigating to determine the cause of the fire, which Mr. Wayne said he could not explain. (Source: Assistant Fire Chief Rex Murphy and Detective O. Farmer)

F. James D. Henley, who is a farmer living on Blackview Road, got up at 6 o'clock this morning to plow his land. He hitched a mule to the plow and started to work. The plow struck something as it overturned the ground near an old stump, and Mr. Henley stopped and investigated. He dug up a dirty brief case. Boy, was he surprised! It was full of money! Mr. Henley took the brief case and money to Sheriff Whorley and told the sheriff the story. An investigation by the sheriff revealed that the money was the $5,000 stolen from the Jackson Trust Company three weeks ago. (Source: Sheriff J. K. Whorley)

II. Clip from a newspaper three short news stories (about three to five paragraphs in length) and rewrite them in chronological order. Put in the details which you think were omitted in the newspaper account.

III. Clip from a newspaper 10 leads. Paste them on a sheet of paper and identify the *W*'s in each lead.

IV. Following are rough notes for story leads. For each story list the 5 W's and then write the lead.

A. Billy Bradley, 4116 Maple Street, wins scholarship worth $5,000
    Will attend State Institute of Technology
    Plans to major in mechanical engineering
    Valedictorian at Central High School last June
    Orphan living with uncle, John Bradley
    Uncle, a textile mill worker, currently unemployed
      (Source: Central High principal, J. E. Smith)

B. Fire destroys home of Mr. and Mrs. C. W. Doakes, 222 Birch Drive
    While couple at movies last night
    Dog, Rover, left in basement, apparently perished in fire
    Mrs. Doakes collapses upon return from movies

Frame building enveloped in flames when firemen arrive
Faulty electrical wiring believed cause
   (Source: Fire Chief H. X. Phillips)

C. City Boosters Club made annual awards at banquet last night
Bernard Cole, club president, presided
Arthur Fiddler, attorney, named "Man of the Year"
For work with the club's youth program
Sam Burton, owner of Burton's Grocery, received "Best Booster" award
For attending all meetings of year

D. Private plane crashes in Green Mountain
In blinding rainstorm last night
Two passengers, A. D. Brown and Walter Smith of Chicago, found dead in wreckage
Rugged terrain
Claude Stokes, farmer, heard plane flying low, crash
Called state police
Bodies removed this morning
   (Source: State Police)

E. Four juveniles arrested last night
Charged with larceny
Stealing school property
Caught in Central High library by janitor, Melvin Strong
Arms full of books
Boys identified as Charles Luster, 14, Danny Burk, 14, Willie Carter, 15, and Don Williams, 15. all freshmen at Central High
Had all copies of American history books library owned when caught
"We needed books for reading assignments," said Charles Luster
Boys turned over to Juvenile Court authorities
   (Source: Policeman Roy Exermine)

V. Clip from newspapers eight leads which feature a variety of the 5 W's. Paste them on sheets of paper and identify all elements in the margins.

VI. Notes for story leads are given below. List and identify (as "who," "when," etc.) the fact or facts which you think deserve the most conspicuous play in each lead. Then write the lead.

A. Two children, Bobby and Sally Jones, left in car by parents
Father, E. B. Jones, 45 Walker Lane, gave children nickel
To put in parking meter at end of hour
Hour later, Patrolman Sam Brown found Jones car illegally parked

Brown heard children crying

They had lost nickel

Instead of giving parking ticket, Brown gives children nickel for meter

(Source: E. B. Jones)

B. Two hunters, William Brown and Charles Green

Driving compact model car on State Highway 1066

Eagle attacks car, crashes through windshield

Unhurt, the eagle claws Charles Green

Inflicted painful face wounds

Driver, Brown stops car

Beat off eagle and shot it with rifle

(Source: William Brown)

C. Farmer Clyde Johnson treated at General Hospital

Had broken arm

Injured when thrown from wagon by runaway team of mules

At his farm near Hayseed Corners

Farmer Johnson vows "I'm gonna sell those mules and buy a tractor"

(Source: Clyde Johnson)

D. Herman Scruggs, age 84, hospitalized at Baptist Hospital

Has fractured collarbone

Suffered injury in City Park

Fell chasing fly ball

Playing center field in baseball game between school youngsters

"Drafted when one team lacked a player"

(Source: Herman Scruggs)

E. Police raid Country Club last night

Confiscate 200 fifths of whisky and 35 slot machines

Dr. John Bradley, prominent physician, E. B. Zimmerman, president of Zimmerman Food Stores, and City Councilman Everett Pate among those playing slot machines

Andrew Maples, manager of Country Club, arrested

Charged with possessing whisky and gambling devices

No members arrested

(Source: Police Chief John Cates)

F. Sam Furrow, farmer, surprises county sheriff

Appears at county jail, holding shotgun on a man

Also leading a goat

Charges prisoner, Willis Lively, stole goat

Tracked goat to Lively's barn at Bugle Gap

Found Lively feeding goat

Sheriff Tod Baker jails Lively on theft charge
Goat is stabled in dog pound as "evidence"
  (Source: Sheriff Baker)

G. Blessed event at zoo yesterday
Elephant, Beulah, has calf
First baby elephant born at City Zoo
Weight 200 pounds
Keepers name him "Tiny"
  (Source: Roy Black, zoo superintendent)

H. Dog killed by speeding automobile at Main and Church streets
Belonged to Arthur Sloan
Driver of car did not stop
Seeing-eye dog
Had just left curb when car sped around corner
Blind owner unhurt
  (Source: Policeman Baker Conroy)

I. Blankville woman failed driver's license test today
Mrs. Horace Walker, 1642 Happy Lane
While taking test, backed her car into parked highway patrol
    cruiser
Patrolman Tom Andrews riding with Mrs. Walker
Gave her traffic ticket charging reckless driving
Marked driver's license application "failed"
  (Source: Patrolman Andrews)

J. Joe Greenleaf, 18, charged with stealing automobile Sunday
Taken from service station
Reported stolen by R. W. Graves, station attendant
Police spotted car on street, gave chase
Greenleaf lost control of vehicle, crashed into utility pole
Youth, unhurt, ran from wrecked car into nearby church
Services under way
Policemen Emmett Jackson and Robert Mills waited until serv-
    ices over
Greenleaf apprehended while shaking hands with minister at door
  (Source: Policemen Jackson and Mills)

K. Robert Smith, proprietor of Smith's Delicatessen, White Street
Robbed of $325 late last night
Almost closing time
Store empty of customers
Well-dressed man came in store
Asked to borrow knife to make minor repair on automobile
    parked outside

When given knife, man pressed blade against Smith's chest
Demanded money from cash register
Man fled on foot
    (Source: Policeman Hobart Books)

L. Carolyn Ballott marries John Mandate
    Bride is daughter of Rep. B. B. Ballott, Republican congressman
    Groom is son of A. L. Mandate, state Democratic leader
    Couple eloped
    Crossed state line for wedding ceremony yesterday
    Married by justice of peace
       (Source: official records)

Chapter 7

The Complex (Several-Incident) News Lead

Previous exercises have dealt only with the "simple" news story—that is, the story of only one incident. If a man is killed and no others are injured in an automobile accident, the reporter should have little trouble selecting a feature. One of the 5 *W*'s pertaining to this death would be featured and the other facts used in the lead; the rest of the story would be but details relative to the one incident.

Sometimes, however, a story has several outstanding incidents or phases of apparently equal importance. How does a reporter handle this several-feature lead?

Suppose a storm causes the following damage:

1. One person is killed by lightning.
2. Flood waters surge through stores and damage $500,000 in merchandise.
3. Fire breaks out and, fanned by a high wind, destroys the $800,000 West End High School.

The general rule in writing any sort of news lead is to place first things (that is, the most newsworthy things) first. The rule applies to the several-feature lead no less than to the single-feature lead. There are two basic methods to follow in writing the several-feature lead:

1. Summarize all features (in order of importance) in the first sentence of paragraph.
2. Play up a salient or outstanding feature in the first sentence or paragraph. (All other features must be summarized in logical order in succeeding paragraphs.)

In either the summary or the salient-feature lead, all the features should be established in the reader's mind *before* the reporter proceeds very far with developing the details of any one feature.

7a *The Summary Lead*

Below is an illustration of how the results of the storm might be revealed in a summary lead. At the left is a diagram of the lead and other beginning paragraphs of the story. In this and other diagrams each geometrical figure represents a separate story-feature. The diminishing size of the figures signifies the diminishing newsiness of the story materials.

The Diagram

Summary of Features

Major details in common to all features (this paragraph or paragraphs not needed in many stories)

Major Details of Feature No. 1

Major Details of Feature No. 2

Major Details of Feature No. 3

Other Paragraphs in the Complete Story ⬇

The Written Story

One person is dead, the West End High School is in smoking ruins, and the Front Street shopping district is flooded as a result of the storm early this morning.

It was one of the most ferocious storms ever to strike Blankville, with winds raging up to 55 miles an hour and five inches of rain pouring down in eight hours.

Tom Henderson, lineman, 2216 Belmont Street, was killed by a bolt of lightning as he struggled to replace high tension wires at Locust Avenue and Fifth Street.

Fire broke out when the smoke stack at West End High School blew down. Firemen were impeded by trees blown across the streets, and the $800,000 building was a total loss. All pupils were safely removed to their homes.

Water from the flooded Ohio stood four feet deep in Front Street stores at 9 a.m. and damage was estimated at $500,000.

(Further details on all features would follow in the body of the story.)

The Salient-Feature Lead   **7b**

If one of the several results of the storm seems of outstanding importance, the salient-feature lead is better. Suppose, for example, that Tom Henderson is not a lineman but is mayor of the city. Then the story could be written:

The Diagram	*The Written Story*
Salient Feature	Mayor Tom Henderson was killed by a bolt of lightning in this morning's storm as he helped direct the rescue work of firemen and police.
Summary of Other Features	Damage to property is estimated at more than a million dollars. West End High School was burned but with no loss of life. Water at 9 a.m. stood four feet deep in Front Street stores.
Other Paragraphs in the Complete Story	(Further details of the salient feature and of the other features would follow in the body of the story.)

Here is a story that is more complicated. A reporter covering a strike obtains the following principal facts which are worth space in the lead:

1. Protesting that their wages were too low, the 800 employees of Maxham Manufacturing Company walked out on strike.
2. The company foremen, J. E. Jones, L. W. House, and T. R. Herring, became involved in an argument with the strikers, and a free-for-all followed. J. E. Jones, found unconscious after the fight, died shortly afterward of a fractured skull.
3. At the request of city officials, Governor Jess Smith stationed the National Guard at the plant to prevent further trouble. Twenty guardsmen were sent.
4. The president of the company Leonard P. Maxham, declared in a statement issued after the fight that the company would rehire none of the strikers. He announced that the plant would be closed "for an indefinite period."

Each of these features is worth a story in itself, but all are related to one event—the strike—and it is the duty of the reporter to weave the several features into one lead. He may do this either by the summary or the salient-feature method.

The Diagram

Summary of Features

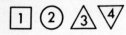

Feature No. 1

Feature No. 2

Feature No. 3

Feature No. 4

Other Paragraphs in the Complete Story

*The Written Story
with Summary Lead*

After a strike at Maxham Manufacturing Company today resulted in death for one man, National Guardsmen were rushed to the scene, and the company president issued a statement that no strikers would be rehired.

The day's developments:

1. The 800 employees of the company walked out on strike for higher wages.

2. J. E. Jones, company foreman, received fatal skull injuries in a fight between strikers and three foremen.

3. Governor Jess Smith stationed 20 National Guardsmen to keep order at the plant.

4. After the fight, Leonard P. Maxham, company president, issued a statement that he would rehire none of the strikers and that the plant would be closed "for an indefinite period."

(Further details of these features in following paragraphs.)

If the leading angle should (under certain circumstances) be the walkout and the closing of the plant:

The Diagram

Salient Feature

Summary of Other Features

*The Written Story with
Salient-Feature Lead*

Demanding higher wages, the 800 employees of Maxham Manufacturing Company walked out on strike today, and the plant has been closed "for an indefinite period."

Immediately following the walkout, a fight between strikers and three company foremen resulted in death for one of the foremen, and National Guardsmen were rushed to the scene. Later the company president declared he would rehire none of the strikers.

| Other Paragraphs in the Complete Story ⟳ | (Details of salient feature and all other features in following paragraphs.) |

The several-feature lead forms, as illustrated above, go beyond the lead sentence and the lead paragraph. Still, they are leads in the sense that they summarize the various features of the story in showcase fashion before the body development begins. In the long stories necessary to develop several features, several lead paragraphs are frequently needed and may be thought of as the "lead block."

Other Leads

The Combination or Scrambled Lead. There are no hard and fast rules and regulations for writing the several-feature lead.   **7c**
The two basic methods of "placing first things first" have been illustrated: the summary method and the salient-feature method. Both lend themselves to variation, and the choice of the exact variety usually will be determined by the facts and incidents of the story. A summary lead, for example, may at times summarize some of the features and not all. The salient feature may sometimes combine some related incidents and relegate others to a subsequent summary. Study the following example:

City Council takes action as follows:

1. Passes ordinance prohibiting riding bicycles on sidewalks.
2. Appoints new delinquent tax attorney.
3. Authorizes purchase of 20 new police cruiser cars.
4. Authorizes $300,000 bond issue for street maintenance equipment.
5. Votes $3,000 pension for widow of slain policeman.

The Diagram

Salient Feature

1 2

The Written Story with Combination Lead

Acting to eliminate a portion of Blankville's antiquated machinery, City Council last night approved purchase of 20 new police cruisers and authorized a $300,000 bond issue for street maintenance equipment.

Further Summary of
Other Features

Other Paragraphs in the Complete
Story

Other business at the meeting included appointment of Fred Porter as new delinquent tax attorney, passage of a law prohibiting bicycle-riding on sidewalks, and authorization of a $3,000 pension to Mrs. Lem Dillard, widow of a slain policeman.

(Details of story in following paragraphs.)

The first paragraph summarizes two of the features by uniting them in a dual salient feature, the elimination of antiquated city machinery. The second paragraph adds other features not related to those in the lead. This method can be called the "scrambled" lead—but a strict nomenclature is unnecessary. If the reporter will organize and relate the several features properly and will place first things first, he will achieve a proper lead, whatever its name.

7d   Tabulations. Illustrated on page 98 is a method of using a tabulation to develop a summary lead within the story itself.

Tabulations may be used either above or within the story or may be set off by boldface type or by some other device. These devices are used to crowd information into small space and to flash essential facts before the reader, thus relieving the lead of cumbersome detail. The lead itself may thereupon proceed without too great a burden. Numerals may be used or omitted in listing tabulated items. Note the following illustration:

A one-column box (or a boldface list):

Highlights in Today's Election

John Doe elected governor.
Richard Roe elected mayor.
Two killed at polls.
Largest vote in 50 years.
Machine power crushed.
Local bond issue defeated.

Simplified lead made possible by tabulation above:

The Republican ticket swept John Doe and Richard Roe into office today as governor and mayor.

Governor-elect Doe issued the following statement:

The Crucible Lead. Instead of presenting all features as in
the summary lead, or some of them as in the scrambled lead,   **7e**
or one of them as in the salient-feature lead, the reporter
may fuse the features into an interpretative lead. In other words, the
reporter throws the separate elements into a crucible, melts them
together, and obtains from them a comprehensive and significant
summary of the story essence.

A crucible lead for the Maxham strike story (see page 98) might
be:

> Violence achieved its goal of death and destruction today in the
> strike-torn Maxham factory district. While federal conciliators looked
> on, labor and management continued to fight each other vigiorously.
> The day's developments:
>   1.
>   2.
>   3.

Since the crucible lead does not present facts and events but gives
overall meanings and significances, it must be followed immediately
by the actual facts and events of the story. These are usually presented in an enumerative summary, though a salient feature may,
even in this case, be important enough to precede the summary. In
no case may the interpretative crucible lead be a substitute for the
essential story features.

It is apparent that the interpretation embodied in the crucible
lead can follow as well as precede the summation of the story facts.
It is only when such interpretation appears to be more important
than the facts that it is lifted from its body position into the lead
position.

Separate Stories. Elections, storms, strikes, wars, and frequently
large fires and other major events may demand separate stories for
the various phases of each. In this case, each story will require either
a single feature or a several-feature lead, and these leads will be
developed in the various forms alrady discussed. Such stories may be
scattered throughout the newspaper under separate headlines of
their own, or they may be placed in sequence. In the latter case,
they probably will be embraced under a large headline, each story
having a dateline of its own and a minor headline.

7f   *Identifying the Features*

The beginning reporter often finds difficulty in distinguishing story features from the mass of story detail. Unless he clearly recognizes the features, he cannot avoid the danger of burying them within the body of the story. Nor can he write the single-feature lead, or any of the several-feature leads, or the body of his story—in other words, he cannot write news stories without definitely identifying the features of his story materials.

Simply defined, features are the highlights, the outstanding and most interesting and most significant items, in any given sequence of events or arrangements of materials. The reporter himself must determine what these are. If he can discern the highlights of a previous vacation, the most interesting chapters of a book, the most telling points in an argument, or the several outstanding results of a storm, he can discern features. No mystery or technicality is involved and yet no rule is available for detecting them.

Ordinarily a speech, for example, contains as features its several main arguments or contentions. Yet, if the speaker suggests that the President should be impeached, or if a fist fight develops in the audience, or if a local issue is touched upon, these would seem to cry out as features of the occasion.

A common fault of the beginner, nevertheless, is to introduce in the body of his story some material that should have been featured in the lead or lead block. When reminded that the body should be used for the development of lead features, he defends this material as developmental detail of the lead feature. Obviously, a broad lead can bracket almost any number of features. If the reporter should lead with "Many interesting events occurred in Blankville today," he could conceivably include in the body development all of the unrelated events of the city. However, such a lead would conceal and not reveal, as the lead must, the story contents.

It is the purpose of the lead not to conceal but to display the true and complete samples of everything for sale (worth reading) later on in the story. Even if it is possible to defend buried features (say, loss of life in a fire story) as being directly developmental of the fire lead in which it is not featured, the reporter has violated the sales (or showcase) function of the lead. If he will keep in mind that he must display his worthwhile wares—all of the them—before he begins to explain them with developmental details, he will not be content to defend buried features. He can display all of them in the summary lead or one of them first in the salient-feature lead, but he will be sure to make the display before he begins the development of the features.

Perhaps the best guide in recognizing a separate and worthwhile feature of a story is this: any incident or detail that is sufficiently newsworthy in itself to be worth reporting as a single-feature story is a feature of, and can be displayed in, the lead of the several-feature story. At least, all such features must be summarized (displayed) prior to their full development.

Under this definition, the several and unrelated actions of a city council, if newsworthy at all, are newsworthy separately. In fact, they might—if they are unrelated in substance—be reported as separate stories except for the identity of place and time and method of their occurrence and their author (City Council). In other words, they have in common the "who," "when," "how," and "where," but they differ as to "what" (happened). A similar identity of some, but not all, of the W's would exist in case of a storm or of any other event presenting several features worth reporting.

It is in the differentiation of the various W's (usually the what) that the several-feature story is appropriate. In the single-incident story the only features available are the W's themselves, and each W is constant throughout the story. In the several-incident story one or more of the W's will vary. That is, different things happen (different what's), or the same thing happens to different people (different who's), or from different causes (why), and so on. Thus the several-feature story has a specific function to perform—that of highlighting, displaying, featuring the variable W or W's. To bury a feature is to violate the function of this story form.

It should be emphasized that the features presented by a variable W must be newsworthy. They are not to be reported merely because they are variables. For example, if a speech contains four what's— say, four main points or logical divisions—only one or two or three of them may be newsworthy enough to be reported. If a fire destroys a valuable painting, a historical shrine, and three chickens, the last item may not be worth reporting. Any item is a feature only as measured by its newsworthiness—that is, reader appeal. The reporter himself must determine what these features are.

Summarizing the Features. Once the several features are recognized, the reporter's concern is to summarize the features adequately for use in the lead or the lead block. Note the following attempts at summations of several features:

7g

Four points in favor of the proposed city playground were given today by John Doe, City School Board chairman, in a speech before . . .

Judge John Doe ruled upon four important cases in Criminal Court today.

Problems of taxation and public health were studied today by City Council . . .

Each of these leads recognizes the existence of several features, but the attempts to summarize the features has sacrificed adequacy for brevity. "Four points in favor" has no particular reader appeal and therefore cannot be classified as a summary of four features. A brief summary of the points themselves is required for an adequate lead or lead block. The features themselves are what the reporter wants in his showcase—not the fact that several features are present. The features are the meat of the story. An adequate summation of the four features in the "four points" could be:

The juvenile crime rate in Blankville would be materially reduced if a city playground were constructed, declared John Doe, City School Board chairman, in a speech before the Lion's Club today.

Mr. Doe also supported the proposed park with statements that it would improve the health of Blankville youth, the playground would provide a recreational area needed by Blankville High School, and tourists would be attracted to the city by the additional facilities.

Combining Stories

Separate stories, naturally, will differ in the content of all their *W*'s—except occasionally when several stories may concern the police or the governor or some other functionary, or occur in the same place or even in the same manner, and so on. When these identities accumulate to any noticeable extent, there is an immediate newspaper tendency to combine them in one way or another. For example, they may be grouped, still as separate stories, under a single headline. But as more of the *W*'s become identical, the stories themselves tend to coalesce into the several-incident, and therefore several-feature, forms.

Exercises

I. Clip from a newspaper leads which illustrate three different methods of writing a several-feature lead.

II. Below are rough notes for several-feature leads. Follow these instructions in utilizing each set of notes:

First—List the various features in the order of newsworthiness.

Second—Write a lead in the summary form, another lead in the salient-feature form, and a third lead in one of the other forms explained in this chapter. Diagram each lead in the margin at the left.

Third—Explain which of the three methods you think yields the best lead and why.

    A. City Council, meeting last night, decided:

        1. To build viaduct across railroad tracks
            At Main Street
            Scene of several automobile-train accidents
            To cost $1,000,000

        2. To dismiss J. Q. Banks
            Welfare director
            Successor not appointed
            Banks recently criticized by auditors
            Irregularities in finances of department

        3. To add new inspector
            In Department of Sanitation
            Appointed J. D. Love
            Now assistant bacteriologist at City Hospital

        4. To hold referendum at next election
            Citizens to vote on $2,000,000 bond issue
            For erection of new high school

    B. Grand Jury met today
       Indictments of four persons reported
       They are:

        1. Paul F. Reece, 28, plumber
            Charged with felonious assault
            On fellow workman, John Holmes, 56
            Holmes struck on head with lead pipe

        2. J. D. Stegall, 33, automobile salesman
            Charged with drunken driving
            Had crashed with another car
            Three injured, including Stegall, in wreck

        3. J. F. White, 46, city clerk
            Charged with embezzlement
            Accused of taking $3,000 city funds

        4. Donald C. Capers, 29, iron workman
            Charged with housebreaking
            Accused of entering grocery

    C. Airplane crash last night
       Four dead

Seventy-five miles north of city
Small chartered plane
Pilot, Judson H. Jones, operator Judson's Areo Service
Located at Blankville Airport
(Source: state police)

Jones warned not to take off
Strong winds and rain threatening
Passengers offered extra pay
(Source: L. M. Watson, Jones' partner)

Jones' wife had premonition
Danger near
Urged Jones not to fly yesterday
"He laughed it off"
(Source: Mrs. Jones)

Jones and three passengers killed
Passengers all television stars
Jennifer Rose, singer, of New Orleans
Spike Williams, comedian, of Brooklyn
Welton White, pianist and master of ceremonies, of
Denver
Crashed into farm home
Of Mr. and Mrs. R. S. Hopper, Route 5, Hurrytown
Plane and home burned
Mr. Hopper suffered severe burns on hands
Tried to recover passengers
(Source: state police)

The three television stars
Here for opening ceremonies yesterday
New station, WWW–TV
Missed commercial plane
Hired charter plane to meet next engagement
(Source: Harry Hoover, WWW–TV manager)

D. Two children lost in mountains near Wildwood State Park
Wandered from cabins where families vacationing
Sammy Stephens, 9, son of Murray Stephens, physicist at
State College; and Donald Crossbow, 8, son of Anthony
J. Crossbow, president, Crossbow Iron Works, Boulder
City
Sammy's Cocker Spaniel, Scout, with boys
Parents missed children when they failed to come for
evening meal

Park Superintendent Amos Moody organizes search party

Heavy summer thunderstorm broke over area at 7 p.m.

Mrs. Crossbow taken to Boulder City hospital and put under sedation

Anthony Crossbow offers ten thosuand dollars reward to anyone "who finds my son"

Searcher, Thomas Winston, 26, park guard, fell from bluff in darkness

Taken to Boulder City hospital with broken leg

Search party finds dog, Scout, near cave entrance

Searchers fan out into twisting corridors of cave which honeycombs mountain

Professor Stephens takes dog into cave, orders him to "find Sammy"

Searchers following dog hear faint cries

Find two boys huddled together in darkness, safe but scared

Became lost while exploring cave

Scout is acclaimed hero

Mr. Crossbow says, "As Scout isn't a man, I don't suppose he's entitled to that reward"

Promises to buy dog a new collar

E. City election yesterday

Polls opened at 9 a.m., closed at 7 p.m.

To elect mayor, five city councilmen, two members of School Board, City Judge

40,000 qualified to vote

Candidates for mayor: Rodney Dodson, incumbent, Frank Wallace

For School Board: Phillip Mason, Dr. Earl Jefferson, Mrs. Alice Whiteside, incumbent

For City Judge: Linton Overcast, incumbent, Robert Miller

For City Council:

First District—J. L. Dodson, incumbent, Wade Burton, H. Hoover Sims;

Second District—Marvin Tompkins, Mrs. Joyce Purdom, F. H. Jones;

Third District—Miles Smith, incumbent, Roy Maples;

Fourth District—Andrew Wilson, incumbent;

Fifth District—David R. Reeves, Abel Curry, Mrs. Ruby Long.

Fight at Maple Street Firehall polling place, First District

John James, election official, knocked down by Charles Smith

James refused to let Smith vote

"Not properly registered," said James

Smith, a truck driver, is a 250-pound brute

Early returns show incumbent Rodney Dodson holding
narrow lead in mayor's race

Final unofficial tally, with 95 of 95 precincts reported,
show

Frank Wallace, 15,263, J. L. Dodson, 12,871.

Dodson concedes at midnight

Results of other races:

School Board—Mrs. Alice Whiteside, 16412,

Dr. Earl Jefferson, 7,210; Phillip Mason, 1,874

City Judge—Robert Miller, 12,892, Linton Overcast,
12,341;

City Council, First District—Wade Burton, 4,833, J. L.
Dodson 3,911, H. Hoover Sims, 1,969;

Second District—F. H. Jones, 3673, Mrs. Joyce Purdom, 1,714, Marvin Tompkins, 822;

Third District—Roy Maples, 4899, Miles Smith, 2013;

Fourth District—Andrew Wilson 2,579;

Fifth District—Mrs. Ruby Long, 3,407, David R.
Reeves, 1,231, Abel Curry, 215.

F. Following is the highlight of a speech by Mayor Phillip
Watkins delivered at a meeting of the Downtown Merchants Association last night.

"For the past decade we have watched the slow death
and decay of our downtown business district, caused by
the undisciplined growth of shopping centers along our
city's perimeter. Although some of you, by establishing
branch operations in these suburban areas, have contributed to this shopping center noose that threatens
to strangle us, I am sure your main interest still lies on
Main Street.

"Therefore, it is my great pleasure to announce
tonight the appointment of a Greater Downtown Committee which will help to reverse this flow of customers, turning them back from the suburbs to your
downtown merchants where they belong. This committee will make plans to revitalize the downtown
area, finding new ways to attract the business you have
lost. The committee will explore all the methods
currently being used by cities to revive dying business
districts—pedestrian malls, multilevel parking garages,

free bus transportation from suburbia to store doors—
and will recommend the best plan for our city.

"And I might add—and this is off the record, gentle-
men of the press—your councilmen and I are considering expanding our city limits through annexation to take
in these fringe area business districts for the purpose
of increasing our revenues and giving us a measure of
control over the future growth of outlying businesses
through our zoning laws."

G. Independence Day parade yesterday

Parade formed at 2 p.m. on Front Street

Line of march extended 15 blocks along Broadway to
Monument Park

Parade composed of military units and bands from Carson
Air Force Base and Fort Holly, local National Guard
unit, sixteen high school bands, veterans from local
American Legion and Veterans of Foreign Wars posts,
floats with patriotic themes contributed by local organizations and merchants

Reviewing stand at corner Broadway and Fifth Avenue

Dignitaries on reviewing stand: Major General C. J.
Brady, commanding officer, Carson AFB; Brigadier
General Charles Dutton, commanding officer, Fort
Holly; General John B. Craig, adjutant general, State
National Guard; Senator Clyde Rawkus; Mayor Walter
Jordan; other city officials

Estimated 100,000 persons line Broadway to see parade

Police arrest civilian marching with army unit

Identified as Charley Green, army veteran

Charged with public drunkenness

Spectator stricken by heart attack near corner of Third
and Broadway

Dead on arrival at Municipal Hospital.

Identified as J. D. Smithwyck, 84

Several women fainted along line of march

Temperature 94 degrees at 2 P.M.

Following parade, Senator Rawkus gave patriotic address
in front of Soldiers Monument in Monument Park

Subject "The Spirit of 1776"

About 10,000 heard Senator's speech

Chapter 8

Devices to Polish the Lead

IN leads, the good is frequently the enemy of the best. A good lead may obey all of the rules and principles so far discussed. It may contain the 5 *W*'s and the proper identification, authority, and tie back. It may play up a satisfactory feature. It may, in short, be entirely adequate and yet lack vividness, style, distinction, attractiveness, brilliance. A merely adequate lead, in other words, may be dull. The reporter's responsibility is to achieve not mere adequacy but also vividness. His job is to polish his lead until it has the maximum reader appeal. There are several devices and procedures for reaching this goal.

8a   *Rhetoric*

Good writing requires the use of incisive language. Another principle of rhetoric is variety of sentence structure. The most usual sentence form is subject-verb-predicate:

> Mayor Thomas M. Elroy will attend the mayors' convention at Cincinnati Aug. 4.

In any single lead there may be no objection to this form. But if the reporter writes all leads in this manner, he cannot achieve maximum reader appeal. His work may be adequate, but it will be dull.

The process of playing up the various *W*'s will probably enforce the use of a great variety of sentence structures. If it does not, the reporter should diligently practice the following forms:

Phrases:

Infinitive: To make Bellevue industry-conscious is the new program of . . .

Participial: Following a practice established 30 years ago, the legislature will . . .

Caught in the cross-fire of officers, the holdup men . . .

Prepositional: In search of buried treasure, the geology class of . . .

Gerund:	Filling big shoes with little men is the nation's political tragedy, in the opinion of . . .

Clauses:

Substantive:	That a moratorium on taxes will be declared is the opinion of . . .
	What they had opposed was of no concern to the . . .
Adverbial:	Because Senator Williams lost his watch, Congress today . . .
	While pickets watched the south exit, strike breakers today . . .

Emphasizing News Values

In the reporter's effort to place the most newsworthy feature first in the lead, a careless analysis of features may fail to shuck the ear down to the golden grain. Certain kernels of news values should be carefully sought. They are discussed elsewhere (Chapter 3) as news values and cannot be considered merely as polish. Their careful use, however, will add luster to the lead.

Timeliness. The words "today" and "tomorrow" characterize most newsworthy leads. Occasionally a story must, however, **8b** concern events which happened "last night," "yesterday," or "last week." In this case the reporter should seek a "today" angle of the previous events.

The Old Story:

The governor's decision yesterday to trim the state payroll $50,000 monthly has resulted in 10 dismissals from the State Highway Department, and dismissals in other departments are expected.

Same Story, Today Angle:

Ten highway employees are out of jobs today, the first victims of the governor's economy move to trim $50,000 monthly from the state payroll.

Proximity. Not merely a "today" angle should be discovered wherever it properly exists, but a "local" angle also should **8c** be diligently sought.

A General Story:

Fifteen thousand teachers will assemble in Centerville Oct. 15–17 for the annual meeting of the State Education Association.

Same Story, Local Angle:

Superintendent John A. White will lead a delegation of 100 Blank-ville teachers to the annual meeting of the State Education Association at Centerville Oct. 15–17. Fifteen thousand teachers are expected to attend.

8d   **Prominence.** Prominent names make eye-catching news.

A General Story:

The new law building of Kenevan College will be dedicated at Homecoming June 6. Many prominent alumni and visitors will attend.

Same Story, plus Prominent Names:

Gov. Carlos Brown of Wisconsin, James Truslow, former Supreme Court Justice, and H. S. Harriman, president of National Steel, will attend the dedication of the new law building at Kenevan College's Homecoming June 6.

8e   *Novelty Leads*

Another method of polishing the lead is the use of novelty forms which do not observe the rule of the 5 *W's*. Most novelty leads depend heavily on suspended interest. The opening paragraph may give one or more of the *W's*, but all five are usually conveyed before the end of the second or third paragraph.

To illustrate all methods of using novelty in the lead would be impossible. Presented below are a few of the more common forms. In these leads the story itself dictates its form, and the reporter should not strain himself to write a novelty lead on a story that does not justify such treatment. Nor does the novelty lead form give the reporter license to practice "fine writing" which violates basic rules of simplicity.

The Question Lead. Serves best when a problem with reader appeal is the crux of the story.

How can traffic deaths be reduced?
Three city officials—the mayor, the police chief, and the safety commissioner—pondered that question today, after receiving news of the seventh traffic death of the month.

The Punch, Capsule, or Cartridge Lead. Uses a blunt, explosive statement, short and to the point, which summarizes the most newsworthy feature.

Mayor Frank Walkons is dead.

After suffering a severe heart attack in his office this morning, the 67-year-old mayor succumbed at Holy Cross Hospital at 11:30 a.m.

The Direct-Quotation Lead. Features a short, eye-catching quotation.

"Give me a big shotgun, and I'll handle any burglar," boasted Mrs. L. R. Sweeney, 1512 Lane Street.

And Mrs. Sweeney lives up to her boasts. Last night she pulled her big shotgun out of the closet and fired away at a housebreaker who was attempting to escape with the family silver. He was taken to General Hospital, peppered with buckshot.

The Contrast Lead. Compares extremes—the big with the little, comedy with tragedy, age with youth, the past with the present—if such comparison is applicable to the news event.

A great celebration was held here 50 years ago, when half of Blankville's population gathered to see the cornerstone for the city's first six-story building set in place. Today, when the cornerstone was laid for the new 15-story Haley Building, only 50 persons were there to see it.

The Direct-Address Lead. Speaks directly to the reader on a subject which has widespread appeal.

Do not expect any pity from the weatherman. He forecasts a continuation of the cold wave.

The Descriptive Lead. Draws a quick word picture of an interesting person, place, or thing.

Tottering precariously, bending over a hand-hewn cane, a 71-year-old man shuffled into the Associated Charities office today.

"I've got a job, and I want to be taken off the relief roll," his voice crackled heartily.

The Parody Lead. Mimics a well-known proverb, quotation, or phrase.

Whisky, whisky, everywhere, nor any drop to drink.

Such was the case at the City Police Station yesterday when officers poured 100 gallons of bootleg beverage into the sewer.

The Historical or Literary-Allusion Lead. Relates a person or event to some character or event of history or literature.

Washington's trip across the Delaware was child's play compared with Dave Jason's span of Big Lick River. Astride a six-foot log, he chopped his way across the ice-bogged stream yesterday.

The Staccato Lead. Consists of a series of jerky, exciting phrases, separated by dashes or dots, used if the facts of the story justify it.

Midnight on the bridge . . . a scream . . . a shot . . . a splash . . . a second shot . . . a second splash.

This morning police recovered the bodies of Mr. and Mrs. R. E Murphy, estranged couple, from the Snake River. A bullet wound showed on the temple of each.

Miscellaneous Freak Leads. Employ ingenious novelty to attract the reader's eye. This list can be extended indefinitely, to the extent of the reporter's writing ability and imagination (tempered with accuracy).

For sale: one elephant.

The City Park Commission is thinking about inserting that ad in the newspaper. A curtailed budget makes it impossible to care for "Bobo," a half-grown elephant lodged in special quarters at Westdale Park, the commission said.

Only two more days . . .

And the city folk will be pulling in their porch furniture. And the rural folk will be putting their gates under lock and key.

It will be Halloween.

Complete Reporting

The best polish a lead can have comes from the inner light shining through essential story elements. If the reporter has chosen the wrong *W*'s or has picked up surface flotsam when data of more significance —more specific gravity—are submerged beneath the surface, no clever language will do more than gloss the defect. There is a notable difference between the following leads:

The Supreme Court this morning affirmed a lower court verdict in the case of R. L. Jameson, operator of Jameson Loan Company.

The "loan-shark" business is outlawed in this state.

The Supreme Court this morning, in affirming the verdict against R. L. Jameson of the Jameson Loan Company, upheld the constitutionality of the recent law requiring . . .

The first lead is so dull internally that it would scarcely take polish. The second shines with essential vitality and invites a higher finish.

The reporter must, however, distinguish between inner light and editorial bias and policy. The second example below emits the strong internal light—but is it a fair light? The reporter himself must be the judge in particular cases. He should not sacrifice fairness and objectivity in order to achieve a polished and colorful lead.

> Two men were killed when an automobile went over the embankment at Fifth and Union Avenues at 7:30 last night. They were . . .

> City "economy" killed two more men last night when an automobile slipped off the unlighted and unguarded Fifth and Union Embankment.

> For weeks the City Council has turned a deaf ear to citizens who . . .

Exercises

I. Rewrite the following leads, striving for variety in sentence structure.
  A. The Brownsville Highway Food Market reported to police that burglars entered the store through a front door last night and stole cigarettes and money from a vending machine.
  B. Dr. William T. Bozeman, president of Berman College, reported that a $10,000 gift had been received from an anonymous donor for use in establishing a new scholarship fund.
  C. Johnny Abbott, 18-month-old son of Mr. and Mrs. C. J. Abbott, 2213 Miller Road, died yesterday afternoon at Children's Hospital, apparently the victim of an overdose of aspirin given by his mother.
  D. Kermit Colter 17-year-old son of Mr. and Mrs. Thomas Colter, 1478 Clifton Drive, shot off two of his toes in a hunting accident near Bailey Lake yesterday.
  E. A Hopkins County man, Boyd E. Bodkins, 32, Carter Valley, died last night of injuries suffered when his automobile collided with a freight train at a crossing near his home.

II. The following leads could be more "timely." Improve them.
  A. Wildwood Boys School, privately operated orphanage, was burned to the ground yesterday, and an anonymous donor today gave $50,000 to help replace the century-old building.
  B. A fire at Dutton Hosiery Mill early yesterday raged for four hours causing a temporary shutdown of operations and doing an estimated $200,000 damage.
  C. An earthen dam, weakened by a week of heavy rains, broke

yesterday, flooding the town of Black Rock and leaving untold damages and several persons missing.

III. "Localize" the following stories. To do so, it is permissible, if necessary, to add a minimum amount of fictitious data.

    A. The Governor today signed into law a bill requiring all automobile drivers over 70 to pass a physical examination before applying for renewal of their licenses.

    B. Beginning Monday, passenger service on the Tri-State Railway will be ended.

IV. Prominent names are not given ample play in the following leads. Improve them.

    A. One person was killed and three were injured in a two-car collision on Highway 41 last night. Dead is J. X. Freeman, county attorney.

    B. Area lawyers will meet here tomorrow for the opening session of the Regional Bar Association Conference, at which Robert G. McDonald, chief justice of the State Supreme Court, will speak.

V. Improve the following leads by adding imaginary "human-interest" data and rewriting them.

    A. Last night's 18-inch snowfall prompted officials to close city school today.

    B. The new city-owned camp for underprivileged children opened this morning.

VI. Clip from a daily newspaper 10 leads employing novelty. Label them according to the classification of novelty leads given in this chapter.

VII. A. Write question leads from the following notes.

    B. Try for better leads using other novelty forms.

       1. Couple drowns when car plunges into Shadydale Lake last night

         Mr. and Mrs. C. K. Davidson of Pondville

         Two teen-age boys and two teen-age girls witness tragedy

         Did not report it until today

         Afraid parents would learn they were "out that late at night"

         Boys went to police this morning after sleepless night

         Said they heard someone screaming as they drove by lake at 1:30 a.m.

         Saw car sink in deep water

         Felt "the situation was hopeless" and occupants couldn't be saved

         Police said Davidson apparently lost control of car on curve

         Automobile found by divers and bodies removed

         Officers declined to identify young couples

2. Frank Barr, city workhouse guard, suspended today

   Prisoner charges Barr beat him last Thusday

   Put in solitary confinement without medical attention

   Barr denies "the entire story"

   Prisoner identified as Sam Floyd, 19

   Serving six-month term for forgery

   Floyd claims beaten with club when he refused to work

   Sheriff John Law promises "to get to the bottom of this matter"

   Asks district attorney's office to investigate

   Workhouse physician, Dr. A. C. Tonick, said he treated Floyd Saturday

   Bruises on head, shoulders, broken rib

VIII. A. Write punch leads from the following notes.
   B. Try for a better lead using other novelty forms.

      1. City's oldest resident

         "Uncle" John McNabb

         Celebrates one hundred and second birthday

         Party at home of youngest son, Abraham McNabb, 11106 Ross Street

         Cake with two candles

         "I'm working on my second century, so I just want two candles"

         Party attended by 112 descendants

         Uncle John's formula for long life: "Eat lots of fruit and stay away from hospitals"

      2. Felix Dutton, 55-year-old painter

         Killed in fall from Palmer Street Bridge into Race River

         Giving bridge annual coat of paint

         Rope supporting scaffold broke

         Arthur Kelly, painter, on scaffold with Dutton

         Saved himself by grabbing girder

         Body recovered by Fire Department rescue unit

         Survived by widow, Mabel Dutton, eight children

         Worked for city maintenance department 27 years

         Unable to swim

IX. A. Write direct-quotation leads from the following notes.
   B. Try for better leads using other novelty forms.

      1. Excerpt from speech made by Robert M. Crosswalk, prominent local businessman and candidate for mayor, in opening campaign speech yesterday:

         "When my opponent took office four years ago, our city had an income from taxes and other revenue sources of twelve million dollars and a surplus in the treasury. Although revenues amounted to eighteen million dollars last year—an increase to which the incumbent constantly points with pride and calls a 'sign of our prosperity'—our city government today is burdened with a debt of more than five million dollars. Ladies and gentlemen, this kind of 'prosperity' is leading us into bankruptcy."

2. Following are several direct quotations from an interview with Miss Lucy Lockett, syndicated lovelorn columnist:

"Everywhere I go women ask me how to be sure they've found the right man for a husband. My stock reply is that if you feel at home with a man, and he can eat your cooking, you've probably found the right man! I think you can tell if he loves you by observing the little things he does for you—not the mink coats or diamonds he lavishes upon you, but things like opening doors for you, being attentive, and listening to you. Really, I am an authority on this subject. I've been happily married four times myself."

X. A. Write contrast leads from the following notes.
   B. Try for better leads using other novelty forms.
      1. A $500,000 damage suit against City of Blankville
         Settled out of court for $10,000
         John Grubb, 8421 Oak Street, complainant
         Struck by police car while entering Police Headquarters last August 4
         Suffered broken leg, dislocated shoulder
         Was on way to station to pay $1 parking fine
      2. Miss Reba Peabody
         Retires after 50 years teaching
         Taught third grade at Emory School entire career
         Plans to enroll at State University
         To get master's degree
         In child psychology

XI. A. Write direct-address leads from the following notes.
    B. Try for better leads using other novelty forms.
       1. One week remains
          To buy state automobile license plates
          State police to set up roadblocks
          At midnight Friday
       2. Drinking fountains at City Park turned off
          Working on water mains
          Visitors must take own water if picnicking in park

XII. A. Write descriptive leads from the following notes.
  B. Try for better leads using other novelty forms.
1. Homecoming football game Saturday
State College (local) plays Berman College
Parade to precede game
Fraternities and sororities to prepare floats
Crowd of 35,000 expected for game
Five thousand State alumni flocking to town
Pep rally on campus Friday night
2. Annual city high school art contest opens today
At City Museum Art Gallery
Fifty students enter
Entries on exhibit at Gallery all this week
Judging tonight by three out-of-town artists
Entries in oils, watercolors, prints, drawings, sculpture
Winning entry in each class receives college art scholarship
Range from surrealism to traditional
Works to be on sale to public

XIII. A. Write novelty leads from the following stories, using any of the forms not mentioned in above assignments.
  B. Try for better leads using other novelty forms.
1. Mayor L. G. Fuller, candidate for third two-year term
Says he will take full salary if reelected
Had taken only one-half salary for past four years
"The city is in sound financial shape now. I think the mayor is entitled to full salary."
Promises to reduce property tax rate if reelected
Only candidate to announce to date
City election two months away
2. John Gray, Ford Street bricklayer, cited to City Court today
Refuses to pay $1 city dog tax
Says his dog, Rufus, "is like a member of the family"
Will go to jail before he will pay the tax
"I'll take Rufus with me, too. He has more sense than the people who decided dogs should be taxed."
3. T. L. Maples, 1506 West Hills
Finds buried treasure in backyard
Digging hole to plant tree
Unearthed metal box full of money
Totals more than $8,000
All in Confederate bills
4. Trained seal escapes from circus
Found this morning in city swimming pool
Early bathers startled

Trainer Claude Duncan retrieves animal

"I don't know how or when she got loose. I guess she wanted to go swimming."

Seal's name is Myrtle

XIV. Review all leads written under exercises in Chapters 6 and 7. Criticize them, and polish them in the light of what you have learned in this chapter.

THE COMPLETE REPORTER
PART THREE

Writing the Complete Story

After the challenge of achieving a distinctive lead has been met, the reporter is next confronted with the difficult problem of developing the body of the story. Just as a lead may be written either as a summary of the five *W*'s or as a novelty form, depending upon the nature of the story, the body of the story can be developed either as a straight news story or as a "feature story"—again depending upon the nature of the story.

Part III presents organizational patterns of both the straight and the feature story. This section also encompasses four other areas dealing with specific techniques and problems in writing complete stories. These relate to the organization of: (1) stories on events about which previous stories have been published; (2) cutlines to go with pictures, which are often important supplements to stories but which sometimes stand alone in reporting a news event; (3) news stories for broadcasting over radio or television; and (4) stories which require special treatment if a newspaper's policy is involved.

The chapters in this section have a bearing on the writing of all types of news stories considered in the chapters that follow.

Chapter 9

The Body of the Story

THE news story is so written that the whole story is summarized as fully as possible in the lead. The lead is the "story in a nutshell." In writing the lead the reporter departs from the chronological order of events and substitutes what is called the logical order. He narrates the incidents and facts in the order of newsworthiness.

If in the lead the reporter has summarized the whole story and has placed first things first, then in the body of the story **9a** he has only the task of retelling the story in sufficient detail —and of placing second things second, third things third, and so to the end, with all facts and incidents arranged in the logical order, the order of descending newsworthiness. A story or parts of it may be retold several times, but in each retelling the additional details are not obviously repetitious.

In logical order the reporter is keeping his "best foot forward." So long as he can hold the reader's interest with one paragraph, he has a chance with the next. One weak paragraph preceding several interesting paragraphs may mean that the latter paragraphs are not read.

In addition, the logical order is necessary to expedite the mechanical process of the newspaper. If the copyreader or makeup editor must reduce the length of a story, he cuts paragraphs from the end of the story. He takes for granted that he is eliminating the least important facts. Hence, the following rule:

Write your story so that, if it is terminated at any point, nothing below this point will be as newsworthy as anything above—and at this point the story will be complete, intelligible, and effective.

The body of the story serves one or both of two purposes: (1) it explains and elaborates the feature or features presented in the lead; (2) it adds and elaborates minor features not summarized in the lead. To achieve these purposes, and at the same time to present facts in a logical order, the beginning reporter might keep the following forms in mind when organizing a story:

9b   *Developing the Single-Feature Lead*

If a story contains but one feature, that feature constitutes the lead. The purpose of the body is to clarify the lead, adding the pertinent facts necessary. In this case the problem is to judge the newsworthiness of all facts so that they may be presented in logical order.

Below is an example of this type of story.

The Diagram	*The Written Story*
Lead: One Feature	Creation of a nonpolitical "Board of Public Welfare" to oversee the State Department of Public Welfare is recommended by the State Welfare Association in a report sent to Gov. John Bryan today.
Details of the Feature	The board is needed to "assure no politics" in handling relief funds and in the general conduct of the entire department, said the report. Board members would receive no pay and would be appointed by the governor to serve six-year terms.
More Details	"Impartial and effective administration of relief is nearly as important to the welfare of our state as a democratic school system," the report said.
	"We have achieved excellent results with a nonpolitical board over our state university, and we can use the same setup to assure no politics in the state welfare department," it said.
Further Details	Under the recommended setup, the proposed board would be the policy-making body for the welfare department. One board member would represent each congressional district, with the initial group serving terms of two, four and six years, and with vacancies filled by six-year appointments.

The Diagram	*The Written Story*
All Other Paragraphs in the Complete Story ▷	(Any additional paragraphs would give more details of the one feature.)

Developing the Several-Feature Lead   9c

Organization of several-feature stories involves problems not encountered in developing single-feature leads. Before noting different forms which can be used in several-feature development, the beginning reporter should review the purposes of the body of the story and be alert to principal difficulties experienced in achieving these ends.

In the first place, the body of the story elaborates features presented in the lead or lead block. After he has found lead **9d** features with particular reader appeal, a beginner sometimes will abandon some of the features entirely, not mentioning them further in the body of the story or perhaps referring to them again only deep within the story. Such errors violate not only the developmental purpose of the body of the story but also the principle of logical order; if a feature has enough reader appeal to deserve a place in the lead, it also deserves a place in the body of the story—and not a place buried beneath less significant facts.

Secondly, the body of the story adds and elaborates other minor features not summarized in the lead. In achieving **9e** this purpose the reporter must be able to distinguish between details of lead features on the one hand and "other minor features" on the other. To make this distinction clearer: *Just as major features are summarized in the lead before their details are presented, all minor features should be summarized at their point of introduction before details of them are presented.* In other words, the lead paragraph is not the only place in the story where features are summarized. If use of logical order eliminates features from the first part of a story, these features must be summarized at their logical place in the body before details on the added features are presented.

Summary Development. If more than one feature is summarized in the lead, each feature should be elaborated in **9f** the order of the presentation in the lead (which is the logical order). Note the following example:

The Diagram	*The Written Story*
Lead: Summary of All Features	Creation of a nonpolitical "Board of Public Welfare," the elimination of untrained social workers in local public welfare agencies, and an increase in state grants for aid to dependent children were recommended by the State Welfare Association in a report sent to Gov. John Bryan today.

1 ② ③

Details of First Feature	The proposed board would oversee the state welfare department and would "assure no politics" in handling relief funds and in the general conduct of the entire department, the report said. Board members would be appointed by the governor for six-year terms.

1

Details of Second Feature	Asserting that some local agencies have employed untrained social workers, the report suggests that the state insist upon properly qualified personnel in all local departments handling state welfare funds.

②

Details of Third Feature	The association said the present monthly allotment is "much too little" to provide for care of a dependent child by a guardian. The recommendation is that a study be made with a view to increasing the grants.

③

Details of First Feature	In advocating a policy-making welfare board, the association suggested an organization similar to the board of trustees of the state university.

1

"Impartial and effective administration of relief is nearly as important to the welfare of our state as a democratic school system," said the report. "We have achieved excellent results with a nonpolitical board over our state university, and we can use the same setup to assure no politics in the state welfare department."

1

The Diagram	*The Written Story*
All Other Paragraphs in the Complete Story ⟱	(Any additional paragraphs would give details of the three features summarized in the lead, presenting details in logical order. The reporter may continue using alternate paragraphs as above until he has exhausted all facts on all features.)

Salient-Feature Development. When one outstanding feature pushes several minor features out of the lead, these minor features can be summarized in the second paragraph (see second method of writing several-feature leads). Following this summary paragraph, the story refers back to the salient feature, giving details. Then, in the logical order, the story considers each of the minor features and the salient feature.   **9g**

The following example clarifies this method:

The Diagram	*The Written Story*
Lead: Salient Feature	Creation of a nonpolitical "Board of Public Welfare" to oversee the State Department of Public Welfare is recommended by the State Welfare Association in a report sent to Gov. John Bryan today.
1	
Summary of Other Features	The association also recommended that steps be taken to eliminate untrained social workers in local public welfare agencies and that state grants for aid to dependent children be increased. The report requested an increase of $1,000,000 in the welfare department budget to provide for "needed expansions of present programs."
	The association's recommendations were adopted at its 50th anniversary meeting held yesterday at Midtown Hotel, attended by a record 800 persons—including Senator Horace Mayes, known as "the father of public welfare legislation" in this state.
Details Common to All Features	

The Diagram

The Written Story

Details of Salient Feature

[1]

The proposed welfare board is needed to "assure no politics" in the handling of relief funds and in the general conduct of the entire department, the report said. Board members would receive no pay and would be appointed by the governor for six-year terms.

Details of First Minor Feature

(2)

Asserting that some local agencies have employed untrained social workers, the report suggests that the state insist upon properly qualified personnel in local departments handling state welfare funds.

Details of Second Minor Feature

/3\

The association said the present monthly allotment is "much too little" to provide for care of a dependent child by a guardian. The recommendation is that a study be made with a view to increasing the grants.

Details of Third Minor Feature

\4/

The $1,000,000 requested to pay for expansion needs was called "a conservative estimate." The report asked the governor to refer the figure to the state welfare department for verification.

Details of Salient Feature

[1]

In advocating a policy-making welfare board, the association suggested an organization similar to the board of trustees of the state university.

"Impartial and effective administration of relief is nearly as important to the welfare of our state as a democratic school system," declared the report.

[1]

"We have achieved excellent results with a nonpolitical board over our state university, and we can use the same setup to assure no politics in the state welfare department."

All Other Paragraphs in the Complete Story ▽

(Other details in logical order.)

Sometimes the minor features are not so important as some of the details of the salient feature. Then the reporter may postpone presentation of the summary paragraph of minor features until he has given the salient-feature details which deserve precedence. This organization still observes the logical order as illustrated by the following example:

The Diagram	*The Written Story*
Lead: Salient Feature	Creation of a nonpolitical "Board of Public Welfare" to oversee the State Department of Public Welfare is recommended by the State Welfare Association in a report sent to Gov. John Bryan today.
Details of Salient Feature	The board is needed to "assure no politics" in handling relief funds and in the general conduct of the entire department, said the report. Board members would receive no pay and would be appointed by the governor to serve six-year terms.
Details of Salient Feature	"Impartial and effective administration of relief is nearly as important to the welfare of the state as a democratic school system," the report declared. "We have achieved excellent results with a nonpolitical board over our state university, and we can use the same setup to assure no politics in the state welfare department."
Summary of Other Features	The association also recommended that state medical care be provided county orphanages and that the state assist counties in aiding the blind. The report requested an increase of $100,000 in the welfare department budget to provide for "expansion needs."
Details of First Minor Feature	To supplement the "meager" medical services furnished by most counties the state might employ several regional "traveling doctors" to visit the orphanages regularly, the report suggested.

The Diagram	*The Written Story*
Details of Second Minor Feature	Assistance to the indigent blind was termed "a state responsibility which in some cases has been assumed by the counties."
Details of Third Minor Feature ▽4	The association estimated the cost of "needed expansion of present programs" at $100,000, but asked the governor to refer this figure to the state welfare department for verification.
More Details of Salient Feature □1	As described briefly in the report, the proposed Board of Public Welfare would be the policy-making body for the welfare department. One board member would represent each congressional district, with the initial group serving terms of two, four, and six years and with vacancies filled by six-year appointments.
All Other Paragraphs in the Complete Story ⇩	(Other details in logical order.)

9h   The Combination Development.

The Diagram	*The Written Story*
Lead: Summary of Two Main Features	Creation of a nonpolitical "Board of Public Welfare" and the elimination of untrained social workers in local public welfare agencies are recommended by the State Welfare Association in a report sent to Gov. John Bryan today.
Summary of Other Features	The association also recommended that state grants for aid to dependent children be increased. The report requested an increase of $100,000 in the welfare department budget to provide for expansion needs.
 Details Common to All Features	The association's recommendations were adopted at its 50th anniversary meeting held yesterday at Midtown Hotel, attended by a record 800

The Diagram	*The Written Story*
	persons—including Senator Horace Mayes, known as "the father of public welfare legislation" in this state.
Details of First Lead Feature	The proposed welfare board is needed to "assure no politics" in handling relief funds and in the general conduct of the entire department, said the report. Board members would receive no pay and would be appointed by the governor for six-year terms.
1	
Details of Second Lead Feature	Asserting that some local agencies have employed untrained social workers, the report suggests that the state insist upon properly qualified personnel in local departments handling state welfare funds.
②	
Details of First Minor Feature	The association said the present monthly allotment is "much too little" to provide for care of a dependent child by a guardian. The recommendation is that a study be made with a view to increasing the grants.
△3	
Details of Second Minor Feature	The $1,000,000 requested to pay for "needed expansions of present programs" was called "a conservative estimate." The report asked the governor to refer the figure to the state welfare department for verification.
▽4	
Details of First Lead Feature	In advocating a policy-making welfare board, the association suggested an organization similar to the board of trustees of the state university.
1	
	"Impartial and effective administration of relief is nearly as important to the welfare of our state as a democratic school system," declared the report. "We have achieved excellent results with a nonpolitical board over our state university, and we can use the same setup to assure no politics in the state welfare department."
1	

The Diagram	*The Written Story*
All Other Paragraphs in the Complete Story ⟱	(Other details in logical order.)

A combination development with some features buried deep in the story (note the example below) is a common form. This is much like the salient-feature form illustrated previously in this chapter. In long stories minor features may be introduced in summary paragraphs at several points in the body of the story.

The Diagram	*The Written Story*
Lead: Summary of Two Main Features 1 2	Creation of a nonpolitical "Board of Public Welfare" and the elimination of untrained social workers in local public welfare agencies are recommended by the State Welfare Association in a report sent to Gov. John Bryan today.
Details of First Lead Feature 1	The proposed welfare board is needed to "assure no politics" in handling relief funds and in the general conduct of the entire department, the report said. Board members would receive no pay and would be appointed by the governor for six-year terms.
Details of Second Lead Feature 2	Asserting that some local agencies have employed untrained social workers, the report suggests that the state insist upon properly qualified personnel in local departments handling state welfare funds.
Summary of Other Features 3 4	The association also recommended that state grants for aid to dependent children be increased. The report requested an increase of $500,000 in the welfare department budget to provide for expansion needs.
Details of First Lead Feature 1	In advocating a policy-making welfare board, the association suggested an organization similar to the board of trustees of the state university. "Impartial and effective administration of relief is nearly as important

The Diagram	*The Written Story*
	to the welfare of our state as a democratic school system," declared the report. "We have achieved excellent results with a nonpolitical board over our state university, and we can use the same setup to assure no politics in the state welfare department."

The Diagram	*The Written Story*
Details of First Minor Feature	The association said the present monthly allotment is "much too little" to provide for care of a dependent child by a guardian. The recommendation is that a study be made with a view to increasing the grants.
Details of Second Minor Feature	The $500,000 requested to pay for needed expansions of present programs was called "a conservative estimate." The report asked the governor to refer the figure to the state welfare department for verification.
All Other Paragraphs in the Complete Story	(Other details in logical order.)

Multiple-Casualty Story Development. Newspapers have a popular form for stories involving several casualties. An illustration follows:

9i

The Diagram	*The Written Story*
	Two persons were killed and three seriously injured at the Jonesboro Pike railroad crossing early today when a freight train crashed with a sedan.

The dead:
Lloyd Torley, 29, of 1206 Truce Street.
Sam Becker, 41, of 101 King Street.
The injured:
John L. Lutz, 30, of 904 Fourth Avenue, fractured skull.
Bernard T. Mooney, 30, of 1704

The Diagram   *The Written Story*

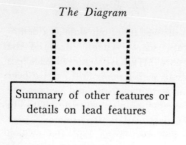

Summary of other features or
details on lead features

Details

Rose Avenue, broken leg and internal injuries.

Kyle O. Felts, 24, of 904 Fourth
Avenue, possible skull fracture.

The five were occupants of the
sedan, driven by Mr. Torley. They
were headed for Jonesboro, where
they were employed in building a
service station.

(Details of accident in chronological order.)

This form is seldom used when the number of casualties is small.
It is designed to single out the casualties and to eliminate the awkward construction of a long list of names within a paragraph.

As diagramed above, this form of story summarizes all features
in the lead paragraph. The same form can be used with several
features which are not all summarized in the first paragraph. In
such case, paragraphs summarizing other features follow, in logical
order, the listing of casualties.

9j   *The Chronological Order*

Strong narrative elements may sometimes demand the chronological order (rather than the logical) in the body of the story. After
the lead has summarized outstanding features of the story, the body
of the story may be developed narratively. In most cases, however,
the narrative paragraphs are interrupted by non-narrative paragraphs. Notice the following example:

The Diagram   *The Written Story*

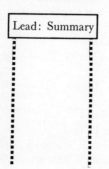

Lead: Summary

An attempted holdup with toy
pistols ended last night with three
12-year-old boys in the Juvenile De-
tention Home, charged with robbing
T. M. Kaye, railroad conductor.

Mr. Kaye said he had started home
from work about 11 p.m. and was un-
locking his car in the railroad yards
when three boys stepped from behind the car, with pistols pointed
toward him.

The Diagram   *The Written Story*

Narrative

Non-narrative
Details

Narrative

"Hands up," one of them shouted. Mr. Kaye recognized the toy pistols. He laughed, thinking the boys were playing with him, and held up his hands.

"Git his roll," one of the boys told another. "We'll cover 'im."

The smallest of the three stepped forward and started to rifle Mr. Kaye's pocket.

"Here, here," reprimanded Mr. Kaye. "This has gone far enough."

"We ain't foolin'. Git your hands up," returned the boys, one of them kicking him on a shin.

Mr. Kaye lunged at the boys, and they scattered frantically. Later they were found by policemen in an empty box car.

The youths, sons of mill workers, live in the Lonneyview neighborhood. Their names are withheld because of their ages.

Questioned by Juvenile Officer Tom Bryant early today, the boys changed their story.

"We was only playing," one said.

Displaying a bruised shin, Mr. Kaye broke in.

"Do you call that playing?"

"He did that!" exclaimed two of them simultaneously, pointing to the third boy.

Feeling he was having to shoulder all the blame, the accused spoke up.

"They told me to."

"We did not."

"You did!"

After stopping the argument and questioning them further, Officer Bryant got the boys to confess they had intended to rob Mr. Kaye.

The Diagram   *The Written Story*

> The boys will face Juvenile Judge
> John Lawson today. Two of them
> have been before the judge before,
> charged with truancy.

┌─────────────────────────┐
│   Non-narrative Details │
└─────────────────────────┘

The chronological order is a popular form for many types of stories—accidents, fires, crime, debates, trials, sports, weddings, and the like. Most of them are stories with strong narrative elements (fast-moving action or events building up to a climax), lending themselves to the chronological order after summarization of the main feature or features. Use of chronological order does not relieve the reporter of the responsibility for adequate summarizations before the chronological order is begun. Care must be taken to avoid jumping into the chronological order too soon; sometimes only one paragraph of summary is needed, sometimes more than one. A story written in chronological order may be either a single-feature or a several-feature story.

9k   *Direct Quotations*

In organizing the body of the news story, a reporter must overcome the problem of monotony in the use of indirect and direct quotations. The story should not be a series of direct quotations. Neither should most stories be wholly indirect quotations or summary statements. It is the "happy medium" that is most effective.

Direct quotations aid a story if used carefully. Sandwiched between indirect quotations and summary statements, they help emphasize certain points, and they are pleasing to the reader's eye, breaking the monotony and giving more life to the story. Some newspapermen frown upon a lead which begins with a direct quotation, but this disfavor arises primarily from slipshod writing. Too many reporters are willing to begin a story with a long, lukewarm quotation instead of troubling their mental capacities with the work of composing a crisp, adequate news lead. If the reporter will remember that the lead is the story's showcase, he will not begin with a direct quotation that does not have the showcase quality of reader appeal. In truth, a poorly written summary is better than a poor direct quotation lead (see special note on "What to Quote," correction key **4q**).

Direct quotations may be phrases, clauses, or words within a sentence, a sentence within a paragraph, or a complete paragraph.

Seldom should more than two consecutive paragraphs be direct quotations, for too many quotations are more monotonous than too few. In some cases, however, an exceptional quotation may be worthy of several consecutive paragraphs. This rule does not apply, of course, in narrating a conversation between two or more persons, though lengthy discourses of this type are usually interspersed by summary paragraphs.

Transitional Devices 91

The reporter must weave together the various parts of a story by the use of connective words and phrases. In attempting to achieve brevity, many beginning reporters sacrifice coherence. Unless the sentences within a paragraph or the paragraphs within a story are obviously related, the reporter must indicate the relationships. Sometimes such common connectives or transitions as *also, on the other hand,* or *meanwhile* may be sufficient, but in many cases the transition must be clarified by reference to previous subject matter. For example: notice the transition in the fifth paragraph of the sample "combination development" story on page 132.

> *In advocating a policy-making welfare board,* the association suggested an organization similar to the board of trustees of the state university.

This transition (in italics) refers to "Creation of a nonpolitical 'Board of Public Welfare'. . . ." Because the paragraph follows other nonrelated paragraphs, the transition is essential to clarify the relationship of the fifth paragraph to former facts in the story. Without the transition, the reader would be confused about the "suggested organization."

In making a transition, care must be taken to avoid the verbatim repetition of previous wording in the story. The **9m** transition in the above paragraph, for example, should not be worded "Creation of a nonpolitical Board of Public Welfare was recommended." The transition should be as short as possible, a mere mention of the feature previously summarized.

Block Paragraphs 9n

The reporter may follow the established principles of English composition in developing paragraphs in the body of the story, though paragraphs should be shorter than those generally used in English composition. Each paragraph may have its topic sentence, or several paragraphs may develop different aspects of the same topic. By observing the topic-sentence principles, most of the paragraphs will be separate units in themselves and can be shifted to other positions in the story without changes in wording or they can be eliminated without requiring substantial revisions in remaining paragraphs. These are called *block* paragraphs. This type of paragraph fits ideally into the newspaper pattern because it expedites the editing of a story when the transposition of paragraphs or the shortening of a story becomes necessary either at the copyreading desk or in the mechanical department.

A paragraph cannot be shifted without editing if a transitional phrase directly connects it with a paragraph that precedes or follows. For example, a paragraph that begins with "on the other hand" could be confusing if it does not immediately follow the appropriate paragraph. In deference to the advantages of block paragraphs, the reporter should avoid transitional phrases which tie consecutive paragraphs together, but he still may employ such phrases from time to time when they are particularly suitable to story construction.

90   *Adequacy versus Trivia*

How much detail should the reporter present in his story? On the one hand, he can clutter the story with boresome trivia; on the other, he can fail to include adequate story data. Beyond the point of an adequate development or explanation (with necessary interpretation) of the features in the story, the reporter is guided by reader appeal in selecting details which go into the story. Any and all details of some events are interesting enough to include in the story, but a large part of the details of most events will do no more than waste newspaper space.

Complete Reporting. At this point the opportunities for complete reporting may be suggested:

If all of the essential information of the story is crowded into the 5 *W*'s of the lead or lead block, the body of the story can do no more than explore and exploit these same *W*'s. Each and every one of them (plus the identification, the authority, and the tie back) is susceptible to endless exploration. Quantity of language is, of course, not the objective—quite the contrary. Quality of information is.

The problem of complete reporting in body development lies not in the writing facility but in research competence. Once the reporter returns from the story scene to his typewriter, the opportunity for complete and competent development of the body of his story must be found in his rough notes, in his memory, and in his background of knowledge. Where these fail, competence fails, for all that logic or language can throw into the breach.

Caught between the irresistible pressure of limitless materials, even in relatively simple stories, and the immovable limits of newspaper space, the reporter has only one recourse: quality and essentiality of story data—unless he is content to fall into the easy habit of superficial reporting.

Certainly it should be clear that the 5 *W*'s cannot be adequately explored in the lead. Yet how many of these *W*'s are wholly neglected in the further development of many stories! How often is the newspaper reader left wondering over this or that deficiency in detail!

Complete reporting requires competence of research—penetrative curiosity—on the part of the reporter. Lacking this, the reporter must depend upon the formal principles of body development to support lame reporting.

Exercises

A REMINDER: Students should keep in mind the points included in the "Important Note" on page 87 in using story notes in the exercises in this book.

  I. Clip from a newspaper five stories which illustrate forms of body development diagramed in this chapter. Paste them upon sheets of paper and draw the proper diagram at the left of each clipping.
 II. Using the following notes, write a story illustrating the first form diagramed (the single-feature form):

> Blankville Parent-Teacher Association
> Met at City High School auditorium
> Last night
> Pass resolution
> Favoring school building program
> Want new high school and three elementary schools
> Would cost approximately $3,000,000
> "All present schools overcrowded."
> "Teaching loads too heavy."
> New buildings would relieve congestion
> Want new high school in Westview neighborhood

New elementary schools in: Oak Park, Glendale, Fountain Park
Draw up petition
To City Council
Asking bond issue to provide money
Committee appointed to present petition: John R. Lowery, attorney; D. V. Dove, principal Fourth Street Elementary School; Mrs. T. M. Collins, 1546 Young Street

III. Adding these notes to those in II above, write a story illustrating the second form diagramed (the several-feature summary form):

Association also votes
To request School Board
To increase salaries of teachers
"Now 20 percent too low."
Compared with national averages
Say elementary teachers should be on par with high school teachers
Elementary teachers now on lower scale
Lengthy statistical study of comparative salaries
To be issued soon
By association
Another resolution
To request School Board
To provide "well-stocked libraries"
For all schools
Elementary and high schools
Claim this is practice
Of other large cities
Say Blankville school system is "behind times"
In this respect
Want libraries "measuring up to best"
"To encourage pupils to read more books" in all grades

IV. Adding these notes to those in II and III above, write a story illustrating the third form diagramed (the first salient-feature form of several-feature development):

Another resolution
To School Board
Asking that local persons
Be given preference
In selection of new teachers
Claim several out-of-town residents
Given jobs last year
Though "local citizens qualified"
To handle positions

V. Adding these notes to those in II and IV above, write a story illustrating the fourth form diagramed (the second salient-feature form of several-feature development):

Association also votes
To request School Board
To provide milk for indigent children
In city schools
The association offers to help finance project
If School Board will cooperate
Also decides
To sponsor health parade
Next month
To promote good health habits
Teachers to rate students
Highest in ranking will march in parade

VI. Using the notes in II, III, and V above, write a story illustrating the fifth form diagramed (the combination form).

VII. Using the multiple-casualty story form diagramed in the chapter above, write a story from the following notes.

Fire yesterday morning
At Fairmont Junior High School, Macey Drive
Originated in furnace room beneath auditorium
Had gained much headway
Before discovered at 9 a.m.
Four hundred students attend school
All were in auditorium at a school assembly
To hear address on fire prevention
By L. X. Huxley, assistant fire chief
During speech, smoke poured
Through west stairway into auditorium
At first Huxley thought it was a joke
Then realized seriousness
Ordered students to file out rear doors, opposite stairways
Directed the exodus of students and teachers
Credited with saving many lives
Auditorium and three classrooms destroyed or damaged
Damages estimated at about $100,000
Fire caused by overheated furnace
One pupil and one teacher killed
Three pupils injured
These did not follow Huxley's instructions
Went out a stairway and were trapped
In small room at bottom of stairway

Attempted to exit from side of auditorium
Outside door to this room locked
Smoke apparently blinded them
Prevented them from finding way back up stairs
Firemen believe pupil and teacher suffocated
Before fire reached them
Injured pupils got out but were burned
(Source: Fire Chief R. N. Weiss)

Pupil killed is James Cox, 13, son of Mr. and Mrs. W. B. Cox, 1042 Strong Street
Teacher killed: Miss Wilma Bailey, 28, seventh grade teacher
Pupils injured: John Spratt, 13, son of Mr. and Mrs. W. N. Spratt of 402 Front Street; Boyd B. Wright, 14, son of Mr. and Mrs. N. O. Wright, 1608 Duncan Street; and Barbara Allen, 13, daughter of Mr. and Mrs. D. J. Allen, Wales Road
(Source: General Hospital records)

Janitor of building, Farley Jones
Had fired furnace at 6 A.M.
Then went home, ill with influenza
Said everything seemed all right
Because of illness, failed to unlock all doors to auditorium
Feels badly about fire and deaths
(Source: F. L. Johnson, principal of Fairmont School)

Four fire trucks answered call
Two from main station
One from each of Fairmont district stations
City school officials and firemen
Still making investigation
Young Spratt not expected to live
Seriously burned about the body
He and others injured in General Hospital
(Source: Fire Chief Weiss)

VIII. Write a story using the chronological order from the following notes:

Robert D. McLean
County tax assessor
Visited this morning
By three persons
Mrs. K. L. Read, Kenneth M. Davis, and James Y. Waite
A committee from County Property Owners' League
Appointed to protest "high" tax assessments
"You know why we are here," said Mr. White

McLean did not answer

Got up from desk

Walked across room; looked out window

"I see we can expect no cooperation from you," said Davis

"We wanted to give you a chance to act before kicking you out of office"

McLean turned around quickly

He glared at committeemen

"What do you expect me to do? Do you want to take over my job?" he said.

"We want an answer. Do you intend to reduce assessments?" said Davis.

McLean replied: "Now get this straight. I'm not wearing smoked glasses for any crackpot organization. When I took this job, I pledged to handle it to the best of my ability. No pressure group is going to tell me how to run this office."

"You need somebody to tell you how to run this offce," said Davis

"You've come down here to kick me out of this office," McLean said angrily. "Well we'll see who gets kicked out."

Then McLean (age 42; six feet tall; 200 lb.) grabbed Davis (age 63; five feet two; 140 lb.)

By back of coat and seat of trousers

Shoved him roughly out the door

Other committee members shocked by episode

Walked out protesting loudly

McLean slammed and locked door

Has refused to give statement

McLean has been in office nine months

Formerly a real-estate agent

Davis said he plans to "see my lawyer"

"No monkey is going to push me around like that," he snorted

IX. Write stories from the following notes, in each case explaining your choice of lead and story form and diagraming the story that you write.

A. Notes taken at City Court session yesterday:

Harmon Timmons, 343 Varr Street

Charged with reckless driving

Policeman Joe Yates testified

Timmons made "U" turn on Selmer Avenue

Car coming from rear

Crashed into Timmons' car

Timmons lost control of car

Car ran up on sidewalk, and into store window

It was Selmer Street Furniture Store
Timmons admitted guilt
Said, "I held out my hand when I turned, and he hit me."
Judge Ernest Bailey fined Timmons $50

Next case:
John M. Mason, 1900 Trent Drive
Charged with shooting in city
Judge fined him $5, and suspended fine
Mason said he was shooting at howling cat
At 2 A.M. yesterday
Because it kept him awake
Judge commented, "I don't blame you. If it were legal, I'd do it myself."

Another case:
Raymond F. Knight, 621 Graff Street
And Thomas Edwards, 825 Yale Avenue
Charged with fighting
Policemen George Stone and Al Ross
Said two men fought in James' Cafe, 2300 Drew Street
Damaged furniture
Threw beer bottles at each other
Both men badly bruised
Knight testified Edwards "insulted my girl"
Edwards denied it
Said Knight had been "gunnin' for me"
Judge fined each $25

B. Skyways Airline plane crashed last night
Plunged into residential section near Municipal Airport
Pilot attempted to land in thunderstorm
Sixty passengers, five crew members abroad
All aboard plane killed
Senator Marvin Caucus aboard plane
Sandra Sheraton, movie starlet, aboard plane en route to Hollywood
Flight 640 from Chicago, due to land at 8:47 p.m.
Was 30 minutes late
Federal officials on scene to determine cause of crash
    (Source: Skyways Airlines)

Wreckage scattered over two-block area bounded by Sanders, Maple, 21st and 23rd streets
Four houses demolished, ten others damaged
Twelve residents known dead but identifications not yet reported
Ambulance en route to scene collided with automobile

Ambulance driver, C. L. Loomis, killed instantly

Automobile driver, Clifford Sutton, hospitalized with multiple injuries, in critical condition

Dead removed to City Hospital, city morgue, several mortuaries

Several residents of stricken area reported hearing explosion prior to crash

Thought noise was thunder

(Source: City police)

Fire broke out in one damaged home, threatened others

Soon brought under control by City Fire Department

Fireman James Driver injured by falling chimney

Admitted to City Hospital with broken shoulder

(Source: City Fire Department)

C. At 10:30 last night

Large, bearded man knocked on door

Of K. C. Johnson home

2472 Fairmont Drive

Mr. Johnson answered

"You the guv'ner?" the visitor asked

Johnson responded

"Guv'ner? What do you mean? My name is Johnson. What do you want?"

"Want to see the guv'ner. You work here? Where is he?"

"I live here. This is my home. There is no guv'ner here."

The visitor suddenly pushed Johnson backward, forced himself through the front door, and closed the door behind him

The visitor drew a revolver from an inside coat pocket

Johnson could smell whiskey on the man's breath

"Take me to the guv'ner," the visitor demanded

At that moment Johnson realized what was happening

Johnson had lived in the house a year

He had heard that a governor of the state had lived there

About 10 years previously

"Listen, man. There was a governor living here a long time ago, but not anymore. It's my house now."

"See the mail," Johnson said, pointing to two invoices on a hall table. "It's addressed to me. My name's Johnson, but I'm no governor."

The man looked at the mail and blinked

He put the revolver back into his pocket

"Where does guv'ner live? I owe 'im somethin. He wouldn't pardon me."

"Man, I don't know. I've lived in this state only a year, and I don't know anything about governors, pardons, politics, or nothing."

The visitor blinked again and looked around the room

He suddenly opened the door behind him, backed out, and disappeared

Johnson called police

(Source of above notes: Mr. Johnson)

Detectives Roy Swann and Philip Askew answered and are investigating

Those recently released from prison being checked

Several will be rounded up today

For Johnson to identify

Ten years ago governor of state was T. B. Brown, who died three years ago

The late Governor Brown did live at 2472 Fairmont Drive at time of his election

(Source: Detective Swann)

D. State Bar Association

To meet here next Friday and Saturday

Annual convention

Approximately 1,000 expected

To be held at Washington Hotel

Following is program:

Friday

10 A.M.—Session on improving requirements for admission to the bar. Speakers: F. D. King, dean of law college, State University; M. O. Sams, president, State Bar Association; K. R. Krauss, of Lynchville. Discussion leader: Attorney Sams .

Noon luncheon—Speaker: Judge James L. Jackson, of State Supreme Court. Topic: "Speeding Up Justice."

2 P.M.—Session on simplification of legal procedure of state courts. Speakers: Harold D. Sparks, vice president, State Bar Association; Judge Warner Pace of second circuit; Attorney U. D. Lacey of Yorktown. Discussion leader: Attorney Sparks.

8 P.M.—Banquet Speaker: Claude F. Ashley, noted Chicago trial attorney. Topic: "Ethics in Law."

Saturday

10 A.M.—Business session

Election of new officers

Final consideration of resolutions considered in other sessions

> > Decide on meeting place for next year
> > Report on president, secretary, and treasurer
> > Installation of new officers

(*Note:* The fact that the association will meet here has been announced in preceding stories. No news has been printed on the program, however.)

E. Tornado struck city suburbs yesterday afternoon
Funnel sighted at 3:40 p.m.
Approached from southwest
Two inches of rain fell in wake of tornado
> (Source: Weather Bureau)

Millwood district hardest hit
Several homes of Brandon Mill textile workers demolished
Most residents took shelter in basements
Family of five wiped out as home demolished
Identified as Willard Johnson, textile mill guard, wife Ruth,
Three children, Janie, 10, Martha, 6, Tommy, 2
Grayson Supermarket near textile mill demolished
Nine customers injured
Several trapped under section of fallen roof two hours
Automobile driven by S. H. Tolliver, a mill foreman, lifted by
    tornadic winds, carried hundred yards
Dropped in vacant lot, rightside up
Toliver, wife, two children unhurt
Flooding of Cross Creek causes damage in downtown section
Basements of several Front Street stores flooded
Merchandise damage estimated in thousands of dollars
> (Source: Police reports)

Fire broke out at textile mill immediately after tornado struck
Broken electrical lines believed cause
Debris in streets delayed fire trucks for 30 minutes
Flames brought under control after two hours
Mill shipping department heavily damaged by blaze
> (Source: Fire Department)

Red Cross rushes food, clothing blankets to area
Homeless families given temporary shelter in Millwood High
    School building
> (Source: Red Cross)

Mayor Todd Sells views stricken areas
Puts loss estimate "in the millions"

F. Hunting prohibited
For indefinite period

In this section state

Ten counties affected

An effort to prevent

Forest fires

More than 800 acres

Already destroyed in area

More than 50 fires in past month

Counties affected: Blank, Smith, Jackson, Washington, Grant,
   Farragut, Warner, Kuhlman, Forest, Sykes

Two fires still burning

Near Whitesville (Grant County) and London (Warner
   County)

Being fought by 500 men

High wind hinders work

One man W. T. Smith, 36, Smith County farmer, killed

In fall down ravine

When blinded by smoke

Panicked; "didn't use good sense"

Dry weather

During past month

Forests dangerously threatened

Worst in 28 years

All precautions possible

To be taken in future
   (Source: W. S. Kirksley, state commissioner of conservation)

Chapter 10

Features and Human-Interest Stories

LEST he suffer utter confusion over the term "feature," the reporter must keep in mind that this word in journalism has several meanings, the precise definition arising from the way the word is used. The features of a story have been described previously as the most newsworthy elements. "Featuring a W" was explained as a technique of writing a lead. In this chapter, however, feature takes another meaning—and several meanings at that! It could be a story based wholly on human interest. It could be a historical treatise. It could apply to materials used in the newspaper that are not classified as news. To understand and assimilate these new meanings, the reporter must have a clear understanding of human-interest and feature stories as conceived in a newspaper office.

Human-Interest Stories. The discussion and practice of story organization in Chapter 9 pertained to the straight news (fact and incident) story plus more or less interpretation as dictated by the the story materials or its context. The importance of all such stories (excluding criticism and promotion) has been measured as news. Reader appeal has been achieved by the news values of newsworthy facts and incidents. Human interest has been included among the news values as characterizing the news story to a greater or less degree, frequently heightening its interest.

It is obvious that as the human-interest values are increased—as the dramatic, emotional, and human background materials of a story are played up—they will become, at some point, more important than the news incident itself. When this point is reached, the story becomes primarily a human-interest (feature) story rather than a straight news story.

Consider, for example, the following brief story, typical of many that are printed daily:

> A four-month-old boy gurgled and cooed his mother to freedom when he served as "defense witness" in City Court today.
> Appearing to plead guilty to a shoplifting charge, Mrs. Jamie T. Lexon, 23, Salem Apartments, had the infant clasped to her breast.

The prosecutors, representatives of City Department Store, conferred among themselves at the sight.

"Your honor," spoke M. W. Edgerton of the department store, "we want to drop prosecution of this case. We did not realize the family circumstances of the defendant, and we do not wish to make the child suffer."

The news value of the story above is virtually nil. Written as a straight news story, it could be disposed of in one sentence: "Mrs. Jamie T. Lexon, 23, Salem Apartments, was freed of a shoplifting charge in City Court today." But does that one sentence do justice to this story situation? In fact, is it worth publishing unless Mrs. Lexon's name has appeared in print before? Obviously, the one-sentence story will be of interest only to those who know or have heard of Mrs. Lexon, but the three-paragraph story contains a dramatic, human-interest appeal for many readers.

A given incident or situation can be handled within the following degrees of human-interest appeal:

1. As straight news with little or no human interest.
2. As straight news plus some or much human-interest treatment.
3. As human interest with little or no news value.

The incident itself, if properly evaluated, will usually determine what treatment it deserves. In general, human-interest treatment, in the third degree above, is decided upon for those incidents which have slight or non-existent news value or values but which suggest a rich background of human interest. Thus, the human-interest treatment not only salvages many stories which would otherwise not be reported but enriches the daily harvest of news with materials which possess definite reader appeal in themselves. In this sense the human-interest story is considered as a separate story type, and it is considered to be one form of the more general feature story.

Feature Stories. The news value is also secondary or lacking in a broad range of materials classified as features. Examples would be seasonal stories concerning Christmas, Thanksgiving, or other holidays; articles of advice and guidance; descriptions of hobbies and avocations; informational and background articles on subjects suggested by the news; biographical or historical sketches; sidelights, analyses, instruction, and information. This type of writing ranges from narration, related to the news and with the news intention, to descriptive and expository articles independent of the news and intended to instruct or entertain. For purposes of study and class discussions, these stories may be called feature stories or articles to distinguish them from human-interest stories.

Both the human-interest story and the feature article are (in the average newspaper office) loosely termed features or feature stories. (In even a looser and broader sense, newspaper features include columns, cartoons, comic strips, and virtually all non-news materials other than advertisements and editorials.) When the city editor says, "It's not worth a story; make it a feature," he will in most cases mean a human-interest story but he could mean a feature article. If he says, "Work up a feature on the city's new industries," he will indubitably have in mind a feature article. But if he says, "What about more feature stories from your beat?" he may mean either one or the other or both. Whatever the terminology, the human-interest story and the feature article are usually quite distinct and distinguishable in form and content and purpose. The former is usually a dramatic story purposing to entertain. The latter is usually an expository article, and its major purpose is to inform.

10a

There are so many borderline cases that no infallible distinction can be made between straight news and features, or between human-interest and feature stories, except where the latter are plainly informational, expository articles. The distinction between straight news and features must be found in the degree of feature treatment and in the story intention.

Sources of Features. Today's straight news stories on the appointment of a new city official, the burning of a large department store, and the signing of a contract for construction of a new library could be developed into tomorrow's features presenting a personality sketch of the official, the history of sizable fires in the city, and the growth of the city's library system. Much feature material is related to the news. Much more could be developed from and around the news if reporters had the time and inclination for the necessary research. Of the regular sources, the police beat yields a wealth of tragedy, humor, and pathos from which many features may be gleaned. The more important news stories such as murders, conflagrations, and wars can be highlighted and sidelighted by supplementary features: comparative size of atomic weapons, how space ships are made, the murderer's life story, how to act if the house is afire, techniques of the fire department. Much of the essay material in magazines is but feature material suggested by the news. The penetrative recognition of features and the aggressive research which clothes them with accurate data can richly supplement the news from the regular news sources.

Many features are developed independently of the current news. The following general classifications of situation and incident suggest the varied fields in which features may be found:

1. *The Unusual.* Oddities, freaks, coincidences, unusual personalities.

2. *The Usual.* Familiar persons, places, things, landmarks, the beggar on the street, the old woman who sells newspapers at the bus station (the feature writer evokes the reader's "I've always wanted to know about that" response).

3. *Dramatic Situations.* Sudden riches, the prize winner, the adopted baby, the lost carfare, rich versus poor, animal heroes, the underdog, perils and rescues, hard luck.

4. *Guidance.* Advice to the lovelorn, recipes, health, etiquette. how to vote, woodcraft, flower arranging.

5. *Information.* Statistics, studies, records, historical sketches, analogies, comparisons and contrasts of then and now, biographies.

10b   *Writing Feature Articles*

Feature stories follow no set rules of syle, form, or content. They may conform to the straight news style with a 5-*W* summary lead, though the novelty lead (see Chapter 8) is quite common. They may be narrative, descriptive, or expository. In other words, they may tell stories, paint pictures, or explain conditions. They are not, however, imaginative except in the matter of style and arrangement of materials. They are not fiction. The incidents, facts, and persons involved are real and are to be reported, not created. Moreover, their intention is to convey information and not, as in the human-interest story, to dramatize events for the sake of an emotional impact. Since the feature story cannot rely upon the news values for reader appeal, it must deal with otherwise interesting and vital subject matter. In brief, the only rule in writing features is "make them interesting from beginning to end."

The following beginnings suggest both the content and the technique of feature articles:

Guidance

The holiday is ended, but the turkey lingers on. Hence these suggestions for the leftovers:

Place slices of turkey and cheese between slices of buttered bread and broil to a golden brown. Instead of pan-frying turkey hash, place spoonfuls between circles of rolled biscuit dough, and press the edges together with the tines of a fork. Bake in moderately hot oven, 425 degrees for 12 to 15 minutes, and serve piping hot.

(Other suggestions follow.)

Information

Drinking intoxicating beverages is a custom dating back to the time of Noah, but few imbibers have taken the trouble to determine why they indulge. Now they can find the answer.

Intrigued by the size of the nation's liquor bill, Dr. Thomas D. Jerney, University of Blankville psychologist, found five reasons why people hoist a few. His "reasons": curiosity, social pressure, escape, appetite and habit, and addiction.

(Full explanation of these reasons follows.)

The similarity of feature articles and magazine articles has been pointed out, as has the writer's freedom in selecting the form used in composing his story. While the reporter may abandon the regular news story organization and apply a narrative or expository form in feature articles, he is bound by other general rules of newswriting: using short paragraphs, observing the newspaper's style, avoiding monotony in the use of direct quotation and unquoted summary, using transitional phrases to bridge paragraphs and achieve smooth reading, and so on. The logical order is used to the extent that the reporter attempts to hold his reader by introducing new features and details in the order of interest or by an interesting narrative. But the general rule of logical order which permits cutting a story from the end may be completely violated, as it is in the "surprise-climax story form" (illustrated later in this chapter). Many if not most feature articles end with a summary or conclusion, a characteristic of expository writing. Hence, feature articles generally must be edited very carefully if it is necessary to cut their length.

Writing Human-Interest Stories 10c

The subject matter of the human-interest story is not the plain unvarnished fact and incident of the news event but rather the human background of the event. Even where a newsworthy event is lacking, there exists here and there predicaments and entanglements of human beings, stresses and strains, and dramatic situations of which the human-interest story weaves its patterns. The thoughts, emotions, ambitions—the varied psychological and social data of humanity—are grist for the human-interest mill. The intention, therefore, of this story is not to convey news or information but to dramatize life itself for an emotional impact upon the reader.

The purpose and materials of the reporter are much the same as those of the dramatist, the novelist, and the short-story writer. There is an essential difference, however, between the art of the human-interest story and the dramatic art: the reporter must present life as it is, whereas the dramatist may present it as it ought to be. In this similarity and difference between the two forms of writing a few principles guiding the reporter may be found.

The temptation of the reporter is to improve upon reality in order to make a better story. Especially is he liable to such exaggerations as the pathetic fallacy, not only with inanimate objects but also in dealing with animals if he needs unusual animal intelligence in his story. The leeway which he does have is not easy to define. He is justified in some rearrangement of events so long as he presents the essential truth of the story. "You suffered greatly after the mines closed down, did you not?" he may ask the striker. And the answer may be "Well, we didn't think much about it." By pressing home his point, the reporter may finally be justified in writing "followed by days of intense suffering." He must not, however, present a false picture for the sake of his story.

The reporter is tempted also to adopt emotionalized language in his effort to achieve an emotional impact upon the reader. To do so is to defeat his purpose. The drama and its impact must be inherent in the facts of the story. Simple language is the best medium for transmitting these facts to the reader.

The human interest story takes no standard forms. Almost any of the rhetorical devices and suspended-interest forms may be appropriate. A novelty lead with the body in logical order is a popular form. The summary lead with the body in chronological order is frequently used. Following are some sample stories.

The Unusual

For 75 years—day and night, winter and summer—a blaze has burned in the fireplace of the Orin Parkey home.

Not once have the stones been cold—not once since Grandfather Parkey built the crude cabin in the mountainous Deer Valley section and struck a match to a pile of twigs. Covering most of a wall in the one-room home, the stone-and-mud fireplace has served as both cookstove and heating plant for the Parkey family.

(The rest of the feature would give interesting details on the Parkey family in relationship to the 75-year-old fire.)

The Usual

"Paper! Paper, mister?"

You hear and see him from early morning till evening time if you are among the thousands passing the busy intersection at Main and Dartmouth. With beard and hair that would rival Old Saint Nick's, he is by far the dean of Blankville's "paper boys."

How many of you know he is virtually blind?

And how many know he was once a wealthy mine operator?

And how many know his name is not "Pop" but Kyle Montgomery Childers, descendant of a famous American statesman?

(The rest would develop the facts above and add other interesting facts and details.)

Surprise-Climax Form. Still another form often used for human interest stories is called the "surprise-climax story." **10d** Notice the following example:

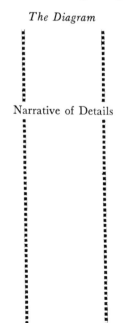

The Diagram

Narrative of Details

The Written Story

Three burly policemen surrounded the brutish figure in the downtown shopping district this morning as a crowd of some 50 persons looked on.

"Grab him around the body," said the sergeant. "He might try to break away before the patrol wagon arrives."

"Look out! He's coming at you!"

"That's all right. I've got him now."

The crowd backed off, but no one left the scene.

"You say he knocked you down, lady? Give me your name. I might need you as a witness."

Two more times the brute attempted to escape, but the policemen held him securely.

The scream of a siren filled the

The Diagram   *The Written Story*

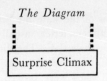

Surprise Climax

air, and the patrol wagon rolled up. The sergeant spoke to the driver.

"Take this Great Dane to the dog pound, Charlie. The darn fool's lost."

The object of the surprise-climax technique is to hold the reader's attention for an O. Henry type of story ending—a climax with a punch. No rules regarding the logical order or the 5-*W* lead apply here; on the contrary, the story builds up as it continues. But its beginning must have an element of suspended interest to attract readers, and its narrative qualities must be strong enough to hold readers to the end.

Other sample human-interest stories follow:

Ten-year-old Johnny LeRoy had good cause, he felt, to make a formal protest to Police Chief Jenkins today.

Johnny, son of Mr. and Mrs. J. M. LeRoy, 412 Fourth Street, was in an indignant mood when he visited police headquarters.

"My dog has been missing more than a week, and you haven't found him yet," he told the chief.

Chief Jenkins explained that police make no special effort to find lost dogs but that the dog might eventually land in the dog pound and could be recovered.

"But you do look for missing kids and people," Johnny objected. "Why don't you look for missing dogs?"

If elephants never forget 5,500-pound Susie of the Blankville zoo will hereafter steer clear of a fire hose.

Susie was curious about a new hose which firemen were using for practice in Blankville Park yesterday. She sauntered over to examine the shiny nozzle, when suddenly—

Gushing water from the nozzle sent the frightened beast scurrying away to her quarters.

Zookeepers finally were able to quiet the perturbed pachyderm, but she refused to go near the fire hose.

Exercises

I. Clip from a newspaper two feature articles. Underline the sentences and phrases you could use from those articles if you were instructed to convert them into straight news stories.

II. Write a feature article using facts presented in the report below. The report is on prehistoric Indians of the state. It was made by T. M. Lowe, University of Blankville archaeologist.

In the middle and western portions of the state the prehistoric groups interred their dead in cemeteries, usually in oblong boxes made of flat limestone or shale slabs. The dimensions of the stone cists conform to the stature of the individual corpses contained within them. The slabs were broken into suitable sizes by means of stone hammers. When the bottom, sides and end had been placed in position, the corpse was deposited in the resulting box in a fully extended position upon its back. Cover slabs were then placed upon the top and the cist covered with earth. During the years which have ensued, the majority of the cists have become filled with earth, since they were seldom constructed with such precision as to prevent the infiltration of soil-laden rain water. In many instances the gaps were sufficiently large to admit rodents which disturbed the anatomical position of the bones and frequently gnawed upon them. The shallow depth of soil which was placed over the stone boxes has in many instances been eroded, thus revealing their presence to relic hunters who have torn up thousands of them in the hope of finding clay vessels and other objects, not realizing that in so doing they were inflicting an irrevocable loss upon the state's prehistory.

In the eastern section of the state stone cist graves occur only occasionally. In that area it was customary to inter the dead haphazardly throughout the village and occasionally beneath the floors of houses. Into shallow pits of small dimensions the bodies were deposited. Before rigor mortis occurred, the legs were bent at the hips and knees and the corpse enveloped in bark or other material and placed in the pit. The deceased individual's closest possessions, such as jewelry, pottery vessels, and implements, were frequently interred with the body. An occasional secondary or bundle burial is encountered, in which some of the bones are lacking and the balance disarticulated. In such instances the assumption is that the individuals died while absent from the village for burial. A few instances of cremated burials have also occurred, the significance of which is unknown.

It was customary to place the houses and shelters in close proximity to each other in these ancient villages, and grave markers, if such were used, might easily have been dislodged, since numerous instances occur in which the bones ef earlier burials were disturbed by later burial pits. It must have been rather disconcerting upon such occasions to discover that the ornaments and implements deposited with the earlier burial had not departed for the "happy hunting grounds" along with the owner. On the other hand, it is quite likely that the earlier groups upheld religious beliefs similar to that of the historic groups, namely the metempsychosis of the spirit of both body and possessions. Frequently unfinished objects and the working tools used in their manufacture are associated with the burials. At other times an object appears to have been deliberately broken in order to "kill" it and thereby relinquish its spirit, that it might depart with that of its owner.

That there was either much contact with the peoples farther to the north and south, or excursions in those directions, is apparent from the vast abundance of ornamental objects made from marine shells, and implements and ornaments made from native copper produced from the mines of the Lake Superior region. Shell disks, often six or seven inches in diameter and cut from large marine univalve shells, have been frequently found in graves of females in a position to indicate that they had been worn from the neck. Upon these shell gorgets the aboriginal artist engraved in a most skillful manner with sharp flint well-proportioned designs which are often paragons of symmetry. These depict fighting and dancing human figures in elaborate ceremonial regalia; zoomorphic representations of the rattlesnake, spider, and turkey; and various geometric motifs. One marvels at the comparative crudity of the design patterns which appear upon the surface of pottery vessels belonging to these same people.

The industrious nature of primitive man is attested by the patience and skill embodied in the thin, narrow blades of flint, which sometimes reach a length of over twenty inches. Occasionally an ambitious individual fashioned a tomahawk, both handle and blade, from a single piece of stone and polished the entire specimen to the smoothness of glass. As many as 15,000 shell beads have been found in association with a single skeleton. To make a globular bead the size of a small pea from a flat piece of shell with no tools other than sandstone and flint, not to mention the drilling of the hole, would require hours. While only an occasional fragment of textile has been preserved by the salts set free from adjacent objects of copper, there is ample evidence to indicate that woven textiles were used extensively. The women pottery-makers often impressed the soft surface of the molded vessel with a woven garment or blanket before placing it in the fire to harden. Careful scrutiny of these impressions indicates a great variety of weaving techniques.

Still another example of the ultra in human patience is exhibited in the form of a dugout canoe 34 feet in length, which was recovered from an old barn on the Little River and presented to the university. It was fashioned from a poplar tree by alternately burning and chiseling with stone implements. Its sides are vertical and about two inches in thickness from top to bottom, with no discernible variation in thickness from bow to stern. The dugout was recovered from the river in 1798.

Seldom did an individual reach senility in those days. From skeletal studies made thus far it has been learned that about 50 per cent succumbed before reaching the age of seven and few attained the 50 mark. The frontal and occipital bones of the skulls of females and an occasional male frequently exhibit artificial flattening. This was accomplished during infancy by binding the head to a cradle board and placing a sandbag upon the forehead. The resulting cranial deformation was probably intended to increase the individual's fascination for the opposite sex. In spite of the numerous allusions which have been made to tribes of prehistoric giants and dwarfs, none such have been discovered and probably never will be. The average male individual seldom attained a height of more than five feet, six inches. Out of hundreds of skeletons awaiting further study in the university laboratories, only one represents a male who approximated six feet in height. No dwarf is among the collection. The teeth of an occasional individual are free from caries, but in general the early inhabitants of the state suffered from dental ills almost to the same degree as do we moderns. The grit contained in corn ground in stone mortars with stone pestles, and the softening of sinews by chewing, hastened dental attrition, but at the same time polished the dental surfaces and arrested decay to some degree.

III. Find some interesting project or activity around your school and write a feature story on it.

IV. Assume that "Journalism Week" (or a week honoring some other vocation) will be observed nationally next week. Gathering the data needed from the library, write a feature on recent trends in the field of journalism (or the vocation you select).

V. Clip three human interest stories from newspapers. Underline the portions of these stories you could use if instructed to convert them into straight news stories.

VI. Write a surprise-climax story using the following facts:
Sally Sewell, 12 Maplewood Apartments, professional photographer's model
Shares apartment with Valerie Collins, also a model
Valerie away last week on an out-of-town assignment

In her absence, Sally borrows necklace

Had heard Valerie say family heirloom worth $10,000

Sally wears necklace in making advertising photograph aboard a yacht

Necklace breaks, falls into sea

Distraught, Sally hurries to jewelry store

Buys necklace similar to the one borrowed

Price tag, $9,500

Valerie walks in while Sally is returning pearls to Valerie's jewelry box

Sally admits borrowing pearls without permission

"Don't be so apologetic," Valerie says. "Use them any time you like. They're synthetic. I keep the real McCoy in my safe deposit box downtown."

VII. Write stories from the following notes:

A. Motorist hits dog

  In front of Bijou Theater

  Boy runs from line of children waiting to enter theater

  Sammy Jones, 9, of 4218 Murdoch Street

  "That's my dog Butch!" he yells to nearby policeman

  Policeman Carl Sanders stops traffic, calls police car

  Car arrives, red light flashing

  Takes dog and Sammy to animal hospital

  At hospital, Sammy learns Butch is dead

  Tearfully, Sammy offers Policeman Sanders his movie ticket

  "I don't feel like going to the show now."

  Movie at Bijou: "A Boy and His Dog"

B. Policeman Charles Grady puts ticket on auto parked illegally

  Out-of-state license plates

  Later two girls bring ticket to police station

  Identify selves as sisters, Molly Rogers, 21, and Susan Rogers, 23, of Darbytown

  Car out of gas

  Had to leave in no-parking zone

  En route to jobs in Blakeville

  Car belongs to their father, a mill worker

  No money to buy gas, food, lodging

  Police check story with Darbytown authorities

  Take up collection at police station for girls

  Policemen donate $25, prisoners chip in $2.38

  Fill tank with gas, send girls on way

C. Maggie, 65-year-old newspaper vendor

  Stands at busy corner, Main and Broadway, for 30 years

  Every day John Wimby, 68, has bought paper from Maggie

John owns shoe repair shop at 412 Main in next block
Last week Maggie began telling customers of wedding plans
She and John to be married
Date set for next Thursday
Yesterday John did not come for newspaper
Maggie went to shoe repair shop
Found it closed
Went to John's room above shop
Found John dead of apparent heart attack
John's newly written will on table
Left all property to Maggie
Shoe shop, bank account valued at $15,000
"I never dreamed he was worth that much," Maggie said
Says she will give money to charity
"I didn't want the money—I wanted John"
Today Maggie was back at her stand, selling newspapers

VIII. Clip two minor straight news stories from a daily newspaper. Add a few imaginary facts which convert each into a feature story. Write the stories.

Chapter 11

Rewrites and Follow-Ups

THE first regular duty of a city editor when he steps into the news-room generally is to read his competitive newspapers. As the last regular duty before leaving, he usually reads his own newspaper. He clips stories from each newspaper (or has them clipped), makes notes in his *log* regarding each clipping, holds some of the clippings that deal with future events for later use, and gives the remainder to reporters. On the clippings from the competitive newspaper he may write "Rew," "RR" or "Rewrite." On the clippings from his own newspaper he may write "Folo" or "Follow-up."

Rewrites

In this case rewrites are stories to be rewritten which appeared in the competitive newspaper—usually stories which "broke" on the opposing newspaper's "time." Other meanings for rewrites are discussed in Chapter 31, "Rewriting Faulty Stories." In re-writing a story from another newspaper the reporter first verifies the facts given in the clipping; then he attempts to get addi-tional facts to use in the rewrite. His object is to have his own story appear to be a new story and not a rewritten one. Therefore, he may start the rewrite (1) by playing up any additional news-worthy fact or facts or (2) by reorganizing the story if no new facts are available. In the second case, the story would usually be a shortened version of the original.

11a Obviously, the first method is preferred, but sometimes there are no new facts to uncover. In any event, the re-written story (especially the lead) should look as much unlike the original story as possible. For instance, the lead in the rewrite below was from the lead in the original story, with no new facts added. (Sometimes an angle featured in the rewritten lead is taken not from the lead but from the body of the original story.)

The original lead:
    Edgar Trillian of New York, secretary of the National Banking Institute, will speak to the Blankville bankers at the Lake Hotel at

7 P.M. tomorrow. His speech, to be followed by discussion, will be on "Cooperation in Banking."

The rewrite:

Blankville bankers will discuss "Cooperation in Banking" at the Lake Hotel at 7 P.M. tomorrow, with Edgar Trillian of New York, secretary of the National Banking Institute, as principal speaker.

If the original reporter had overlooked the fact that one of the matters to be discussed is cooperation in increasing charges for bank services, the rewrite would feature this new fact: **11b**

Increased charges for bank services will be studied by Blankville bankers at 7 P.M. tomorrow in a called meeting at the Lake Hotel, and Edgar Trillian, secretary of the National Banking Institute, will come here from New York to lead the discussion.

Facts omitted purposely or otherwise by the reporter of the original story are often featured in the rewrite because they give the story a fresh aspect. In striving for a fresh angle, however, a reporter must guard against distorting the essential facts and significance of the story. Sometimes new events occur which give the rewriter a feature which was not available to the reporter of the original story. In the latter case, the story is a combination rewrite and follow-up.

Follow-Ups **11c**

Stories giving later developments of events already reported are called follow-ups. Though "nothing is so cold as yesterday's news," the reporter is usually forced to repeat part of the preceding story in writing the follow-up. He features new developments, but he must summarize enough of the background of the new story to satisfy those who did not read the preceding story and to refresh the memories of those who did. Because this summary refers back to an earlier story, it is called a *tie back* (see reference to this in Chapter 6).

The tie back often consists of one paragraph which immediately follows the lead, but no set rules govern its length or position. One sentence or phrase within a paragraph or within the lead itself may be sufficient to make new developments clear. In some stories several paragraphs may be necessary, particularly when the follow-up is published some time after the preceding story appeared.

11d The common method of using the tie back is as follows:

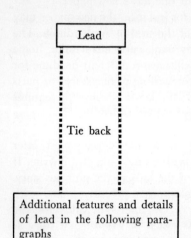

Thomas D. Folks, manager of the Knott Street Grocery, will go before City Judge John Kerney tomorrow to answer charges of operating his grocery in violation of the city's Sunday "Blue Law."

Mr. Folks was arrested last Sunday following passage of the Sunday law by City Council the previous Thursday. The grocer had openly defied the council to "tell me how to run my business" and had advertised that he would be open on Sunday.

The hearing tomorrow is expected to attract a large number of spectators, including many grocers who maintain that the city cannot force them to close on Sundays.

The follow-up is handled in the same manner as the rewrite, the reporter using the facts already in hand and diligently seeking new developments. Except for the tie backs, the follow-ups are written in the same form as new stories.

Most rewrites are brief and rather insignificant items, for the reason that a newspaper rarely overlooks events which deserve reporting. If a big story breaks on the competitor's time, the story is not rewritten, in the usual sense of the term. Indeed, reporters are sent to the sources of the initial story, and only the subsequent stories are follow-ups—just as they are when the newspaper's own first account deserves later exploitation. Most stories of importance are pursued through later developments for days or even weeks. The fire or the storm is followed by accounts of relief and reconstruction. The election is followed up by statistical recountings and by announcements of winning candidates. The crime is followed through the trial and sentence. Gradually the force of the first explosive event plays out, and the follow-ups dwindle away.

Sometimes the follow-up is augmentive rather than diminutive. A very small paragraph in a first edition or on a given day is followed by larger accounts until a great story burgeons from insignificant beginnings. Embezzlements, scandals of all sorts, Congressional investigations may come to light, and the story will build up slowly.

The Developing Story. Another type of follow-up which offers problems of rewriting is the story requiring "latest develop- **11e** ment" changes in several editions of one day's newspaper.

If a major court trial is in progress, for instance, the newspaper may want an up-to-the-deadline report of the trial in every edition. The newspaper with four editions (early mail, early street sales, home distribution, and late street sales) will have a different deadline for each edition, and it may require the rewriting of one story (or parts of it) four different times to include the latest newsworthy features in each edition. This type of story can be called the *developing* story.

This story is a follow-up because it includes developments later than those in the previous story. It is also something of a rewrite. It usually does not entail a rewriting of the bulk of the previous story. A new lead, including latest developments properly linked with previous developments, may suffice. Or inserts or adds for the original story may fill the need. As much of the original story as possible is left undistributed.

Story in the first edition:

A youthful purse-snatcher netted $50 early today when he escaped with the pocketbook of Miss Grace Horner, 437 North Drill Avenue, near her home.

Darting out of an alley between Third and Fourth Streets, the young man ripped the purse from Miss Horner's arm with such force that the strap was broken. He fled up the alley.

Miss Horner, who was on her way to buy a new coat with the $50, joined police in the search for the thief. "Nobody's going to keep me from getting that coat," she stormed.

Examples of changes that could be made to include up-to-deadline developments in later editions are the following:

New lead:

Eighteen-year-old John Doe of Huntville was arrested by police today on a purse-snatching charge after he admitted taking a purse containing $50 from Miss Grace Horner, 437 North Drill Avenue, early today.

"Insert" after second paragraph:

Police surrounded Doe in an empty house on Fourth Street. Doe gave himself up without resistance.

"Add" to end of story:

A tip that someone was breaking into the vacant house at 807

Fourth Street led to Doe's arrest. Miss Horner's empty purse was found in a closet, and $50 was taken from Doe's pockets, police said.

If later features do not offer new developments of note, the original lead is left intact.

If time does not permit the revision of a story in an earlier edition, a short (usually one paragraph) "bulletin" is written to precede the lead of the earlier story. However, this is usually done only for the leading stories on the first page and only in event later developments are significant enough to warrant such special treatment.

Exercises

I. Using only the facts given, rewrite the following story which appeared in a competitive newspaper.

> The Better Business Bureau warned today that itinerant termite eradicators from other states, most of them unlicensed here, are doing house-to-house soliciting in this area.
> "Often they use scare tactics with elderly couples, widows and others, and charge exhorbitant prices," the BBB said.
> The BBB urges the public to beware of the transient, unlicensed termite control operators who prey on gullible homeowners to the tune of thousands of dollars annually.
> "When they finish their jobs, they leave behind so-called 'bonds' and 'guarantees' which are not worth the paper on which they are written. They bear fictitious addresses and telephone numbers," said the BBB statement.
> The BBB suggested that no one be rushed into buying termite control and that this service be bought only from a known, reliable firm.

II. Rewrite the story in Exercise I with the following additional facts.

> Police late this morning arrested two men on charges of selling termite control without a city license. The men were identified as Franklin Lee, 24, and Wayne Sharp, 31, both of Longviewville. After the arrest it was found that the equipment the two men were using had been stolen from the Bugs-Out Control Company of Longviewville and that Lee formerly was employed by that firm. The two were also charged with larceny and possessing stolen equipment.

III. Two days later the cases of Franklin Lee and Wayne Sharp are heard by City Judge Sam Howard. The defendants admitted guilt in selling termite control without a city license, but they claimed that they had purchased the equipment "from a junkyard in Williamston" and they denied guilt of other charges. They presented no proof of the purchase from the junkyard. The judge held that larceny had not been proved, and he dismissed the charge. But he fined each of them $150 on charges of possessing the stolen equipment plus another $15 for selling without a city license. Write a follow-up story.

IV. Using two daily newspapers published in the same city, clip three rewritten stories and the original stories of each as published in the competitive newspaper. Underline any new facts appearing in the rewritten versions.

V. Clip from a newspaper three follow-up stories and the original story on each of the three. Underline the tie back in each of the follow-ups.

VI. Clip from today's newspaper three locally written stories which you believe will result in follow-up stories in the future. List the possible future developments which should warrant a follow-up for each story, then add some reasonably expected imaginary facts and write the follow-ups.

VII. Clip from today's newspaper three locally written stories which are several paragraphs in length. Rewrite them without using new facts. Rewrite them adding a minimum amount of imaginary new facts which might be available.

VIII. Clip from several editions of one day's metropolitan daily newspaper all versions "developing story" appearing that day. Underline the changes and additions made in each edition.

IX. Assume that you wrote the story in Exercise I above for an early edition. Later in the day, facts in Exercise II become available. Write the necessary changes to bring the story "up to deadline."

Chapter 12

Pictures

THE handling of pictures is an essential "sideline" in the work of a reporter. A picture may be either the story or a part of the story, but in either case the reporter may have certain writing responsibilities in the steps necessary to prepare it for publication. In some cases a reporter also doubles as a photographer and must take the pictures as well as attend to the written matter.

Pictures have become a vital part of the modern newspaper. They take the place of many words in portraying the day's news. Pictures speak quickly, vividly, simply, and they give the newspaper a more colorful and more readable typographic appearance.

In general, pictures will supplement and be used in connection with news stories, on the same page adjoining a story, on a different page in the same edition, or even in subsequent editions with or without follow-up stories. Frequently, however, a picture may tell its own story and stand alone, supported merely by a short headline and a paragraph or two of type.

These news pictures will, if possible, feature vivid action or a prominent or interesting personality in a new pose, preferably both in a dramatic combination. If pictures of this sort cannot be obtained, the newspaper may content itself with formal head-and-shoulders photographs drawn from the morgue or taken by the staff photographer.

A good photographer will achieve good pictures, just as a star reporter will achieve excellent stories. Except for head-and-shoulders photographs (called "mug shots"), the photographer will avoid the stiff "facing the camera" pose and will have the subjects looking toward a focal point in the picture rather than "mugging" or looking into the camera.

He will seek drama, human interest, conflict, and other news values. All of this is important to the reporter in the sense that he frequently must aid the photographer in picture-making. In such cases the reporter records the exact names and initials of the persons, "from left to right," while the picture is being made. And it is the reporter who often must plan the pictures related to his own story.

Picture Process. The reporter will naturally be familiar with the picture process:

1. The picture is taken by a photographer; the film is developed and printed (a new photographic process eliminates the film or negative stage and produces a finished print in the camera). The glossy print is handed to the proper editor—usually the city editor for local pictures. The Sunday editor, the movie, or television, or sports, or society editor also will receive many pictures from other sources, such as news bureaus or press agents.

2. The proper editor determines the news value of the picture, marks the picture where it should be "cropped," and indicates the size of the cut (or negative, in offset printing) which should be made of it. If the picture has flaws that can be corrected, the editor submits it to the staff artist, who may "retouch" it to strengthen weak lines or "paint out" objectionable features. If several pictures are to be combined into one, the artist makes a "layout" showing the arrangement.

3. The retouched print goes to the engraver, who makes a metal "cut" of it. (This is for the letterpress printing process; for the offset process a screened negative instead of a cut is made.)

4. One print of the cut (or negative) is returned to the proper editor, who may mark it for a special place in the paper.

5. The editor submits the print either to the copyreader or the reporter for the writing of "cutlines." Often, however, cutlines are written during the time a cut is being made from a picture.

6. The print with its cutlines (checked by copyreader or editor) is returned to the composing room, where the cutlines are set and assembled with the cut or negative in the page where it will appear.

Writing Cutlines

In addition to his responsibility for planning and obtaining pictures and assisting the staff photographer in the picture-taking, the reporter must, therefore, be prepared to write cutlines, not only for his own pictures but also for any others assigned to him. Cutlines consist of the lines of type below and above the picture, explaining what the picture is about. The lines below are called *underlines;*

those above, *overlines* or *captions*. Most pictures have no overline or caption, and in such cases the underlines commonly are preceded by a few words in boldface type which highlight the main point of the picture. The boldface phrase serves the same purpose as the overline or caption and is, to all intents and purposes, a headline.

Cutlines should be very brief. The overline or the boldface phrase in the underlines may be written as any other headline, though it is usually a simple crossline style of head. The underlines are much like a story lead, narrating the 5 *W*'s of the picture. All rules for writing a story lead apply in writing underlines. For example, "Pictured above are . . ." is certainly not the proper beginning for underlines, if the reporter remembers that the most important feature should be presented first. If the facts concerning the picture would ordinarily make a straight news story, the underlines should be written as that type of story. If the explanation of the picture would make a feature story, a feature story lead would be appropriate for the underlines.

Use of the 5 *W*'s in the underlines is especially necessary for a picture published without an accompanying story, since the reader does not have the explanatory facts usually included in a story. On the other hand, all of the *W*'s are obviously not essential in cutlines of a picture used with an accompanying story. Duplication (that is, featuring the same facts and using the same phrases) should be avoided in writing cutlines for a picture which accompanies a story.

Examples of overlines and underlines follow.

12a **Picture Not Accompanied by a Story.** Frequently, as in the example below, pictures are used as a follow-up of a story published previously, usually because the pictures were not available at the time the story was used. In this case all 5 *W*'s are adequately presented and explained in the underlines.

Trains Crash Head On

Picture is aerial view of wrecked train

At least 106 persons were injured Tuesday in the collision of a freight train and a commuter train carrying several hundred workers to their construction jobs near Sunnydale, Idaho. In this aerial view twisted masses of cars are strewn about the junction at which the trains crashed. Many victims were riding in the splintered passenger coach which lies on its side in the center foreground.

Straight News Picture Accompanied by a Story. Not all *W*'s
are introduced here, and the cutlines feature an angle not   **12b**
played up in the lead.

The Story Lead	*The Cutlines*

Allen V. Edwards, textile-mill
executive, was instantly killed this
morning when his small, single-
engine plane nose-dived 500 feet
to earth at the city airport.

Picture of wrecked plane

Fatal Plane Smash—A smashed
twisted wreckage, this $10,000 plane
contained the lifeless body of its
owner, Allen V. Edwards, after a
500-foot crash.

Feature Picture Accompanied by a Story. Cutlines are written
in feature-story style, stressing an angle not emphasized in   **12c**
the feature-story lead.

The Story Lead	*The Cutlines*

Young Harry Davis, who
planned to be a lawyer, has sat
helpless for eight years with a
mysterious nerve affliction.

Picture shows Davis watching television in his room

Happy Birthday Present—A new
television on his twenty-third birthday was a more-than-welcome gift to
Harry Davis, above, for watching
television is a daily pastime for the
young man who has been a shut-in
for eight years.

Exercises

I. Following are brief notes for cutlines. Explain specifically what kind of
pictures you would suggest for use in connection with each story.
Next, write the cutlines for each of the suggested pictures. (*Note:*
These are to be used without accompanying stories.)

A. Automobile accident
   Sam D. Dons, 33, automobile salesman
   Killed yesterday
   Car skidded on wet pavement
   Smashed into telephone pole
   A new automobile

       Car badly demolished

       Dons suffered broken neck, broken shoulder many lacerations

  B. Thomas K. Briggs, 28, taxi driver

       Yellow Cab Company

       Inherited $100,000 yesterday

       Distant cousin died in California

       Left all to Briggs

       Briggs plans to give up job at end of week

       Will enter some business for himself

  C. Baby abandoned

       In busy railroad station here

       Early this morning

       Girl, black haired, about seven months old

       Put in babies' home

II. Clip from a newspaper three local stories which might be improved by the use of pictures. Explain what type of picture you would use with each story, and write cutlines. Hand in clippings with cutlines.

Chapter 13

News for Radio and Television

HAVING learned the techniques of organizing a story for a newspaper, the reporter can apply many of these methods in writing news for radio and television. But some of the newspaper procedures of preparing the story must be ignored or violated to achieve the most effective style of newswriting for the broadcasting media. Writing for a newspaper is designed for readers; material prepared for broadcasting is designed for listeners or for both listeners and viewers. The differences in newswriting procedures for the two media arise chiefly from these reader-audience and time-space contrasts.

Similarities of the Media

Everything that has been learned (and will be learned) on the gathering of news, the analyzing and selecting of newsworthy features, the treatment of stories as straight news versus human interest, the summarizing of features in the news lead or the lead block, and general principles of attribution and identification are vital to the writing of news for radio and television. All of these are basic techniques, applying to any media of journalistic communications. The similarities greatly outweight the differences in number and importance.

Differences in the Media

The differences between the newspaper and broadcasting media range from the average age of the audience to the details of structuring sentences for listening rather than reading. In between are many other factors which influence the newscast writer in his daily assignments.

The average educational age of the radio-television audience is lower than that of newspaper readers, principally because of the many children (and, to a lesser degree, the illiterate and nonreading adults) who are listeners but not readers—except perhaps of the comics. Because of the large number of children listeners and viewers, radio and television must go an extra mile in observing good taste and avoiding indecencies, indelicacies, and indignities (see Chapter 5 on ethics).

The "reception rate" of words per minute is considerably faster for radio and television listeners than it is for newspaper readers. This, of course, means that radio and television can pack more information into the same amount of time. Announcers deliver newscasts at a rate ranging from around 125 to around 150 words per minute.

While newscasting can outstrip newspapers in the reception rate of words per minute, newscasting is at a considerable disadvantage because its listeners cannot "rehear" a word, phrase, or sentence that was not fully understood, but newspaper readers can go over a sentence as many times as desired. Such a disadvantage puts an extra burden upon writers for radio and television.

The complete job of the radio-television reporter in preparing material for a single newscast (corresponding to a single edition of a newspaper) differs in several respects from that of a newspaper reporter. First, the newscast writer must incorporate a large number of different stories in his assignment, but he does not begin to cover any one of those stories as fully as the newspaper because of limitations on the time allotted for news. Consequently, the newscast writer's assignment consists of putting together what amounts to a number of leads and lead blocks—in effect, he is producing an abbreviated version of the principal news appearing in the entire edition of the newspaper.

Another difference, growing out of the first one, lies in the organizational procedure which a newscast writer must follow in preparing his material for the announcer. The newspaper writer can devote all of his attention to one story at a time, handing in each story as completed for the editors to take over the responsibility of displaying that story in the newspaper. The newscast writer has to assume the "display" as well as the writing tasks, which means that he must group and organize the different stories in accordance with their news values and also in an appealing pattern.

Newscast reporters may take advantage of a format which is not possible for the newspaper reporter. Both the newscast and the newspaper reporter use the interview process, talking with persons who are authoritative sources of information or are eyewitnesses. The newspaper reporter can do no more than quote these individuals in print, but the newscast reporter can put them on the air. Obviously, this format requires a different type of writing, including summary statements of the news, the introduction of individuals to be interviewed, and pertinent questions that should be asked those interviewed.

In preparing copy to be read on radio and television, the newscast writer does several things which are different from **13a** the general practices of newspaper writers. Many of those who read the newscasts prefer that copy be triple-spaced to facilitate reading, whereas most newspaper writers double space their copy. Newspaper reporters have to pay particular attention to the accurate spelling of names (of persons, places, and things), but the newscast writer is more concerned about transmitting the proper pronunciation of names to the announcers who read the written newscasts. In such transmission newscast writers use the device of inserting the pronunciation within parentheses immediately following unusual names. The correct pronunciation of questionable names is spelled out in easily recognized syllables, with accented syllables usually indicated by capitals—such as Buehler (BEE-ler), Spivey (SPY-vee), Iglehart (EYE-gull-hart), and Smythe SMEYE-th). In accord with the preferences of those who announce his newscasts, the radio-television newswriter also uses punctuation marks freely in his copy. For example, in some cases an announcer desires three periods (. . .) to indicate pauses.

One other difference in preparing copy—employed by only a minority of radio and television stations—is the use of all-capital letters in typing newscasts. The regular news style of capitals and lower case has proved to be more easily read than the all-capital style; however, some announcers still prefer the all-capital style because they have become accustomed to it in reading all-capital teletype news.

Differences in Writing Newscasts

The most important difference between writing for radio-television and for newspapers is in the construction of sentences. In general, newscasts are written in the informal manner in which a person ordinarily speaks; sentences are short, simple, and straight to the point, with emphasis upon the ending. Complex words and phrases are avoided because they are more likely to be misunderstood when heard than they are when read. These and other differences are outlined and illustrated in the sections that follow.

13b   Sentence Structure

1. The inverted sentence structure used in newspaper writing is usually not followed in newscast writing, particularly when the source of authority or the attributive phrase is used at the end of the sentence. The strength of the sentence should be at the end rather than the beginning.

2. Sentences are shorter than those generally used in newspaper stories, but variety in sentence length is still a desired quality.

3. Only one principal thought ordinarily is given in each newscast sentence. If longer sentences are used, they tend to be compound rather than complex. (One newspaper sentence will sometimes be divided into two newscast sentences.)

4. Verbs and their subjects are kept reasonably close together. This practice rules out the use of long interrupters between verb and subject. Especially avoided are appositives which introduce a second proper name between the subject and verb (such as "Mary Roe, secretary of Mayor John Doe, died this morning."). A listener may not hear the opening words in such sentences.

5. Identifications of persons quoted are shortened as much as possible and placed before instead of after the names. Sometimes the identification only is used in one sentence and the name in another to break up extraordinarily long combinations of the two.

6. Incomplete sentences, if used only from time to time, are permissible in newscasts.

13c   Language

A. The present instead of the past tense is used whenever possible to give the newscast a sense of immediacy. This should not be carried too far, however. It can be used in cases such as "Mayor John Boring say the city will prosper" but not in such sentences as "Mayor John Boring dropped dead with heart attack today." Exception: when phrases from a series of top news items are read preceding a regular newscast (see later section on "Some Special Devices in Newscasts").

B. To prevent awkward pronunciations by the announcer, such combinations as alliteration in the sequence of words should be avoided. (Example: "the professor protested provisions.") Also, the use of too many sibilants will result in noticeable hissing. (Example: "just a sister should.")

C. The overworked "quote" and "unquote" are no longer used; instead, direct quotations are implied by other methods, such as "Mayor Smith said he is tired, bone-tired, of hearing complaints on garbage collections," or " 'I'm tired, bone-tired, of hearing complaints on garbage collection' was Mayor Smith's answer today . . ."

D. If possible, numbers should be rounded off. "A city budget of one million, two hundred and fifty thousand dollars" is acceptable (even if the actual figure is $1,250,997), but "a tax rate of one dollar and fifty three cents" cannot be rounded off. Newscasts, in general, use figures sparingly.

E. Contractions, generally taboo in newspaper stories except in quotations, are acceptable in newscasts but should not be employed to extremes. This license does not extend to the use of slang.

F. Newscasts are sparing in the use of adjectives. Often adjectives can be turned into nouns, which are much stronger words from the standpoint of listeners, especially if the adjectival pronunciation has a different sound from that of the noun. Example: "Floridian weather descended upon Blankville today" could be strengthened by "Florida weather."

Following is an illustration of the newspaper and newscast versions of the same story. Numbers and letters on the far right refer to paragraphs under *13b* and *13c*.

The Newspaper Version	*The Newscast Version*	*See Under* *13b, 13c*
Taxes will rise in Blankville unless wholesale revisions are made in property appraisals, Walter Jonness, city director of finance administration, said this morning.	The city finance director says taxes will rise in Blankville unless wholesale revisions are made in property appraisals.	1, 5, A
Mr. Jonness made his statement prior to testifying at a closed hearing before the special City Commission committee which is investigating ways of avoiding further city tax increases.	Director Walter Jonness (JOE-ness) made this statement today prior to testifying at a closed hearing of a special committee of City Commission.	2, 3, 5, C B

The Newspaper Version	*The Newscast Version*	See Under 13b, 13c
Present property appraisals, which have not been altered in 13 years, total $250,000,000, but "they should be twice that amount," said the director.	A Committee is investigating ways of avoiding further increases in city taxes.	2, 3, 6
	Mr. Jonness declared that appraisals should be twice their present amount.	1, 2, 3, C
	Present appraisals total two hundred and fifty million dollars.	2, 3, D
	This total hasn't changed in thirteen years.	3, E
Mr. Jonness, who last month succeeded John Q. Smith, has assailed these appraisals ever since taking office.	Three months ago Mr. Jonness succeeded John Q. Smith, and since then the new director has assailed these property appraisals.	3, 4

(THE NEWSPAPER STORY WOULD PROBABLY HAVE ADDITIONAL PARAGRAPHS.)

13d   *Special Devices in Newscasts*

Since a newscast is composed of a number of stories, there is often a need to "bridge the gap" from one story to another, particularly when the two have common denominators. Transitional phrases of many types can do this effectively. Some examples: "Meanwhile, at City Hall, Mayor John Smith took action to . . ." (which follows a story that resulted in action at City Hall); "Today's hazardous weather conditions had no effect upon Mayor John Smith, who . . ." (which follows a story on weather conditions). "However," "on the other hand," and other such phrases are applicable at times—but *not* such editorialized transitions as "Here's an interesting item" or "You will like this story." Datelines are often used not only to identify where each item originates but also to serve as transitions from one story to another.

As a teaser to attract listeners, a newscast sometimes begins with a series of three or four rapid-fire, headline-style phrases from leading stories of the day. This is followed, generally, after a commercial break, with the regular form of newscast. Example: "Fire destroys tobacco warehouse . . . Doctor's wife asks for divorce . . . Kiwanis Club dismisses president . . . These and other local developments will be on your six o'clock news roundup immediately after the following announcement."

Stories in chronological order can be used in newscasts just as they are in newspapers. However, they should be very short, and they usually end with a surprise or a punch line.

The Extra Job of Television Writers 13e

Newscast writers for television have the added job of illustrating their presentations with visual materials. While television newscasts show the announcer reading the script for much of the time, periodic cutaways to visuals should help tell the story. Used for this purpose are film clips, photographs, artwork and signs, and persons in the news who are interviewed in the television studio. Films used for newscasts can be either silent (with the announcer reading the story off-screen) or "sound on" (in which case the announcer lets the sound system take over).

Visuals are as important to a television newscast as pictures are to newspapers. Visuals add materially to both the effectiveness in reporting the news and the viewer appeal of the newscast program itself. For the viewer a long sequence of an announcer reading news reports will become monotonous, no matter how well written the reports or how handsome the announcer. Moreover, television is wasting its most distinctive feature when it fails to make the best possible use of video in presenting the news.

Planning and selecting the visuals are usually part of the responsibilities of the newscast writer, and in many cases he also gathers them with a motion-picture camera. To get timely and interesting film clips on the news of his local community, the newscast writer must keep abreast of and often ahead of news developments in order to schedule the cameraman at locations where significant news may occur. For fires, accidents, and other unpredictable events, the cameramen are rushed out on an emergency basis. But for most news events the cameramen fill specific assignments given to them when they report to work.

The quality of judgment used in making assignments will determine the extent to which the finished newscast will have visuals on the principal local news stories of the day. Therefore, the newscast writer must weigh the day's story possibilities carefully and then schedule the filming of only the leading events of the day.

This method of operation will require the writer to decline many requests of publicity seekers who plan such hackneyed events as the mayor's signing a "special day" proclamation, the election of a beauty queen, and the awarding of a "best salesman's cup" to a club member or a good-conduct medal to a member of the military.

Even if the newscast writer does a fine job in scheduling the filming of events, the excellence of the finished visuals depends primarily upon the competence of the cameraman. This applies not only to the technical but also the artistic aspects of motion picture production. Good filming for television is like good photographing for newspapers (see Chapter 12), except that the television cameraman should take advantage of motion instead of still pictures by planning sequences involving movement rather than frozen figures.

Like the newspaper photographer, the television cameraman should make his work tell the full story or an interesting part of the story that is being depicted. Sometimes such pictures can be shot while the actual event is occurring, but often the cameraman must set up a sequence which permits him to accomplish his purpose. Pictures of people eating at a banquet table or of a group listening to a speaker rarely tell the real news story involved in the banquet or the meeting. The cameraman must study each assignment carefully to arrange an interesting and meaningful motion picture sequence.

The newscast writer selects the film strips he will use from the sequences shot by the cameraman, and to these films the writer will add photographs and other visual materials in planning the video portion of the television newscast. All of these extra duties require precise timing to designate cues for the newscast announcer and others who have a part in putting the visuals on the air. Hence, the script for television newscasts must give instructions on synchronizing the video with the audio part of the program. A portion of a television newscast script is illustrated below.

```
ANNCR:               Drought . . .the dread word that

                     sends fear through famers, forest

                     fire fighters, and conservation-

                     ists . . . .
```

PIX #1   Drought . . . it's getting out

                          of hand . . . parched farmlands

PIX #2   such as these . . . and forests

                  which rangers say are nothing

                  but tender boxes . . . ready to

                  explode into the worst forest

                  fire in modern history.

FILM 3   Arkansas is drier now than
(from file)   in 1953 when 260-thousand acres
                  were burned in uncontrollable
                  forest fires. Hunting seasons
                  have been cut short. Laws
                  against smoking in or near state
                  parks and preserves have gone
                  into effect in states from Mich-
                  igan to Pennsylvania, from New
                  York to North Dakota.

ANNCR: What's the situation in our

                  local forests? State Forester

                  Richard Bruce had these com-

                  ments...

FILM 4   SOUND ON FILM: 38 secs. (OUTCUE:

                  "IN THE NEAR FUTURE.")

Exercises

(*Note:* If any name in the following exercises requires a pronunciation insert, the student may determine what that pronunciation will be—except in the cases of names of existing places.)

I. Write a newscast version of each of the following opening paragraphs of newspaper stories:

   A.

   City College's new women's dormitory will be named in honor of Miss Henrietta Lotck, emeritus dean of women who retired five years ago after serving 30 years with the college, President J. M. Clark of City College announced today.

   Miss Lotck, the college's first full-time dean of women, was succeeded by Miss Grace Henry present dean.

   B.

   The home of Henry Toney, attorney, of 1617 Chance Street, was looted last night, and a safe containing an undetermined sum of money plus jewelry and valuable papers was carted away, according to David Droery, chief of city detectives.

   Mr. and Mrs. Toney are out of the city on a southern cruise, and the Toney housekeeper discovered the theft this morning, said Mr. Droery. A typewriter, pistol, clothes, and other items were stolen along with the safe.

   C.

   The annual convention of Regional Builders Association is expected to attract between 150 and 200 delegates from 11 states here March 10–12, according to M. J. Bruenstalar, association secretary.

   Mr. Bruenstalar said early convention arrivals would be feted at the Sky Lodge March 9. The annual convention officially starts March 10 at Uptown Hotel.

   D.

   TRUNKTOWN, Jan. 28—An inquiry into rumors that older boys were "shaking down" younger pupils at the city's high school will be conducted by the Trunktown School Board.

   The rumor is that a group of boys has been charging other students 25 cents to use lavatories and water fountains, threatening to beat pupils who "squealed" about their operations.

   The school board will discuss the allegations "as soon as it can get together," said John S. Crullizter, board chairman.

   E.

   CAMPTOWN, Jan. 28—A committee appointed by the State Supreme Court today recommended that disbarment proceedings be instituted against James S. Shue, Camptown attorney.

The recommendation was made by three attorneys who investigated alleged unethical practices by Mr. Shue, reported Associate Justice B. S. Brown.

Mr. Shue recently was convicted of contempt of court charges after four hotel bell hops said the lawyer advised them to lie during a trial for illegal whisky sales.

II. Write a one-minute newscast (make it about 150 words) from each of the following groups of newspaper stories:

A.

1. BENGHAZI, Libya, Feb. 28—The town of Tolemaide today was terrorized by a series of earth tremors, but whether there were any casualties was not known.

A town of about 500 people settled by the Greeks before the birth of Christ, Tolemaide is only 18 miles from the scene of an earthquake which killed 261 people at El Marj last week.

2. A law that has not been overly popular was another year older today.

This is the anniversary of the day when three-fourths of the states ratified the federal income tax amendment to the U.S. constitution.

3. FLUSHING, Holland, Feb. 25—A 2,776-ton Panamanian tanker carrying a cargo of crude oil caught fire after colliding with a 3,333-ton British tanker in the Scheldt River here today, and at least 20 persons are believed to have perished in the accident.

The entire length of the Panamanian craft was in flames within minutes after the collision. The British tanker did not catch fire, but it was damaged.

4. A. J. Trustine of Philadelphia today filed suit in Federal Court asking $900,000 for damages from Interstate Steel Company for injuries resulting from an accident involving one of the firm's trucks.

Mr. Trustine, a salesman, said in his petition that he was driving on Highway 72 north of the city on Jan. 23 when a truck belonging to the steel company and driven by J. M. Smith swerved across the center line and collided with the Trustine car.

Mr. Trustine said he suffered a broken back and skull fracture in the accident.

5. A fleeing youth was captured by two Downtown Clothing Store clerks and two policemen today after he was accused of stealing three shirts from the store and tried to escape from his accusers.

Charged with shoplifting, the youth was identified as Homer Hustings, 18, of 4081 Tulip Avenue.

B.

1. Part of a nationwide effort to raise money for the Heart Fund, 352 volunteers will join in a home-to-home canvass here today.

The City Heart Association hopes to raise $20,000 during the campaign, surpassing last year's figure of $19,000, according to Mrs. Jane Stulting, chairman of the Heart Fund.

2. A 17-year-old City High School student walking to school this morning, was hit by a car on Main Avenue, police reported.

The youth, Harvey Lettfinger of 2218 King Avenue, suffered cuts and bruises in the accident, according to City Hospital attendants.

3. TANKVILLE, Feb. 25—An explosion here today injured two men, crushed oil tanks, overturned trucks and railroad cars, and caused a spread of dangerous fumes from a one-mile-square area.

Fire and police units blocked off the area and were helping to dissipate the fumes from broken lines leading to the terminal plant of Home Oil Company.

4. HURRYVILLE, Feb. 25—A Hurryville man who faces murder charges in the death of a Booneville man over five years ago was arrested by police here today.

Elmer J. Harvey, 61, was taken to Booneville by Deputy John Loberelli, who said a warrant was sworn out last October charging Harvey with the murder of Samuel F. Lemmons, who was found dead on the banks of First Creek.

5. BROWNBURG, Feb. 25—A 25-year-old mother today saved two of her children from the family's burning home, but she died when she returned to the home because she thought her third child was still inside.

In the confusion the mother forget that the third child was spending the night with his grandmother.

Mrs. George W. Hixshure, wife of a traveling salesman, perished in the fire. She had saved Ronnie Joe Hixshure, 8, and Susan Grace Hixshure, 6.

III. Write a two-minute newscast (about 300 words) from each of the following groups of newspaper stories:

A.

1. TOKYO, Feb. 26—A Japanese ferry rammed into a Japanese freighter and sank today, and 13 persons were reported dead by the Maritime Safety Agency.

The 238-ton Tokiwa Maru and the 9,547-ton Richmond Maru collided about five miles south of Cape Wadamisaki, off western Japan.

The agency said the freighter reported no casualties. All who died were aboard the ferry.

2. CAPITALVILLE, Feb. 26—The three-judge court handling a recount in the recent governorship election today tossed out 466 disputed ballots, leaving the Democratic candidate with a slight advantage, but there are still more disputed votes to be considered.

In the first four of 24 groups of disputed ballots, the court's decision gave Democrat Holbert Franz a 35-vote unofficial lead over Republican Lloyd Henderson. Disputed ballots now remaining in the 23 other groups will total between 1,000 and 1,500.

3. A Westside electrician, Clyde O. Stambough, has been charged with fraudulently obtaining a car from a local automobile dealer by giving a worthless check for the vehicle, police said today.

Mr. Stambough has been charged with obtaining merchandise under false pretenses and passing a $1,000 worthless check.

4. Three former employees of the State Revenue Department, indicted yesterday by the County Grand Jury on charges of conspiracy to defraud the state, today posted bonds in Criminal Court.

Charged with cheating the state of sales tax revenue, the three posting bonds were Leonard B. Harrold, James T. Simmerman, and McConnell Hyde. Bonds were set at $10,000.

5. The Rev. Huey R. Smith, pastor of Lakeside Congregational Church, suffered a heart attack this morning and is in critical condition at City Hospital.

Dr. Smith, 56, was driving from his home to the church when he suffered the attack. He has been pastor at the church since it was founded eight years ago.

6. MILAN, Italy, Feb. 26—Four hundred of the University of Milan's architecture students, participating in one of the most unusual strikes in history, have spent the seventh day barricaded in their classrooms.

The students refuse to permit their professors to enter until courses and tests are made more difficult, to weed out the incompetent.

The students also demand guest lectures by practicing modern architects, and they want a voice in what their courses should include.

Their professors are declining to give in, claiming that the students are attempting to assume too much authority.

B.

1. NEARVILLE, Feb. 26—Dr. Freberg Hamilton, professor of economics and business administration at Nearville College, is the author of a new college textbook, "Basic Economics," which will be published soon by the New York Book Company, it was announced here today.

2. CAPITALTOWN, Feb. 26—State Supreme Court Justice Hawley H. Huenemann was removed from the bench today after the court ruled he "engaged in unethical and improper conduct."

Charles F. Fritz, clerk of the court, announced that Judge Huenemann was found guilty of obstructing a judicial inquiry and investigation into "ambulance chasing" by lawyers in Capitaltown.

The judge's removal was the first such action taken by the court.

3. Charges of drunk driving, reckless driving, driving without a license, and resisting arrest were lodged against a 20-year-old college student by police here today.

Traffic Officer H. D. Simpson said Oliver C. Burnett of Pike Road crossed a double yellow line in passing a bus in the 1800 block of Main Street and nearly hit the officer's police cruiser.

The officer said he had to chase the car down and, when forced to stop, Mr. Burnett "put up a fight."

4. TORONTO, Feb. 26—An estimated $250,000 worth of jewelry was stolen by a group of masked robbers last night from the home of a Canadian millionaire, Daniel M. Cooke.

Mr. Cooke, financier and mining promoter, and his wife were away at the time of the robbery, but their 21-year-old son, Morris Cooke, was there alone.

Young Cooke said the gunmen forced their way into the mansion and, after tying him up, ransacked every room in the house for jewelry.

5. Four new members were named to the Chamber of Commerce board of directors today, elected by the 12-member board to succeed those whose terms were expiring.

The new members are Eugene T. Betts, Frank Hillory, J. Basil Troop, and Prentice N. O'Steen.

6. FAIRBANKS, Alaska, Feb. 26—Eight persons were killed here today when an Air Force jet tanker crashed on take-off at an Air Force Base.

Seven airmen aboard the plane and an air policeman on duty at the main gate were fatally injured, according to Air Force officials.

The jet failed to rise in the take-off and smashed into the main gate of the base.

IV. Complete the following exercises:

A. If you were limited to five of the 10 stories in Exercise II (A and B), select the five best stories that you would use and write pre-newscast teaser headlines on those five.

B. If you were limited to six of the 12 stories in Exercise III (A and B), select the six and write pre-newscast teaser headlines on them.

V. Complete the following exercises:

A. List the television visuals that you would suggest for each of the five stories in Exercise I.

B. List the visuals that you would suggest for the local stories in Exercises II and III.

Chapter 14

Policy in the News

THE chapter on policy in the news fits in the book at this point because it treats a subject that is something of a hybrid between the journalistic techniques considered in preceding chapters and the story types to be considered in following chapters.

The newspaper is a privately owned business enterprise. As such, it can be operated as the owner sees fit for any purpose he has in mind, including financial, political, or social gain. It can promote the political or other fortunes of the owner or his friends or of any special interests.

The newspaper is also—whether it wishes to be or not—a social instrument. It enters thousands of homes and is read by, or indirectly influences, every member of the family. It purveys not merely news but information and entertainment. It promotes—whether it intends to or not—social, economic, and political philosophies. It creates the atmosphere in which character is nourished. It is the Fourth Estate in power and influence, coloring and dominating character, ideals, and institutions—the individual, the family, and the community.

Under these conditions the first duty of a newspaper is to keep the people fully and accurately and truthfully informed. So long as it does this, a newspaper can promote its own policies without being accused of perverting the news.

Devices to Promote Policies

Editorials. The editorial column is generally recognized and accepted as the editor's (or owner's) platform and pulpit. He has the same liberty to voice his opinion as the newspaper reader has to reject it.

It is an open question whether a newspaper should adopt strong policies or pursue a middle-of-the-road course—whether to attempt to shape public opinion or merely to reflect it. Some newspapers assume a strong position in one issue and keep hands off in another. Some newspapers take pride in their fighting qualities, but others boast of disinterested judgment. The answer is largely to be found in the newspaper's circulation and advertising accounts. Its editorial policy may be, and usually is, determined on the basis of profitable reader appeal. In any event the reader and society as a whole cannot object to the newspaper's pursuing any policy it pleases so long as it labels the policy as such by confining it to the editorial page.

In cities and towns served by only one newspaper, the editor is sometimes reluctant to adopt an outspoken editorial policy on controversial issues or political candidates. His policy is that, as the city's only newspaper, his publication should be nonpartisan and independent, neutral in printing all the facts on all sides of public issues or campaigns for public office. However, this general policy does not prevent the editor from making certain exceptions and giving his opinions, pro or con, on questions and candidates when he feels that the public welfare of the community justifies his taking a stand, but he should keep the columns of his newspaper open to those who disagree with his views. Indeed, even newspapers which admittedly have strong partisan or other unneutral general policies should be willing to print news and public statements detrimental to their policies.

The Front-Page Editorial. Occasionally, to reinforce the importance of an issue, the newspaper resorts to front-page editorials. Though this may be a confession of editorial-page weakness, the practice is generally accepted as permissible. The column, or double or triple column, is usually labeled "editorial," and the reader is therefore apprised of the fact that he is receiving not news but editorial opinion.

Other Policy Devices. Policy may be legitimately promoted not merely by editorials but by cartoons. The "visual editorial" plays an important part in political campaigns and other editorial promotions, and it makes no pretense of being unbiased. It is frequently a frank and open criticism of an antagonist and in support of a definite policy. The columnists and other byline writers also may freely express opinions, and local citizens may be invited to contribute letters or articles to strengthen a campaign or crusade. Sometimes a newspaper will adopt a slogan which promotes a policy.

The Newspaper Platform. Some of a newspaper's policies may be long-range programs. Others have immediate objectives. Thus there are Democratic, Republican, and Labor newspapers whose policies in time of elections can be predicted. Then, there may be local programs which a newspaper may list at the head of its editorial page as the year's objectives—for example, a city park, a reduction in debt, a new high school, traffic lights, better salaries for policemen. All of its policies taken together, including its more permanent attitudes, constitute the newspaper's platform. Upon this platform it has a right to stand. And so long as it is a constructive platform, the newspaper's policy is a powerful influence for the common good. In promoting such policy, the editorial, the cartoon, the signed article, and the slogan are legitimate devices beyond question.

14a   *"Slanting" the Policy Story*

There is a natural temptation for a newspaper engaged in the vigorous promotion of a policy to utilize other resources at its command. Its most potent other resource is the news column.

Methods which have been used to promote a policy through the news channels are of several kinds:

1. Featuring (and sometimes overplaying) an event in line with the newspaper's policy. This may be done with a large headline, a prominent position in the newspaper, and a detailed account of the event. For example, if a newspaper is campaigning for safe driving, it may emphasize all automobile accidents, major or minor, thus saying in substance, "I told you so."

2. Ignoring or "playing down" events opposed to the newspaper's objectives. If mentioned at all, such events may be hidden under small headlines on an inside page or "buried" at the end of a story. If a newspaper opposes a candidate for public office, it may give the candidate comparatively little space in which to present his side of an issue. More space may be devoted to the candidate's faults.

3. Garbling news, emphasizing certain story phases and omitting certain others, and thus interpreting an event so that it will best suit the newspaper's policy. Sometimes, unfortunately, facts themselves may be distorted or falsified. For example, suppose a speaker should say: "The working man does not deserve unemployment insurance. He deserves employment insurance, and it is the duty of the employer to see that he gets it." If the reporter should play up the first sentence and purposely ignore the second, the story would certainly be colored. From the first sentence, one would conclude that the speaker is against labor. Good reporting and honest newspaper policy would condemn such a purposely colored account.

4. Editorializing in the news. For example, if a newspaper favors a reduction in the tax rate, it may always refer to the existing *high* tax rate, taking it for granted that everyone agrees the rate is high. The newspaper's opinions may be injected throughout the story in this manner.

5. Gathering special stories which support the newspaper's policy. For example, the newspaper can always find prominent local persons who agree with the policy. These persons are interviewed, and their statements are played up in the newspaper. Persons against the policy are not usually interviewed. Another example: if a newspaper wants the city to build a new jail, it might have a reporter investigate and report the "disgraceful" conditions existing in the present jail.

Justification of Policies in News Stories

Is there any justification for promoting a policy by means of the news? Are all of these and other such devices to be condemned? Obviously so, if their intent or their result is to deceive. Obviously so, if their use prevents the complete, accurate, and truthful presentation of the news. Under certain circumstances, however, there is some excuse, if not justification, for "policy reporting."

Subjectivity. An editor of a metropolitan daily, under fire because one of his men had reported a speech with evident bias, made the following statement in defense of his paper: "If I sent any seven reporters to cover a speech, I probably would get seven entirely different interpretations of that speech."

Though this may be an overstatement, it is based upon sound observation. Theoretically, a speech has but one interpretation. Actually, every person in the audience may get a different impression of the speaker's message, and the reporter is no exception. The reporter summarizes the speech as it impresses him, using quotations from the speaker to support his interpretation. He is an experienced interpreter, of course, but even then he may give a speech a misleading slant. Yet he may be reporting the facts as he sees and hears them.

The complete objectivity necessary to perfect reporting is scarcely to be achieved by the human being. All facts reported to newspaper readers must pass through the mind of the reporter. He observes events and understands facts against the screen of his past experience and through the film of his own emotions. He is not a perfect mirror nor a nonrefractory lens. This human frailty must excuse faulty reporting when the intention is honest and the effort adequate.

Self-Censorship. A newspaper may carry in its masthead the slogan, "All the news that's fit to print." It thus acknowledges itself a censor standing between the facts and the newspaper reader. The obscene language of the law court, the oaths of the gangster, the "inside" story behind the politician's downfall, or the "real dope" about the divorce may be censored from the story. The reader thus may not be given either all the information about events reported or reports on all events. The newspaper to this extent fails to report the news fully.

Just how far this censorship in behalf of decency should go is determined by public taste. If it goes no further, if the newspaper does not take advantage of its censorship powers in behalf of a special interest, its policy reporting (and the slogan) will be defensible.

The Moral Purpose. Another excuse for faulty reporting and for policy reporting may be the intention to do good. A story may be warped to point a moral—to teach a lesson. Many feature stories become thoroughgoing fiction in the process of passing from the scene of action, through the reporter's mind aglow with an honest emotion, to reach the printed page. The boy who might have been saved from drowning by the faithful dog which actually plunged in only when his master staggered into shallow water—not every reporter resists the temptation to make a hero of the dog. Photographers rush to the home for the dog's picture. No harm is done? And it does make a good story? Perhaps. Perhaps, too, many superstitions which have persisted through the ages have been perpetuated by the moral purpose. But the function of the newspaper is to present the news fully, accurately, and truthfully, and this type of story is neither accurate nor truthful.

Dilemma in Weighing Stories. Another excuse for playing up a story in behalf of a policy may be found in an occasional dilemma. When two stories are of approximately equal value, it is almost too much to expect a city editor to "bury" the policy story. It is easy for the whole editorial staff to value the policy stories highly. If the newspaper is campaigning for a bond issue, every item bearing upon the need for the bond issue may appear to be important. The newspaper cannot recuse itself like a judge whose son is to be tried for murder. Must it not either favor its own child or commit the equal error of "leaning over backward"? Here again the reporter and the staff need almost superhuman objectivity to present the news fully, accurately, and truthfully.

Complete Reporting

In pursuing a policy, the newspaper and the reporter have an opportunity to serve the community by placing emphasis on fullness, accuracy, and honesty in reporting. Not all newsworthy material is to be garnered on the regular beats. The encyclopedia, the librarian, the school teacher, the laboratories of science are rich in background material outside the boundaries of established news beats. The people of a democracy are attempting to govern themselves. They need the fact foundation for right decisions and intelligent actions. Yet the issues reported in the press are too commonly the plain unvarnished facts—lacking the intelligible background which an enterprising reporter would gather from library investigations, from studies of experiences of other communities, and from other sources of information. The reporter can offer a service to his community of a rare order of usefulness. Let him but utilize the cultural tools which his community affords—tools which the average citizen lacks the time and ability to use—and he can report not only accurately and truthfully but also with the fullness needed by a people trying to manage their own processes of government.

Exercises

I. You are working for a newspaper which advocates the widening of the main thoroughfares in the uptown business area. Write policy stories using information in the following stories appearing in a newspaper which is neutral on the matter.
A.

A $60,000,000 project to widen five uptown thoroughfares, providing four lanes of traffic plus on-street parking, will be submitted to City Council at 7 p.m. tomorrow, and opposition to the plan is expected.

The project has been developed by the Uptown Merchants Commission, a private group of businessmen, after a series of studies and discussions which have involved approximately 85 percent of the merchants of the business area.

Opposition to UMC's plans is sure to come from another group of businessmen, the Uptown Business Development Board, which was formed in opposition to the street-widening proposal and includes some merchants formerly associated with the UMC.

The project calls for the widening of Main, King, High, Brewer, and Swift Streets from First Avenue to Court Avenue. Costs involved would cover the acquisition of properties as well as street construction.

"This project is a matter of life and death for the uptown business district," said Frank P. Hensley, president of Frank's Department Store and chairman of UMC.

"Unless we do something to relieve traffic congestion and to provide accessible parking spaces, the uptown business houses will continue to suffer business losses," he said.

Harley J. Brakebille, chairman of the board of Economy Drug Stores and head of the opposition group, said the UMC is making "entirely the wrong approach in attempting to solve this problem."

The UBDC is preparing an alternate plan which will be ready to submit in "about a month," Mr. Brakebille said.

"The UMC plan is ridiculously costly, and it will force many of our merchants to reduce the size of their stores to provide for the street widening.

"This is high-cost parking space, if you ask me," he said.

B.

City Council last night deferred action on the $60,000,000 uptown street widening project submitted by the Uptown Merchants Commission and opposed by the Uptown Business Development Board.

However, in preparing for further consideration, council requested the City Engineering Department to make a detailed study of UMC's plans and also asked Mayor James Guinn to survey the sentiments of all uptown businessmen regarding the proposal.

Frank P. Hensley, president of Frank's Department Store and chairman of UMC, presented the proposal to council asking for "immediate action to save the life of our uptown business district."

The proposal calls for four lanes of traffic plus on-street parking on five uptown thoroughfares—Main, King, High, Brewer, and Swift Streets—from First to Court Avenues.

Harley J. Brakebille, board chairman of Economy Drug Stores, was spokesman for UBDB in opposing the plan. He asked council to wait until his group submitted an alternate proposal before taking action.

"The Uptown Merchants Commission no longer represents the majority of the businessmen of that area, and the proposal you have is really a minority report," he said.

"This is too large and too costly a project for you to take hasty action, and I think you owe us the courtesy of considering our plan—the majority plan—before you go into the matter any further," Mr. Brakebille said.

Councilman W. H. Poore asked Mr. Brakebille when council would receive the UBDB report.

"Soon," said Mr. Brakebille.

"Next week? Next month? Next year?" asked the councilman.

"A month at the most," replied Mr. Brakebille.

A large group of businessmen attended the council session but, by agreement, only Mr. Hensley and Mr. Brakebille spoke on the proposal.

II Rewrite the stories in Assignment I, adopting policy against the street widening proposal.

III. Search local newspapers for examples of the promotion of policy, other than in editorials. Clip examples that you find and paste the clippings to sheets of paper, making marginal notations in pointing out policy materials.

THE COMPLETE REPORTER
PART FOUR

WRITING THE GENERAL STORY TYPES

While most story types are labeled in accordance with stratum of subject matter within which they fall, there are three types which cut across many if not all of these strata. Such types are presented in the following section as "general" in nature.

Personals and brevities; speeches, publications, and interviews; meetings and occasions—all are different types from the standpoint of categories of facts available for a news story. But none of them is confined to one subject matter. All of them can be used for stories gathered on the business beat, the religion beat, the government beat, and other beats. At least one or two of them can be used on every beat.

Logically, therefore, these general types should be considered before the reporter studies the various "simple" and "complex" subject-matter types.

Chapter 15

Personals and Brevities

PERSONALS and brevities are, as the names indicate, short items. They may fill whole columns, as on the society page or in "gossip" columns, or may be scattered among the longer stories as fillers. Their filler function is apparent, as they facilitate makeup by filling in small spaces left after longer stories are placed in the page form. Even when serving this purpose, however, they should be carefully selected and written and should be essentially interesting.

Personals and brevities are arbitrarily classified here as a separate story type. Actually, they are a type only in the sense that they emphasize personalities and that they are short, rather insignificant news items. In subject matter they run the whole gamut of human activities. All of the subject-matter story types discussed more fully in later chapters are represented among them. They are considered to be merely elementary stories which the beginning reporter finds himself assigned to write and which the seasoned reporter also recognizes as well worth the little time and effort required to get them as he covers his beat.

Personals

Aside from stories which may be of major interest because of the prominence of the persons they involve, newspapers recognize the news value of names of quite ordinary persons. The names of visitors, guests, committee members, those sponsoring or attending dinners, banquets, conventions and so on are listed by newspapers as fully as space permits. Lack of space, and not failure to recognize the essential news value of names, excludes many of these smaller items from newspapers in large cities.

Recognized as personals are announcements of trips, visitors, parties, newcomers, and a large assortment of interesting, even if insignificant events. The society page (discussed in Chapter 27) usually contains many such items, and other personals generally serve as fillers throughout the paper.

News Values. What is the news value of the personal item? Since personals are news stories, they should, like other stories, be susceptible to measurement by the accepted news values. The element of interest in these items apparently is not conflict. Is it progress or disaster? Many of the items reveal slight changes in the status of the persons mentioned. "Mrs. L. E. Strickland is in St. Mary's Hospital" would indicate a slight deterioration in the status of the person—toward disaster. Similarly, "L. E. Strickland is the new manager of Westside Hardware Store" suggests progress. But if these items were of any great consequence, they would be expanded into longer stories—stories to be classified as illness, or death, or business. They are very seldom novelties. They contain little human interest of an emotional or dramatic nature. They partake somewhat of eminence—that is to say, very local eminence.

Miniature Measurements. There would seem to be no news value which characterizes the class as such. Personals, as a class of stories, would seem to be a microcosm which would have to be measured by a miniature composite of all the news values. Considered separately, each personal item is measurable by the regular news values in miniature. When Mrs. Strickland goes to the hospital, it is a miniature disaster. That a given personal may be of little consequence, of little human interest, of little novelty, is to be expected, for they are little stories. The gossip at the card party or the Tuesday Woman's Club may concern trivial matters, but, by and large, it includes virtually all human interests—birth, death, illness, conflict, novelty, eminence, and the rest. These gossip values would seem to characterize the news items called personals.

Rural and Urban Interests. Since the news values of the personal item exist in miniature, its magnitude or importance is definitely measured by proximity. "Garden Club members" may lack sufficient eminence to be interesting at a distance. But if "members of the Hometown Garden Club" are planning an event, it is local news of the personal type. Thus the personal flourishes best in the columns of the rural or small-town press. In the small town it is usually unnecessary to belong to an organization or to take part in a "movement" to be mentioned in the news columns. The purchase of a new tractor or the planting of rose bushes may be sufficient for one to get his name in the local newspaper. In the large city dailies the personal is somewhat confined to the more or less eminent and to the activities of local groups and clubs and the personalities of formal society. Rural or urban, however, the newspapers consider the personal items as an important reader interest and circulation builder.

Sources of Personals. Most personals are telephoned, mailed, or brought to the newspaper office by interested persons. Hostesses report their guest lists and plans. Mothers announce the school or vacation plans of their daughters. Dinners, parties, and entertainments of one sort or another are similarly brought to the attention of the society editor of the paper. Every regular beat yields both personals and brevities to the alert reporter. Public officials and employees go on business trips and vacations. They have sons and daughters going off to school, babies at home. Behind the public front of every person on every beat there are many personal items of interest. Hobbies, along with other recreation and sports activities, are fertile fields for personals.

Writing the Personals. Since the personal is distinctly a news story, it can be measured by the news values and written **15a** in the news style. The general principles of the well-written lead will provide an adequate formula of necessary information for most personals. They require:

1. The 5 *W*'s. These are essential in all stories, of course, though some of them may be implied.

2. Identification of the persons mentioned. If a long list of persons is given—for example, the names of new club members—it is not necessary to identify each one. But if the item reports the activities of only a few individuals, each should be identified. Where possible, a descriptive identity should be included to intensify reader-interest. The descriptive identity, lacking in the first of the following personals, is italicized in the second item:

Mrs. J. B. Linton, 824 Forest Drive, is spending the holidays in Los Angeles, Calif., where she will make a special study of Los Angeles gardens.

Mrs. J. B. Linton, 824 Forest Drive, *whose rock garden won first prize in the recent city-wide contest,* is spending the holidays in Los Angeles, where she will make a special study of Los Angeles gardens.

Stressing an Interesting Feature. Reporters should search for interesting features of a personal and not be satisfied to use **15b** a mere name with a skeletal statement. To say that "Atty. Paul R. Barton will leave for New York Friday" is interesting to friends. But what is he planning to do in New York? Is he on public business? Does he have relatives there? Who are they? Is anyone going with him? If Atty. Barton is willing to answer a few such questions, the reporter may find an interesting feature somewhere.

Notice how the bare personal has been improved by the addition of "clothing" in the second version:

> Mrs. Chester Williams is recuperating from illness at her Morgan Street home.

> While recuperating from a severe cold, Mrs. Chester Williams is penning the last pages of her new novel, "Trillium." The author is at her Morgan Street home.

15c On the other hand, puffs should be avoided, such as calling a person "a well-known and popular citizen of this community." This is editorialized matter which should be pared from personals and brevities.

Brevities

Distinguishing between a personal and a brevity is difficult with some items, and in these cases there is little or no advantage in attempting to do so. Is the appointment of L. E. Strickland as new manager of a hardware store a personal regarding Mr. Strickland or a brevity regarding the hardware store? Whether it is one or the other would make no difference. However, some brief items do not pertain to persons and are easily identified as brevities. A story giving hours that the city's library will be open during a holiday, for example, might be a brevity (unless this information is incorporated in a longer story on the holiday). Other examples of brevities would be stories on such minor developments as the installation of new steps on a school campus and the announcement of the date set for fines to go against delinquent city taxes.

15d Brevities are usually one- or two-paragraph stories dealing with incidents or occasions which have a limited reader appeal. They may be rewrites from other papers or new stories picked up by reporters on their regular beats. They may be telephoned or sent to the newspaper office. They are used because they are news, and they may be grouped together in a "news briefs" column or used as fillers by the makeup editor.

The dividing line between a brevity and a longer, more important story cannot be established. Some events which are worthy of no more than two paragraphs in some newspapers may be "blown up," with the inclusion of more details, to five or six paragraphs in other newspapers. The size of the newspaper, the availability of local news, and the interests of townspeople all are factors which must be considered by the reporter. A story's relative significance—the proportion of readers it will interest—is the only space-measuring device for the reporter.

Like a personal, a brevity is obviously a single feature story—and hardly more than a lead at that. The 5 W's, with the proper play given to the most important W, usually compose the whole story. Further explanation of one or more of the W's may call for a second paragraph.

Careless reporting, notably the lack of an inquiring attitude, sometimes makes long stories into brevities. If the beginning **15e** reporter becomes "brevity conscious," feeling that every story should be completed within two paragraphs, he may fail to inquire thoroughly enough into a matter to develop possibly a hidden, page-one story. On the other hand, insignificant news events should not purposely be blown up and overplayed.

Fillers

Besides brevities and personals, the makeup editor sometimes uses two-, three-, four- or five-line fillers to "plug" the small spaces in a page. These fillers are usually small bits of information, not necessarily news, and their chief purpose is to fill the crevices of makeup, since five lines or less will seldom accommodate even a brevity.

Fillers are obtained from various sources—news magazines and almanacs, government reports and census data, history books and encyclopedias. They are carefully selected, whether they be "fascinating facts" or descriptive items highlighting the local scene. They may be used with or without headlines. Examples are:

Owls are dumber than the average bird, according to many scientists.

___

Australia has become an increasingly important source of lead for the United States, according to the Department of Commerce.

___

Special galleries for children are to be opened at New York's Metropolitan Museum of Art this autumn.

___

Three minutes of snowfall would pile up more than two feet of snow on your sidewalk if snow fell as fast as rain does in a tropical cloudburst.

Exercises

I. Clip from the papers a dozen personals and brevities and make sample news analyses.

   NOTE: *In making these and other assigned analyses of news story types, follow the form illustrated by the "sample news analysis," pages 37 and 38.*

II. The brevities and personals below are faulty. On a separate sheet of paper, answer the following questions about each of them: (*a*) What additional questions would you ask in an attempt to get an adequate, interesting story? (*b*) What statements would you eliminate from the story as it is, and why?

   A.

   Edward P. Stokes has taken employment with Johnson Motor Company.

   B.

   Charles O. Turley, beloved science teacher at Blankville High School, will go to London, England, next summer to attend an international science meeting. This is an honor of great distinction for Mr. Turley.

   C.

   The Woodlawn Book Review Club, which meets bimonthly, will meet at 7 p.m. Monday.

   D.

   The office of the city tax assessor today was moved from Room 305 to Room 107, City Hall.

   E.

   First Baptist Church will hold a covered dish supper at 7 p.m. Wednesday. Everybody come!

III. Write personals and brevities from the following notes.

   A. Harold T. Utley
      Today is smiling broadly
      Giving out cigars
      Is father of 8-pound boy
      First child, named Harold Jr.
      Mr. Utley is city trial attorney
      Mrs. Utley is former Miss Grace Smith

   B. Local Criminal Court
      Judge Hugh Green presiding
      Visited this morning
      Group of 23 students
      Political Science
      Blankville Teachers College

Dr. C. C. Moffitt, professor
Visit to learn court procedure

C. Mrs. D. Rodney Richards
Former Miss Catherine Wilkes
Here to visit parents
Mr. and Mrs. L. M. Wilkes, Cansfield Drive
To stay a week
Now lives in New York City
Mrs. Richards former beauty queen
Of Blankville Teachers College
   (Source: Mrs. Wilkes)

D. Past state legislature
Appropriated fund
To purchase school library books
Blank County today received
Thirteen hundred books
Purchased with county's share, $1,500
Books on all subjects
To be distributed
Among all schools
   (Source: James T. Karns, county superintendent of schools)

E. The Rev. Glenn R. Powell
Pastor First Baptist Church
Announced entire church debt
Amounted to $2,200
Now paid, after 10 years
Last $350 raised
In special campaign
During past month
Debt for furniture
And remodeling building

Chapter 16

Speeches, Publications, Interviews

JOURNALISTIC techniques in writing stories on speeches, publications, and interviews are closely akin even though there may be vast differences in the subject matter of these stories. The principal characteristic common to the writing of all of them is in the treatment of quotations. Every speech, publication, and interview is a collection of direct quotations from the speaker, writer, or the person interviewed, and the work of the reporter is much the same in presenting any of the three in proper news story form.

Speeches

All speeches—whether formal addresses on special occasions or impromptu remarks during an unplanned gathering—are handled very much alike. Three elements are considered in all speech stories: (1) the speaker, (2) the audience, and (3) the speech. A fourth consideration is the possible interpretation which any of the three elements may need. The proportion of the story to be devoted to each element varies with the comparative importance of each, but no speech story is complete without all three.

16a The speaker should be properly identified. Sometimes a title or sentence, sometimes a separate paragraph, or even a biographical sketch may be needed. This is an amplification of the basic principle of identifying persons named in the news. The reader needs to know who the speaker is and why his statements are worth quoting. Even a description of the speaker, his distinctive characteristics and his manner of emphasizing certain points, is sometimes woven into the story to give it more color.

16b The audience also should be described. How many were there? Who were they? Why did they meet? The reporter looks over the crowd, talks with the leaders, and reads any available program carefully to answer these questions. He need not give names of persons present, unless he wishes to mention a few notables in the crowd, but he should tell whether they are bankers, teachers, mill workers, taxpayers. These facts are, of course, implied at regular meetings of civic clubs and similar organizations, when nothing more than the name of the organization is required. Audience reaction is also frequently worth noting.

The speech is usually the most important of the three elements. "What did the speaker say?" is logically the first **16c** question one asks about a speech. If what is said has interest, the story has something. It becomes more than a drab "a meeting was held" story. The meeting itself then becomes just a news peg or a vehicle to carry the speech.

Some interpretation of one or more of these elements may be needed. Perhaps the audience is not as representative as it appears. It may represent special interests and may have been "drummed up" for the occasion. Applause may be staged by claques. Perhaps the speaker has affiliations or a record that should be presented to clarify his significance. Perhaps the speech content should be related to larger national movements, editorial campaigns, or other programs. Frequently the speech will have significance in local issues. For example, if the speech concerns public recreation and if the community is campaigning for a national park, a story ignoring this relationship would be inadequate and noninterpretative. Interpretation, however, must avoid editorializing. The interpretative reporter is not authorized to express opinions. Interpretation must be merely the presentation of pertinent facts.

Getting the Speaker's Words. If the reporter is able to obtain a written copy of the speech, his job is much easier. Never- **16d** theless, he attends important occasions to gather other facts. Without the advance copy, he must attend and take down a "running story." He does not attempt stenographic notes. He jots down only the important statements and turning points, now summarizing an argument by the speaker, now quoting directly. He should make an effort to place only the speaker's exact words within quotation marks, particularly in matters that may be controversial. Because direct quotations tend to add emphasis, the reporter should avoid quoting routine, obvious, or minor points from speeches. Accurate paraphrasing is usually sufficient to convey most of the newsworthy substance of a speech.

In organizing the material of a speech story, the reporter should look for the theme, the logical divisions, and unusual or provocative quotes, for a speech may have one or several features just as any other type of story. *A rambling speech is no excuse for a rambling story.* Good speeches have a principal theme and supporting arguments. However, the reporter does not have the responsibility of playing up the theme or of summarizing the entire speech. He is responsible to his readers only for an accurate and newsworthy story. He may play up what he selects as the feature with the most reader appeal, and he may report only the parts of the speech which he feels are of interest to the general public.

16e   *The Speech-Story Lead*

The lead will usually feature the salient point or points of the speech. Exceptions are (*a*) if the speaker is very prominent, his name may be substituted; (*b*) if the occasion itself is important or embraces several speeches, it may be featured; or (*c*) the entire program may be keynoted or thematized. The following examples illustrate these three exceptions:

a. The President of the United States today addressed the National Congress of Parents and Teachers at Washington.
b. Parent-Teacher Association delegates from all states in the Union assembled at Washington today to hear speakers debate the responsibility of the American home in the life of adolescent youth.
c. That the home has the greatest influence upon adolescent youth was the theme of most speakers appearing before the National Congress of Parents and Teachers at Washington today.

These exceptions, however, are not strictly speech leads. They are leads for meetings and conventions. They bracket several speeches or lay the groundwork for speeches to follow.

The speech lead and story will be considered here as applying to a single speech as the sole important, or most important, element to be reported. To include this story along with other speeches and debates in a larger convention story will not alter principles in the following pararaphs.

The speech lead will feature the newsworthy substance of the speech. It will do so either by summarizing the entire speech or by presenting a salient feature. In this sense it follows precisely the methods of the several-feature lead. In either the summary or the salient-feature lead, the reporter can use direct quotations, indirect quotations, or interpretation. Following are examples of speech leads:

Summary—Interpretation:

Closer ties between the United States and nations of South America, as predicted by a Latin American expert, promise a stronger solidarity of the Western Hemisphere.

Summary—Indirect Quotation:

The United States will improve South American relations because of industrial expansions, improved shipping, and the work of goodwill organizations, Dr. James Ward of the University of Blankville told the Civitan Club at its luncheon yesterday.

Summary—Direct Quotation:

"The United States will gain in trade with South American countries because industry is expanding, shipping is adequate, and goodwill organizations are preparing the way," said Dr. James Ward, Latin American expert of the University of Blankville.

Salient Feature—Indirect Quotation:

Industrial expansions in both the United States and South American countries should lead to gains in trade between these nations, said Dr. James Ward, Latin American expert of the University of Blankville, in a speech before the Civitans today.

Salient Feature—Direct Quotation:

"The excellent work of goodwill organizations will guarantee the United States its share of increased South American trade," said Dr. James Ward, Latin American expert of the University of Blankville, in a speech before the Civitans today.

The Body of the Speech Story

Throughout the body of the speech story, direct quotations, indirect quotations, and interpretative summaries of the speech should be interspersed. (See discussion of "Direct Quotations" in Chapter 9.)

"Quote-Summary-Quote Story." Through years of handling speeches (and publications, interviews, and similar assignments), newspapermen have developed a popular story **16f** form for stories containing a large portion of direct quotes. Considered as a "quote-summary-quote" story, it can best be described by an example and a diagram.

The Diagram	*The Written Story*
Lead Summarizes All Features or a Salient Feature (This example summarizes a salient feature) □ 1	Ineffective budgetary systems cause many cities to pile debt on debt, having to borrow money to meet current expenses which should be paid by current revenues, declared Dr. Boyd F. King, director of the United States Credit Association, in a speech to the State Municipal League here today.
Quote on Feature or Features in Lead □ 1	"Chronically unbalanced budgets are probably more responsible than any other factor for excessive debts and an inferior quality of debt management," the credit expert told the 200 officials from 76 municipalities.
Summary of Other Features or Details ② △3 ▽4	Dr King said other causes of poor debt control are borrowing beyond resources, operating under defective systems of taxation, and adopting unwise plans for retiring debts.
Quote: Details □ 1	"Unbalanced, annual budgets, resulting from ineffective budgetary systems, lead not only to frequent loans for current expenses but also to borrowing for small projects which should be financed from current revenues, and then to the perpetuation and pyramiding of debts," he said.
Summary: Details ②	Borrowing beyond resources was attributed to the disregard of proper limitations upon public debt. A debt of 10 percent of the full value of taxable property is a safe maximum for communities of average stability and resources, but this figure should be reduced to 7 or 8 percent in communities of limited resources, and it may be increased to 13 percent in exceptionally well-to-do communities, he explained.
Quote: Details	"Inadequate local taxation systems reveal a variety of defects, chiefly the restrictive tax limits imposed on local

The Diagram	*The Written Story*

Summary: Details

governments by state constitutions and legislatures," Dr. King said.

"Other shortcomings arise in the valuation of property, enforcement of delinquent tax liens, and dependence on poorly collectible intangible taxes."

Debt retirement plans of some counties and municipalities are ill-founded because they do not cover the costs during the useful life of the improvement which the debt has financed or because little consideration is given to planning repayment of these costs out of future budgets without causing sharp increases in debt payments, he said.

Notice in the example that a number of references, made throughout the story, attribute all statements to the speaker. **16g** A common error of beginning reporters is the omission of these attributive phrases (the source or authority) down in the story, where they serve to keep reminding the reader that the speaker—not the reporter—is making the statements. Such phrases are not needed with every sentence if the reporter will so put the story together that the source of each quoted statement is clearly evident. The omission of the phrase with a directly quoted statement is permissible under these circumstances. Generally speaking, however, every paragraph containing indirect quotations should include the phrase.

Complete Reporting. The foregoing example of the quote-summary-quote story is straight news reporting. If the occasion had required it, the following paragraphs of interpretation might have found a place closely following the lead:

> With the city elections only 30 days off, Dr. King's address was dismissed as "political" by members of the city administration.
>
> Mayor Fred Bonham has consistently refused to follow the league's recommendations for installing a budgetary system under league supervision, and it was after the latest refusal that the league decided to meet here.

The importance of such interpretative reporting—if the occasion requires it—is apparent. Without editorializing, the paragraphs above merely assemble additional pertinent facts. Nevertheless, it gives the whole story an altered significance and enables readers to understand the possible motivation involved.

Story Contents. A speech-story formula:

Facts	*Sources*
A. Speaker	A. Speaker, various "Who's Who"
1. Present position	publications, members of group
2. Experience	before whom he speaks, observa-
3. Description (if apropos)	tion of reporter.
4. Unusual speaking charac-	
teristics	
B. Audience	B. Officials of organization, observa-
1. Name and type of organi-	tion of reporter
zation	
2. Number present	
3. Purpose of meeting	
4. Reactions to speech	
5. Description	
6. Important persons present	
C. Speech	C Speech
1. Theme	
2. Divisions	
3. Title	
4. Quotations	

16h   *Publications*

When the reporter is handed a written speech and nothing of interest develops on the occasion of its delivery, his task is essentially that of reporting the contents of a published article. Dozens or even hundreds of prepared speeches, pamphlets, business publications, etc., may be analyzed and "written up" by the reporter in the course of the year. An article in a national magazine may relate to the local community. Or its author may be a local citizen. Or the chamber of commerce may issue a publication. Or a railroad may submit a handsome travel prospectus. These various written documents may deserve stories.

Reporting in this sense is a routine procedure. It is not to be confused with a book review or with "criticism" in the higher brackets. It is not evaluation, and it is not art. The reporter is not supposed to judge the document but to report it. His review or report will follow the general principles and forms useful in reporting speeches.

There is very little difference between a story of a speech and a story on a published article. The author of an article is, in other words, a "speaker," though he uses written words. A news story on an article is, therefore, similar to the report of a written speech. A description of the publication (name, type of publication, frequency of publication) may be necessary, just as a description of the occasion (audience, time of presentation) is necessary in reporting a speech. As in the speech story, the content of the article and not the fact that an article has been written is usually the substance of the lead. Thus the assignment can be handled effectively as a quote-summary-quote story.

Personal Interviews 16i

Virtually all news stories are results of interviews. The reporter must talk with someone to get facts and quotations for a story, even though he may be an eyewitness of the event. Policemen, hospital attachés, eyewitnesses, and others are questioned for facts concerning an automobile accident. A club president is interviewed concerning the program of the next meeting. A public official is asked for a statement on charges brought against him. Or a reporter may interview a number of persons to get either a sampling of professional opinion or a "man in the street" poll of opinions on a question of current interest. All such interviews directly related to some news event or public issue are to be called "fact" interviews. They deal with and emphasize the news event or public issue rather than the personalities of the interviewees.

The personal interview is of another type. The subject of such an interview may be an eminent scientist, a world traveler, a famous screen star. Or he may be a drug-store clerk who has recently attracted public attention by capturing two bank robbers. If the story interest and emphasis concern a person's life, mannerisms, personality, achievements, reactions, or the like, the story is to be considered a personal interview. The purpose of many of these interviews is to give readers an intimate "close-up" of a famous, infamous, or at least notable personality.

The personal interview calls for a certain amount of advance preparation. "Interview L. K. Whiffle at Salem Hotel" would be an assignment requiring forethought on the part of the reporter. He must know, at least, what sort of person he is going to interview. Various "Who's Who" publications may give him a brief biography. The newspaper's library or morgue may contain photographs and biographical data in news clippings and press bureau material. Or someone in the city may supply the needed background. With a background knowledge of Mr. Whiffle's achievements, failures, hobbies, and dislikes, the reporter can begin to formulate a few questions that might be asked in an interview.

16j **Planning Questions.** In general, questions should pertain to the work, life, or personal interests of the person interviewed, but also they should elicit answers that will interest the newspaper reader. Questions should be *timely* and, to whatever extent possible, *local*. Comments of a prominent person on a current national event (in that person's field) are timely, and on a current local event both timely and local. Obviously, visitors in the city will not feel justified in commenting on most local matters, but sometimes one may be familiar enough with a local problem to venture a suggestion.

One question should lead to another, and the interview should move along in a conversational, informal manner, the reporter jotting down on paper or in his memory the answers and attitudes revealed. Constantly taking notes is inadvisable except for dates, figures, and the like, though in some cases it may be permissible to keep the pencil busy throughout the interview. The reporter will have to sense whether note-taking makes the person interviewed self-conscious and "quote timid," and if so the use of the pencil should be spared. As soon as possible after the interview, however, the reporter should fill out his written notes.

16k The reporter should watch as well as listen. The interviewee's mannerisms, dress, distinctive features, and other personal characteristics make copy for the personal-interview story. No matter how important the statements, there is always room for a few phrases describing the interviewee.

Interview Story Forms. In the personal interview, the reporter finds that he has another story requiring many direct quotes. He can again make use of the quote-summary-quote form in the body of the story. The personal interview is somewhat similar to the speech story, and the lead may be either summary or salient feature. In some cases a novelty lead is justified. Usually the lead will contain the substance of the interview, though a bold word picture of the speaker may be desirable if his personal characteristics are particularly striking. By all means, somewhere in the lead or the first few paragraphs, the importance of the interviewee must be established.

There is a tendency for a reporter to bring himself into the story of a personal interview, but this should not be done unless the circumstances of the interview justify it.

Exercises

I. Clip from newspapers and analyze a story on a speech, a story on a publication and an interview story.
II. Write a story using the following excerpts from a speech on "Rocking Chairs and Rockets" given by Dr. Harvey W. Lewellen, president of the American Society of Scientists, at an assembly of Blankville High School students here today:

> "Several generations ago ambitious young people sought to satisfy their adventurous urges by explorations in the vast areas of the earth that were unknown regions in the geography of their era. Today the expeditions of those predecessors are pages in the history of civilization, and the earth—from pole to pole —holds few geographical secrets to entice the exploratory spirit of youth. What has this wrought? Is there no longer a call for the pioneer? Is youth's lot nothing more than that of rocking-chair occupants in a ready-made society—heirs to all the comforts and the conflicts abounding in today's civilization? The answer is a stout 'No!'

> "Instead of the unexplored reaches of the earth, the unknown and the unused facts about the world we live in are the horizons that beckon today's ambitious and adventurous youth. Not alone the dark mysteries of space or the intricate laces of the atom, but also such things as the indestructible fibers of an automobile tire, the functional design of a new building, and the peaceful settlement of an international crisis are among areas for the young person of today to explore. New and unused facts are there, awaiting 'discovery,' for those who would seek them in business or manufacturing, in medicine or dentistry, in engineering or science, in teaching or law, in all of the areas of modern civilization. Here are the horizons for the modern pioneer!

> "But today's pioneer is not one armed with sword or gun. His added power must be knowledge—knowledge acquired in high schools and colleges, and extended even beyond this formal education by a never-ending desire to keep abreast of new developments as they occur throughout an individual's life. Today's pioneer must be a rocket instead of a rocking chair,

constantly ascending into new realms of knowledge in search of the betterment of civilization.

"So what does this mean to the high school student? Those courses in English and mathematics, in science and languages, in history and the other high school subjects are the launching pad for youth's career. High school must be taken seriously, for the knowledge that is offered at this level is basic to future success. No rocket can rise from an ill-constructed launching pad.

"But the ambitious and adventurous youth of today must prepare himself with more than a high school education. There is so much more knowledge available to the modern generation than there was to the pioneers of old. A college education has become an essential ingredient in the building of a rocket.

"The decision of every young man and woman is his own: will he be a rocking chair or a rocket?"

III. Write a story on the following excerpts from a speech by William D. Patt, president of the United Corporation, at the annual meeting of the State Press Association here today:

"As a newspaper reader, I can tell you that you newspapermen need a scope of knowledge broader than that required by any other profession. You need to know a lot about everything. That's because you have to write about every subject under the sun, and you also have to interpret what's going on so that we, your readers, can understand the significance of the day's news.

"The newspaper occupies a unique position in our civilization today. On the one hand, it is a public enterprise, and every person who pays his nickel or dime to buy a paper feels as though he is a stockholder and has a right to tell the publisher what should or shouldn't be printed. We subscribers demand that the newspaper keep us informed on developments of city government, of county government, of state government, and of federal government and world affairs. In addition, we want detailed information on church socials, on who is marrying whom, on the high school football game, on the traffic accident that occurred at Main Street and Depot Avenue, etc., etc. So the newspaper is a public enterprise that belongs to the readers.

"On the other hand, the newspaper is a private enterprise. We subscribers are quick to tell you publishers about what to put in your newspaper, but we are nowhere around to give advice on payday when you have to pay off your reporters, pressmen, paper salesmen, and the like. Unfortunately, those nickels and dimes that we pay for the newspaper will cover only a small portion of the amount needed on payday. Hence, you publishers have to be good businessmen to stay in business so that we subscribers can tell you how to run your newspapers.

"Therefore, it takes a great amount of knowledge to be a successful publisher and editor. Knowledge about advertising, job printing, accounting, law (to avoid libel suits), personnel management (hiring the right people), public relations (keeping from being put 'in the middle' on political and factional arguments which may not concern the publisher), and many other subjects. On top of this, as we mentioned earlier, you must have enough knowledge to interpret the important events that occur in your city, in your county, in your state, and in the world. Otherwise, you will be fired by your subscriber stockholders. If we should forsake you, you are out of business.

"Not many people realize, when they come asking your support of a special community cause, that the space in your newspaper is worth money. You should use it for news stories and other articles which will sell your newspaper to your readers, or for advertisements for which you are paid. It is not easy for you to give your space away on matters which won't sell newspapers, but you do it when you feel that you are serving the best interests of your people. That's what makes a newspaper different from other types of businesses.

"I know that you publishers have been told by many speakers that you are the most important people on the face of the globe—that you mold public opinion, that you hold the power to make or break a person. Those are broad statements. The power of the press is that strong. You publishers have been placed in an honored position in the American way of life, but that is not what has made the power of the press so great.

"That power has come from the fact that people like you are the publishers of our newspapers. People who realize their responsibilities as well as their rights. People who are in the newspaper business not for the purpose of wielding great power or making a great amount of money but who find, in operating a newspaper, that this is the way they can serve their fellowman."

IV. Attend some speech or listen to a radio speech, take notes, and write a news story on it. Hand in your notes as well as the story.

V. A special committee of the State Legislature met here today in the City Auditorium to hear testimony on the needs of legislation pertaining to the forests of the state. Write a story from the following excerpts of comments made to the committee:

Said Sidney H. Johnson, state forester:

"Nearly half of the state's acreage is covered with forests, and our forestlands contribute substantially to the state's economy. Forest industries provide jobs for more than 50,000 persons who earn more than $175,000,000 a year in woods and mills, turning out products that are valued at more than $400,000,000 a year. One of our most important needs is the improvement of our forests, and this requires some measure of control over the quality of trees that are planted. Basic to this requirement is a strong program for the certification of forest seed, requiring guaranteed statements on the origin, germination, and purity of seeds that are sold in our state."

Said Donald H. Bruner, president, State Conservation League:

"Forests are vitally important to the conservation of the state's natural resources. They are important to soil conservation and the prevention of erosion, to the preservation of wildlife, to the conservation of water resources, and to the recreational facilities of the state. Collectively, the owners of forestlands control a large portion of the state's land surface, and most of the acreage they own is suited only to forest purposes. The future conservation of the state's resources is in the hands of these land owners, and both they and the state must be made aware of the importance of this situation. In effect, the land owners hold a public trust. The state must see to it that the strongest possible measures of conservation are followed. An adequate forest fire prevention organization is one of the most important steps that can be taken. Expert assistance and advice given to the forest owners by our State University to bring about wise utilization of forestlands is another step."

Said Connelly T. Ruttenburg, professional forester:

"Those who can do the most about protecting our forests and about the proper use of forestlands are the professional foresters of the state. You notice that I said PROFESSIONAL foresters. We must be sure that the men who are advising and instructing forest owners really know their business and have a real appreciation for the conservation of natural resources. We can do this with the proper set of licensing laws to raise the level of forestry management and to protect owners from pseudo-foresters. I know that it is difficult to enforce such licensing laws of this kind, but this must be done. You take such characters as Philip Lonas of Horse County, for example. He poses as a forester, but he is no more of a forester than he is a Doctor of Medicine. We have to do something to put the Philip Lonases out of the forest business."

VI. Write a news story on the following article, by Dr. Franklin T. Eager, political science professor at the University of Blankville, appearing in the current *National Government Review,* a monthly magazine published by the Political Science Society of America.

Surburban Trend Poses Governmental Problems

Lively interest has developed recently throughout the country in a characteristic feature of the development of cities— namely, the tendency shown by such aggregations of population to develop at their fringes or peripheries. This outer-ring development which usually extends beyond the corporate boundaries of the central city is indeed found typically in all modern industrial states, and the problems to which it gives rise face local governments in all regions of the nation.

Similar tendencies can be seen in operation in this state, although not so clearly as in some other states. The recent census indicates a decline in the population of some of the cities of the United States, a decline which can in part at least be explained by the movement of population to the suburbs on the outer ring of the urbanized area beyond the central city's boundaries.

A variety of causes has contributed to this movement to the suburbs of our large cities. The movement is probably made up of the migration of central city dwellers to the suburbs and rural outskirts, and the migration to the same sections of persons from other parts of the state and country. Improved means of transport enable persons to live at considerable distances from their places of work. Thus many persons have found it possible to move to country surroundings close enough to permit them to retain the economic and cultural advantages of the city.

The characteristic soft-coal smoke of cities undoubtedly contributes to the flight of citizens to rural suburbs. In all probability the inadequate protection offered house owners from commercial encroachments by zoning practice also leads residential property builders to seek safety at considerable distances from commercial sections. The taxes within corporate limits are often given as the cause of migration outside those limits. All these causes probably contribute to the peripheral movement, but it would be difficult to determine just how great a part each cause plays.

Serious problems for local government units are posed by the growth of population and of residential and commercial building in the areas outside city limits. Some idea of the scope of the problem is revealed in a recent statement by the Blank County Planning Commission. According to this source, the city of Blankville comprises 22.3 square miles, and the city of Belle Meade, 2.8 square miles, of Blank County. Outside of these areas, 30 square miles in the unincorporated area of the county are being developed in an urban maner.

If the urban development outside corporate limits is very extensive, the county government may be burdened with the provision of the various governmental services, although such urban sections may often by allowed to become deficient in the quality of services provided for residents.

Insofar as a flight from the central city takes place, that governmental unit is faced with serious financial questions. It has increasing difficulty finding revenues to support services which do not diminish as people move to the outskirts. Indeed, the spread of building aggravates the situation, since the cost of certain services such as streets, sidewalks, water, and sewage disposal are made greater by the development of thinly scattered building.

In the meantime, the center of the city experiences serious decay in the sections immediately surrounding the principal business area. These "blighted areas" are familiar sights in modern cities. They constitute a problem for the city in terms of low income, public-welfare costs, and unsightliness. In addition, the spread of such sections is contagious, as they inevitably pull down the desirability of neighboring areas for residential purposes.

VII. Write a news story on a byline article dealing with current events appearing in some magazine.

VIII. Interview an interesting person and write the story.

IX. Make a list of questions you would ask the governor of the state if he were visiting your city and you were assigned to interview him.

X. Write an interview story from the following notes:

Joseph Beckman, famous pianist, is in city. To give concert at City Auditorium at 8:15 p.m. tomorrow. Staying at the Brooke Hotel. From the morgue and from a press release you learn he is 54 years old. Left native Poland more than 40 years ago. Now an American citizen. Is also a composer of note.

When you meet Mr. Beckman for an interview, you notice: He is short and plump. His hair is graying; his eyes are blue. He speaks with a strong accent. He moistens his lips continually as he talks. He is wearing a gray suit, black tie, black spats. There is a dirty spot on his tie.

Quotations taken in the interview:

"Do you want to ask me if I am sane? Or am I eccentric? No. I should say not. Of course, it's very hard to say. There's my dislike of meeting a great number of people, but that is because I don't like to become involved in things too far outside my work when I'm on tour. No, I should say I lead a very normal life. The time has passed when everyone thought a musician had to be a freak—that is all gone now.

"I make a habit of placing my hands in warm water before each concert. It is not a whimsical trick of a musician but a very practical measure since it warms and relaxes the muscles of the hands—a thing that would ordinarily require a half hour at the piano.

"After a concert I eat a sandwich, drink a glass of milk, and go to bed.

"I never know until I have played a half hour or so whether I'm playing well or not. Playing music is my duty, my profession, and my gospel, but whether or not I play good music often depends on such a prosaic thing as the condition of my liver. I am happy when I am playing music and feel like playing, but that is not always the case. On the night of the concert, when 8:15 comes around, one goes on the stage and plays, regardless of how one feels.

"I have three specially built pianos. They have special keys to give quicker response to the fingers and a special sounding board to make the music more luscious. I send them ahead by express to the cities in which I will give concerts.

"My tours usually last four months. My ability to sleep almost anywhere at any time of the day is a very lucky thing since it keeps me from becoming fatigued by the strain of traveling.

"My home is on a small island in Balboa Bay, south of Los Angeles. Harbor Island is the place where myself, my wife, and my assortment of children dwell in peace. I have three boys, aged 12, 13, and 15, and they have a great time together, sailing and riding a motor boat in the bay."

(*Note:* His reference to his wife and children is a surprise to you because you have heard the rumor that he does not get along with his family.)

"My children like today's popular music and hang on the

radio all day. A little of it is all right, but I was not brought up on that kind of food.

"My boys have been rather slow in learning to appreciate my music. The first time the eldest boy heard me play at Carnegie Hall in New York he listened quietly throughout the concert, and when it was over, Mrs. Beckman eagerly asked him how he liked it. 'Not at all,' was his reply.

"My hobbies are connected with mechanics. I am an inventor on the side. I constructed my own oil-burning furnace at my former home in Merion, Pa. The quick-responding piano key is also an invention of mine which greatly lightens the work of a long concert but has not been widely adopted yet.

"I never played with soldiers and cannons. My toys have always been steam engines, electric lights, and phonographs. I have a shop, and for my own pleasure I work with hydraulics, pneumatics, and mechanics.

"I have lived in the South 20 years, you know, at Aiken, S.C. The people of the South have a special charm that I like very much."

XI. Suggest newsworthy pictures and write appropriate cutlines on the following preceding assignments in this chapter: Exercise III, Exercise V, Exercise X.

XII. Write a newscast from the following preceding assignments in this chapter: Exercise II, Exercise V, Exercise VI, and Exercise X.

Chapter 17

Meetings and Occasions

THE variety of meetings reported in the newspaper is very large. Among the most common are those of civic, fiscal, religious, social, scholastic, and professional organizations as well as legislative, administrative, political, literary, and technical bodies. The types of meetings would include regular periodic gatherings, specially called meetings, and annual conventions. Almost any group meeting —large or small, organized or unorganized—may deserve a news item but (a) the larger the group the more newsworthy and (b) the more consequential its program the more newsworthy. Routine meetings are routine news (often brevities), and important meetings with real issues involved are important news.

Amid the multitude of meetings, the bare fact that "a meeting was held" (or "will be held") is of minimum news **17a** value. If a very large number of persons is involved, it may be permissible to write as a lead: "More than 7000 persons assembled this morning in the fifth annual convention of . . ." Or, if nothing at all is involved and the reporter must hand in a story, it may be necessary for him to write: "The Tuesday Bridge Club met at the home of Mrs. J. W. Sutherland yesterday." Otherwise the reporter should eschew the "meeting was held" vehicle and seek his features in the substance of the meeting, just as he must seek the substance of a speech, publication, or an interview.

Features of Meetings

Most meetings worthy of more than a bare announcement will yield one or more of the following features for a lead and for the development of a story:

Substance. (1) A definite action—passage of a law, adoption of resolutions, pronouncement of plans, rejection or adoption of reports, authorization of bond issues, budget adoption, increasing or decreasing activities, and the like. (2) One or more speeches. (3) Discussion and debate—conflict, differences of opinion, voicing of views, criticism, probing of problems and difficulties may deserve narrative treatment even if subject matter is not otherwise significant.

Other Features. (4) Personnel—election of officers, nominations, new members, resignations, membership drives, visitors, prominent members or guests, interesting personalities, hence interviews. (5) Miscellaneous features—music and other entertainment and program elements, unexpected interruptions, and the like.

17b These types of possible features are available to the reporter in writing stories of future as well as past meetings. Before a meeting, for example, the feature might be "A new speed-limit law will be studied by the city council . . ."; after, "A reduction in the speed limit from 40 to 35 miles an hour was voted . . ." Though little difference exists in the substance of stories before and after meetings, the before-meeting report must be more detailed in two of the *W*'s, the "when" and the "where," to benefit those who plan to attend. The "when" should be "at 8 p.m. Friday" instead of "tomorrow evening"; the "where" should specify "at the University of Blankville auditorium" instead of "at the University of Blankville." It is undesirable to be so specific regarding the time, and perhaps the place, in reporting the meeting in the past tense.

17c   *Leads of Meeting Stories*

The story lead for an important meeting will frequently be of the several-feature variety. It will either summarize the entire meeting or open with a salient feature to be followed by a summary of other features. In either case it may be possible and desirable to keynote or thematize (crucible lead) the entire story:

> Higher prices for farm products were demanded by speakers and conference committees of the State Farm Bureau's annual convention here today.

Thematization of a meeting (before or after it occurs) is desirable if it does not violate the principle of logical order. Often some feature that is far from the main purpose of a meeting but is strong in reader appeal will deserve lead play. The reporter's responsibility is to his readers, not to the sponsors of the conference, and he selects and presents available features with reader interest in mind. While guided by reader interest, however, the reporter must guard against conveying a distorted view of the meeting.

Conventions

Handling the stories necessary in the coverage of a large convention is the heaviest meeting assignment a reporter can undertake. Only a few of the available meeting features are usually present in an ordinary meeting story, and only a few stories concerning the meeting are necessary; but a big-scale convention report is in reality a long series of meeting stories offering a large number and a wide variety of features and requiring multiple news stories. Several staff members may be appointed to help a "reporter in charge" achieve complete coverage of such heavy assignments.

Many newspapers make special effort to "cover all angles" of a large convention held locally, frequently devoting more space to it than the event justifies (in local reader appeal). Any such overplay can be justified, however, on the basis of civic spirit. The newspaper joins with other organizations of the city in welcoming the visitors and in accommodating them with all conveniences. Some of the news stories may hold little local interest, but they will appeal to those attending the convention.

On the other hand, a large convention has many angles of local interest. Though they may attract little attention in the largest cities, several hundred visitors in the average city will create news in themselves. If pride of being host has no appeal, then the economic benefits (sales to visitors) should spark attention. Other local reader attractions include prominent visitors, newsworthy speeches and discussions, resolutions pertaining to important issues, unusual persons or incidents, and participation of local persons.

Preliminaries. If the editors of a newspaper decide to give maximum attention to a convention, a reporter will have weeks or months of work, which intensifies with the approach of the event. Long before the date of the meeting, the reporter takes the role of a promoter, writing story after story to feature all phases of the forthcoming convention. Frequently he has the assistance of a publicity manager or a publicity committee representing the convention, but his responsibility for gathering and writing stories is not relieved by such aid. The convention's publicity manager (sometimes the secretary) can serve him best in helping to gather data needed for advance stories. These data include pictures and biographical sketches of speakers and convention officers, a history of the organization sponsoring the convention, an explanation of important subjects to be discussed, oddities or "human-interest stuff" regarding the convention or its delegates, and—probably more important and harder to get than any other material—advance copies of speeches. The reporter cannot reveal the contents of a speech before it is delivered, but he is able to give an adequate explanation of the speech subject and to give the speech the play it deserves if he has an advance copy. And the reporter can ease his job of handling stories during the rush of the convention by writing an advance story on the speech for use after the speech has been delivered.

The speech and other needed advance data are usually obtained by writing to speakers and officers of the convention. Though a convention publicity manager will agree to perform the chore of letter writing, the reporter should assume an advisory capacity in determining which pictures and speeches are desirable. Sometimes the number of speakers and the variety of sectional meetings of a convention are so large that the newspaper must omit details of the less important features.

Presenting Convention Features. In preparing a number of advance reports on a convention, the reporter must schedule **17d** his stories to avoid repetition of the same features. In other words, he should play up a new feature or features in the lead of every new story. The first story lead generally announces that the convention, attracting an approximate number of persons, will be held in the city. Story leads of follow-up stories will highlight different phases of the program (speakers, discussion, officers). A summary (minus details) of other features will be included in the body of the story. If a summary of all other features runs the story length beyond limitations, it is permissible to omit some features. It is also permissible to play up—in the lead—features which have been summarized in the body of preceding stories, even though the features are not new developments. Hence, some of the convention stories are to some extent promotional (see Chapter 26).

From the day before a convention opens until the day after it closes, there is a real rush. Photographers and other reporters team with the reporter in charge to gather speeches, interviews, and other material which was unavailable in advance. In addition to reports on business and speeches of the convention, some effort may be made to report interesting sidelights—the oldest delegate, comments of delegates on scenic points of city, or other matters.

All features of a convention may be thrown together in one long several-feature story, or they may be divided into a number of stories.

If they are divided, one main several-feature story will contain announcements of the whole program, number in attendance, and general information, and other stories will present sectional meetings, speeches, interviews, and sidelights. It is, of course, possible to combine a few of the principal features in the main story.

Special Occasions   **17e**

Fairs, festivals, dedications, exhibitions, and other large occasions which attract a great number of persons, offer much the same sort of problems as do convention stories. The element of promotion and the multitude of available features are also present, however different the other aspects. Advance preparation is necessary to obtain details. Several stories, each playing up a different feature, are required before the occasion takes place, and adequate coverage of all features is necessary while the occasion is in progress. If the program of the special occasion is merely substituted for the convention program, the whole assignment involves the same procedure.

Exercises

  I. Clip and analyze three meeting stories, including one convention.
 II. Write a story on the monthly meeting of the Blankville Boosters Club which will be held at the Civic Auditorium at 7 P.M tomorrow. The program for the meeting follows:

      Presiding, L. L. Platt, president
      Secretary's report—Mrs. Mark Andrews
      Reports of Committees—
          Uptown Beautification Committee, J. Q. Johnson, chairman
          Auditorium Enlargement Committee, Frank Jackson, chairman
          Membership Campaign Committee, Royce Holly, chairman
      Speech, "Blankville's Recreational Needs," Mrs. William S. Knott, city recreation director
      Election of new officers for the coming year
      Adjournment

III. The annual State Highway Conference will be held here, at the University of Blankville, tomorrow and the next day. About 250 engineers and state and local highway officials will attend. Write a news story on it, including newsworthy facts from the following outline of the program:

      Tomorrow—

9:45 A.M.—Welcome, Dean F. W. Horace, College of Engineering, University of Blankville

10:00 A.M.—"Recent Progress of the State Highway Program," Thomas Waggoner, State Commissioner of Highways

10:45 A.M.—"Highway Changes in the Past 40 Years," Dr. Earl Folger, Professor Emeritus of Civil Engineering, University of Blankville

11:30 A.M.—"The Need for Better County Roads," Kenneth Williams, Near County Superintendent of Roads

2:00 P.M.—"Unusual Problems in the Construction of Expressways," Felix J. Rothberg, Construction Engineer, State Highway Department

2:45 P.M.—"The High Cost of Cheap Rural Bridges," Brooks T. Snyder, Engineer, High County Highway Department

3:30 P.M.—"Pouring Street Maintenance Costs Down the Drain," Wallace F. Keats, Chief, Homeburg City Streets Department

4:15 P.M.—"The Use of Aerial Photography in Road Construction," H. T. N. Dudney, Supervisor, Maps and Surveys, State Highway Department

7:00 P.M.—BANQUET SESSION
Address: "The Economic Impact of Better Highways," Rutland H. Jones, Philadelphia, President, National Road Construction Association

THE NEXT DAY—

9:25 A.M.—"Using Electronic Computers for Highway Design," Paul K. Shraine, Consulting Engineer, King-Shraine & Co.

10:00 A.M.—"Cooperative Buying to Cut Equipment Costs," Henry T. Long, Superintendent, New County Highway Department

10:45 A.M.—"Traffic Control Relative to Interstate Highways," Capt. Ernest F. Wing, State Highway Patrol

11:30 A.M.—"How Much More Taxing Will the Motorist Take?" Frank H. Niles, State Manager, Associated Automobile Association

IV. Attend some meeting and write it up in news story fashion. Hand in notes as well as news story.

V. Write a story from the following notes on the final session of the State Press Association convention this morning. The convention lasted three days. About 200 publishers and editors from throughout the state attended. Your paper has already had stories on previous sessions. At the final session the following occurs:

Speech on "What to Print," by Robert B. Warthage, editor of the Belleville Sun; excerpts:

Printing all the news all the time is rather a difficult problem for the small-town editor. Disagreeable stories arise, and then a decision must be made as to whether they should be published or not.

Recently a radio program, discussing this same problem, attempted to show that news must be published regardless of how disagreeable. The main idea, however, was whether the public would be served best through publishing the story or not.

In cases of persons who are unfaithful in public trust, or one who is guilty of serious crime, it is not difficult to decide, because the public interest as well as the public's right to have the news demands that it be printed.

There are some cases, however, where the offense is purely personal, and where publication would bring sorrow and embarrassment to innocent persons. In these cases it is often not an easy matter to decide. If such a story is printed, relatives and friends of the person feel that it is unnecessary; if it is suppressed, the scandal mongers will be disappointed, and there are those who will insinuate that the editor was "bought off."

Some of the people who shout the loudest may sometime be placed in a position where they too could be embarrassed. Thus our readers can see it is hard to please everybody, and that the editor must let his conscience and judgment be his guide. However, we always weigh the merits of news items which may cause sorrow, and if they serve a better purpose by not being published, then we leave them out of the columns of the Sun.

Our policy has been not to cause sorrow to any family or person insofar as we can help. So if we err on the side of kindness and sympathy, our error will be forgiven by our subscribers, we know. Yet, we will not suppress news, whether under pressure or any other way, which we believe the public should know.

Elections. The following new officers were elected: Charles C. Cobb, editor of the Plainview Herald, president; Raymond D. Turley, publisher of the Union County Democrat, vice president; Jackson L. Letter editor of the Worth County Tribune, secretary and treasurer (reelected). Mr. Cobb is a native of the state. Has been editor of the Plainview paper 14 years, a newspaper man 28 years.

Resolutions. Two passed. One expressed appreciation of the association to retiring officers, to this city, to convention speakers, and to all persons "aiding in making this convention the most successful one ever held." The second resolution favored "a strong state citizenship program" in public schools of the state. "In no one class in our public schools is attention given to the state's public affairs, or to the place of a citizen in his state and local government," the resolution read. It was recommended that attention be given to "state citizenship" in the social-science classes.

Discussion. Proposed that a resolution be adopted to support Horace L. Smith, Lonville attorney, for governor in the forthcoming campaign. Following are excerpts taken from discussion:

John D. Lundy, editor of the Jonesboro Record, sponsored the resolution. He said: "Mr. Smith, as a member of the state senate, was an ardent supporter of our association and of a free press. He deserves all the support we can give him. And when he takes over the governor's chair, he will not forget that we supported him."

Hall D. Tress, editor of the Salem News: "While I am personally in favor of Mr. Smith as governor, I do not believe the association should adopt this resolution. It will be taking the association into open politics, and it will harm us in the long run."

Thomas A. Cummings, publisher of the Youngstown News: "I agree with Mr. Tress."

Jackson L. Letter, editor of the Worth County Tribune and association secretary: "Mr. President, our bylaws prevent the association's supporting any political candidate for office."

Fred M. Collins, editor of the Highville Weekly, president of the association: "That being the case, I rule the resolution out of order."

Next convention. Decided to hold the next annual convention at Centerville. Date to be announced later.

VI. Write a news story using the following quotations and explanatory facts on a meeting of University of Blankville student leaders, held last night at the Student Center. The meeting had been called by Jackson Jurgeons, president of the school's Student Governing Council, for the purpose of "improving school spirit at U–B." The meeting was attended by nine students, principal officers of various campus organizations.

JACKSON JURGEONS—The Student Governing Council believes that school spirit is at a low ebb at U–B, and we think it the responsibility of you student leaders to correct the situation. That is the reason I have called this meeting. I would like to see some constructive suggestions come out of this meeting, and I can assure you that the council will follow through on any good proposals you make. The floor is open for suggestions.

PHILIP FLIPP, head cheerleader (who is also a candidate for president of the Student Governing Council, running with the support of the All-Student Party, opposing a candidate of the Progressive Party, of which Jackson Jurgeons is a member)— Listen, Jack. This meeting is a farce. It is a political attempt to defeat me in my race for president of the council. You and your misnamed Progressives are trying to smear me because I am head cheerleader and you think you can make students think I didn't do a good job in boosting school spirit. You think you are clever, but everyone knows this is a political trick.

JURGEONS—There is nothing personal in this meeting. The Student Council ordered me to call it, and that's why we are here. If we are stepping on anyone's toes, that's too bad. We are thinking of the welfare of old U–B, not of the political ambitions of one student. Besides, we asked for constructive suggestions, and all that Phil the Flipp has given us is a bowlful of sour grapes. Any remarks from anyone else?

SUSAN SWEET, president of the Women's Dormitories Association—I think it's nice that the council is thinking of school spirit. I like school spirit. I think Phil has done a wonderful job with school spiirt. I like the way he turns those flips when he leads cheers. We can always use a lot more school spirit, and we hope everybody will work together to get more school spirit. That's not too much to ask of any student. Get more school spirit!

STEPHEN L. SIMMONS, president of Phi Kappa Phi—This whole business is ridiculous. The interpretation that you make of school spirit is yelling at football games, turning flips when we make a touchdown, and in general making a lot of noise and commotion for dear old Alma Mater. School spirit must be much deeper than that. It must be in the classrooms where the students will demonstrate school spirit by their academic achievements. The victories that our University wins on the football field are shallow things that are soon forgotten. The victories of our students in the classrooms and laboratories make them leaders of tomorrow in our nation's advancement —and perhaps its struggle for existence. My suggestion is that we pitch the tone of school spirit on the work of students in the classoom rather than the football antics of a bunch of screaming adolescents.

BEN BRAWN, captain of the football team—Steve made some good points, but I believe he went too far in trying to put football in competition with academic work. I agree that school spirit is displayed by high scholarship, but I also believe that football is a beneficial and wholesome recreation for college students—for spectators and players alike—and it is another way for them to display school spirit. All of you know that most of the members of our football team do quite well in the classroom as well as on the football field. And you will find, Steve, that many of today's leaders of our nation were football players when they were college students. So let's not confuse the issue by turning this meeting into a procedure to condemn college football.

JURGEONS—That's not the purpose of the meeting, Ben. I hope we can get back on the right track and come up with some suggestions to improve school spirit. We need some concrete, constructive suggestions.

FLIPP—One way to get more school spirit is to have the members of the Progressive Party can all their hot air and use it to blow a steam whistle at football games.

JURGEONS—We've had enough of that, Phil. If you want to try to turn this meeting into a political rally, we don't need you here. I've been asked to hold this meeting, and that's exactly what I'm going to do.

SIMMONS—I move we adjourn.

JURGEONS—You're out of order. Anybody who wants to leave may do so, but we are not breaking up until we accomplish what we came to do. What's wrong with the rest of you student leaders? Are you going to let Flipp and Simmons ruin this meeting? Where's your school spirit?

SUSAN—Let's help Jack. Let's stop fussing and get school spirit.

BRAWN—You're one hundred percent right, Jack. If you need a sergeant-at-arms to keep this meeting running, I'll be glad to volunteer.

JURGEONS—Thanks, Ben. You are it.

BOB BELLOWS, president of the Debating Society—I was feeling sympathetic for you, Jack, but now that you are bringing physical coercion into the meeting I've changed my mind. This is America, the home of free speech. We shouldn't be subjected to the threats of a 200-pound football captain and made to get in line because we might fear physical harm. I, for one, will not be intimidated.

JURGEONS—Nonsense. Having a sergeant-at-arms to keep order at a meeting is an American tradition. Nobody has threatened you.

BELLOWS—But the way this appointment was made constituted a threat to Phil and Stephen to keep them quiet. I resent it.

BRAWN—Nuts! I wouldn't lay a pinkie on either one of them, but I would insist that they leave if they try to disrupt this meeting—as you are trying to do right now.

SIMMONS—What manner of fascism is this?

SUSAN—Now you be quiet, Stephen Simmons. All of you be quiet and help Jack. You are just fussing and not talking about school spirit at all. Now behave yourself, Phil and Steve.

SIMMONS—And you behave yourself, too, you sweet little vacuum head.

BRAWN (*rising to his feet*)—One more crack like that and I'll see that you leave. Who do you think you are that you can insult everyone here?

SIMMONS—George Bernard Shaw.

WILMA WISE, president of the Women's Honor Society—What a meeting this is! Politics, football versus classrooms, free speech, and little Susan trying her best to get a date with big Jackson Jurgeons—all in the name of school spirit!

SUSAN (*rises and stands in front of Wilma*)—I am not so trying to get a date with Jack, and you take that back, Wilma Wise.

WILMA—Methinks the lady doth protest too much.

Susan Sweet grabs Wilma Wise by the hair and yanks. Wilma screams. Ben Brawn steps in and forces Susan to release her hold. As soon as she is released, Wilma slashes with her fingernails, but she hits Ben instead of Susan. Ben receives a long scratch down the side of his face. Ben and Jackson force the two girls to calm down. Meantime, all of the others at the meeting were enjoying the "proceedings" immensely.

BRAWN (*wiping the blood from his face*)—Nuts. I'm going to my room. I've got some studying to do.

Ben Brawn walks out.

SIMMONS (*stands and moves out of room*)—Meeting's adjourned.

Others follow, Susan and Wilma sobbing as they leave.

JURGEONS—Well, we didn't get anything done on school spirit, but nobody can say we didn't have a spirited meeting.

VII. Suggest newsworthy pictures and write appropriate cutlines on the following preceding assignments in this chapter: Exercise V, Exercise VI.

VIII. Write a newscast using the following preceding assignments in this chapter: Exercise II, Exercise III, and Exercise V.

THE COMPLETE REPORTER
PART FIVE

WRITING THE SIMPLE STORY TYPES

Any city editor would assign a beginning reporter the simpler stories. The more complex would be handled by the more experienced staff men. In no other sense does the classification of stories as simple and complex presume to have any general acceptance or technical significance. It is merely a convenient and arbitrary division.

In general, single-incident stories would seem to be simple—automobile accidents, deaths, illness, funerals, crime. Those stories requiring little interpretative writing and little background on the part of the reporter might be added to the list. The truth is that any single story may turn out to be either simple or complex, regardless of its type. For purposes of proceeding from the less difficult to the more difficult stories, however, the chosen classification has proved useful.

Chapter 18

Illness, Deaths, Funerals

OFTEN a neophyte reporter begins his journalistic life by writing about death. That is because deaths, along with illnesses and funerals, are among the simple story types published by the newspaper.

News Values. All of these events are newsworthy on the disaster side of human experience. They are disruptions of the status quo, and they are of consequence in the community. The removal of almost any human being from the local scene requires social and economic readjustments among relatives and friends. His place must be taken; his job must be filled by others. His home may be offered for sale; his widow may move to another city; his daugther may withdraw from college. All such changes touch the lives of others. Universal emotion and drama surround disaster and death as common experiences to which all must come. Even when the individual is comparatively unknown, the community can spare a little meditation over misfortune in general.

Factors of Magnitude. The magnitude of the event (the importance of the news story) is determined by several factors. Illness is measured by its gravity (intensity), approaching death as its climax. And both illness and death are measured by the number of persons affected (extensity) in the community. Thus the eminence of the person and the nature of the illness may determine story importance. A very rare disease or accident is interesting because of its unusualness, but of even more importance may be the threat of epidemics of quite common diseases. Since eminence usually means being well known, as well as holding a position of importance, the community is more generally affected by matters involving eminent persons. Multiple deaths or cases of illness extend the news importance. Though the story of illness or death (and of the funeral) may frequently stand stripped to its disaster appeal, its news importance may sometimes be heightened by eminence, novelty, consequence, human interest, and even conflict.

Illness

Illness—grave illness—is reported less frequently than its news importance justifies. Patient, family, physician, and hospital are frequently loath to have the illness known. Physicians and hospitals usually shun publicity. Family and patient may wish to avoid unnecessary alarm to friends or employer or employees, and sometimes the family wants to hide information from the patient. Business matters, contracts, and various obligations may be affected. Always there is the thought in the background that tomorrow or the next day the patient may be well and the less uproar about the matter the better. If the patient's family, physician, and hospital all refuse to give a statement on the illness, the reporter should use information available to him with extreme caution.

Illness is not easy to report properly. Highly technical or tenuous conditions may characterize the illness itself. The optimism or pessimism of a given moment may prove to be ill-founded. Delicate sensibilities and emotions are involved. Moreover, once the brief bulletin on the patient's condition is announced, little substance is left for the reporter to take hold of and expand. In the prolonged illness of an eminent person, say, the governor of the state, the comings and goings of delegations, the friends and relatives "at the bedside," and the sympathetic comments of other officials may provide copy. The illness stories of lesser persons will usually be brief.

Though a list of patients admitted to and dismissed from the hospitals may be published from day to day, the reporter gives individual attention to only a few. In addition, sometimes "tips" will lead him to desirable stories.

18a **Story Contents.** Many accounts of illness may contain only one, two, or three paragraphs (most being handled as personals) and contain the following material:

1. Name and identification
2. Cause of illness
3. Condition (fair, serious, critical—an accurate quotation from the doctor or hospital regarding condition)
4. Name of hospital (sometimes "at a local hospital" for patients at mental or tuberculosis hospitals)
5. Duration of illness

Other matters sometimes included:

1. Members of family at bedside
2. Effect of illness upon person's business or public position

The "who" is the most important *W* in most illness stories,
and it takes first place in the lead. For variety, or if the   **18b**
disease or operation is unusual, the cause of the illness or
the condition of the patient may be featured. However, if the story is
a follow-up, the condition of the patient is usually the feature. Note
the examples below.

Who:

Howard P. Barnes, city superintendent of education, is critically
ill at the Westview Hospital today, following an emergency operation
for acute appendicitis.

Cause:

Stricken with acute appendicitis, Howard P. Barnes of 126 Front
St. was in critical condition following an emergency operation at the
Westview Hospital today.

Condition:

A slight improvement in the condition of Howard P. Barnes, city
superintendent of education, was reported today by the Westview
Hospital, where he underwent an emergency operation for acute
appendicitis yesterday. His condition is still "serious," however.

Hospital Notes. Some newspapers carry regularly a hospital column.
It may be merely a list of "Entered" and "Left" with no details
given. Some hospitals frown on even this practice, while others adopt
a more liberal policy of publicity. With or without the cooperation
of the hospitals, many personals deal with hospitalization. Following are common examples:

Mrs. Nadine Rock of Washington, D.C., has been admitted to the
St. Thomas Hospital. Her illness is not thought to be serious.

Mrs. May Polk, 815 Carrol Street, was taken to the Outland Hospital today for treatment of injuries suffered in a fall. Mrs. Polk, who
is 82 years old, was working in her rock garden when the accident
occurred.

James A. McKendrick of Millington is seriously ill in the Ballard
Hospital, where he was taken Saturday for blood transfusions.

Deaths

Death is an important item of news. It may contain all of the news
values discussed above. Regardless of news values, the death is re-

ported as a public record. No person ever becomes so unimportant that he is not valuable for vital statistics. The public-health records chart all deaths, and state laws fix standard forms for physicians' reports. Even the nameless tramp dead on the railroad tracks is not overlooked. He fits in somewhere in a chain of persons and events. Though practices may vary in the treatment of death stories, all newspapers report deaths.

18c **Obituaries.** A distinction must be made between obituary columns and death stories because these differ in newspapers which publish both. Many newspapers make a per-word charge for notices in the obituary column, the same as they do for classified advertisements, and such charges become part of the funeral costs. Other newspapers publish obituary notices free of charge. Whether the obituaries are paid items or not, the form used by the newspaper is standardized to get all essential information into a compact space. For the preparation of the obituaries many funeral homes use a report similar to the one on the opposite page.

From the report a rather standard death notice or obituary is printed in the "death column," including funeral arrangements when these are available, as follows:

> MEEK—Saturday, Jan. 7, at 8 a.m., at Reams Hospital, John Louis Meek, 1514 Utley Street. Age, 52. Survived by his wife, Mrs. Lucille Meek; two daughters, Miss Lucille Meek, and Mrs. L. D. Hall of Montgomery, Ala. The body is at the Brown Funeral Home. Funeral from the First Street Methodist Church, Monday, Jan. 9, at 10 a.m. conducted by the Rev. J. B. Snow. Elders of the First Street Methodist Church will be honorary pallbearers. Active: U. T. Denton, Sam Harris, J. E. Weatherly, Henry Smith, George Manners, Horace L. Wilson. Interment, Rosemont Cemetery. Brown Funeral Directors in charge.

18d **Death Stories.** In addition to or in lieu of the formal type of obituary notice, the newspaper may carry death stories written in the regular news style. In newspapers which carry obituary columns, separate stories are written only on deaths which are newsworthy enough to justify this extra attention. In a large city, the death of a person who has gained no eminence and who died of natural causes would be reported only in the obituary column.

The information in the obituary notice provides the basic facts for the death story, but the reporter often seeks additional information by telephoning or visiting relatives or others mentioned in the

THE BROWN FUNERAL HOME
DEATH REPORT

Date   January 7

Full name   John Louis Meek   Age   52

Home address   1514 Utley Street

Occupation   Mechanic for the Southern Railway

Place of death   Reams Hospital   Time of death 8 a.m.

Cause of death   Pneumonia

Length of illness   Two weeks

Affiliations   Member of First Street Methodist Church

Remarks

Survivors, with relationships and addresses Wife, Mrs. Lucille
Meek; two daughters, Miss Lucille Meek, 1514
Utley Street and Mrs. L. D. Hall, Montgomery, Ala.

FUNERAL

Time   10 a.m., Jan. 9

Place   First Street Methodist Church

Officiating   Rev. J. B. Snow

Burial Place   Rosemont Cemetery

Active Pallbeareres   U. T. Denton, Sam Harris, J. E.
Weatherly, Henry Smith, George Manners, Horace L.
Wilson

Honorary Pallbearers   Elders of the First Street
Methodist Church

Remarks   Body at Brown Funeral Home

notice. The following story is typical of those where only one or two
additional facts (italicized) are obtained by the reporter:

John L. Meek, *former city councilman and past president of the
local Railway Workers Union,* died at 8 a.m. today at the Reams
Hospital after a two-week illness of pneumonia. He was 52.

Mr. Meek, *for 25 years a machine-shop superintendent with the
Southern Railway,* was a Mason and a member of First Street Methodist Church. He resided at 1514 Utley Street.

Surviving are his widow, Mrs. Lucille Meek, and two daughters,

Miss Lucille Meek, 1514 Utley Street, and Mrs. L. D. Hall, of Montgomery, Ala.

The body is at the Brown Funeral Home.

18e **Story Contents.** The routine story thus provides the following information:

1. Name and identification (address, occupation, and affiliations)
2. Age
3. Day and time of death
4. Place of death
5. Cause of death
6. Duration of illness
7. Names of members of the immediate family

Most obituaries in the news columns include facts on the person's affiliations with fraternal and religious organizations, past offices held, notable achievements, and interesting or significant experiences. If plans for the funeral services have been completed, they are announced in the last paragraph of the notice. Otherwise they may be published later.

If John L. Meek happened to be the city's mayor, or centenarian, or the victim of a rare disease, the story would be much longer and more detailed. It would be far from a routine story.

The death story of a prominent person usually contains a complete biographical sketch and a picture and perhaps comments from eminent persons. Outstanding achievements, details of the death, and other data are mentioned in initial paragraphs, and the life history may follow in chronological order. Such biographies are often written in advance by reporters during unhurried periods and kept on file in the newspaper's morgue for use as needed with stories not only on the newsworthy incidents which occur in the lives of these individuals but also on their deaths.

18f The reporter must write death notices from a dispassionate, objective point of view. He should report only the facts as he obtains them, and he is not bound by the proverb, "concerning the dead, nothing but the good." The reporter does in general avoid derogatory remarks concerning a person who has died, but if facts of that nature are required for an adequate story, they are used. The language of the death story should be simple and precise, avoiding circumlocutions and euphemisms. A person "dies" instead of "passes away"; he is "buried" instead of "interred."

Funerals

The funeral announcement is simply the follow-up of a death story. As in any follow-up, a brief summary of the preceding story must be included, but the lead features the funeral.

Story Contents. The funeral story should provide: **18g**

1. Time
2. Place
3. Public or private (open to the public unless otherwise stated)
4. Who will officiate
5. Place of burial
6. Active pallbearers
7. Honorary pallbearers

Following is a typical funeral announcement:

Funeral services for John L. Meek, 52-year-old Southern Railway mechanic who died Thursday, will be held at 2 P.M. tomorrow at the Brown Funeral Home. Burial will be in Rosemont Cemetery.

The Rev. J. B. Snow, pastor of First Street Methodist Church, will officiate. Active pallbearers are U. T. Denton, Sam Harris, J. E. Weatherly, Henry Smith, George Manners, Horace L. Wilson. Honorary pallbearers: board members of First Street Methodist Church.

The funeral story of a prominent person would be greatly expanded with such information as expressions of loss by other prominent citizens and an account of the arrival of relatives.

Exercises

I. Clip from the newspapers a death story and an illness story and make news analyses.
II. Write stories from the following notes.
   A. While visiting Grace Elementary School
      At 10 a.m. today
      William F. Roberts, 60, city superintendent of schools
      Fainted in school hallway
      Rushed to General Hospital by ambulance
      Mr. Roberts supt. here 15 years
         (Source: L. R. Pruitt, principal of Grace School)

      At press time, had not regained consciousness
      Exact cause of illness undetermined

Suspected to be heart attack
Condition considered critical
  (Source: hospital officials)

B. Mrs. Ralph N. Wells, 37
Wife of State Senator Wells
Daughter of Judge J. D. Dorry
Entered at General Hospital last night
  (Source: hospital records)

Hospital officials
And members of Mrs. Wells' family
Decline to state cause of illness or give condition
An orderly at hospital
Said he believes cause is cancer

C. Fred M. Weese, 50
Pastor of Central Baptist Church
Had surgery at 11 p.m. yesterday
An emergency situation
Suffered Merkle's diverticulitis
Is resting well today
In fair condition
  (Source: hospital officials)

III. Write an obituary using information in the following report.

THE BROWN FUNERAL HOME

DEATH REPORT

Date __January 7__

Full name __James William Denton__ Age __66__

Home address __1980 Salem Road__

Occupation __Operator of Cross-Roads Grocery Store__

Place of death __Christ Hospital__ Time of death __9 p.m. today__

Cause of death __Pneumonia resulting from influenza__

Length of illness __Three weeks__

Affiliations __Member of Brother Grocerymen of Lakeville, Salem Presbyterian Church, Masons__

Survivors, with relationships and addresses __Wife, Mrs. Sarah
Smith Denton; one son, James William Jr.; two
daughters, Miss June Denton and Mrs. R. E.
Talley. All live at home except Mrs. Talley, of
Coppertown, N. C. Also one brother U. J.
Denton of Long Falls, N. Y.__

IV. Write a death story using the information in the report in Exercise III plus the following notes on Mr. Denton.

> For three years Mr. Denton served as a member of City Council, 20 years ago, representing the Seventh District. He is a native of the city and has operated Denton's Grocery for 43 years. He was president of the Brother Grocerymen of Lakeville for 10 years and held that position at the time of his death.

V. The next day Brown Funeral Home sends you the following announcement of Mr. Denton's funeral. Write the story.

FUNERAL REPORT: James William Denton

Time   2 p.m., January 10

Place   The Brown Funeral Home

Officiating Rev. H. J. Masterson, pastor Salem Road Presbyterian Church

Burial Place   Lakeville Cemetery

Active Pallbearers K. L. Thomas, H. J. Knight, R. R. Gill, V. H. Stone, T. T. Butler, and M. M. Nance

Honorary pallbearers Members of the Brother Grocerymen of Lakeville

Remarks   Body will be removed to home at 3 p.m., Jan. 8, to remain until funeral

VI. Write a death story on a prominent individual of your school or community. Use all available sources in gathering biographical information, which must be accurate. You may use a reasonable amount of imaginary facts in giving cause of death, funeral details, and statements of prominent people regarding the "death" of the individual about whom you are writing.

Chapter 19

Fires and Accidents

Most fire stories and accident stories are gathered by the reporter after the event from records of the police and fire departments and from interviews with eyewitnesses—policemen, firemen, spectators. The stories are usually picked up as routine on regular beats—police, fire headquarters, and hospitals—or by calls from spectators.

On the other hand, major fires and accidents (floods, storms, train wrecks, and the like) will find reporters routed from their beds on special assignments which may require hours or days of actual observation and investigation.

In either case, facts are important. The newspaper reader is eager to know who was injured and the amount of property damage. If, in addition, the drama of major events can be effectively presented, so much the better. But drama should be implicit in the facts (incidents) and not explicit in the language of the story.

Overemotionalized:

> The throng, eyes glazed with horror, shrieked aloud as the ledge collapsed and the hapless firemen plunged headlong into the flaming inferno. Many women swooned from the very horror of the spectacle.

Better:

> Some three thousand spectators in Bolton Square saw the ledge collapse and the firemen plunge into the flames. Three women fainted.

Facts and Sources

19a **Story Contents.** The following formula indicates the facts (and sources) usually available in a major fire or accident story. Minor stories use few details.

Facts	*Sources*
A. Casualties 1. Name and identification of every person killed and injured	A. Police, firemen, hospitals, funeral homes; friends and relatives of dead and injured; witnesses; neighbors

Facts   *Sources*

  2. Manner in which persons
     were killed or injured
  3. Nature of injuries
  4. Disposition of dead and in-
     jured
B. Damages   B. Police, firemen, and property
  1. Damages to property   owners
  2. Description of property
  3. Owner of property
  4. Insurance
  5. Other property threatened
C. Description   C. Police, firemen, persons involved,
  1. Cause   witnesses
  2. Time and duration
  3. Chronological account of
     incidents
  4. Relief work of firemen,
     police, or others
  5. Spectators
D. Escapes   D. Police, firemen, persons involved,
  1. Rescues   witnesses
  2. Experiences of those escap-
     ing
E. Legal Action   E. Police, firemen, fire marshal,
  1. Investigations   property owners, lawyers em-
  2. Arrests   ployed
  3. Suits
F. Sidelights (human interest, as
    part of the main story or as
    separate story)

In a major fire and accident story the number of persons injured and dead is usually featured. The amount of the **19b** property damage is the most common feature. But a prominent person involved, an unusual cause, a dramatic rescue, or any one of the 5 *W*'s may sometimes be featured in the lead.

Story Forms. Fire and accident stories can range in form and size from the brevity to the lengthy several-feature story. **19c** The multiple-casualty story form is often used when such treatment is justified.

Vocabulary and Fact Reporting. In reporting accidents— notably automobile accidents, because of their frequency— **19d** the reporter must use words carefully, with an eye to precise meanings. Only moving objects collide, strictly speaking. Therefore, *"struck* a parked car" is better than *"collided with* a parked car." "The accident occurred *when the car in which they were riding"* is an awkward circumlocution, yet *"their* car" is usually inaccurate. Libel actions may grow out of inaccurate phrasing, and the short cuts of language should be used with care. Except in reports of storms, earthquakes, and other "acts of God," colorful language should yield to fact reporting. The phrase *completely demolished* (or *destroyed*) is not only tautological but usually inaccurate. A statement that a person is *not expected to live* generally should be reported as *critically injured.*

Fact reporting and careful language will also help the reporter to write without purposely or unpurposely expressing an opinion on who may be responsible for a fire or accident. The reporter does not attempt to fix this responsibility. The guilty person may seem apparent from the facts, the arrests, and the statements of officials as reported in the case. But the reporter makes no effort to point out the guilty party, for that is the job of the courts. To the contrary, if the reporter has information in his story which he thinks may tend to point a finger of guilt at a person, the ethics of fair play require that he make an effort to get that person's side of the story.

Complete Reporting. Isolated disasters may usually be treated adequately as straight news, with little interpretation. As they accumulate into a daily threat to the security of life and property, they confront the reporter with a different sort of responsibility. Most communities face the serious continuing problem of automobile accidents. Occasionally there may be a series of fires, and there are epidemics of disease or of crime. What causes these disasters? How do they occur? How could they, how can they, be avoided? Before the community can protect itself or take the proper remedial steps, it must know the facts. The reporter is frequently the only research agent on the job. Only as he can see—or foresee—and report, not merely the surface event but the underlying causes and trends, can the proper programs of reform be undertaken. Is the electric wiring of the whole community defective? Are there danger spots for traffic or unsound or unsanitary structures or practices? Surface reporting of simple events may not reach the heart of the community problem. Complete reporting would in these cases require independent thought, under-the-surface investigation, and interpretative analysis.

Exercises

I. Clip from newspapers a fire story and an accident story and make news analyses.

II. Write stories using the following notes.

    A. L. J. Jamieson driving
       Huge beer truck
       Weight two and one-half tons
       On Marion Highway
       Noon yesterday
       Tire blew out
       Three miles from Blankville
       Truck ran off road and overturned
       Truck badly damaged
       Thirty cases beer smashed
       Jamieson escaped serious injury
       Suffered minor bruises
          (Source: Police report)

    B. Dan T. Howell
       Blankville orchestra leader
       On way home from honeymoon
       Married Miss Juanita Stokes of New York
       Last week
       Car struck telephone pole
       Just within city limits
       At 9 p.m. yesterday
       Howell blinded
       By headlights of another car
       Howell in Grace Hospital
       With deep cut in neck
       And few minor lacerations
       Mrs. Howell escaped injury
       Couple had motored to Florida
          (Source: Mrs. Howell)

    C. School bus carrying 40 children collides with automobile this morning
       Accident occurred at intersection of Highway 31 and Bailey Road
       Six children suffer minor cuts and bruises
       Driver of car, Ellis Pierce, 55, of Bailey Road, taken to City Hospital
       Suffering broken leg, possible internal injuries
       Automobile's front end badly damaged; bus slightly damaged

Bus driver, Calvin Watts, said car entered highway from side road without stopping

Empty whisky bottle found in Pierce's car

Pierce looks like a whisky drinker

Pierce said bus was exceeding speed limit

No charges placed pending further investigation
(Source: Deputy Sheriff Melvin Speers)

D. B. A. Ridges

Salesman with Truant Machinery Company

Travels throughout this region

Keeps loaded gun in pocket of car door

Slammed door shut

This morning

Gun went off

Ridges shot through left arm

Treated at Westview Hospital
(Source: Police report)

E. Children living in

Harwood Street neighborhood

Play "Tarzan of the Apes"

Every afternoon

In wooded lot on street

Accident there yesterday

Proves that parents should pay more attention

To activities of children

Raymond Salley, eight

Son Mr. and Mrs. D. M. Salley

424 Harwood Street
(Source: Mrs. Salley)

Fell from tree

Rushed to General Hospital

Died shortly afterwards

Neck was broken
(Source: General Hospital attendants)

Raymond in third grade

At Frankwood School

A frail child but star pupil
(Source: Miss Jewel Smith, teacher)

F. Mountain Home Methodist Church

In Mountain Home Community

One mile from Blankville city limits

Started services

At 10:45 a.m. yesterday

The Rev. C. L. Briggs, pastor
In church pulpit
Had started sermon
Someone yelled: "The place is on fire"
Congregation of about 150
Moved most of furnishings
From building
New $1,500 organ saved
Song books and many of pews also saved
Church burned down
No water supply to fight blaze
One city fire truck did answer call
Not able to extinguish flames
Helped remove furnishings
Building valued at $78,000
Large auditorium and eight small rooms
Only outer brick wall remains
Insurance covered $25,000
Fire believed started from flue
Exceptionally cold day
Hot fire built in furnace
Church janitor obviously at fault
Caught eaves of church first
No one hurt
    (Source: The Rev. C. L. Briggs)

G. Plane accident at Blankville City Airport
Two-engine passenger plane
Of State Airlines, Inc.
Collided shortly after take-off
With privately-owned, single-engine plane
Passenger plane rose through low-lying bank of clouds
Crashed with private plane
Which was getting in position to land
10 passengers and crew of 3
On passenger plane
2 in private plane
Crew members and 6 passengers killed
2 other passengers critically injured
Remaining 2 in fair condition
2 in private plane killed
Those in passenger plane killed—Capt. William J. Needham, 29,
    pilot; Capt. Felts S. Sommes, 32, assistant pilot; Miss Juanita
    Lopez, 22, stewardess; Dr. Fred S. Faley of Central City,
    dentist; Homer J. Hecklefield of Blankville, local radio station

announcer; James T. Jett, home unknown, destination Phillipsville; Mrs. Helen F. Wellsman, housewife of Marysville; Dr. Samuel K. Sells, dean of the University of Blankville; Charles W. Jamsey, a child, of Hartsville.

Killed in private plane were Mr. and Mrs. Virgil T. Hartley, are owners and operators of the Hartley Motel of Blankville

Airport officials investigating

Why Hartley plane was in line of passenger plane taking off

Federal authorities also expected to investigate

(Sources: Saul T. Wilhelm, Manager of City Airport, and personal observation of wreckage)

Mr. and Mrs. Hartley were returning

From visit with son, daughter-in-law, and two grandchildren in Centerville

Were celebrating 25th anniversary

(Source: son, Henry F. Hartley of Centerville)

Critically injured were Mrs. Fred F. Faley and 16-year-old daughter, Ann Faley

In fair condition are John Alivine of Centerville and Lloyd Jamsey, father of Charles Jamsey of Hartsville

(Source: General Hospital)

Passenger plane broke into flames after striking ground

The body of Captain Needham was torn into a hundred pieces

Rescue workers from airport

Credited with saving lives of survivors

(Sources: Mr. Wilhelm and personal observation. Mr. Wilhelm has not been cooperative with your newspaper in the past.)

H. 60-car freight train
    Of Midwestern Railway Company
    Headed toward Blankville
    Last night at 8:30
    On Smithtown to Blankville line
    Carrying coal
    Had two engines
    Three miles from Blankville
    Ran into rear
    Of motionless 30-car Midwestern freight train
    Loaded with coal
    Stopped on line
    To repair overheated bearing
        (Source: Mr. Fremens)

    Had warning flares
    But stopped near curve

Heavy freight
Had no time to stop
   (Source: Engineer Simon)

Both engines of moving train
Jumped the track
Engineer, Tim Dozier, 43
In front engine
Killed when thrown
Against top of cab
William Simon, 41, engineer
In second engine
Suffered fractured wrist
And minor bruises
Larry Clements, 39, brakeman
Riding in second engine
Suffered burned face
Injured, in General Hospital here
   (Source: General Hospital attendants)
No person working
On motionless train
Was injured
Caboose and two freight cars
Torn to splinters
Other cars on both trains
Damaged slightly
Coal scattered extensively
Tracks badly torn
Now being repaired
And wreckage removed
Other trains detoured
Via James City
Damages estimated at $118,000
Accident being investigated
By S. T. Fremens
Local superintendent of company
   (Source: Mr. Fremens)

III. Suggest newsworthy pictures and write appropriate outlines on the following preceding assignments in this chapter: Exercise II, C; Exercise II, E; Exercise II, G.

IV. Write a newscast using the following preceding assignments in this chapter: Exercise II, A; Exercise II, B; Exercise II, F; Exercise II, G; and Exercise II, H.

Chapter 20

Seasons and Weather

Seasonal Stories

IN keeping tabs on day-by-day activities of the city, the city editor watches the calendar. The approach of Independence Day, Labor Day, St. Valentine's Day, and other holidays, anniversaries, and seasons results in timely feature stories, readable news. The reporter is assigned to "work up a feature" on seasonal events.

The chart on p. 255 points out some of the seasonal events and dates which receive attention by newspapers throughout the nation.

Not all of these events are reported by any one newspaper, though all are potential stories. Local interest and space available in the newspaper are the deciding factors.

To this list may be added many seasonal events which are of local interest only: anniversaries of battles, admission of the state into the Union, anniversary of founding of city, and various "weeks" (Book Week, National Newspaper Week, and so on) are proclaimed during the year. Once in a while an astronomical phenomenon, such as an eclipse or sun spots, is also noted in the newspaper.

20a **Weaving the Story.** The woof of the seasonal story is the present; the warp is the past. Together, they tell the reader just how his neighbors will observe a certain day and just why that day will be observed. Something is lacking if a feature on Columbus Day fails to recall highlights of the discovery of America. Something is lacking if the story mentions nothing of the plans of local residents to observe that anniversary.

The sources for the seasonal story are evident. In developing a feature, the reporter must go to reference books to obtain facts of the past. He must interview informed persons for facts of the present. He must weave these two together, and to give his story timeliness he usually plays up the present in the lead.

Sometimes the cause of the celebration does not date back to a historical event—for example, the vernal equinox—and the reporter would develop a scientific rather than a historical background. The reporter may assume that many persons will approach a certain

January
1—New Year's Day
8—Jackson's Birthday
17—Franklin's Birthday
19—Lee's Birthday

February
2—Groundhog Day
12—Lincoln's Birthday
14—St. Valentine's Day
15—Women's Suffrage Day
22—Washington's Birthday
29—Leap Year Day (every four years)

March
17—St. Patrick's Day
21—Vernal Equinox
Last of month—evidence of spring, first robin, spring fever, outside activities
Between March 22 and April 25—Easter, First Sunday after full moon following equinox. Good Friday, Friday before Easter

April
1—All Fool's Day
13—Jefferson's Birthday
26—Arbor Day (varies in different states)

May
1—May Day
Second Sunday—Mother's Day
30—Decoration or Memorial Day

June
First two weeks—school commencements
14—Flag Day
Third Sunday—Father's Day
22—Summer Solstice
During month—many vacations start, trips, picnics

July
4—Independence Day

August
During month—height of "dog days," last from four to six weeks.

September
First Monday—Labor Day
17—Constitution Day
23—Autumnal Equinox
During month—most schools open, harvest time, fairs held

October
12—Columbus Day
30—Hallowe'en

November
First Tuesday after first Monday—Election Day (not every year)
11—Veterans Day
Last Thursday—Thanksgiving
During month—beginning of winter evident, sports, migration of birds

December
First of month—Christmas shopping
22—Winter Solstice
25—Christmas
28—Wilson's Birthday

"day" with interest, and it is permissible to predict what will be done as an unplanned observance of that day. Depending upon the tenor of the story, the reporter sometimes may make his predictions imaginative as well as factual.

Seeking information on local celebrations, the reporter naturally will question leaders of clubs and organizations. The American

Legion would be the principal source for a Veterans Day story, the labor unions for a Labor Day story. Schools observe most of the anniversaries by class programs. Most other organizations will announce such special programs in advance.

20b **Story Contents.** The formula for a seasonal story:

Facts	*Sources*
A. Explanation of seasonal event	A. Reference books or reliable persons
1. History or definition	
2. Past observances	
B. Observance	B. Officials of organizations, predictions of reporter
1. Formally by organizations	
2. Informally by whole city	

20c *Weather Stories*

Related to the seasons, but much more important from the news standpoint, is the weather. Farmer, businessman, clerk, housewife—all talk about the weather. It is everyday news, whether or not conditions change.

Every day the various communications media convey regular weather reports furnished by the United States Weather Bureau. These usually include facts on temperature, precipitation, wind velocity, pressure, humidity, river stage (if a river is near), and clearness of atmosphere. The forecast, concerning temperature, precipitation, and clearness for the local area, is usually given a place on the front page of a newspaper, while more general statistics may be printed on an inside page.

To break the day-by-day routine of weather forecasts, a reporter sometimes searches for human-interest approaches in writing a weather report. In so doing, he must exercise caution to prevent his addition of human-interest and imaginary elements from changing or misinterpreting the forecast. It is a violation of federal law to falsify a weather report.

Special Weather Stories. Often the weather gets more space
20d than the brief forecast and formal statistics. A special story is demanded if:

1. The weather results in disasters—floods, hurricanes, tornadoes, droughts, dust storms, blizzards, lightning, and other weather quirks which cause deaths or serious damages.

2. There are sudden changes—cold waves, early snows, heavy rains, or other out-of-the-ordinary conditions.

3. Records are approached or broken—highs and lows in monthly and annual temperatures or rainfall.

4. A special event may be affected by the weather—football and baseball games, parades, other outdoor events, and even a few indoor events Readers are interested not merely in data but in the social and economic effects of unusual weather.

Such news is obtained from a variety of sources: the hospital, for deaths, injuries, and illnesses; the police station, for accidents and traffic problems; the fire hall, for fires and rescues; the charity agencies, for suffering of the poor; the government buildings, for relief work; the transportation and utility companies, for interruptions in service; and a variety of reports which usually trickle into the newspaper office. All are usually bound together in one weather story.

The multiple-casualty story (page 133) is a popular form to use for weather stories concerning a number of deaths and injuries. Even if there are no casualties, this same form may be used as a convenient method of presenting a wide variety of property damages and other effects, the list of damages taking the place of the list of dead and injured.

Story Contents. Facts sought in getting various weather **20e** stories:

Facts	*Sources*
A. Statistics	A. Weather Bureau
1. Temperature (high and low)	
2. Precipitation	
3. Visibility	
4. Humidity	
5. Wind velocity	
6. Flood stage (if any)	
B. Forecast warnings	B. Weather Bureau, police, fire department, relief workers
1. Crop warnings	
2. Sea or lake warnings	
C. Casualties	C. Police, fire department, hospitals, friends and relatives, witnesses
1. Names and identification of dead and injured	
2. Cause of deaths and injuries	
3. Nature of injuries	

Facts	*Sources*
4. Disposition of dead and injured	
D. Damages	D. Police, fire department, rescue workers, owners, witnesses
1. Damages to property	
2. Description of property	
3. Cause of damage	
4. Property threatened	
E. Relief	E. Police, fire department charitable agencies, city hall, relief workers
1. Relief done	
2. Relief needed	
F. Escapes	F. Police, fire department, relief workers, witnesses
1. Experiences of those who escaped	
2. Rescues	
G. Legal action	G. Police
1. Arrests	
2. Investigations	
H. Tie in or tie back	H. Newspaper file, reference books

Exercises

I. Clip from newspapers a seasonal story and a weather story and make a news analysis of each.

II. Write stories using the following notes:

  A. Prepare a feature on Groundhog Day. Place the date as "tomorrow."
No formal observance.

  B. Prepare a feature on Franklin's Birthday. Place the date as "tomorrow." Include the following facts:
Several schools will have programs
On "thrift"
Relating them to Franklin's Birthday
High school to have short play
During assembly period
Depicting highlights in Franklin's life
    (Source: J. K. Jackson, superintendent of schools)

Dr. J. C. Ward, history professor
At State Teachers' College
To speak on
"Franklin's Service to the United States"
At Rotary Club Meeting
    (Source: S. O. Snow, club president)

C. "Last night" was Hallowe'en. Write a story using the following notes:

Thousands costumed children
Paraded during evening
Most satisfied with "trick or treat"
Some engaged in vandalism
Thirty extra policemen
Assigned for night
Police received 189 calls
During three-hour period
Rotten eggs hurled
At houses, cars, people
Fences dragged into street
Street lights smashed
Porch furniture removed
Windows marked with soap
Car tires deflated
Store window of Brooks Cafe, 109 Main Street, broken
Three youths, boys, arrested
Taken to Juvenile Home, released to parents
   (Source: Police Department records)

Five false alarms received by fire department
Traffic tied up in uptown area
Answering false alarms
Four grass fires extinguished
   (Source: Fire Department)

III. Write stories using the following notes:

A. Weather forecast:
Warmer tonight and tomorrow
Clear, broken clouds
Temperature above 50
Low this morning, 47
At 5:30 a.m.

B. Cold wave expected tomorrow
Weather Bureau forecasts
Drop of 22 degrees
During night
Lowest about 10 degrees
Hourly temperatures today:

1 A.M.—31	5 A.M.—30	9 A.M.—36
2 A.M.—30	6 A.M.—31	10 A.M.—41
3 A.M.—29	7 A.M.—32	11 A.M.—42
4 A.M.—30	8 A.M.—34	Noon—44

Mean temperature yesterday, 34 degrees
Normal
May have snow flurries
During night

C.   Storm hits Littletown
Early this morning
Small town, near this city
Population 1800
Believed to be
Seventy-mile gale
Heavy downpour rain
Intermittent with severe wind
Lasted about one hour
    (Source: Weather Bureau)

Filling station
Blown over on two cars
Damages $5,400
    (Source: M. H. Randolph, station operator)

Thomas D. Franks, 39, laborer
Seriously injured when home caved in
Ancient, wooden structure, valued $1,200
Franks brought to General Hospital
Believe his back is broken
    (Source: Red Cross workers and hospital)

Large oak tree
Blown over on home
Of F. D. Parker
Six-year-old son F. D. Jr., injured
Cut by shattered glass
Damages to home, $1,900
    (Source: Mr. Parker)

Electricity off
Communication cut off
Wires snapped
Trees across roads
Citizens clearing roads
Fire breaks out in home
Of J. D. Williams
Unable to fight
Fire truck blocked
Damages to home $6,000
Not all damages reported

Other persons
May be injured
Red Cross has sent help
Many local citizens
Have gone there to aid
In clearing debris
    (Source: Red Cross workers)

D. Today 34th day
With no rain
None in sight
Cloudy skies
Forecast for tomorrow
No rain expected
Above normal temperature
Registered again yesterday
For 12th consecutive day
High yesterday, 86 at 2 p.m.
Low 52 at 5 a.m.
Mean 69, normal 60
    (Source: Weather Bureau)

Other cities in U. S.
Also have drought
And "heat wave"
Beaches crowded
Animals in Chicago zoo
In outdoor cages
First time in 16 years
During this month
    (Source: Associated Press)
Local crops suffer
Ground hard and dry
Damages not estimated
    (Source: L. M. Jones, county agent)

E. Blankville covered by
Snowfall 12.1 inches
Began falling yesterday
At 2 a.m.
Fell almost continuously
More expected tonight
Already heaviest
In 14 years
When 12.9 inches fell
Expected to surpass that record

If so, will be heaviest in 22 years
When 16.5 inches fell
Temperature remained below freezing
All yesterday
No letup expected
Low of 12 degrees tonight forecast
Low yesterday of 11 at 5 a.m.
High 29 at 2 p.m.
   (Source: Weather Bureau)

Public schools closed
Until later announcement
Because transportation difficult
   (Source: School superintendent's office)

Many streets packed
Uptown streets cleared
Extra cleaning crews working
   (Source: City Streets Department)

Highways being cleared
Curves being sanded
Traffic moving slowly
No serious accidents reported
Few damaged fenders
Reported to police
Buses off schedule
Taxis at premium
   (Source: State Highway Department)

Most businesses suffer
Few persons uptown
Many auto-supply stores
Sold out of tire chains
Sleds almost sold out
Boots, overcoats also selling fast
Postal deliveries
Reported delayed
   (Source: Various businessmen)

Welfare agencies taxed
Many requests
For fuel, food, clothing
   (Source: Welfare Bureau)

Two persons
Treated at hospital

For slight injuries
Mrs. D. W. Booth, 48, 1010 Wood Avenue
Sprained hip in fall
David T. King Jr., 12, 407 State Street
Injured arm
In sled accident
   (Source: General Hospital)

IV. Suggest newsworthy pictures and write appropriate cutlines on the following preceding assignments in this chapter: Exercise II, B; Exercise III, E.

Chapter 21

Crime

FROM the city police station, the county jail, the federal building, and some state offices, the city newspaper gathers its news of crime. These four branches of government cooperate in fighting the criminal, sometimes enforcing identical laws, but each has its separate law-enforcement machinery.

The chief source of crime news is the city police station. Indeed, a wide variety of important news is reported to the police—murders, robberies and other criminal acts, accidents, fires, missing persons. Policemen enforce state laws (on murder, larceny, and other felonies), in addition to ordinances which apply within the city limits.

The county jail, where the sheriff and his deputies and other county law-enforcement officers imprison persons who violate state and county laws, is also an important source of crime news. These county officers function chiefly outside the city limits, though they also have authority within the city.

Federal officers make few arrests compared with city and county officers, but these few frequently result in lengthy, featured news stories. Their routine work is the enforcement of federal laws, dealing with the sale of narcotics, fraud by mail, federal tax evasions, kidnapping, counterfeiting, violation of national park regulations, manufacture and sale of illegal beverages, unlawful flight to escape prosecution, interference with civil rights, and similar matters.

The state may maintain fire marshals, tax collectors, and investigators, highway patrols, game wardens, forest rangers, and other units of law enforcement yielding news.

Often the first beat assigned to a new reporter is the police beat, which includes some if not all of the law-enforcement agencies. The police beat is a splendid training ground for beginning reporters because it offers good practice in the fundamentals of reporting, in cultivating news sources, in gathering all of the facts needed to write an adequate story (which often-times requires checking several sources), and in writing under the pressure of approaching deadlines.

Crimes

Before examining the content of the typical crime story, the reporter should know what is meant by crime. A breach of law may be either a felony or a misdemeanor. A felony is one of the more serious crimes, usually carrying a penalty of imprisonment and sometimes of death. A misdemeanor is a minor breach of law, usually resulting in a fine and no imprisonment. A study of most state laws will show that the following crimes are usually regarded as felonies:

Homicide (killing a person)
1. Manslaughter
    a. Voluntary (intentional, in a fit of passion)
    b. Involuntary (unintentional, through negligence)
2. Murder
    a. First degree (with evident premeditation)
    b. Second degree (no premeditation but intent to kill)
Assault
1. Assault with intent to kill or maim
2. Felonious assault
3. Mayhem (maiming)
4. Kidnapping
Violating property rights
1. Larceny (illegally taking property)
2. Burglary (entering dwelling to take property, housebreaking)
3. Robbery (larceny with assault, threatened or committed)
4. Embezzlement (larceny through trust)
5. Forgery
6. Arson
7. Receiving stolen property
Obstructing justice
1. Interfering with officer
2. Perjury
3. Bribery
4. Contempt of court
Conspiracy in crime
1. Accessory before fact
2. Accessory after fact
Others
1. Gambling

2. Manufacture, possession, or sale of illegal beverages and drugs
3. Disturbing peace (fight, riot)
4. Sexual crimes
5. Criminal libel

Misdemeanors include violations such as drunkenness, speeding, the unlawful sale of certain merchandise (milk, beer, coal), improper parking, and simple assault.

21a In crime stories the reporter must be sure to write only privileged facts gathered from public records, and he must be accurate. Of course, accuracy is important in every news story, but it is vital in crime stories because a libel suit lurks behind every one of them. If a person has been arrested and charged with a certain crime, the reporter can say just that. It is a matter of public record. But publication of a detective's chance remarks that a certain person committed a crime is not a matter of public record and therefore is not privileged. It may result in a libel suit.

A person arrested is not necessarily guilty of a crime. No matter how damaging the evidence, the reporter must not "convict" him in the newspaper story. He can report the evidence that police have against the prisoner, but he cannot conclude that this evidence shows the person is guilty. A prisoner is always arrested *on charges* of a certain crime, not *for* the crime.

If doubt exists that the prisoner gave his right name, the newspaper reports that "he was booked at the city jail as John Smith," or "He gave his name as John Smith." The same method is used when the address of a prisoner is in doubt. However, reporters should use directories and other available sources in checking doubtful information. If a prisoner refuses to give his address, the reporter may write: address not given.

Police Records. Two types of records commonly yield local crime news: (1) the city and county jail "blotters" and (2) the complaint bulletins. The first is an entry book for persons arrested; the second, a record of compliants made to police and of investigations by police. The following illustrations of these records have been condensed to conserve space.

These records give the reporter only a few bare facts about a case. If he wants others, he must interview the officers or the persons involved. Some cases are so trivial that he ignores them altogether.

The reporter is privileged to use reports from the jail blotters, but

POLICE BLOTTER

Date	Time	Name	Age	Color	Sex	Occupation	Residence	Offense Charged	Arresting Officers
1/17	9:01 P.M.	John L. Tukes	38	W	M	Mechanic	101 W. Rhodes St.	Larceny	Stamps & Edd.
1/17	10:10 P.M.	Nathan F. Burkhart	27	W	M	Laborer	712 N. 4th St.	Drunk	Jones

COMPLAINT BULLETINS

COMPLAINT	INVESTIGATION

COMPLAINT

Date 1/17	Time 9:01 AM.	Taken by Larson

Complaint:
Name: J. D. Hornsby
Address: 3102 S. Ailor St.
Telephone: 6-2907

Complaint: Someone entered house: Stole silver, watch, money

Assigned to: Fox and Knell

INVESTIGATION

Date 1/17	Time 10:30 A.M.

Complaint:
Home of J. D. Hornsby
3102 S. Ailor St.
entered last night

Investigation: Following articles missing: Set Rogers Silver Value $40.00. Elgin Watch #6430973, value $25.00 Money $19.07 No suspects

By: Fox and Knell

he must be careful with information from the bulletins. These bulletins are simply a form of interoffice correspondence between the officers and the desk sergeant, who acts as a clearing agent for all complaints. There may be errors in the spelling of names, in addresses, and in other information, and the reporter must check carefully. Also, the reporter is expected to use good judgment in handling reports marked "Not for Publication," observing this request if publication would aid a suspect in escaping or if there are other justifiable reasons.

While the records illustrated above pertain to city police, records of a similar nature are kept by other types of law-enforcement officers—county, state, and federal.

The coroner is another public official whose records are often important in crime news, although he does not fit exactly into the law-enforcement picture. The coroner makes an inquest into deaths from "unnatural causes"—those in which foul play, violence, suicide, or unusual circumstances may be involved. His report, if it shows that the cause of a death points out evidence of crime, may result in arrests by law-enforcement officers. However, it must be kept in mind that the coroner's functions are limited to ascertaining cause of death and he does not "try" a case against persons accused of the death; any arrests arising from his reports must go through the courts in the usual manner.

21b **Story Contents.** The formula of usual information and sources for a crime story might be outlined as follows:

Facts	*Sources*
A. Casualties	A. Police, hospitals, friends and relatives of dead and injured, witnesses.
1. Name and identification of persons	
2. How persons were killed or injured	
3. Nature of injuries	
4. Disposition of dead and injured	
B. Damages	B. Police, property owners
1. Value, property stolen or destroyed	
2. Description of property	
3. Owner	
4. Insurance	
5. Other property threatened	
C. Description	C. Police, persons involved, witnesses
1. Chronological account	
2. Description of persons involved	
D. Escapes	D. Police, persons involved, witnesses
1. Rescues	
2. Experiences of those escaping	
E. Legal Action	E. Police
1. Investigation, clues, evidence	
2. Arrests	
F. Tie backs	F. Morgue Library

21c The length of a crime story is usually determined by the seriousness of the crime. Other factors which add paragraphs and increase the size of the headline are the prominence of the persons involved, the place of the crime, unusual circumstances, and incidents of human interest. Often one of these factors causes a reporter to write a feature story about an incident he might have ignored as "straight news." In selecting facts to go into his stories and in the treatment he gives those facts, the reporter must be careful to observe the ethics of his newspaper with respect to crime news. A review of the ethics of newspapers (Chapter 15) would be appropriate in considering this chapter.

Suicides   21d

Another type of story gathered from the police beat is the suicide. The official record, and not the reporter's own judgment, should determine whether a death is suicide. This record may be established only by action of a coroner.

Even if John Doe plunges from a 14-story window in front of a large crowd, there may be no suicide. Even if Mr. Doe is found dead on a lonely road, a pistol in his hand and a bullet in his head, there may be no definite evidence that he fired the bullet. Hence, until the coroner completes his investigation, the reporter can say only that John Doe was "found dead," or that he "plunged" or "fell." The reporter can give all of the facts surrounding the case, in keeping with the ethics of his newspaper, and the reader must draw his own conclusions as to whether it is suicide.

Suicide notes are sometimes found, which may seem to assure the reporter that he may safely call the death a suicide. Nevertheless, it is always best to wait until a public official makes the pronouncement. In other words, the reporter should use only unvarnished facts in a suicide story and let the suicide statement be a fact obtained from the coroner.

It may be possible to discover a motive, after suicide has been clearly established, but here again the reporter must be careful. He must not piece together certain facts about the person's ill health, financial difficulties, or love affairs, then conclude what he thinks is the motive. If he has a definite, authentic statement of motive, from the suicide note or a close relative, he probably will be safe in using it. If no apparent motive is found, the reporter should say so.

Even more caution is necessary in reporting attempted suicides. Unless the suicide attempt is evident and backed up by statements of authorities, or unless the person admits he attempted to end his life, the reporter must give only facts pertaining to the person's actions, rescue, and so on.

The method of suicide is usually described in general terms, with few details of methods which might be suggestive for others contemplating suicide. For instance, the name of a poison is seldom used in a suicide story. It is simply called "a poison." Gory details are omitted in suicide accounts, as in most crime stories.

21e **Story Contents.** A formula for the usual suicide story:

Facts	*Sources*
A. Name and identification	A. Officers (coroner's report), hospital, relatives and friends
1. Disposition of body	
B. Method	B. Officers, witnesses
1. Cause of death	
2. Circumstances surrounding death (when and how found)	
C. Motive	C. Officers, relatives, friends, physician
1. Suicide note	
2. Statements from relatives, physician, friends, business associates	

21f Each of the three principal facts named above may be the feature of the suicide. An unusual method or motive is usually the feature, unless the person's prominence overshadows that feature.

Exercises

I. Clip and analyze a crime story and a suicide story.

II. Following are several bulletins on investigations by police. On a separate sheet of paper explain what you would do with each of them.

   A. Loye Rankin, 34, 13 Front Street, arrested in alley behind Truax Food Market on Twenty-Second Street at 2:30 a.m. Burglar tools in his possession. Screen on store rear window cut. Charged with attempted burglary.

   B. Sammy Slye, 15, 3215 Temple, and Curtis Moon, 14, 8437 McAdams Drive, charged with theft of automobile. Property of C. J. Knox, 8435 McAdams Drive. Owner left keys in ignition switch. Taken from driveway at 11 p.m.

   C. Mrs. Beulah Castor, 36, Avondale Apartments, attempted suicide. Took overdose of sleeping pills. Found by maid at 7 a.m. today. Estranged from husband, John D. Castor, 1212 Wilkins Street. Taken to General Hospital.

   D. Amos J. Andrews, 46, industrialist, arrested at office this morning. Charged with murder. Body of wife, Charlene Andrews, 42, found by gardener in Andrews' home on Glencliff Trail. Gun found near body. Andrews admits argument with wife before breakfast.

  E. Thad Hopkins, 84, hit-run victim. Corner Sixteenth Street and Wallingford Boulevard. Crossing with light. Hit-run vehicle light brown sedan, hotrod. First four numbers of license, 4X-91.

III. Write stories using the following notes:

  A. Obadiah Sellers, 56, farmer recluse
      Charged with felonious assault
      Shot and wounded Andy Maples and Randy Maples, 17, twins
      Said boys were stealing wagon
      Victims taken to Community Hospital
      Buckshot wounds in back, legs
      Boys told Sheriff V. C. Rawlins they intended to put wagon atop barn
      Happened Hallowe'en night

  B. Unidentified body found
      On Arthur Greenway farm on Leeward Road
      Victim male, about 35
      Wearing business suit, diamond-studded ring
      Two neighborhood boys with dog found body in shallow grave
      Boys were Jim Ward and Philip Hilands
      Greenway heard car late last night
      Drove up private lane into woods
      Casts made of tire marks near site
      Sheriff Oliver Purdy investigating
      May call State Bureau of Investigation

  C. Two high school girls
      Arrested on charge of shoplifting
      Mary Dawson, 15
      Father, R. C. Dawson, president, First National Bank
      Theresa Brewster, 15
      Father, Carl (Red) Brewster, coal dealer
      Wilfred Boggle, manager, Ajax Variety Store
      Caught girls with school supplies, perfume in handbags
      Referred to juvenile authorities
        (Source: Policeman Henry Lang)

  D. Two masked men robbed Grant Supermarket
      At 1:45 p.m. yesterday
      Fled in stolen car
      Took $4,100 in cash, $3,500 in checks
      Robbery executed with clockwork precision
      Took less than two minutes
      Customers unaware of robbery
      Harold Conrad, store manager, had money in bag

On way to deposit it in bank

Bandits' car pulled up beside Conrad as he left store

Took money bag at gunpoint

Getaway car later found abandoned

On Merchant Street four blocks away

Witness said two men got out of car

Got into blue sedan parked nearby

Did not get license number

Three-state alarm sent out

Police believe bandits still in city

Conrad said trip to bank daily routine

"They knew when to expect it," Conrad said

E. Roderick Benet, 68, arrested for public drunkenness

Gave address as rooming house on Front Street

Benet former movie idol

Also played Shakespearean roles on stage

Most famous role that of Hamlet

No acting parts for past 25 years

Now working as vacuum-cleaner salesman

Police arrested Benet on downtown street

Reciting Hamlet's "To Be or Not To Be"

Three towering policemen surrounded the frail actor

Like wolves on a rabbit

At Police Station, Benet listed occupation: "television victim"

F. Police searching for missing 20-year-old girl

Donna Sarvid, daughter of Mrs. Ethel Sarvid, 8321 Plaza Place

Sophomore at Lakeville College

Believed kidnapped

Message scrawled in lipstick on diner wall

Latest clue

Found this morning by waitress at Playland Diner

After serving breakfast to girl, two men

Message said: "Call Lakeville 489-2201. I'm being kidnapped."

Mrs. Sarvid said daughter missing since last night

Did not return home from date

Was with John Jerguns, 22, senior at Lakeville College

Waitress, Molly Lumley, said girl answered Miss Sarvid's description

Neither man looked like Jerguns' description

Girl was extremely nervous

One man was about 40, short, dark, thick black mustache

Other man about 25, medium height, fair, blue eyes, crewcut

Police also looking for Jerguns

Did not return to his dormitory last night

Believe he may have met foul play
Twelve-state alarm sent out
FBI to be called in

G. Frank Wright
Alias Frank Warren, 30, "of Florida"
Drove into State Avenue Filling Station
Yesterday afternoon
Purchased six gallons gasoline
Handed $10 bill to attendant, R. L. Fisher
Fisher pretended he had no change
Went to nearby drug store
Called federal officers
Marshal S. E. Arms rushed to station
Arrived just as Wright
Drove off after becoming suspicious
Arms stopped car
Arrested Wright
Charged with counterfeiting
Several similar bogus bills
Passed in Blankville stores
In recent weeks
    (Source: Marshal Arms)

H. Policeman Joseph D. Hurst
Killed at 3 a.m. today
Southern Drug Store, 920 Main Street
James D. McGhee, 31, of Chicago
Arrested for murder
McGhee captured by Policeman Dale Sumner
And Assistant Police Chief L. B. Cross
Murderer shot in arm
Before captured
Three officers answered robbery call at drug store
McGhee got in through window
Was attempting to get in safe
Hurst shot through heart by "surprised" thief
Other officers jumped to cover
Shot it out with murderer
Preliminary hearing set
Tomorrow afternoon, 1:30
Robbery reported to police
By Q. D. Stanton, just getting off from
    night work at Blitzer's Mill
Stanton, 42, lives at 2901 Highland Street

McGhee gave up when shot through arm by Chief Cross
Fight lasted 30 minutes
Woke whole neighborhood
Rescue police came just as McGhee surrendered
  (Source: Chief Cross)

"If he had held out another minute, he'd be a dead
  man," said Cross
Hurst, 44, had been with department 23 years
Known as "Old Joe"
Much feeling against murderer among policemen
McGhee, small, well-dressed, refused to talk
Police checking up on past
He looks like a ratty gangster

I. James S. Walker, 40, and wife, 36
    Registered at Woodward Hotel
    Two days ago
    As "Mr. and Mrs. James S. Wilson of Chicago"
    Went on "spending spree"
    Bought most expensive meals
    Gave generous tips
    Attended all shows
      (Source: K. L. Lumpkin, hotel manager)

    At 2 A.M. today
    Leaped from window
    Of 27th floor
    Coroner pronounced it "double suicide"
    Walker was bankrupt
    Also in ill health
      (Source: Coroner D. B. Russell)
    Had threatened to "end it all"
    After financial reverses
    Married 15 years
    Had only $121 dollars
    Spent all but $1
    On "one last party"
      (Source: R. E. Layman, Walker's former business associate)

IV. Suggest newsworthy pictures and write appropriate cutlines on the
    following preceding assignments in this chapter: Exercise III, D;
    Exercise III, H.

 V. Write a newscast using the following preceding assignments in this
    chapter: Exercise III, A; Exercise III, C; Exercise III, F; and Exer-
    cise III, I.

The subject-matter stories examined so far have been of the simple type, rather well defined in form and content. Mostly they have been straight news stories with a minimum of interpretation and explanation. Interpretative summaries, it is true, have been necessary in the leads and in the body of those stories having salient-feature leads—to make clear the relationship of story parts, one to another. Interpretation in this sense has been merely the culling and arranging of items present in the materials. The reporter has not had to supplement the story materials with independent information of his own.

In the example below, the second paragraph is explanatory material drawn from within the story. It gives the background of the news event. It explains why the telegram was sent. This paragraph could have been written by any reporter covering the story, even if he had lacked any previous knowledge of the labor troubles. This characterizes straight reporting.

A charge that Ku-Klux methods were used in the flogging and tarring of two union organizers Thursday night near Kingville was made today by William W. Bewley, president of the local Industrial Union Council, in a telegram to the governor.

The two men said they were fired upon, dragged from their automobile, and beaten and tarred by six masked men following a union meeting in Kingville. Later, they said, they made their way to a farmer's house and notified Kingville police.

Thursday's episode apparently was another incident in a long struggle between two factions of the IUC to control the local textile union. The group led by Mr. Bewley replaced one headed by I. L. Tomsky two years ago, and since that time the Tomsky followers have been attempting to regain leadership.

In General Hospital today, the two organizers . . . (REMAINDER OF STORY WOULD GIVE REST OF NEWSWORTHY FACTS).

The third paragraph is an interpretation drawn from the reporter's independent information. It supplements and is not a part of the particular news event. This is interpretative news reporting.

It is impossible to draw a sharp line between stories which can be straight news reporting and those which require interpretative treatment. However, in the fields of law, business, government, politics, and other areas the need for more interpretation is clear. In these fields the reporter encounters new problems of reporting:

1. Stories often involve a web of conditions and events stretching into the past and into the future and into related fields.

2. The reader must be told not merely the facts but the significance of the facts.

3. Since much interpretation is necessary, the reporter needs a general background of information.

4. And generally he needs a technical vocabulary.

Because of these requirements, the beginning reporter will need study, practice, and experience for successful reporting in fields represented by the complex story types.

Chapter 22

Courts, Trials, Lawsuits

MOST court stories (trials and lawsuits) will concern events that have already appeared elsewhere in the news. They are in a sense follow-up stories. The crime, already reported at the time of commission and arrest, will reappear as a trial for murder, or larceny, or arson, or embezzlement. Fires and accidents, already reported, reappear as lawsuits developing from them. Many business conflicts may result in litigation. After evaluating the importance and newsworthiness of a trial or lawsuit, the reporter may ignore it, write a brief summary about it, or give it lengthy coverage.

In two previous chapters references were made to the freedom of the press (Chapter 1) and the right of newspapers to publish judicial proceedings as privileged copy (Chapter 5). In this chapter it is necessary to point out that judges have the power to limit those freedoms and rights insofar as the cases in their own courts are concerned. The judges can back up their power by having stubborn newspaperman jailed on contempt-of-court charges. This is not to say that judges use this power wantonly, although a few judges have gone beyond the bounds of both reason and law in such matters.

The conflict here (if any) is between two different provisions of the United States Constitution, one guaranteeing freedom of the press and the other guaranteeing an individual a fair and impartial trial. No ethical journalist would want to deny an individual a fair trial, but at times judges feel otherwise about newspapers. If a judge thinks the presence of newspaper reporters, newspaper photographers, or television cameramen in a court will affect court proceedings to the extent that the rights of the individual in receiving a fair trial may be impaired, and justice obstructed, the judge has the power to ban any and all of these communications representatives from the courtroom. Even more serious, if a newspaper is ruled guilty of "trying a case" in its columns through the use of stories which attempt to show that an individual is guilty or innocent, the judge can take action against those responsible for the stories. The judge's contempt of court penalty can carry a fine and/or a sentence in jail. The press does have the right of "fair comment and criticism" on the action of a judge or his court, but not while litigation on the case in point is still pending, and caution must be taken even after a decision is reached because of the possibilities of a new trial or an appeal. The power of judges to bar the press from a case is generally used discreetly even though some cases have resulted in animosities between judges and journalists.

22a **Story Forms.** For reporting trials and lawsuits no definite forms can be prescribed. The general principles of news writing will suffice. The lead will either summarize the trial events of the day or emphasize a salient feature.

Summary:

J. L. Carson was seen near the scene of the alleged murder, his fingerprints were found on a windowpane, and the death weapon was registered in his name, according to testimony presented at the opening session of Carson's trial in Criminal Court here today.

Salient Feature:

J. L. Carson's fingerprints were discovered on the windowpane of the room in which Edmund Ralston was found shot to death, a fingerprint expert told the jury when Carson went on trial in Criminal Court here today.

22b The body of the story will amplify the lead as in other types of stories. Direct quotations, indirect quotations, and interpretative summaries will be interspersed, and there will be frequent use of the chronological order. Quotations from the opening and closing arguments of attorneys or from opinions handed down by judges are similar to speech forms and can be handled effectively as quote-summary-quote stories. Quotations from testimony are usually of the short question-and-answer type similar to discussions and can be handled effectively in the chronological order (direct quotations interspersed with indirect quotations or unquoted summaries) after the features are summarized.

22c The reporter may choose one of two forms in relating the questions and answers. The following style is common for brief excerpts:

"Were you there at the time of the murder?" demanded Attorney Jones.

"No!" exclaimed Miss Smith. "I was at my mother's, 10 miles away."

Such phrases as "demanded Attorney Jones" and "exclaimed Miss Smith" are not needed throughout, if it is evident who is making each statement quoted.

The second form is used for extended questions and answers in cases of considerable importance or interest:

> Q.—Were you there at the time of the murder?
> A.—No! I was at my mother's, 10 miles away.

Quotation marks are not necessary in the Q–A form. Before testimony is given in this form, it must be preceded by an explanation, such as "Miss Smith's testimony follows."

In addition to noting feature highlights in court proceedings, the reporter should take notes on the background of court actions—descriptions of the crowd, witnesses, jury. Sometimes a lead feature comes from an event not included in regular court procedure. The courtroom is an excellent source of human-interest stories.

Court stories may be reported as straight news, and such an account may be effective. A considerable amount of interpretation may be necessary, however, to enrich and to make perfectly clear the significance of facts and procedures.

Background and Interpretation. In the first place, the reporter needs a background of the facts and relationships of the **22d** particular case at trial. Is the embezzlement of bank funds related particularly to a previous bank failure or perhaps to business conditions? Is the case a striking parallel of other cases? When, where, and how and by whom was the suit filed, the crime committed? Have there been any previous consequences? Are other suits or indictments pending? What consequences will develop from the case? Is there a particularly interesting problem of law, court jurisdiction, *corpus delicti,* or other novel feature involved in the case? Only with such a background can the reporter do full justice to the case and render a clear account to his readers.

A full interpretation also demands of the reporter a knowledge of law terms and procedures. He must know the difference, for example, between "evidence" and "testimony," and he must use these and other legal terms properly in his stories. He must not only possess a legal vocabulary himself but should be ever alert to help the reader over the rough spots. No helpful, interpretative reporter would leave readers struggling with a sentence like this:

"The grounds for the demurrer was repugnancy of counts."

The reporter should explain both the terms and the consequence of the action. "The Grand Jury returned a no-true bill against J. S. Sallings. . . ." might not be understood by most readers, but "The Grand Jury did not uphold charges against J. S. Sallings" or "The Grand Jury freed J. S. Sallings of charges" would be clear. If the case involves the constitutionality or validity of a certain law which is being tested in the courts, the reporter must explain the consequence of court rulings. For example, "The new state income tax was declared unconstitutional by the State Supreme Court today in its decision in the J. S. Sallings case" is infinitely more important than "J. S. Sallings was freed by the Supreme Court today." Readers are hot expected to be interpreters of court decisions. The newspapers must tell them, in the language of the layman, exactly how a decision affects their routine of life.

Actual experience and contact with the courts may be necessary to acquire an adequate technical background. The following definitions and procedures are more or less uniform in the various states and may be used as a foundation.

The Law and the Courts

Two general types of law are recognized: *civil,* under which may be brought suits for damages involving two or more persons, and *criminal,* under which charges of offenses against society may be brought by a governmental officer or a citizen against one or more persons. The authority for enforcing the two types of law comes from the constitution (constitutional law), the acts of legislative bodies (statutory law), and customs and judicial precedents (common law).

A further classification of the two types would be:

I. Civil Cases
   A. *Cases in law,* which abide closely by the law.
      1. *Contracts*—cases in which the *plaintiff* (the person bringing the suit) claims the *defendant* (the person against whom the suit is brought) did not follow the terms of an oral or written contract.
      2. *Torts*—cases which treat of private injuries not arising from a breach of contract. For example, it is usually a tort for a man to damage someone or his property, purposely or negligently.
   B. *Cases in equity,* which are distinguished from cases in law

because the judge can render "equitable" judgment by not following definite laws. Persons go to this court when they can get no relief from the definite writs existing in the regular law courts, this relief often being obtained by compulsory or preventive decrees (*mandates* and *injunctions*) issued by the judge. Controversies over property are usually brought to this court.

II. Criminal Cases

    A. *Misdemeanors,* minor criminal cases usually resulting in fines, sometimes in imprisonment.

    B. *Felonies,* major criminal cases usually resulting in imprisonment, sometimes death. (See Chapter 21 on crimes.)

State courts—which include county and city courts serving by authority of the state—and federal courts deal with the two types of law. Local affairs and cases concerning state laws are tried by the state courts. Cases concerning federal laws and interstate cases are tried by federal courts. The dual system of courts is outlined in the chart on pages 282 and 283.

To obtain a better understanding of this chart, and at the same time to learn a few of the most common legal terms, it is necessary to trace the route of a criminal case and a civil case in a state court. (Be sure to learn the meaning of each italicized term.)

Route of a Criminal Case

I. In the Court of Limited Jurisdiction (county or city magistrate).

    A. A *warrant* is sworn out, charging person with crime, enabling officers to bring him before magistrate.

        1. If the person has been arrested because he is wanted in another state, an *extradition* is obtained, which will enable officers in the other state to take the prisoner back.

        2. If the prisoner feels that he is held illegally, he may obtain a *writ of habeas corpus* from a superior court and get an immediate hearing. Then the officers holding him must prove that the prisoner is held for a just cause.

    B. The magistrate hears the case.

        1. If it is a *misdemeanor,* he may (within prescriptions of state law) *fine* the prisoner.

            a. *Fines* may be *appealed* from this court to a *Court of*

STATE SYSTEM

State Supreme Court

Appellate Court, usually of last resort for state, though some cases may go from here to U.S. Supreme Court if they involve federal questions.

(Criminal and Civil)

↑

Court of Appeals

Intermediate Appellate Court, created to relieve Supreme Court.

(Civil only)

↑

Courts of General Jurisdiction

(Where cases are first tried)

In the various states these courts have different names: Circuit, District, Superior, Common Pleas, Chancery. Jurisdiction is in criminal law, law, and equity. Each district court may be divided into units, a separate judge passing on each of the three phases of law named above. Or one judge may have jurisdiction in all three. Petit juries hear many of the cases.

↑

Grand Jury

In many states no person may be tried in a court of general jurisdiction on a criminal charge unless indicted by a grand jury.

FEDERAL SYSTEM

U.S. Supreme Court

Appellate Court of Last Resort in the United States.

(Criminal and Civil)

↑

Circuit Court of Appeals

Intermediate Appellate Court, created to relieve Supreme Court.

(Criminal and Civil)

↑

District Court

The Court of Original Jurisdiction in the federal system. One judge hears cases in *law,* in *equity,* and in *criminal* law. This judge also appoints a Bankruptcy Referee who relieves the district judge of these cases.

↑

Grand Jury

This body must indict every person who is to be tried in the district court on a *criminal* charge.

↑

U.S. Commissioner's Court

This official is appointed by the district judge to give preliminary hearings on criminal cases.

282

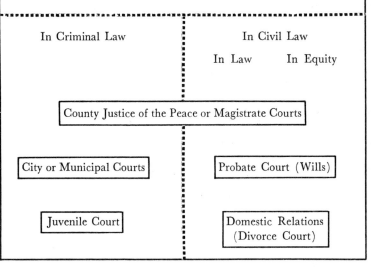

State Courts of Limited Jurisdiction

These inferior courts handle only petty cases. They enforce local laws in addition to state laws. They serve as courts for *preliminary hearings* in major *criminal* cases, and the *civil* cases they handle are *limited* to *stated amounts* (except in probate courts) by the state code or constitution. The most common inferior courts are shown below.

In Criminal Law

In Civil Law

In Law   In Equity

County Justice of the Peace or Magistrate Courts

City or Municipal Courts

Probate Court (Wills)

Juvenile Court

Domestic Relations
(Divorce Court)

General Jurisdiction, where such cases are tried anew.

2. If it is a felony, the magistrate may *bind the prisoner over* to the Grand Jury.

   a. The prisoner may *waive* the preliminary hearing and be bound over to the Grand Jury.

3. In binding the prisoner over, the magistrate *sets the bail bond* which the prisoner may post in order to be released until trial.

   a. In some very serious cases, the magistrate may not allow the prisoner freedom from jail but will bind him over *without bond.*

II. In the Grand Jury.

  A. Evidence is given to members of the Grand Jury *ex parte,* or without the presence of the defendant.

    1. Only the evidence against the defendant is heard. This is not a trial body. Cases are not heard in public.

  B. If the Grand Jury feels the evidence against the defendant warrants a trial, it may return an *indictment,* or *true bill,* against the defendant, arraigning him for trial in a Court of General Jurisdiction.

C. If the Grand Jury feels the evidence is not sufficient or in order, a *no-true bill* is returned, and the defendant is released.

III. In the Court of General Jurisdiction. (Officers of this court usually include the judge, clerk, attorney, jury, bailiff.)

A. The trial opens with charges made against the defendant.

B. Pleas and motions are made by attorneys. Below are some that could be made:

1. "Guilty" or "not guilty."

2. Motion for *continuance*.

3. *Demurrer*—Challenges the sufficiency of the indictment.

4. *Plea in abatement*—Contention, among others, that the indictment is illegal.

5. *Motion to quash indictment*—Contention that indictment is unfair or defective.

6. *Nolo contendere*—Defendant does not admit guilt but declares he will not fight case.

7. *Nolle prosequi*—Prosecuting attorney announces he does not wish to prosecute the case, because new evidence has convinced him of the person's innocence or because the attorney does not feel he has a strong case against the defendant.

8. *Plea of insanity*—Claiming defendant is irresponsible.

9. *Motion for change of venue*—Attorney contends he will not get a fair trial in that district and asks to have the case transferred to another district.

C. The judge acts on pleas or motions.

D. *Petit* (or *trial*) *jurors* are selected if case continues.

1. The jurors are selected from a *panel of veniremen,* or a list of persons who have been *summoned* for jury service.

2. Attorneys on both sides may *challenge* certain veniremen and prevent their serving on the jury.

3. The judge also excuses from jury service those who show evidence that they may be prejudiced in the case or are disqualified for other reasons.

E. Opening statements of the prosecutor (in some states) are made to the jury.

1. He outlines the case and explains what he will attempt to prove.

F. Testimony is given by witnesses who have been subpoenaed to testify for the prosecution.
   1. Prosecuting attorney questions witnesses—the *direct examination.*
   2. Defense attorney questions same witness—the *cross-examination.*
   3. *Depositions,* usually written sworn statements, are given for witnesses who are forced to be absent or are not present for other reasons.
G. Opening statements of the defense attorney are made to the jury.
H. Testimony of witnesses for the defense is heard. (Same procedure as for prosecution.)
I. The trial is concluded with arguments of attorneys to jury.
   1. The prosecutor speaks first, reviewing what he has proved.
   2. The defense attorney speaks next, reviewing his side.
   3. The prosecutor speaks again.
J. The judge instructs jury on case.
   1. He explains what decisions it can return.
   2. He explains certain points of law in the case.
K. The jury deliberates.
   1. If jurors cannot agree unanimously, it is a *mistrial.*
   2. If they can agree, they report their *verdict* to the judge.
L. Motions may be made by the attorney of defendant losing case.
   1. He may ask for a *new trial,* claiming errors were made in trial or new evidence has shown up.
   2. He may ask for an *arrest of judgment.*
M. The judge passes sentence if the defendant is found guilty and if the judge rejects motion for new trial.
   1. He may send defendant to prison immediately, issuing a *mittimus,* a court order of commitment to prison.
   2. He may (in some states) declare a *suspended sentence,* holding up imprisonment of the person. He may later put the sentence into effect, placing the person in prison. Or he may keep it suspended indefinitely, so long as the defendant gets in no more trouble.
   3. He may (in some states) place the defendant on *probation,* which might be called a suspended sentence on good behavior for a certain period of time.

      4. He may fine the person.

IV. In the Appellate Courts (appeal made on errors, with a *transcript* or *record* of trial sent to Appellate Court).

    A. The decision may be *reversed*.

    B. The decision may be *affirmed*.

    C. The case may be *remanded* (and reversed or affirmed) or returned to the court in which it originated and a new trial ordered.

V. After the Appellate Courts.

    A. The governor may *commute* (or decrease) the sentence.

    B. The governor may issue a *reprieve,* staying for a time the execution of the sentence.

    C. The governor may *pardon* the prisoner outright.

    D. The prisoner may be put on *parole* and allowed his freedom after he has served part of the sentence. But he has to report to parole officers periodically.

Route of a Civil Case

(Similar in some respects to a criminal case. Explanations of similar steps and terms are not repeated.)

I. In the Court of Limited Jurisdiction. (The case may be heard here if the amount involved is lower than the maximum fixed by law for such courts.)

    A. The plaintiff submits his *declaration* or *complaint* that he is due relief or compensation.

        1. If the case involves recovery of property, the magistrate may issue a *replevin,* which is a court order enabling officers to take the property.

        2. The magistrate may also issue a writ of *attachment,* usually when the plaintiff convinces him that the defendant may dispose of certain property involved in the suit. By that writ, the court takes charge of the property until the case is settled.

    B. The defendant is summoned to answer the complaint.

    C. The magistrate hears the case and passes judgment.

        1. Either party may appeal the case to higher court, where it is tried anew (*de novo*).

    D. The magistrate may attach the funds of the defendant (if he loses) to carry out the judgment. This order may be served on a third party, who may owe, or will owe money to the losing party. In other words, the magistrate may *garnishee* the losing party's income if the court's judgment is not paid.

II. In the Court of General Jurisdiction. (Cases may originate here, or they may come up from courts of limited jurisdiction. In either case, they are handled similarly.)

    A. The plaintiff submits declaration, which is recorded with the clerk. (The declaration sometimes is not necessary in appeals from courts of limited jurisdiction.)

    B. The defendant is summoned.

    C. The defendant may submit motions and demurrers attacking the complaint.

    D. The defendant submits his *answer* or *plea,* which is recorded with the clerk.

    E. The plaintiff submits motions and demurrers attacking the answer.

    F. The case is set for trial.

       1. Trial may be held by judge without a jury.

    G. If the trial is by jury, the jury is selected.

    H. The attorney for plaintiff makes an opening statement (in some states).

       1. The plaintiff's attorney explains case and outlines arguments.

    I. The attorney for defendant makes an opening statement.

    J. The plaintiff presents evidence.

    K. The defendant presents evidence.

    L. The plaintiff may present more evidence in rebuttal.

    M. The defendant may also present more evidence in rebuttal.

    N. The plaintiff's attorney makes his closing argument.

    O. The defendant's attorney makes closing argument.

    P. The plaintiff's attorney makes his rebuttal.

    Q. The judge renders a decision in the case (if tried without jury) or he instructs the jury.

    R. The jury deliberates and returns verdict if agreed upon unanimously.

    S. Motions may be made by the attorney on either side.

       1. He may ask for a new trial or arrest of judgment.

    T. The judge renders his judgment on any motions.

    U. The judge acts on the verdict.

III. In the Appellate Courts.

    A. The decision may be reversed.

B. The decision may be affirmed.

C. The decision may be remanded (and reserved or affirmed) to the lower court and a new trial ordered.

Cases in equity are usually not tried before a jury. The judge (sometimes called a *chancellor* when there is a separate court of equity) hears cases and renders verdicts and judgments.

The *Probate Court,* named in the chart above, has a limited jurisdiction in the disposition of a deceased person's property. If the person dies *testate* (having written a will), the probate judge has the *executor* named in the will carry out its provisions. If the person dies *intestate* (without a will), the judge appoints an *administrator* for the property.

Only a small portion of cases will be followed through the full routine outlined above. Still, nearly every step may result in a separate news story if the case is important enough. The outline should be checked against local variations because each state determines its own court procedure.

Exercises

I. Clip from the newspapers a court story and make a news analysis.

II. Visit a court hearing and write a news story on what occurs.

III. Write news stories from the following notes:

A. Case decided today
   Circuit Court jury trial
   Judge J. F. Judicious presiding
   Action by Jimmy Cooper, 11, 960 Carson Camp Pike
   Against Bobby Bails, 14, 6400 Calf Street
   Assault and battery charged
   $20,000 damages asked and $10,000 awarded
   During school class four months ago
   Bobby, without just cause, kicked Jimmy in the leg
   Teacher was lecturing at the time
   Jimmy's leg became infected
   Hospitalized for two months
   Leg permanently disabled
   Bails' attorney says he will appeal decision

B. The Grand Jury today returned "true bills" on two indictments, one against Elsie Kidwell, 4607 Marigold Manor, charged with shoplifting, and the other against Sam Slasher, 4 Cheathim Arms Apartments, charged with murder.

   Upon checking the police files, you find:

That Elsie Kidwell is a waitress at the New Hope Tavern. That on September 30 of this year, Elsie was caught leaving the Fair Way Department Store wearing five skirts, only one of which belonged to her. That Elsie had taken six skirts to "try on" in the women's dressing room, had purchased none, but had returned one. That she was apprehended by Morris Greeley, store detective, as she left the store. You were also informed that she is the sister of Prof. James K. Lentz of the University of Blankville.

That Sam Slasher, unemployed, was apprehended on October 3rd of this year and charged with the murder of Rocky Rass on Oct. 1. That Rocky was found dead in a ditch outside the Blue Goose Tavern under very suspicious circumstances. That a knife was imbedded between his shoulder blades. That there had been reports of an altercation between Slasher and Gass in the tavern shortly before the death.

C. City Judge Mahlon Marks passed on the following cases in court this morning:

1. Mayme Munn, 5407 First Street
   Saleslady at the Deluxe Department Store
   Fined $50 for public drunkenness
   A result of a raid on the Good Luck Tavern
   Last Saturday night

2. Terry Taylor, machine operator of Circletown Mill
   Pleaded guilty on charges of reckless driving
   Ran 3 stop signs
   Speed 80 mph estimated by Patrolman J. Ketchum
   Fined $150.00

3. Resulting from burglary last Oct. 15th
   Of Easy-Way Construction Company
   Three men bound to Grand Jury
   Those charged—
      X. Y. Fingers, manager of H & J Finance Company
      T. G. Krunks, laborer with the Easy-Way Co.
      H. M. Handle, accountant with Easy-Way Co.
   Police said burglary was an inside job
   $100,000 taken and none recovered
   Defendants waived hearing

IV. Write a story from the following notes:

Francis S. Cain, local critic, had written a review-criticism of a book, "Solving the Labor Problem," by Daniel T. Krantz, professor of economics at the state university. In the review, Cain said the book "contains the logic of a fourth-grade student," severely attacking the author's proposed solution of labor problems. "This is just another quack remedy, attempting to alarm laborers to crises which do not exist," wrote Cain. "The book isn't worth the paper it is printed on." Krantz sued for libel. Cain won the case in Circuit Court. Krantz appealed to the Court of Appeals. Today the Court of Appeals affirmed the decision, issuing the following statement prepared by Judge John Fulton:

"No malice was shown on the part of the defendant in this case. And we find that the personal character and reputation of the author are not attacked, though his theories are. In no matter is there any misstatement of fact or of propositions set forth in the book. The critic was at liberty to attack or denounce them with sarcasm and ridicule.

"It appears that the plaintiff in this case would attempt to throttle free speech in this state if he feels that a person is not free to criticize an article set forth for public consideration and approval. This great state and nation was founded upon the right of man to speak his mind and cast his vote in line with his convictions on matters of public interest. The publication of a book, which is distributed among the people of this state, is a matter of public interest. Although the criticism is undoubtedly severe and caustic, it does not exceed the bounds of legitimate criticism."

V. Write a story using the following notes:

This assignment deals with a trial which was held in Circuit Court. Sam Sears, a former employee of the Maynard Steel Yard, is charged with the murder of Wayne Wear, who was a foreman at the Yard. The state contends that Sears frightened Wear into stumbling into an open culvert, causing the death.

The defendant's attorney is Benedict Jones. The district attorney handling the case for the state is Abraham Smith. The state's case was presented first with Attorney Smith calling Raymond Burns as its first witness. Excerpts from the transcript follow.

SMITH—Just prior to the deceased's fall, where were you standing?

BURNS—I was standing about ten feet from Sam, directly under the big crane.

SMITH—Did you see the altercation between Sam and Foreman Wear?

BURNS—Yes, I saw Sam hit Wear.

SMITH—You say Sam struck Wear.

BURNS—Yes, Sam and Wear had been arguing. I did not hear what either of them was saying, but all at once Sam yelled "you no-good stoolie." At that, I turned around to face them when Sam hit Wear across the face with a wrench.

SMITH—Did this knock Wear down?

BURNS—Yes.

SMITH—Did he get back up?

BURNS—Wear got up and started running. Sam was chasing him, wrench in hand. Then I saw Wear trip beside the open culvert and stumble in.

SMITH—Did you offer assistance?

BURNS—Yes, about four of us ran to see if Wear was okay. When we reached him, he was unconscious. Somebody called an ambulance and the police. They told us that Wear had died instantly from the fall.

SMITH—Were you well acquainted with both Sam and Wear?

BURNS—I had been acquainted with Wear for 5 years. He has been my boss the whole time. But with Sam it was different. We have been fairly good friends for about three years.

SMITH—Was there animosity between Sam and Wear?

BURNS—What's ana er ana er whatever you said?

SMITH—Did ill feelings exist between the two?

BURNS—Oh. Well for about 3 weeks before the death, I felt there was bad blood between them. You see, they both were seeing Jane Mead, a girl who worked at the Yard. I heard them argue about her several times, and once they almost fought. As a matter of fact, Sam told me that Jane was stepping out on him and he would not stand for it.

SMITH—Were there other instances?

BURNS—No. They worked together okay.

SMITH—Thank you, Mr. Burns. I have no further questions.

The state next called Steve Williams.

SMITH—Mr. Williams, did you overhear the conversation between the deceased and the defendant just prior to the death?

WILLIAMS—Just before the fight Sam and I were working on the wrought iron job for the new City Hall. Wear was our foreman. There had been a rumor going around that one of us was going to be canned. Well, Wear came over and told Sam that the superintendent wanted to see him. Sam left.

SMITH—Did Sam and Wear fight then?

WILLIAMS—No, as I was saying, the superintendent wanted to see Sam. When Sam came back, he was boiling mad. It seems that the super had just fired Sam for drinking on the job. Personally, I never saw Sam drinking on the job, but that didn't help.

SMITH—Did Sears go to see Wear about it?

WILLIAMS—Yes, he and Wear argued about that for a couple of minutes and then Sam hauled off and cracked Wear with a wrench he had been using.

Williams went on to describe the fight and the fall in substantially the same manner as the previous witness. The state completed its presentation of the case and the court recessed until the next morning. Write your story for publication in the next morning's edition of your newspaper.

VI. Write a follow-up story to the one in Assignment V, for publication in the next day's newspaper, using the following notes.

The next morning the defense of Sam Sears was begun. Attorney Jones called Sears to the stand. Excerpts from the testimony follow.

JONES—Did you strike Wear with a wrench?

SEARS—Yes, but not until he threatened to kill me—to shoot me.

JONES—When did Wear threaten to kill you?

SEARS—After I returned from the super's office. The super called me in for a talk and told me what Wayne had said about me.

JONES—What occasioned this threat?

SEARS—Well, I returned and started picking up my tools and putting them away. I had just quit my job. Wear came up to me and accused me of taking some of his tools. I told him just to stay his distance. He said he was going to take his tools away from me, but I didn't have any of his tools and I wasn't about to let him run all over me. I hit him with the wrench because he had an iron pipe in his hand and was getting ready to use it.

JONES—Did you force Wear to run from you?

SEARS—No! I was trying to get him away from me. After I hit him, he said he was going to get his gun and kill me. He went after his gun. I didn't chase him.

JONES—You didn't chase him?

SEARS—No. I took a few steps toward him, telling him to calm down, but I didn't chase him. I don't see why I'm on trial at all. I didn't hit him hard. His death was caused by the fall, not by me.

JUDGE TORTS FACTO—Here now, Mr. Jones, I suggest that you instruct your client to refrain from any such outbursts.

JONES—Yes, your honor. Mr. Sears, just answer my questions. Do you known Jane Mead?

SEARS—I certainly do. I'm going to marry her.

JONES—Did you and Wear fight for her favor?

SEARS—Wayne tried to beat my time, but he didn't have a chance, so why would I want to fight him over Jane?

SMITH—Objection.

JUDGE—Sustained. Strike that answer from the record.

JONES—I repeat. Did you and Wear fight for her favor?

SEARS—Of course not.

On cross examination, District Attorney Smith hammered at the defendant.

SMITH—You liked working at the yard, did you not?

SEARS—Certainly I did. I've worked there for 10 years, three of these with Wear as the foreman.

SMITH—So you were upset when the superintendent fired you?

SEARS—He didn't fire me. I quit.

SMITH—Do you drink?

SEARS—I am a moderate drinker, but I never drink on my job. Wear told the super I did, but it was not true.

SMITH—Is it not true that you were mad and resentful toward Mr. Wear because he was dating Jane Mead?

SEARS—That's not true. Jane was my girl. He didn't stand a chance.

Jones, the defense attorney, next called the "mystery girl," Miss Jane Mead, to the stand. She testified that her affections were at one time divided between the two, but that recently she had decided that she loved Sam Sears.

JONES—When did you decide this?

JANE—Well, Sam asked me to marry him, and I decided that I loved him most. I told Wayne that we could not see each other anymore.

SMITH—How did Wear react?

JANE—He became very mad and said that I was his woman. He left saying he would "settle with Sam."

After Jones completed his defense, District Attorney Smith called Myron Tyme, the superintendent, in rebuttal. Tyme stated that he fired Sears because Wear had reported that Sears was drinking on the job.

The state then rested its case and the jury retired to consider its verdict. After deliberation of one hour, the jury returned and acquitted the defendant of the charge of murder but found him guilty of voluntary manslaughter. The jury recommended leniency. Voluntary manslaughter can carry a sentence of from one to twenty years. The court recessed until tomorrow morning at 9:00 A.M. for sentencing.

VI. Write a newscast using the following preceding assignments in this chapter: Exercise III, A; Exercise III, B; and Exercise V.

Chapter 23

Government and Politics

GOVERNMENT is the biggest business and the biggest problem of the people. It is the people's own business. For its operation they furnish the money and select the managerial personnel. Properly financed and managed, government ensures the various benefits of "life, liberty, and the pursuit of happiness" through private initiative. Improperly operated, it may mean insecurity of life and property. At a hundred points, day in and year out, the complex machinery of democracy touches and influences the daily lives of citizens. It affects their jobs, businesses, education, health, safety, transportation—all aspects of public welfare.

A function of the newspaper is, or should be, to keep the people informed about all of the affairs of government. Without complete reporting, the stockholders in this enormous business are without the knowledge to select proper representatives in government or to judge their acts thereafter.

Government News. What do people want to know and need to know about government? What is meant by government news and by political reporting? Much news that emanates from government offices is of the various types discussed in other chapters. Among these stories might be listed:

Type of Story	*Sources*
Crime and accidents, suicide	Police, sheriff, state patrol
Illness, death, accidents	Public hospitals
Fires and accidents	Fire department
Trials and lawsuits	Courts
Weather	Weather bureau
Meetings	Legislative bodies, boards

In other words, government yields all types of news. And in reporting upon these matters the reporter is rendering an account to the public of governmental activities. Over and beyond these reports of daily activities there lie ill-defined but important materials that need reporting as government news by a political reporter. They do not constitute a story type, perhaps, nor are they easily defined. Nevertheless, they can be illustrated and studied, and they must be written if the public is to have a complete report of its government.

The Political Reporter. The political reporter, for example— or any journalist reporting politically—would, in this ca- **23a** pacity, center his attention not upon the policeman but upon the commissioner of police (or safety). He may not visit the state hospitals but he would talk to the health commissioner. He may be only mildly interested in the construction of a bridge or a street but very much interested in traffic or an entire highway program. He may collect personals and brevities (in his general reporting capacity), but as a political reporter he is looking for attitudes and theories and plans and programs. He would, in short, be interested in going beneath the surface of routine government news, coming up with stories on issues and policies and the broad aspects of government.

There are specific matters—and others not so specific—that the political reporter would look for and report. The specific items would include:

Legislative actions (whether of the state legislature, the city council, the governing body of the county, or Congress)

Executive dispensations (whether of the governor or mayor, or department heads)

Judicial decisions (of the supreme courts usually—not trials and law suits but precedent-making decisions)

Financial and budgeting matters (including bond issues, debt reduction, taxes, and tax delinquencies.)

The less specific or nonspecific items would include any of the following matters pertaining to any governmental office—whenever they should be of sufficient importance to affect policies and trends:

1. Daily records
2. Periodic reports
3. Changes in personnel
4. New projects and programs
5. Speeches
6. Discussions
7. New laws
8. Enforcement of laws
9. Taxes imposed and paid
10. Publications
11. Changes in policies
12. Interviews and features

Just what the substance of these items would be can only be determined by the reporter in contact with, and thoroughly conversant with, a specific office or official of government over a period of time. The political reporter should be so versed in the activities of a governmental office and its officials that he can detect any significant changes deserving public notice, whether or not such changes are announced by the office. Often the unannounced changes involve political developments that should be exposed.

Since the reporter's duties (as both a government news and political news reporter) require a thorough knowledge of government itself, including the various governmental forms and their news potentials.

Forms of Government

In general, there are four layers of government: city, county, state, and federal. Each offers the citizen certain services, paid for ultimately by taxes. Each has a legislative, an executive, and a judicial branch. The legislative branch, composed of representatives elected by the voters, enacts the laws which make possible those services and imposes the taxes which bring in revenues to support the services. The executive branch, composed of persons elected and appointed, carries out the laws of the legislative branch, actually performing the services and collecting the taxes to pay the bill. The judicial branch, composed of persons either elected or appointed, administers justice, interpreting laws enacted by the legislative branch as well as common laws and constitutional laws. In addition to these four layers of government, there may be others, such as special districts created by legislative act to perform and charge for special services (such as water and sanitation).

City Government. In the accompanying charts are presented sample forms of city government. The specific form of any particular city can be ascertained from its charter which is granted (enacted like any other bill) by the state legislature. The charter will define the duties and powers of city officials and otherwise outline the corporate structure of the city. No reporter should attempt to cover city hall or otherwise to report city governmental or political affairs without mastering the city charter. He will find that no one else (probably including the mayor) is thoroughly acquainted with it, and his peculiar knowledge will lend strength and luster to his reporting.

The charter (and even a chart which should be drawn from it) will suggest the many important phases of city government which should be reported. Major issues should be checked with the proper city officials from day to day. The current problems will change

FIVE SAMPLE FORMS OF CITY GOVERNMENT

Bicameral Plan

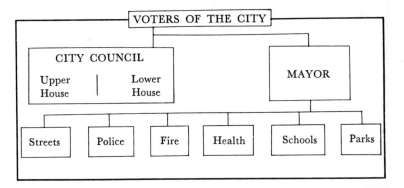

Mayor–Alderman Plan

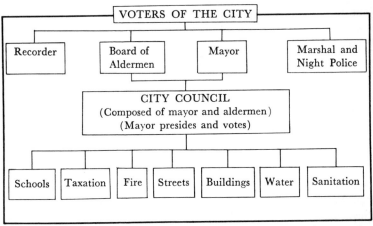

from time to time. One month may find the live public issue to be higher salaries for teachers. The next month a street-improvement program may be current, or the city water may be in question, or revised zoning regulations may be under debate. Knowledge and background and personal acquaintance with city officials and employees are far more important tools than even pencil and paper and typewriter for successfully reporting city affairs.

County Government. Forms of county government (see sample charts) vary somewhat and must be mastered by the local reporter

Mayor–Council Plan

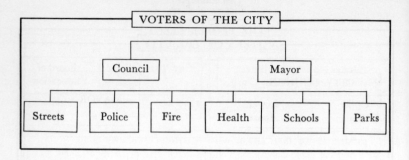

City Manager Plan

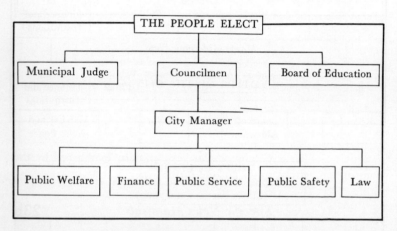

covering the county building. Unlike the city, the county has no charter. It derives its forms and powers from acts of the state legislature and from the state constitution and perhaps from precedents. Nevertheless, the county reporter must learn his county government. Let him go to all the legislative acts for a hundred years (unless a state code has brought them into focus) if he must. For unless he knows the facts he cannot recognize the special political interests that will attempt to bias the news. He should draw a chart of his county government, list officials and their duties, and become familiar with the enabling acts under which the county operates.

State Government. A sample state government is shown in the accompanying chart. The reporter must, however, master his own state government. Knowledge of the state constitution will be the chief staff to lean upon. But there will be many reorganization bills

Commission Plan
(An Example)

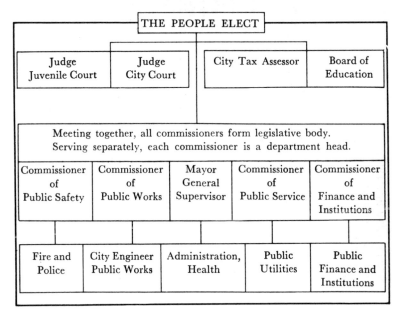

THE PEOPLE ELECT			
Judge Juvenile Court	Judge City Court	City Tax Assessor	Board of Education

Meeting together, all commissioners form legislative body.
Serving separately, each commissioner is a department head.

Commissioner of Public Safety	Commissioner of Public Works	Mayor General Supervisor	Commissioner of Public Service	Commissioner of Finance and Institutions
Fire and Police	City Engineer Public Works	Administration, Health	Public Utilities	Public Finance and Institutions

(statutes) which have altered the basic pattern established by the constitution, setting up the current form.

Specific News Materials   23b

All of the story forms previously discussed and diagramed are employed in reporting government and politics. They are used to present the following types of specific story materials.

Legislative. The state legislature, the city council, and the governing body of the county should be covered faithfully. New laws are important news, but even more important are proposed laws. The public depends upon the reporter for information. Citizens may want the opportunity to be heard. Carefully observing and reporting the trend of legislation, the reporter is the watchdog of the public welfare. He will not only cover the legislative sessions but will also follow the bills into committee rooms. He will poll authoritative opinion. He may canvass similar legislation in other states or communities to determine whether it has been successful and constructive.

THREE FORMS OF COUNTY GOVERNMENT
"Long Ballot" Plan Used by Some Counties

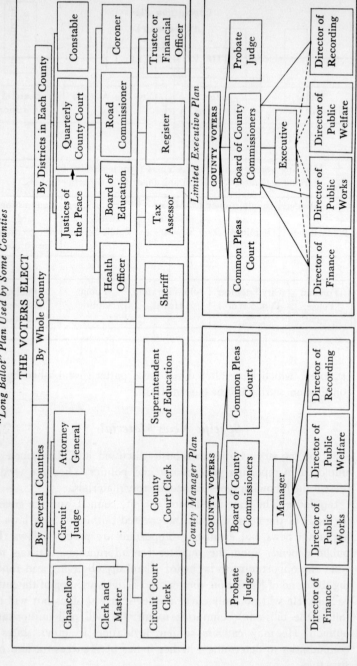

ORGANIZATION OF A SAMPLE STATE GOVERNMENT

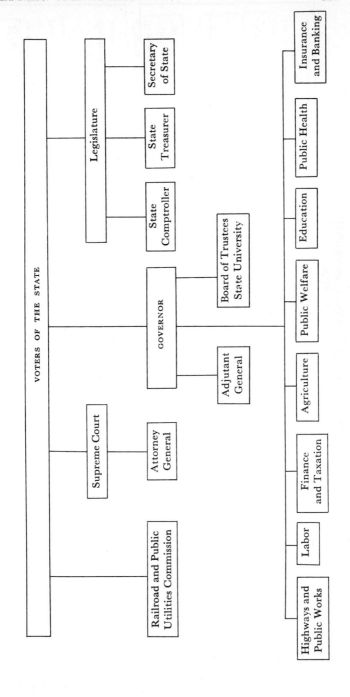

VOTERS OF THE STATE

Railroad and Public Utilities Commission

Supreme Court
Attorney General

GOVERNOR
Adjutant General
Board of Trustees State University

Legislature
State Comptroller
State Treasurer
Secretary of State

Highways and Public Works
Labor
Finance and Taxation
Agriculture
Public Welfare
Education
Public Health
Insurance and Banking

A SUMMARY OF GOVERNMENTAL SERVICES
PROVIDING SOURCES OF NEWS

Services and Activities	City	County	State	Federal *
Protection of person and property	Police Fire Courts Building inspectors	Sheriff Magistrates Deputies Constables Courts	State police, courts, fire marshals, rangers, game wardens, National Guard	Army Navy and Marines Air Force Coast Guard FBI inspectors
Promotion of health	Water supply Health Department Garbage and sewage disposal, Hospitals	Health Department	Health Department	Public health service
Regulation and promotion of agriculture	None	Agricultural agents and departments	Department of Agriculture	Department of Agriculture and other agencies
Regulation and promotion of business of industry	City ordinances enforced by inspectors	Licensing	Department of Commerce (may have another name)	Department of Commerce and other agencies
Regulation of working conditions	Usually none	Usually none	Department of Labor	Department of Labor and other agencies
Construction and maintenance of public roads	Department of Public Works, Streets	Department of Highways	Department of Highways and Public Works	Bureau of Public Roads and other agencies

Education	School boards Superintendents Libraries	School boards Superintendents Libraries	Department of Education and state institutions	Office of Education and other agencies
Conservation of natural resources	Parks Planning agencies	Agricultural agents Planning agents	Department of Conservation	Department of Interior, Regional agencies
Regulation, control, and operation of public utilities	City water Power Light	Rural electrification corporations	Utilities and Railroad Commissions	Interstate Commerce Commission
Promotion of general welfare Social Security	Department of Welfare, almshouses Hospitals	Almshouses Hospitals	Department of Welfare, mental hospitals Special schools	Social Security and programs of many other agencies
Other major services		Property and other records	Regulations and controls	Post Office, Department of State (foreign relations)
Administration	Taxes Budgets Regulations Routines	Taxes Budgets Regulations Routines	Taxes Budgets Regulations Routines	Taxes Budgets Regulations Routines

* Federal agencies form too vast a network to permit detailed analysis here. Only standard services are suggested.

Executive. Once a law is enacted, it may become a permanent news potential. If it is a tax law, for example, the reporter can follow its effects, checking with the proper executive officer, probably the commissioner of finance. What is its yield? Is it popular or unpopular, easily enforced? Aside from its function in the execution and enforcement of new legislative measures, the executive department of government (governor, mayor, county judge or manager, and chief department heads) is a permanent news source. Are the laws being enforced? Too strictly? Not strictly enough? What specific problems arise from day to day? What new policies are in effect? The reporter not only keeps the public informed; he also is an aide to the executive offices which need to educate the public and to popularize programs. Without the news channel the interaction of government and the people would be difficult.

Judicial. The political reporter keeps an eye on the courts. Here the same laws which he saw enacted and put into operation may come up for adjudication. The trials and lawsuits will usually be covered by other reporters, but sessions of the supreme court or any court in which decisions are fraught with economic and social consequences—in which the constitutionality of laws is involved—will find the political reporter present.

Fiscal. The revenues and expenditures—the budget of state, county, and city—will have the close attention of the political reporter. Bond issues, taxes, delinquent taxes, assessments, and the whole financial structure, fixed and current, badly need interpretation to the people. Wrapped in technical terms and difficulties as this system is, no auditor or financial expert will take the trouble to explain it in plain language. Only the reporter who will equip himself thoroughly for the task can serve the public as interpreter. Such a task is both a responsibility and an opportunity for complete reporting.

Public Records and Meetings. In covering government offices, a reporter will want access to public records and the right to attend public meetings. Questions and even conflicts sometimes arise over these matters. There are questions over what is and what is not a "public record" or a "public meeting." National and state journalistic organizations have conducted crusades charging officials with too much secrecy in government, demanding that all public records and meetings be open to the public (hence, open to the press, for the press must base its claim for access upon the public's right of access). The Tennessee Press Association, for example, sponsored such a campaign with a slogan, "What the People Don't Know WILL Hurt Them," and was able to obtain a state law requiring that all public records be open to the public and the press. Such laws still leave unanswered, however, some pertinent questions on what constitutes a public record or a public meeting.

Of course, there is no quarrel over certain types of public records and meetings, such as property transfers, delinquent tax notices, arrests, periodic fiscal reports, city council meetings, and sessions of the state legislature. The disputes have been over certain types of records which officials claim are not open for public purview and on certain types of meetings (special committees of a city council, for example) to which the public is not invited. The mayor or governor would not want his correspondence files open to the public. A public hospital would not want the detailed medical records on its patients available to anyone desiring to see them. Nor would a special council committee want to give frank discussion to personalities involved in a hiring or firing episode if members knew that the press was there to quote them. Newspapers have had varying success in opening records and meetings which had been closed for unjustified reasons. In any event, the press can demand the right to see records and to attend meetings which are accessible to anyone other than specified government officials and employees, and the press can insist that final action on a legislative matter (such as the action of council on a special committee's recommendations) be taken in open session. If government officials persist in closing records and meetings for unjustified reasons, the press must resort to public opinion, legislative action, and the courts.

Elections   23c

Periodically the people must choose many of their public servants in elections. With no constitutional provisions for this important task, the system of political parties and election practices has grown up by trial and error. Somewhat stabilized now in various state laws, the election machinery is nevertheless still animated by informal political agreements. If a fixed system of government is so complex that it needs professional interpretation, the primary and general election practices require even greater political acumen in those who are to report the multiform facets of political campaigns.

The charts on the following pages are simplified pictures of party

PARTY ORGANIZATION AND METHODS OF
CALLING CONVENTIONS
(Democratic and Republican Parties)

National Executive Committee

Composed of representatives from each state and territory chosen by the national convention. In general, manages the national party affairs and issues the call for the national convention.

State Executive Committee

Composed of representatives from each congressional district chosen at biennial primary elections. In general, manages state party affairs and, in response to call of National Executive Committee, issues call to County Executive Committees for the election of delegates to the State Convention.

Congressional District Executive Committee

Composed of the chairman of, or other delegates from, the County Executive Committees of the particular district. Frequently inactive.

County Executive Committee

Created usually by party usage. Its organization is different in each of the political parties and is not uniform in the counties, even in the same party. The committee issues call for county convention or primary election to nominate party's candidates.

---

organization. The national party system is well fixed, but the states show considerable variation in their forms and practices. The political reporter will need to make the same serious investigation of his state's election laws as of his state and local government to report political campaigns adequately.

The reporter is also expected to evaluate candidates for office. He must understand not only machinery but personalities and issues. Without editorializing—unless he is conducting a signed column— he must, as a reporter, present these subtleties to his public in factual accounts. Obviously he can do so only from careful study or long

STATE PRIMARY ELECTION MACHINERY
(*Democratic and Republican Parties*)

State Primary Board
or
Primary Election Commissioners

Composed of representatives from each congressional district, or otherwise as local election laws may determine.

County Primary Board

Composed of members appointed by the State Primary Board upon recommendation of the county executive committees from lists furnished by the candidates for office.

Officers of Election
(For each voting place)

Officer-in-charge, Judges, and Clerks

Appointed by the Primary Board, which also appoints an adequate number of watchers—all watchers and officers selected from lists furnished by the candidates.

---

experience and close contact with the politics of his community or state or nation. He may interview candidates, propound questionnaires, compose biographical sketches. He must report adequately from day to day the reactions of candidates to issues. Finally he will perhaps accompany the candidate through the campaign, reporting speeches and audience reaction, and end by tabulating the results precinct by precinct on election night.

Interpretation of Politics. Especially is it true in government and political reporting that essential news is frequently **23d** cloaked behind policy. Stories of the handout variety (stereotyped releases, "canned" information) must be carefully interpreted, or the reporter may find himself innocently conniving in partisan policies. In other words, the reporter must "know politics." He must see the facts behind the news, the motives of governmental actions, the underlying party machinery as it grinds meal for its supporters, mud for its opponents. The public more or less depends upon him to expose the bad and commend the good deeds of public officials.

STATE GENERAL ELECTION MACHINERY

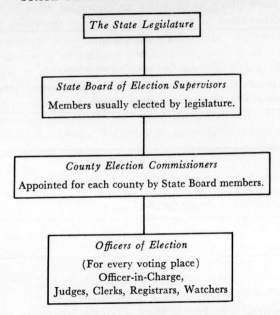

To represent his readers faithfully, the reporter of governmental news must be a student of public opinion and political philosophy, and he must work his way to the "inside" with many politicians and with political organizations in order to keep a finger on the pulse of action. This does not mean, however, that he bargains his rights as a reporter to obtain an inside seat. In most cases the political reporter is one of the oldest and best reporters on the staff—one who has the ability and personality to be an important figure in the political life of the city.

Reporting politics and government is a year-round job, but the field calls for special additional attention during election time. The newspaper must inform the public about the candidates for office, the issues at stake, political alignments and maneuvers. The reporter must debunk propaganda from the material supplied him by both sides. He must tell the voters what they want to know about the candidates. And when the votes are counted, he must analyze election statistics so that they mean something to the reader.

Frequently newspaper policy (see Chapter 14) is involved in reporting politics and government. This will arise if the newspaper has partisan views on those holding or running for office or if it has a policy relating to governmental affairs. Such policies may range all the way from efforts to eliminate an outmoded office in the city welfare department to a campaign to change the entire form of city government. More than all other communications media, newspapers have taken the lead in crusading for governmental reforms. The public has come to expect newspapers to be not only a guardian of governmental conduct but also an adviser on progressive steps needed in governmental organization. Candidates for public office, in declaring their platforms, are swayed by opinions of the press. With such great responsibilities, the reporter who covers government and politics must have the competency to live up to his obligations.

Exercises

I. Clip from newspapers three political stories and make news analyses.

II. Diagram the organization of your:
1. City government
2. County government
3. State government
4. State election machinery

III. Visit the city hall in your community to obtain a list of departments and records which a reporter should check daily for news stories. What types of stories are available from each department?

IV. N. D. Wiggs, city service director
Today announced that Carl D. Larson
Had resigned position with city as garbage truck driver
Larson was with city for nine years
Four years ago appointed superintendent of city garage
By former mayor, T. S. Martin
Martin defeated eight months ago
By present mayor, John M. Wyatt
Larson's salary as superintendent of city garage was $6,000 year
Position changed to superintendent of mechanics
When Wyatt elected
Salary reduced to $5,000 year
Larson was strong supporter of former mayor
When Martin ran against Wyatt
Larson is civil service employee
And cannot be fired without sufficient cause
Six months ago was made garage mechanic
"We are doing away with the position of superintendent of mechanics for economy's sake," said Mr. Wiggs at that time

Larson's salary as mechanic was reduced to $3,600

Last week Larson transferred

To Division of Sanitation

Made driver of garbage truck at $2,400 a year

"We need more truck drivers and have too many mechanics," explained Mr. Wiggs

Wiggs was appointed service director by Wyatt

Larson refused to take truck driver's job

"I haven't a chance," Larson said today

"There's no use trying to stick it out until Wyatt is defeated," he said. "Next they'll try to make me clean streets at $10 a week."

Larson says he will sue the city

Will ask for reinstatement to position equivalent to

Superintendent of city garage with salary of $6,000 a year

V. Write a story from the following notes:

> Fred J. Troll, retired Army colonel, has announced that he will run for the City School Board in the coming election. He is a native of this city and has lived here since his retirement five years ago. He has never before run for public office. His announcement is not news, but you have interviewed him to get his stand on campaign issues. A report of the interview follows.

> *Q.* Are you in favor of an increase in pay for teachers?

> *A.* I think teachers should have more money. They are very poorly paid. On the other hand, the tax rate in our city is very high, and I am not sure that we can afford to increase the pay of teachers. I believe a School Board member should protect both the schools and the taxpayers, and if elected I shall see to it that both are treated as fairly as possible.

> *Q.* Are you in favor of retaining Superintendent D. T. Rule as head of the school system?

> *A.* I certainly am not. One reason why I am running is to get in a position to discharge Mr. Rule. We have had no harmony in our school system since Mr. Rule became superintendent. Though it may not be his fault, I feel that a change is needed for the good of the city.

> *Q.* Do you oppose him because he has been fighting to get an increase in the pay of teachers?

> *A.* That is one of the reasons. He has made the teachers feel that the School Board is antagonistic in the matter, I believe.

> *Q.* Do you really believe it will be possible to raise the salaries of teachers, Colonel?

A. I believe I've already answered that question.

Q. In other words, you aren't sure?

A. This is a matter to be explored.

Q. To change the subject, what do you consider as other problems of our schools?

A. Upgrading the curriculum is a matter of tremendous importance.

Q. Do you have any specific proposals?

A. Yes. For one thing, I believe we should cut out the frills in our schools and get back to fundamentals—the three "R's." Our schools are spending too much money to give vocational subjects and such frivolous things as teaching students to drive automobiles.

Q. Do you mean that these courses should be eliminated?

A. Yes. That's where we may find the money to raise salaries. Cut out the frills and spend our money on solid education.

Q. What would you cut out?

A. I've already mentioned them. Mechanical arts, home economics, secretarial work, and even some of the foreign languages, and psychology and sociology and other courses that are not fundamental. They don't belong in our public schools. We are supposed to give them a solid education. If they want to learn a trade, let them go to a trade school.

Q. Should trade schools be operated by the city school system?

A. Definitely not. That's a private matter. The public schools should give a general education, free of costs, but a person should pay his own way for a vocational or professional education.

Q. What about the young people whose families cannot pay?

A. There's always a way if there is a will to earn it.

Q. Where did you attend college, Colonel?

A. West Point. I graduated from West Point.

Q. Isn't West Point a publicly supported institution training students for professional careers?

A. That's quite different. Quite different! See here, now. Aren't you becoming disrespectful? From your questioning it is apparent that you are looking for something to put me in an unfavorable light. That's yellow journalism and I'll submit to no more of your abuses. Good day, sir!

(With that, the Colonel walked out of the room.)

VI. Attend a meeting of the city council or its equivalent in the community and write a news story on the meeting.

VII. Write a story which presents a current, local governmental issue or problem, analyze it, and survey public opinion.

VIII. Write a story using the following notes:

> In a city election held "yesterday" the votes for candidates and their party affiliations were:
>
> For Commissioner of Administration (and mayor):
>
> | | |
> |---|---:|
> | Robert E. Davis, incumbent (Democrat) | 20,173 |
> | Herman DeBerry (Independent) | 3,392 |
> | W. E. Miller (Republican) | 21,409 |
>
> (Note: This was a particularly bitter race. Davis served two terms. Recently opposed by churches because led fight to eliminate restriction on sale of whisky near churches. Miller is Presbyterian elder.)
>
> For Commissioner of Safety:
>
> | | |
> |---|---:|
> | Howard Gernt (Republican) | 5,476 |
> | James P. Stockton, incumbent (Democrat) | 36,942 |
>
> For Commissioner of Health:
>
> | | |
> |---|---:|
> | Henry D. Barry (Republican) | 14,243 |
> | Wayne Oliver (Democrat) | 25,242 |
>
> For Commissioner of Education:
>
> | | |
> |---|---:|
> | Thomas Folkner, incumbent (Republican) | 22,004 |
> | Jones D. Maddox (Democrat) | 23,409 |
>
> (Note: Folkner has been commissioner of education for eight terms, 16 years. Maddox was formerly a high-school principal, but was dismissed by Folkner because of "insubordination in office" after Maddox refused to require his teachers to take a prescribed "oath of allegiance.")
>
> For Commissioner of Public Works:
>
> | | |
> |---|---:|
> | Paul D. Dunlap, incumbent (Democrat) | 30,122 |
> | Joe B. Hale (Republican) | 9,803 |
> | Calvin James (Independent) | 2,122 |
>
> City Judge:
>
> | | |
> |---|---:|
> | Warren R. Cockrum, incumbent (Democrat) | 40,109 |
>
> (*Notes:* Cockrum was unopposed. Seventy-two years of age, he has been city judge for seven consecutive terms, 28 years. Number voting was about average. Only one disturbance reported at polls: man ejected from Fifth Ward polls after church people complained he was "drunk, disorderly, and insulting those opposing Mayor Davis.")

IX. The Joint Finance and Ways Committee of the State Legislature today released its recommendations on state appropriations to the various branches and departments of the state government. Analyze these recommendations as given in the table below and write an interpretative news story on them.

	Appropriations for Present Fiscal Year	Appropriations Recommended for Next Fiscal Year
Legislative Branch (Legislature meets every two years)	$ 400,000	$ 150,000
Judicial Branch	2,620,950	2,718,000
Secretary of State (Dept. of State) ..	106,000	180,000
State Comptroller (Dept. of Audit ..	596,005	845,000
State Treasurer (Dept. of Treasury) .	275,000	318,000
Public Service Commission (which regulates public utilities)	305,000	343,000
Governor's Office	145,000	180,000
Department of Finance and Administration	1,591,500	1,925,000
Department of Personnel (which supervises civil service system)	135,000	166,500
Department of Purchasing	152,000	210,000
Division of Veteran's Affairs	195,000	210,000
Department of Agriculture	1,460,500	1,645,000
Department of Conservation and Commerce	2,588,690	3,345,000
Game and Fish Commission	2,050,000	2,100,000
Department of Correction	4,662,900	6,577,000
Department of Education	153,652,518	180,011,072
Department of Insurance and Banking	791,000	851,000
Department of Labor	345,900	420,000
Department of Mental Health	11,213,000	14,700,000
Department of Military	766,475	927,000
Department of Public Health	7,981,000	9,210,000
Department of Public Welfare	13,573,000	15,600,000
Department of Revenue	2,728,000	3,225,000
Department of Safety	3,126,400	3,937,000
Emergency and Contingency Fund ...	500,000	500,000
TOTAL	$211,960,838	$250,274,172

Appropriations recommended for the fiscal year following next year were the same as for next year, except the amount for the Legislative Branch was increased to $400,000 because the Legislature will be in session.

X. Suggest newsworthy pictures and write appropriate cutlines on the following preceding assignments in this chapter: Exercise IV, Exercise V.

Chapter 24

Business, Industry, Agriculture, Labor

THE economic life of a community is reflected in the local developments of business, industry, agriculture, and labor. Obviously, then, the news from these areas of activity deserves space in the local newspaper. The newspaper itself is a business which derives its financial support as an advertising medium for the establishments which compose the economic structure of the community. While not expected to convert their news columns into free advertising space to please advertisers, newspapers are expected to carry legitimate news on these establishments to serve their readers.

Even the routine business stories are usually of much local consequence, affecting the pocketbooks, the jobs, the household budgets, and in general the plans of the local citizenry. The stereotyped real-estate transfers reported in a "column" without benefit of lead or language will be read by adult members of the family. The price paid for the corner building lot may reflect the value of every piece of property in the block. Will a service station be located there? Or perhaps a grocery or a poolroom? If so, it may be the first sign of decay of a substantial residential neighborhood. Progress and disaster thus may move below the surface of the routine business story.

24a Though such dull nuggets of news await the reporter's labor for exploitation, many a shining "gold brick" is proffered him in finished form. Handouts, publicity, and promotional stories of various sorts from business, industry, agriculture, and labor seek newspaper space. Fashion shows, Santa Claus promotions, circuses, carnivals, department stores, beauty parlors, summer resorts—all afford stories, many of them beautifully prepared by press agents. But are they news? Always the reporter must be on guard against free advertising that may creep into the news columns. The policy of the individual newspaper will determine how much and in what manner such material will be accepted. Many newspapers join with local merchants in promoting some events. Some national "weeks" and "days" with a commercial tinge may be publicized. Mother's Day, Father's Day, and other worthy though special-interest occasions may find the reporter writing not news

314

but promotion and publicity. In all such cases the safeguard of honest reporting is the ability to distinguish the wolf in sheep's clothing.

Types of Establishments. Establishments and organizations that come within a community's economic complex include:

Retail stores
Wholesale distributors
Banks and finance firms
Real estate agencies
Insurance agencies
Transportation firms—passenger and freight—highway, airway, railway
Industries
Communications—telephone, telegraph
Business and industrial organizations—chamber of commerce, Better Business Bureau, various trade associations, automobile club
Farms
Agricultural markets
Agricultural organizations and agencies—state, county and federal
Labor—organized and unorganized
Plus various types of service establishments, some indigenous to the locality

The extent to which a newspaper will cover each of these activities may depend upon local characteristics. If a sizable number of the newspaper's subscribers are engaged in one of the activities, special sections of the newspaper may periodically be devoted to news and timely information published for the benefit of those subscribers. Such sections range from the fairly common farm page used in regions which have substantial agricultural interests to a special section on railroad news which might be used in a city whose principal industry is a railroad terminal. Whether or not any special sections are carried, stories from all of these economic activities are published as the news may become available.

Types of Stories. The great variety of stories from business, industry, agriculture, and labor will not conform to any simple general type. Some will be reported as meetings, speeches, interviews, and publications. Some will appear in trials and lawsuits. Even crime, accidents, fires, illnesses, deaths, and funerals may affect the economic life of the community and thus require an interpretation of this influence.

Following are some general varieties (rather than special types) of news on economic developments which appear from day to day in the newspapers:

1. *Markets*. Stocks and bonds, livestock and commodities—mostly tabulations and stereotyped reports, national and local, but accompanied by interpretative stories.

2. *Real Estate*. Routine transfers, new additions, large sales, improvements and expansions of buildings.

3. *Merchandizing*. Retail and wholesale stores—expansions and improvements, new corporations and partnerships, fashion mergers, bankruptcies, prices, cost of living.

4. *Finance and Banking*. Stockholders' and board meetings, dividends, bond issues, discounts and interest rates, the money market in general, refunding, trends.

5. *Industry*. New industries, new products, improved processes or methods, expansions, removals, bond issues, mergers.

6. *Transportation*. Changes in schedules, rights of way, board meetings, stocks and bonds, refunding, rates.

7. *Labor*. Wages and hours, unemployment, strikes, lockouts, relief, policies.

8. *Business and Government*. Taxes, legislative acts and court decisions affecting business, regulations and enforcement.

9. *Agriculture*. Crops, sales, droughts, new methods of farming, regulation by government, new varieties.

For all of these varieties, stories on personnel changes (including human interest stories on retirements) are available.

Story Forms. Just as these story varieties run the gamut of **24b** different story types, so also will the story forms vary.

Straight news stories, simple and complex; human interest stories; feature articles—all will be used in presenting the news on business, industry, agriculture, and labor.

In reporting the various incidents, facts, trends, policies, struggles, factors of progress, expansion and contraction of programs and projects involved in business stories, the reporter will need an adequate background and an ability to interpret—both of which he can gain from experience and study.

Interpreting the News 24c

As in covering other types of activities which employ technical terms in describing day-by-day procedures, the reporter writing on business, industry, agriculture, and labor must enrich his stories with interpretation whenever and wherever needed. For example, he should simplify statistics. The average person probably would not stop to read, "A total of 30,612 of the 147,604 persons in Blankville own automobiles, according. . . ." He has no time to analyze the figures. But he may be interested in "One out of every five Blankville residents owns an automobile. . . ." In other words, the significance of statistics should be made clear. Usually a comparison is needed. How do the figures compare with other figures? Are they high or low? How do they compare with figures of past years and other sections of the nation? Most figures are meaningless unless comparisons are given.

No less important than simplifying statistics is the need to interpret technical language. Sometimes reporters are so **24d** familiar with certain technical terms that they use them without thinking of the reader. How many persons can explain the difference between *debt* and *deficit* or *gross* and *net?* Yet such terms are often used as if every reader knows their precise meaning. The reporter should either translate such terms or take care to use them within a context which enables the reader to understand their meaning.

The following list of technical terms used by business, industry, agriculture, and labor will emphasize the need for interpretation: partnership, corporation, articles of incorporation, charter, bonds, refunding bonds, serial bonds, sinking-fund bonds, common stock, preferred stock, bankruptcy, referee in bankruptcy, "bull" and "bear" markets, collateral, call loans, strikes and lockouts, clearing house, assets and liabilities, discounts, interest, dividends, premiums, exchange, liquidation, credit, trusts, monopolies, receiver, Federal Reserve, surplus, socialism, communism, fascism, state capitalism, contracts, overhead, trustees, directors, interlocking boards, pyramiding, holding companies, public utilities, municipality, debt and deficit, "blue sky" laws, audits, balance sheet, tariff, parity, balance of payments, gold reserve.

Some economic terms may require only simple definitions, but some involve analyses which are possible only if the reporter knows the language of business and industry. Such documents as an auditor's report, a profit and loss statement, a bank statement, and a market report require special knowledge in economics to read and translate.

The Reporter's Background

Such academic subjects as economics, sociology, economic history, and political economy give the reporter a foundation for covering business, industry, agriculture, and labor. These are subjects generally studied by the college graduate, and the assumption could be that a college education is sufficient background for depth reporting in the economic structure of the community. However, while a college education helps, the college graduate stands at the entrance —not at the exit—of his economic education.

In addition to the general theories, principles, and history of economics, the reporter covering business, industry, agriculture, and labor must learn the specifics of these activities in the locality where he serves. He should have ready answers, in a handy notebook if not in his head, to basic questions on the area, population, wealth, chief sources of income, chief occupations, tax rates, school enrollment, bank deposits, labor force, value of properties, and other vital facts about the community and the people whose economic life he will attempt to interpret.

Knowing the basic information on his community, understanding the technical language he must interpret, and mastering the techniques of organizing news stories, the reporter must go even further in establishing himself as a competent journalist on economic affairs. Additional effort is required in each of the four areas of economic coverage.

Business. To cover the economic activities of his community
24e effectively, the reporter must develop a thorough knowledge of the business houses and better than a passing acquaintance with the business executives of the city. Retail and wholesale stores, finance houses, transportation agencies, and other firms, particularly the principal officers of these firms, are news sources for the business reporter. He must know enough about these business firms to ferret out the real news, to separate free advertising from legitimate news, to present an accurate picture of the city's economic progress or decline.

Obviously, business firms cannot be subjected to interviews, but their executives can, and the reporter should develop a friendship with them which not only will make them willing to answer penetrating (and sometimes distasteful) questions but also will encourage them to volunteer tips which can lead to important stories. Everything from minor shoplifting problems to major mergers of large business firms can be scented by the reporter even before they are ripe for public print if he has the thorough knowledge and the cultivated contacts he needs in covering the business beat.

Industry. Local industries generally are not so close to the community's daily news events as are the business firms **24f** because the industries usually have their sales sights on a regional or national rather than a local market. Nevertheless, the people employed by a local industry are local citizens, and their activities as well as the industry's well-being are of interest to all the people of the community. The reporter covering industries should known them well—the products they manufacture, the number of persons they employ, the distribution of their products, the sources of their raw materials, and the people who manage and operate them. As in the case of the business beat, the reporter must cultivate and keep alive his news sources in the industrial life of the community.

Agriculture. The agricultural constituents of a newspaper are, of course, as widely dispersed as the number of farm units **24g** in the circulation area. However, the agricultural interests are more closely knit than one might surmise. The local agricultural and home demonstration agents, farm bureaus, and other offices of agricultural agencies and associations have long-standing affiliations with the hundreds or the thousands of individual farm operators, and these offices are the primary sources of agricultural news. The reporter, then, must know the officials and the scope of services of these organizations, and he must cultivate them as news sources.

Some knowledge of agriculture is also required of the reporter when he delves into the how and why of farming. It is all too easy for a "dude" reporter to make a screamingly funny mistake in writing about planting peas or milking cows. A few such errors will cost a reporter the confidence of his readers. A background of farming, therefore, is helpful to an agricultural reporter. However, books, bolstered by visits to farms, can substitute. Even reporters with farm experience must rely on books to keep up to date with agricultural advances.

Labor. The labor force of a community, which constitutes **24h** much of the total population, cuts across the areas of business, industry, and agriculture. Some of the laborers are organized by crafts, some by industries, and some not at all. Therefore, covering the labor beat involves developing many sources of news. The general run of labor news offers no more than brevities on elections, routine meetings, barbecues, and the like, but when strikes are threatened or are in progress it becomes front-page matter. News sources cultivated by the handling of routine stories often become quite valuable during periods of labor strife. Moreover, to develop latent interest in labor news, the reporter needs to search for stories and features unrelated to labor strife.

A labor reporter is not expected to be a crusader for labor or a spy for management. He is a reporter and no more. However, he should be well versed in the advantages and disadvantages of organized labor, in the structure of labor organizations, in the extra benefits of labor membership (such as welfare funds), in the salary scale of laborers, and in other data important in his locality. This knowledge will enable him to enrich his labor stories with accurate interpretation, but it does not follow that he should become labor's champion. When he is writing of strikes and lockouts, for example, he should make his interpretation an objective one—giving the facts but not swerving to one side or the other. On the other hand, his knowledge of strikes will lead him to treat them as the result of disagreements between management and labor rather than as military warfare (which sometimes happens when a police reporter is assigned to cover a strike).

24i   *Complete Reporting*

The most important form of interpretation in reporting the economic life of a community is that which reaches below the surface of events and brings forth significances and trends. The stock-market figures, commodity prices, car loadings, and other financial data are usually not significant in themselves. Compared with what they were a year ago or last month, they yield a meaning and a prophecy of the future. This does not mean that the reporter should become a forecaster; on the contrary, he must be cautious about making forecasts on business conditions because serious consequences may result—stock shifts, sales slumps, and the like. Nevertheless, the reporter can point up the trends of the past. Although analyses of business conditions may be the prerogative of "business analysts" or special columnists, the reporter himself cannot afford to restrict his questions to the obvious facts.

Is a factory to be established in the community? What, then, will be its effect upon the labor situation, unemployment, housing, taxes? No columnist or analyst exists to interpret this sort of local story to the citizens. Only the reporter can render this service. Complete reporting is a public service expected of him. Concerning a new bridge, a new street, a strike, or the status of retailing, the question is not alone "What is happening?" but "What does it mean in the lives of local people?"

Exercises

I. Clip from newspapers and make news analyses of three stories representing different aspects of business, industry, labor, and agriculture.

II. Define the following terms:

Stocks and bonds
Monopoly
Mortgage
Overhead
Voucher
Workmen's compensation
Audit
Common and preferred stock
Depreciation
Dividends
Insolvent and liquidate
Public utility
Collective bargaining
Open and closed shop
Corporation and partnership

Bull and bear markets
Earnings versus dividends
"Blue sky" law
Craft and industrial unions
Receivership
Holding company
Trust
Clearing house
Index numbers (economic conditions)
Lockout
"Yellow dog" contract
Lease
Parity prices
Principal and interest

III. Write stories using the following notes:

A. Brick warehouse building
   At 1100 Truitt Avenue
   Leased for past four years
   By Humbolt Warehouse Co., Inc.
   Sold today for unannounced figure
   To Holquitz Investment Corporation
   About 70,000 square feet in building
   Sale made by City Realty Co.
   Humbolt Company has 10-year lease
      (Source: Franklin Lamb, president, City Realty Co.)

B.   State Power Association announces safety awards
     City Power Company wins first place in state
     Award presented yesterday to Emmett Clark, president, City Power Co.
     At annual convention of State Power Association
     City Power Co. cited
     For 2,500,000 man-hours during year
     With only 26 lost-time accidents
     No permanent disabilities

C.   Trumpet Industries, Inc.
     Located on River Road
     One of city's oldest industries
     Well respected by businessmen
     Employs 900 persons
     Craig LeRoy Kennedy
     Has been with firm 14 years
     In engineering department
     Today was appointed vice president
     Announced by Carwell West, president
     Mr. Kennedy a native of this city
     Married, one child
     Lives 1402 Vineyard Drive
     Former president Kiwanis Club
     Graduate of City College
     As a small child, Mr. Kennedy was retarded
     Because of deficiency in hearing

D.   State Life Insurance Company
     Of Centerville
     Opened branch office here today
     J. T. Reed, manager
     Located in General Building
     Rooms 711-12
     Employs six agents
     Reed is local man
     Represented company here
     For 13 years
     Policies issued by
     State Life Insurance Company
     Are best in country
     Cost is less
     But returns are more
       (Source: Mr. Reed)

E. State Restaurant Association to meet at Capitalville
    Next weekend
    Local restaurateur, Lee M. Regastar, is vice president
    President of Regastar Restaurants, Inc.
    Expected to be elected president
    Approximately 500 restaurant operators to attend convention
    Principal speaker to be Senator T. M. Glumwater
    President of association is Fred S. Whipplepole of Hydeville
    Mr. Whipplepole has been a restaurateur for 30 years
    Is a great golfer
        (Source: Frank Fleming, secretary of association)

F. Sterling Clothing Company
    Located on Railroad Avenue
    Employs 880 persons
    Has been in city six years
    Established by group of local businessmen
    Ben H. Dummeridge is president
    Is a well regarded gentleman
    Now on chamber of commerce board
    A subscriber of your newspaper for 17 years
    Prior to heading up this new company
    Mr. Dummeridge was vice president, City Bank & Trust Co.
    Mr. Dummeridge said today
    That company is installing new equipment
    To quadruple production
    Will seek large government contracts
    If successful, will more than double number of employees
    Making all types of clothing
    New equipment costs $2,000,000
    Will take six months to install
    A few of employees do not like new machines
    But most approve of expansion plans
    Sterling's Board of Directors
    Jubilant over whole situation
    So is chamber of commerce

G. City National Bank
    Established 49 years ago
    Farris C. Johnston is president
    Bank has been located
    In old building at Commerce Avenue and Fifth Street
    Planning to relocate in new building
    A 20-story building to be constructed by bank
    Will house bank and offices for rent

Building permit obtained

For $5,000,000 structure

Will be one of city's largest buildings

Everyone is happy about this development

Building will be completed next year

Fiftieth anniversary of bank

Strong Construction Company

Will construct structure

New building located at Main Street and First Avenue

Home Drug Store now located there

This building will be razed

Is a quarter-block area

Home Drug Store to move

To new building at 403 First Avenue

Architects for new bank building

Williams & Sons, Architects

New building to have 367,000 square feet of floor space

Will be set back 25 feet from Main Street

Will rise 314 feet

An underground garage planned

For 200 cars

Eight elevators to serve building

To be modern design

Air conditioned throughout

H. Write a story using the following statement issued by Henry D. Lee, county agricultural agent:

"Extremely dry weather prevailing throughout the state has created an acute problem with respect to pasture and hay for livestock feed, and has to a great extent upset the cropping system on many livestock farms.

"Farmers are faced with the problem of providing supplemental pasture to replace a seriously decreased lespedeza crop, and additional hay to take the place of decreased production of red clover, lespedeza, alfalfa, and grass.

"There are certain things that can be done now to relieve the probable feed shortage. (1) Sow Sudan grass, which will provide grazing in about six weeks after seeding, and will last until frost. This applies particularly to dairymen. (2) Sow soybeans for hay, as they normally make considerable hay when seeded. (3) Arrange for additional acreage of corn or cane silage, which can be put up in a trench pit or temporary silo.

"Most of the clover and grass and some of the lespedeza

seeded in small grains perished during the drought. To secure returns from this land, in providing livestock feed that would have been obtained had there been no drought, is a problem on nearly half a million acres in the state. Some of this land may be used for Sudan, soybeans or silage. However, the majority of it should probably be prepared for summer seedings of winter cover crops."

I.   The following statement was issued by John D. Miller, president of Miller Realty Company, in answer to a prediction by the Blankville Builders Association that prices of building materials will rise and a warning to "build now."

"I don't know whether or not the prices on building materials will rise, but I'm reasonably sure that such price-boosting propaganda is a bad thing to be putting out—bad for the building industry and everybody connected with it.

"People will just stop building and wait if prices go up much. That's what they did, to a greater or less extent in times of the so-called 'recessions.' It was a consumer's strike in the face of rising prices which the public did not expect and could not stand. And that's exactly what will happen if unjustifiable price boosts are attempted.

"It may be remarked in this connection that for some years the prices of building materials, and especially of lumber, have followed a pattern all their own. How these prices maintain themselves through good times and bad is not understood by the average man."

IV. Following are three news releases which were given to you by the public relations agent of a local manufacturing firm on three different days. Explain what changes, if any, you would make in each of these releases before handing it in for publication.

A.

Wiley S. Knudsen, an engineer with the Gay Plastic Company here for the past nine years, is the firm's new chief engineer.

Mr. Knudsen succeeds H. S. Wilson, who resigned last week to accept a federal assignment overseas.

A graduate of the University of Blankville, Mr. Knudsen is a native of Hopesville. He was a civil engineer with the State Department of Highways for five years before joining the Gay firm.

B.

Now is the time to brighten up the home, and the Gay Plastic Company has several new products which will do just that.

The toothbrush holder, for example, can be an ugly thing in the bathroom—but not the colorful "Gaybrusher" which has recently been developed by the Gay Plastic Company.

The Gaybrusher is not only colorful but compact, and it has individual protected places for up to eight brushes.

Other items recently developed by the Gay Plastics Company are:

1. Combs and brushes which add flash to bedrooms and are as durable as steel.
2. Dishes and glasses which make the kitchen and dining room more cheerful.
3. Lamps and many other items which add color and happiness throughout the house.

C. (The following item submitted with picture of Miss Holdbrook in swim suit, holding a toothbrush holder):

MISS HOLDBROOK HOLDS HOLDER. Miss Marilyn Holdbrook, selected two days ago as "Miss Blankville," believes not only in romance and marriage but also in a large family.

"I love children and would like to have at least six of them," she said.

The new Miss Centerville also expressed her preference for color in the home where she will raise her large family. She was particularly praiseful of the "Gaybrusher," the beautifully colorful toothbrush holder now being manufactured by the Gay Plastics Company.

V. Complete the following exercises:

A. Write a story on the stock market based on the 15 imaginary stocks listed below (figures in first column are total shares sold; second, closing price; third, net change since yesterday).

Aching Motors	80,100	52	+ ½
Alley Bowling	28,395	38	− 4
Blue Thermometer	74,700	120	+ 6
Castor Oil	65,700	67¼	− ½
Dagger Steel	63,200	27¼	+ 1
Easy Tel and Tel	81,000	111	+10½
Fudge Wire	46,948	17½	− 2
Greasy Oil	58,948	48¼	− 1
Hair Corp	26,947	153	+ 2
Itchy Steel	85,376	38½	− 2
Junebug Industries	37,486	73	+ ¼
Kilroid	85,467	59½	+ 5
Messy Tobacco	36,286	19¼	2¼
Nosecovers	48,254	33	+ 1
Open Sesame	36,745	99¼	− 7

B. Write a story from the following monthly report on business activities issued by the Business Research Bureau of the University of Blankville:

THE PAST MONTH COMPARED WITH THE SAME MONTH LAST YEAR

	Percentage Change
New car registrations	+22
Construction contracts awarded	+15
Ordinary life insurance sales	+ 6
Mortgage loans	+ 4
Manufacturing employment	− 1
Bank debits	− 2
Prices received by farmers	− 4

THE ENTIRE YEAR COMPARED WITH THE SAME PERIOD LAST YEAR

Construction contracts awarded	+40
New car registrations	+28
Bank debits	+ 6
Ordinary life insurance sales	+ 4
Mortgage loans	+ 4
Manufacturing employment	+ 2
Prices received by farmers	+ 1

C. For some time
   Employees and employers
   Of local soft drink distributors
   Engaged in fuss over wages
   Both sides stubborn and unreasonable
   Today 200 salesmen, truck drivers, and warehouse workers
   Discourteously walked off job
   Broke off contract talks
   Between local Bottle Drink Union
   And representatives of soft drink distributors
   Said Lem D. Hopkins, spokesman for distributors,
   "We were negotiating in good faith, but they just walked off and
      left us."
   Mr. Hopkins has fought organized labor many times
   It is said he is an enemy of decent labor conditions
   Said Hugh D. Nelms, business agent of union
   "After trying time after time to get a settlement, we have come
      to the end of the line."
   Mr. Nelms is known as a domineering sort of person
   It is rumored that he would prefer a strike instead of a settlement

Union wants cent a case increase for salesmen for first year, two cents second year

Also 15 percent raise for truck drivers and warehouse workers

Soft drink distributors offered $2 base pay raise per week for salesmen and 2 percent increase for others

Said Hopkins: "The price of drinks has not changed in three years, but the workers have been given raises all along. We cannot afford to give what they are asking and stay in business."

Said Mr. Nelms: "With their increased business, they can well afford our requests. We are just asking them to share the wealth."

Distributors affected by the strike are City Bottling Company, Drane's Drinks, A and S Distributing Company, Health Bottlers, and Heaven Kist Drinks, Inc.

Officials of these companies absolutely refuse to talk, referring reporters to Mr. Hopkins

VI. Write stories from the following notes:

A. City Transit Authority
Has been having trouble with bus drivers
Drivers want 24 cents an hour increase
And shorter work week
Over 1,000 drivers involved
Strike had been planned and announced
But Superior Court held last week
That Bus Drivers Union could not strike against city agency
Averted walkout which would have stranded over 250,000 passengers
City Transit Authority today agreed
To submit disagreement to arbitration
The president of the union, Robert F. Parker
Said union would meet tomorrow
To consider arbitration offer
The offer is fair enough and we hope the union will accept

B. Report from the Agricultural Experiment Station of State University
Recommends steps to be taken now
To fertilize pastures
To produce healthy plants for early grazing
"Get your soil tested to determine the lime, phosphate and potash needs of your pasture"
Pasture production can be doubled
If no soil test recommendations for lime and fertilizer are followed

However, if no soil test is taken

You should fertilize straight fescue and orchardgrass pastures now with 500 pounds of 6-12-12 per acre,

If fescue or orchardgrass pastures were fertilized last fall

With phosphate and potash

These pastures should have top dress with 100 pounds of ammonium nitrate or its equivalent per acre

Fertilizing small grain with nitrogen can also help supply early feed

Use of 100 pounds of ammonium nitrate or its equivalent

Recommended for small grains

(Source: Harold S. Grimley, agronomist with Agricultural Experiment Station)

Chapter 25

Education, Research, Science

EDUCATIONAL institutions constitute one of the most important sources of news in a city. Everyone is (or should be) interested in the schools, for commencement speakers are unquestionably accurate when they point out the unstartling fact that today's school children are tomorrow's adult citizens. The press has a special interest in the fact that today's school children are learning to read tomorrow's newspapers. Furthermore, everyone has a direct personal connection with the community's schools; he or she is or has been a student, or is a parent, a grandparent, or some other relative of a student. Even if a local citizen does not fit into any of these categories, he or she is among those who give a substantial portion of their state and local taxes to support public education. Therefore education is of great public concern.

The newspaper should report newsworthy activities and developments of all educational institutions in its locality, from kindergartens to universities, particularly the public, church-related, and privately endowed schools. A community may also have a number of trade schools and "colleges" (secretarial, beauty, and technical) which are private commercial enterprises operated for the profit of the owners; these also deserve coverage, as would business houses, with stories limited to bona fide news to the exclusion of free advertising.

Research and education go together. Those in the field of education, especially those on the upper levels, seek not only to teach the knowledge already accumulated but also—through research—to add new knowledge to the annals of man. Research, of course, is by no means confined to educational institutions. Government agencies, industries, hospitals and clinics, and private laboratories sponsor many research programs. However, a large percentage of these programs are linked to educational institutions, either through special contracts or through the services of educators as consultants. In any event, educational institutions must train most if not all of the personnel qualified to operate research programs.

The word *science* has not been used so far in the discussion of

330

research. This word was purposely avoided because science and research are too often considered as synonymous. Research in the basic sciences, medical sciences, and engineering has become tremendously important, dramatically so, and some newspapers have recognized it to the extent of appointing science editors. Science deserves this recognition, but not to the exclusion of research in all other fields of knowledge. Studies in the humanities and the social sciences must not be neglected.

Since research is characteristic of the higher levels of education, it is one of the important types of news which the education reporter could gather in covering a college or university. As pointed out, research stories will also originate from other sources, but the procedures and problems of handling them are much the same regardless of the source.

Covering Education   25a

To cover the education beat effectively, the reporter must know the organizational structure of the institutions in his community. Whether it is a single school or a large education system, the organizational pattern of each will be much the same. At the top is some type of board, elected or appointed, on which membership is considered a public service. Generally composed of prominent individuals who meet as necessary from time to time and who serve without compensation, the board is responsible for the total operation of the school or the school system. Either the board employs or the voters elect an individual, preferably a professional educator, who serves as the chief administrator (superintendent, president, headmaster) of the school or system, and from that point on the functions of the board and the administrator are clearly defined.

The board, after consultation with the administrator, should set the basic policies for the operation of the school or the system, should decide on capital-outlay measures, and should formalize appointments, retirements, leaves of absence, and terminations of faculty and staff members. The administrator should be in complete charge of operating the school or system within the policies set forth by the board, and he should also make recommendations on the appointments, terminations, and other matters requiring formal board action. Board members are not (indeed, they must not be!) expected to move into the professionalized area of administration, nor should the administrator extend his authority beyond the policies fixed by the board. Unless the top echelon of the school or the school system functions under this accepted pattern, the operation is doomed to suffer controversies and diversion from its primary objective of educating young men and women.

The top organizational officials, as well as the subordinate ones (supervisors, principals, deans, directors, department heads), are vitally important to the operation of a school or an educational system, but the most important function is the teacher-student relationship. Everything else is done for the purpose of getting the teacher and the student together, giving them adequate facilities needed for the learning process, hoping that the student will absorb the desire for learning as well as the knowledge that the teacher can inspire and transmit. Presumably, if the organization is efficient and effective at the top levels, it will achieve these goals at the teacher-student level.

Scope of Coverage. The education reporter usually is expected to cover the activities of all levels in the institutions in his locality, from the policy-making boards to the teachers in the classrooms. Large or small, the education beat offers many routine stories as well as special articles which arise with particular developments in an individual school or an entire school system. Some of the routine stories:

1. Scheduled dates—opening and closing, holidays.
2. Enrollments—statistics, comparisons, trends.
3. Honors—citations of students and faculty.
4. Changes in curricula—courses added and dropped.
5. Commencements—speakers, graduating students.
6. Personnel changes—appointments, resignations, retirements.
7. Board meetings—policies, budgets, capital-outlay plans.
8. Activities of affiliated organizations—education associations, parent-teacher chapters, "booster" groups, alumni.

25b **Story Forms.** Education stories range from the one-feature brevity to the multifeature report of a significant board meeting. In between can be found all story forms, including human interest stories on students and teachers and feature articles on school activities.

Covering Research, Science   25c

Scientists and other scholars engaged in research are the fact-finding agents of society. Every advance the world can hope for is largely based upon new knowledge and constructive theories erected upon the new facts that are proved through scholarly research. Yet research is not enough. So long as science or scholarship remains enshrined in technical language, society cannot understand it fully. It must be interpreted to the people, reduced to terms which laymen and legislators can comprehend. As the chief medium of interpretation, the newspaper is a tool which research must learn to use, and research is a fertile field which the newspaper must explore.

The science editor or any other reporter covering research has problems and responsibilities which he must understand and master to do a creditable job. Reporting a research project—giving the public an understandable explanation of research findings—is quite often an assignment unlike any other that is given a journalist. He faces three challenges: first, the researcher (or researchers) ; second, the research project; and third, the accurate and interesting interpretation of that project to the public. Any one of those three can give the journalist a very difficult experience.

The Researcher. In interviewing a researcher, the reporter must keep in mind that the subject of the interview is usually not eager for (or perhaps even mildly interested in) newspaper publicity. A researcher sometimes fears publicity. He is afraid of both inaccuracies and sensationalism. Having spent days or months on a carefully worded paragraph, he is averse to having it slashed to bits in a three-minute effort by a reporter on the excuse of emphasizing an "interesting" feature. Dullness, often attached to preciseness, is the researcher's prerogative. Frequently he does not see—and may be indifferent to—the utility or human interest aspects of his work, and consequently he may have no sympathy whatever with the reporter's problems in writing the story for the general public.

The researcher may even be antagonistic toward publicity. A newspaper article on his project will mean little if anything to his professional career; the only publication that really counts is one in a professional journal which he himself prepares. More trouble-some, a researcher is sometimes untrusting of all newspaper reporters because of the experience that he (or his colleagues) may have had with slipshod or sensation-seeking or jokester reporters who have interviewed him in the past. Reporters have been guilty of mishandling research stories—of publishing serious errors and of poking fun at things the reporters have not understood—and this is a problem which competent reporters must avoid.

Obviously, then, the reporter's opening task is to establish himself with the researcher, winning enough confidence for at least a chance to show a sincere desire for accurate interpretation. An explanation of the need for public appreciation of research is the reporter's main approach, a need to which a researcher should agree. Although they may be publicity-shy individuals, secure in the cloisters of their laboratories and libraries, researchers are generally understanding people who will respond to sincere expressions of interest and cooperation. Some of them need more persuading than others. While the reporter must admit local newspaper publicity may not add to a researcher's professional stature, the points can be discreetly made that such publicity does enhance the prestige of the researcher's institution or organization and that it will attract favorable attention to him (and his family) in the community.

The Research Project. A reporter must recognize the two broad types of research: (1) basic or fundamental research and (2) practical or utilitarian research. Further, he must understand that a basic research project, even though it may make little sense to him, is the predecessor of practical research, the value of which is evident. The atom was not split until numerous basic research projects uncovered fundamental secrets of the atom. Andrew Johnson was not vindicated as an able President until research brought to light the intimate facts regarding his tribulations and decisions. If the reporter does not understand the value of a basic research project, that does not make the project one whit less justified. Neither the average reporter nor the general public is competent to judge its value.

Many thousands of research projects, basic and practical, are being conducted at considerable cost to the people of the nation. Some projects will turn out as failures, but others will pay spectacular practical dividends that make the total cost of research look small indeed.

It is fairly easy to report a project dealing with an improvement in automobile windshield wipers. But what can be done, for example, with a project "concerned with the synthesis and biochemical evaluation of drugs which influence psychological processes through their effects upon the central nervous system"? The answer calls for interpretative skill.

Interpretation of the Research Project. While dullness is the researcher's prerogative, it is the reporter's enemy. Given **25d** a task of writing an interesting story, the reporter seeks to humanize the research project, spelling out what it means to the public. If the reporter can find what the discovery or theory means to the average person, he has the key to the story—the lead feature. The rest of the story provides the details necessary to give the layman a clear picture.

The keys to research projects designed to fill specific practical needs are ready-made, but the secrets of many basic projects are not easily unlocked. For basic research the reporter must interpret the nature and findings of the project without stretching facts in an attempt to indicate practical value. The interpretation can perhaps explain that a project reveals knowledge that *may* contribute to the solution of practical problems, but this must be done with extreme caution. Between the following two paragraphs, for example, is a world of difference:

> The reaction of cells to certain acids manufactured by the human body is being studied by Dr. A. B. Count, Blank University zoology professor, who hopes his findings will contribute basic knowledge to science's fight against cancer.
>
> A cure for cancer is being sought by Dr. A. B. Count, Blank University zoology professor, in studying the reaction of cells to certain acids manufactured by the human body.

If the first paragraph is accurate, no one can blame Dr. Count for becoming furious with the reporter who takes the liberty of "interpreting" the basic research project as is done in the second paragraph. As a researcher who demands facts and accuracy, he cannot shrug off such "sensationalizing" reporting. He considers such extravagant claims as damaging to his professional career, and he remembers this the next time a reporter approaches him for a story.

While the reporter (with the researcher's consent) attempts to indicate a practical use of a research project, however remote that use may be, there are times when no practical angle is available. These are cases of pure basic research being performed solely for the purpose of discovering new knowledge. Sometimes that new knowledge (or the search for it) is itself interesting enough to give the reporter the key to his story. Other times it may be so complicated and so far from public interest that the reporter must abandon the story.

In gathering information to interpret a research story the reporter must ask many questions. He must convert technical terms into common language, and this requires many questions. He must be sure the possible lead angles that he detects are accurate, requiring more questions. In other words, the reporter himself should have a clear understanding of what he is attempting to explain or he may garble the whole story in pursuit of an erroneous idea.

25e **Story Forms.** All forms can be used in writing research stories, which could range in length from one paragraph to several columns. If the research has significant practical value, the straight news format is generally used. As the practical value diminishes, there is a rise in the use of the feature story form to achieve a more interesting presentation.

Exercises

I. Clip and analyze four stories on different aspects of education, research, and science (at least one on science).

II. Outline the different school systems, schools, and agencies from which research and science stories would be available in your locality.

III. Write stories using the following notes

A. Riverside College
On River Park Boulevard
Founded five years ago
Dr. John L. Park is president
Has 40 faculty members
Over 400 students
A junior college
Dr. Park received notice today
Riverside accredited
By regional accrediting agency
This is great
Dr. Park says it means
All students completing courses at Riverside
Accepted by other institutions without question

B. Western College at Whitesburg
Gives scholarships
For chemistry competition
Local City High School senior

Charles Killory
Son of Mr. and Mrs. Howard J. Killory
1835 Greer Street
Wins $450 scholarship
For first place
Al G. Allenberg
Local East High senior
Son of Mr. and Mrs. M. M. Allenberg
140 White Avenue
Wins second prize
Of $300 scholarship
These two have been
Outstanding science students
At respective schools
According to their principals

C. Announcement made
   By City College President H. D. Smith
   Commencement activities
   May 25 and 26
   At college auditorium
   Baccalaureate at 7 p.m. May 25
   By Rev. Leon Ring
   Pastor, First Baptist Church
   Graduation exercises at 10 a.m. May 26
   Thirty-five to get bachelor's degree
   Speaker Dr. William Sawyer
   Director of Winstill Laboratories
   Annual Alumni Dinner
   To be in college cafeteria
   At 7 p.m. May 26
   President Smith to speak
   To tell of college's new development plans
   Will ask alumni for money, of course

D. Dr. David Clinton
   Retired last year
   As dean of business
   City University
   After 35 years of service
   Was a good dean
   His successor is
   Dr. George Artista Jr.
   Head of accounting department
   At Trist College

Was named today
By Board of Trustees
Of City University
Appointment effective first of next month
Dr. Artista has B.S. from City University
M.S. and Ph.D. from Columbo University
At Trist College for 14 years
Previously taught at Columbo for 10 years
Author of three textbooks
Married, three children
Native of this state
Father was noted Presbyterian pastor

E. The following enrollment figures were released today by Dr. Z. D. Kress, registrar of City University:

ENROLLMENT BY COLLEGES

	Today	5 Years Ago	10 Years Ago
Arts and Sciences	2,007	1,402	912
Business	1,630	1,420	1,101
Education	1,211	1,001	710
Engineering	1,511	1,360	1,202
Law	130	95	72
Graduate School	1,000	501	200
Grand Total	7,489	5,779	4,197

F. City University faculty met yesterday
Adopted following courses to be added
To University curricula

ENGLISH 21E. *Composition for Technical Students.* Designed to give writing experience for students in the various sciences. Three hours.

CHEMISTRY 41E. *Radiochemistry.* An advanced study of nuclear chemistry and radiochemistry. Four hours.

HISTORY 33K. *Diplomacy and Foreign Policy of the United States Since 1898.* The development of foreign policies after the United States became a world power. Three hours.

ZOOLOGY 40G. *Radiation Biology.* A basic course devoted to a study of radiation techniques and research and their application in the various fields of biology. Four hours.

PHYSICS 44 F. *Experimental Physics: Atomic and Nuclear.* Measurements of e, e/m, h/e, resonance potentials, X-ray absorption, half-lives, beta-ray and gamma-ray absorption, gamma spectra, specific activity, alpha-particle ranges, and radiation dosage. Two hours.

PHYSICS 54D. *Cosmic Rays and Relativistic Phenomena.* Dealing with the field of cosmic rays. Topics include relativity theory, interaction of cosmic rays with matter, shower theory, properties and production of mesons. Three hours.

ASTRONOMY 31F. *Celestial Mechanics.* The mechanics of systems of gravitating particles, with emphasis upon the calculation of orbits, theory of perturbations. Three hours.

G. West Southeast Association of Colleges and Schools
    Regional accrediting agency
    For high schools, colleges, and universities
    Held annual meeting
    Opened here today
    At Uptown Hotel
    1,000 delegates attended
    To meet again tomorrow morning
    Will close with noon luncheon
    Speeches and discussions held throughout today
    On many different subjects
    Harvey Hewey, librarian of Triview College
    Explained new phases of library cataloging system
    Applied to cataloging of periodicals
    Made very interesting talk
    Of interest to librarians and educators
    Dr. William Ford Frye, president
    Of Whoopla University
    Spoke on freshman admission policies
    Of colleges and universities
    Said admissions standards at most institutions
    Still too low
    Too many unqualified students
    Permitted to enroll
    A waste of time and money, he says
    "The idea that, in a democracy, every student should have the
        opportunity of a college education is not based on wisdom.
        Everyone in a democracy does not have the same capabilities.
        For example, everyone is not qualified to receive an automobile
        driver's license. It is sheer nonsense that an unqualified
        person be permitted to enter college."
    Panel discussion held
    On policies pertaining to salaries
    Of elementary and high school teachers
    Panelists were Jackson Switch, president Blank City School
        Board; Dr. Whipple Bornfree, superintendent of schools of

Zero County; and Miss Grace Slowglue, seventh-grade teacher
of Switchville Junior High

All panelists favored

"Merit policy" in

Fixing salaries of teachers

Were against set salaries

Based solely on years of service

Said Dr. Bornfree, "Individual initiative is discouraged under a
system where all teachers get the same salary based on the
number of years they manage to hang on as a faculty
member."

Miss Slowglue said a great majority

Of teachers themselves

Favor merit system

Mr. Switch pointed out

Dangers of favoritism in merit system

He said, "However, risking this danger is more desirable than
the annual increment system of fixing salaries."

At sessions tomorrow morning

Will discuss ways of relieving teachers

Of unnecessary chores

And also will talk about

Year-round employment of teachers

As a means of increasing their annual income

IV. Write stories using the following notes:

A. Meeting of Dental Research Section
Of State Dental Association
Held at Fleming Hotel this morning
Speaker was Dr. Karl J. Williams
Of Blank City General Hospital
Who is chief of prosthetics
Dr. Williams said
Research shows direct relationship
Between occlusion of teeth
And ailments of muscles and joints
"The tensions of a person are affected by occlusion far greater
than dentists formerly realized," he said.
Dr. Williams predicted
That further research will enable dentists
To contribute more
To neurology, physiology, and anatomy
As well as "mending the teeth"

B. Blankville Medical College
   Experimenting with new therapy
   Three hundred inmates Western State Hospital
   All victims of paresis
   Placed in hospital (here)
   Infected with malaria fever
   By bite of malaria-carrying mosquitoes
   To induce temperature
   Which will arrest paresis
   Research men hope to obtain
   More exact information
   On this therapy
   Through experiment
   Careful record of all patients kept
   Paresis is disease caused by syphilis
   Eventually kills victim
   Malaria method only cure known
   Statistics show 60 percent
   Those taking treatment
   Have been cured.
   (Source: Dr. J. D. Moore, administrative officer of Blankville
   Medical College)

C. Radioisotope Conference scheduled
   Here the 4th and 5th of next month
   At City University
   More than 400 scientists expected to attend
   Will be an important affair
   Meeting in Science Building auditorium
   Dr. Lester R. Ward, head of physics department, in charge
   Scientists from throughout nation and several foreign countries
   will attend
   Leading authorities will present papers on following subjects,
   which will be discussed:
   Trends in Nuclear Instrumentation
   A Wide-Bandpass Transistorized Ratemeter for Alpha-
   Gauge Measurements
   Alpha Particle Energy Resolution in the Liquid Scintillator
   A liquid Densitometer with Improved Sensitivity Employ-
   ing X-ray Transmission Techniques
   Neuron Flux Perturbation in Activation Analysis
   A Radiometric Determination of an Adsorption Isotherm
   of a Surfactant on an Organic Subtrate
   The Application of Radiochemistry to Semiconductor Re-
   search

Study of the Vacuum Distillation Process and Thin-Film
Deposition with the Radioactive Tracer

The U.S. Atomic Energy Commission Isotope Development Program

Measurement of Diffusivity in a High-Viscosity Liquid

Removal of Radioiodine from Hot-Off-Gas Systems by
Charcoal Adsorption

Use of Radioisotope Technique in Undergraduate Research

Radiotracer Analysis of Catalyst Flow Distribution

Large-Scale Use of Radiotracers for Leak Detection in the
Space Vehicle

Radiotracer Technique for Determining Stream Flow Rates

Power Applications of Radionuclides

Silage Density Measured by Gamma-Energy Attenuation

Nuclear Transducers for Digital Control Systems

Some Applications of Radioactive Isotopes to the Measurement of Coating Thicknesses and Analysis by Means of
X-Ray Fluorescence and by Compton Effect

V. Many persons have been calling the newspaper office about the
recent appearance of locusts in your vicinity. They fear the insects
are ruining trees. You call Dr. John L. Church, state entomologist,
and get the following quotations for a story:

Since they make their appearance at such lengthy intervals,
most people are not familiar with them. Hearsay has led many
to believe that they poison trees on which they deposit their
eggs, but they are harmless in every way. They are commonly
called 13-year singing locusts, but the entomological name for
them is *periodic cicada* or *cicada tredecim*. Take your choice.
I don't know whether or not many people want to know the
true name. The life of this insect is interesting. They live in the
ground for 12½ years; then come up to develop into adults,
reproduce, and die. As adults, they look a lot like flies, particularly jar flies. They do no harm because they eat nothing
after they come out of the ground. They are more of a beneficial than a harmful insect to the farmer. When they fall to
the ground, the swine eat them. Not only are they very palatable
to the swine, but they are very fattening. The only damage they
can do is done by the female. She has a javelin-like appendage
on the bottom of her body, and uses it to cut into the bark of
trees to deposit her eggs. This constitutes a sort of general
pruning, not especially injurious to large forest trees, but hard
on fruit trees and disastrous to young trees and nursery stock.
The insects will all be dead in a few months. Their shrill noise

is made by the male, who has small cymbals on the bottom of his body, which he vibrates at different speeds. The male courts his mate by calling to her with the cymbals. The mate can make no noise. The female will deposit her eggs on a tree. After 10 days the eggs hatch, and the young fall to the ground and burrow in. They attach their mouths to roots, from which they get their food. This does not harm trees, either.

VI. Interview some faculty member of your institution engaged in research and write a story on his research work.

VII. Suggest newsworthy pictures and write appropriate cutlines on the following preceding assignments in this chapter: Exericse III, D and Exercise V.

VIII. Write a newscast using the following preceding assignments in this chapter: Exercise III, A; Exercise III, E; Exercise IV, A and Exercise IV, C.

Chapter 26

Religion, Philanthropy, Promotion

RELIGION and philanthropy both involve man's subordination of his own interests to those of serving his fellow man. Religion preaches this philosophy; philanthropy practices it. The two are intertwined insofar as service to mankind is concerned, but from the newspaper's standpoint the expressions of such service desires are made through a variety of news sources which are not closely related. In this respect religious institutions form a large category of similar news sources; philanthropic movements involve many different news sources. Promotion deals with the newspaper's editorial support of these efforts in behalf of public welfare.

Religion

The vital force of spiritual life in a civilized society leaves no question of the newspaper's responsibility to report religious activities and developments. Of course, the newspaper of general circulation should advocate no one religion but should be a channel of communications for all religions. Freedom of religion, like freedom of the press, is protected by the Bill of Rights of the United States Constitution, and the press must recognize both the place of religion and the right of religious choice in its columns.

The proportion will vary from community to community, but a conservative estimate is that substantially more than half the people served by a newspaper are members of a church or synagogue. Hence, news on religion will have many potential readers. While religious institutions have a large total membership, the news interest of an individual member is, first, in his own church; second, in his denomination; then, to a milder degree, in other churches. Sometimes the churches are competitive to the point that publicity given to one may stir up jealousies of the members of others—even of the same denomination. Religion news must therefore be broad enough in denominations, diverse enough in the same denominations, and selective enough in the newsworthiness of materials used that readers will recognize the stories on religious activities as solid news rather than puffy publicity.

Religion news is published by some newspapers as a special section or page. A member of the staff may hold the title of religion editor or church editor (often in addition to other duties), and it is his or her job to gather and write the special section.

Not all news on religion appears in the special section. Sometimes church activities make front-page news. A hotly contested, pastor-versus-a-faction-of-the-congregation controversy is one example. A church's entering the political arena to persuade members to vote for or against an important issue or a candidate for public office is another. News sources cultivated by the religion editor in handling routine stories often prove valuable in gathering information when such special stories develop.

The religion reporter must learn the organizational patterns of the churches he writes about, for the sources of news on religion include church-governing officials as well as local churches. Church organization varies widely between the different denominations. Some are completely independent, and they select their ministers and set up their own programs. At the other extreme, local churches are under the strong control of a central governing body, which assigns the ministers to the various churches and also has a strong influence on the local program of each church. The program of a church encompasses many activities in addition to worship services and Sunday schools. It may also include the sponsorship of such projects as foreign missionary work, local relief projects, kindergartens, grade and high schools, and colleges and universities. All of these activities make news, in the religion section, in the education section, or on the front page or other sections when there are special news breaks.

The Religion Section or Church Page. Newspapers which carry a regular page or section on religion use a well-organized **26a** plan of compiling news for that section. Church officials are informed that they must submit materials for the section by a specified deadline, which puts the burden of getting publicity on the churches and thus protects the religion editor from some of the criticism of members whose churches are not mentioned in the news.

Some highly newsworthy stories can often be harvested from the materials submitted by the churches, but for the most part these handouts must be condensed into one- or two-paragraph stories if used at all. On the other hand, the reporter may have to get additional information to build up the better stories that are submitted.

A religion editor or reporter, to be a good one, must take pride in his assignment, for he can make the news on religion as important as he makes his job. If he looks upon his work as a chore, news on religion will be no more than a compilation of briefed-down handouts. If he wants his section to be strong influence in the spiritual life of the community, he can make it reflect accurately the community's religious tone. The religion reporter who depends wholly upon church handouts for his news is a victim of one of three (or a combination of three) serious ailments: (1) lazy habits, (2) little interest in writing religion news, or (3) poor newspapermanship. To do an acceptable job, the reporter must plan his section in advance, scheduling significant stories and features on the most newsworthy developments, on timely or seasonal events, and on important trends in the religious life of the community. Such stories as these require that the reporter seek out his information. In some of these cases the church handouts can give him ideas and can be incorporated in the stories, but in all cases the reporter must do some interviewing, analyzing, and writing.

Following are some subjects and types of stories which the reporter may garner from materials submitted by the churches and from his own efforts:

1. Regular worship services (some newspapers publish a weekly listing of church services).
2. Sermons—if unusual.
3. New buildings or other facilities.
4. Changes in church personnel.
5. Special events and campaigns—evangelistic efforts, fund-raising drives for worthy causes, attendance promotions.
6. New policies of local church or denominational groups.
7. Meetings of denominational groups, ministerial associations, and lay groups.
8. Human interest and feature stories—on unusual church members, historical anniversaries, retiring pastors, interesting projects of Sunday School classes, work of missionaries.

Interpreting Religious Terminology. In stories on religion, as **26b** in so many other story types, there are technical words and phrases to deal with. One denomination's language is often another's jargon. What is called the *pastor* in one story may be the *father, rabbi, elder* in other stories. The *parsonage* in one story is the *manse* or *rectory* in another. These and other religious terms must be understood by the reporter, must be interpreted if necessary, and must be used correctly if used at all.

Philanthropy

The basic meaning of philanthropy is "love for mankind." However, a secondary and more general meaning has developed which entails the expression of such love and concern for others in terms of hard cash. Fund raising is the objective of drives, campaigns, civic projects, and numerous other efforts in behalf of philanthropic movements to contribute to the health, welfare, and betterment of the community.

Philanthropy includes a wide diversity of activities, among which are projects designed to promote and support religious and educational institutions and programs, the cultural arts (music, drama, art), character-building youth groups, welfare agencies of all types, senior citizen organizations, Christmas charities, disaster relief, hospitals, community civic projects, historical observances, recreational facilities, the treatment of and research for the cure of diseases and disabilities, and other promotions which culminate in fund-raising efforts. Not all philanthropic movements ask for money, however. Some solicit a person's time; others, a pint of blood; or housing accommodations for visitors; or old clothes and newspapers; or a pledge to drive safely or to eliminate fire hazards. Whether for money or for blood, all of these movements are in the public welfare—the service of mankind—and, as such, are associated with philanthropy.

Sponsors of philanthropic movements are many times more numerous than the types of movements. Included are the Community Chest or United Fund organizations; Red Cross; Salvation Army; the YMCA and YWCA; Boy Scouts and Girl Scouts; all types of civic and service clubs and fraternal groups; drama, music, and art societies; recreation organizations; health associations such as those serving in the areas of tuberculosis, heart disease, and various paralytic afflictions; societies to assist the blind, deaf, and physically handicapped; and churches, schools, colleges, hospitals, and similar institutions. Newspapers also sponsor their own philanthropic promotions. Some of the various philanthropic movements are short-term drives; others are long-term continuing efforts.

The newspaper, a public service institution itself, is by its very nature interested in philanthropic programs and promotions. Much space and the time of reporters and editors will be contributed to the success of worthy causes. In these cases the newspaper often will make an exception to its regular demands for stories based strictly on newsworthiness, and it will accept material that is more promotional than informative.

Problems in Publicizing Philanthropy. Handling news of philanthrophy poses some special problems for a newspaper. Often an editor must take the responsibility of deciding whether the publicity being sought is intended to promote the self-interest of an individual or organization rather than a charitable or other social goal. If a newspaper uses all of the publicity that certain groups wish, it risks loss of reader interest and consequently of circulation. On the other hand, if it restricts such publicity sharply, the newspaper risks loss of the goodwill of the groups involved.

The number of different philanthropies has increased to the point that the public has insisted upon the consolidation of many of the fund-raising campaigns under the Community Chest or the United Fund plan. At one time several different campaigns were being conducted simultaneously almost every week of the year, and frequently the same volunteer workers were called upon to assist in most of them. The United Fund plan has combined most of these campaigns, with givers urged to make larger donations to cover many services, and this has sharply reduced the number of campaigns and the demands upon volunteer workers. Newspapers, having to bear a heavy portion of the promotional work, were among the chief advocates of the United Fund plan. Some newspapers decline to participate in campaigns which the editors believe should be part of the United Fund, but this restriction applies only to permanently organized philanthropic groups and not to short-term campaigns organized on a one-time basis by service clubs, fraternal organizations, and other public groups.

26c **Promoting Philanthropic Movements and Civic Projects.** Various media are used in campaigns and drives—letters, brochures, meetings, radio, television—but newspapers serve as the principal channel of communication for most of the promotional efforts. However, it must be recognized that newspapers (and other news media) have a limited role in the success of such campaigns, particularly those involving fund raising.

The most effective method of soliciting funds is the person-to-person approach—the volunteer worker visiting the prospective donor. Solicitation by mail and other means are used when the number of prospective donors is so great that direct contact is impractical. How does the newspaper fit into these approaches? Publicity given a project in the press will "set the stage" and help develop a climate of genorisity among prospective donors. And of course the recognition afforded by publicity stories is important in obtaining and encouraging volunteer workers. However, the sponsors of the project will be greatly disappointed in expecting such publicity to do the whole job. While many people may be inclined to give to a worthy cause publicized in the press, very few remember to respond to their inclinations unless a solicitor visits them or a letter reminds them. These are things that the reporter and the campaign sponsor should keep in mind, or they may expect too much from newspaper publicity.

A newspaper can publish many promotional stories for philanthropic movements and projects. Following is a listing of some of the developments which could be reported:

1. Initial announcement of campaign or project.
2. Appointment of person in charge of project.
3. Appointment of personnel or committees who will assist.
4. Various meetings of campaign workers—goals set, campaign plans, time schedules.
5. Series of straight news stories, features, and human interest stories reporting recent benefits of the project.
6. Special stories on large donations.
7. Progress reports on campaign.
8. Stories on conclusion of campaign and its achievements.

Exercises

I. Clip from the newspapers four different stories on religion and philanthropy and make analyses.
II. Define the following religious terms:

Diocese	Synod
Congregational Church	Presbytery
Fundamentalist	Predestinarian
Unitarian	Transfiguration
Trinitarian	Consistory
Christian Scientist	Arminian
Ban	Calvinists

Adventist	Sacrament
Pentecostal	Plenary
Orthodoxy	Liturgy

III. Attend a church service (or chapel program) and write a story on the pastor's sermon.

IV. Write stories using the following notes:

A. Westside Presbyterian Church
   Has been without pastor for two months
   Lay members and visiting preachers
   Have filled pulpit each Sunday
   Since death of the Rev. William H. Knox
   New pastor was appointed last month
   The Rev. Hewlett J. Roddy
   Pastor of Bradfield (Fla.) Presbyterian Church
   Accepted call as pastor here
   Mr. Roddy has moved here
   Will deliver first sermon here next Sunday
   He and family settled in
   Westside Presbyterian Church manse
   At 1619 Little Road
   Three children: Ann, 15; Frank, 12; Susan, 10
   Mrs. Roddy is piano teacher
   All members of family play piano
   Family's two pianos being moved here
   Mr. Roddy is graduate of Triview College and Chicago Seminary
      (Source: Mr. Roddy)

B. First Baptist Church
   Will have big revival
   Services will be held at church
   Every evening at 7 p.m. next week
   Will close with Sunday morning services
   At 11 a.m. Sunday week
   The Rev. Harry Towne Meyers, pastor of West End Baptist Church, Bigtown
   Will be guest evangelist
   Guest music director will be Thomas H. Everrett, noted music director, also with West End Baptist
   Dr. Meyers had conducted revivals in 25 states
   Is well known as an inspirational speaker
   The Rev. Garrett Wilkerson, pastor of First Baptist
   Will assist in the special services
      (Source: Mr. Wilkerson)

C. Jewish congregations here
   To participate in observing
   Festival of Purim
   Also called "Festival of Lots"
   Begins at sundown
   A traditional observance
   Arising from historical episode
   When Haman, prime minister of ancient Persia
   Ordered death decree for all Jews as of specific day
   But Queen Esther persuaded king to overrule Haman
   For this festival
   Children given noisemakers to use
   When Haman's name mentioned
   In reading of Old Testament Book of Esther
   Purim services planned at 7:30 p.m. Saturday
   To be repeated at 8:30 a.m. Sunday
      (Source: Rabbi Max Strauss)

D. Each Sunday morning
   Young Adult Class of Hillsboro Methodist Church
   Sunday School
   Will "roll out the barrel"
   Members bring gifts to fill barrel
   Gifts are sent to the Rev. and Mrs. James E. Coleman
   Methodist missionaries in the Congo
   Clothing of all types
   Sewing materials and cloth
   Blankets, thread, yarn, etc.
   Placed in barrel
   Project was started at suggestion
   Of Mrs. Horace E. Saunders, class president
      (Source: Mrs. Adams Lovett, class secretary)

E. St. Thomas Episcopal Church
   At church supper last evening
   Turned out to be surprise birthday party
   For Henry (Old Hank) L. Winters
   Custodian for the church
   On 70th birthday
   Has been with church for 30 years
   Mr. Winters had been told to be there
   To help clean up after supper
   Was called before group and given many presents
   Including plane ticket to visit daughter
   And new suit of clothes

Mr. Winter visibly shaken by event

Thanked church members profusely

"I've always been poor as a church mouse, but I'm rich with friends like you," he said

Dr. David M. Seymour, rector

Said Mr. Winters has always been reliable, energetic worker

And one of most loyal church members

    (Source: Dr. Seymour)

F. State meeting to be held here tomorrow

    Representatives of Roman Catholic Churches

    Directors and co-chairmen

    Of periodic census

    Taken by church

    Next June will count all Catholics in state

    Also number of children

    Also the number of marriages of Catholics to members other faiths

    For last census the state diocese

    Had over 175,000 Catholics

    Increase expected since then

        (Source: the Rev. Michael Brady)

G. The Rev. John T. Black, pastor of St. John's Lutheran Church

    Gave special services for college students

    At noon yesterday

    Excerpts from sermon follow—

        "There are four words which lie at the very heart of life's problems today. They are freedom, authority, worship, and obedience. There is no such thing as absolute freedom: that is freedom to do whatever I want to do. You can wreck your own life and the life of others by doing exactly what you want to do . . .

        "There is what is known as a vested authority; that which belongs to government officials and others in our society representing us in places of leadership. There is another authority which rests upon truth and right. Jesus spoke with authority. He exercised authority in cleansing the temple. . . .

        "In cleansing the temple Jesus was speaking for an inalienable human right, the right to worship. It is here we find the principle that justifies the right of revolution. If authority is abused and the rights of men are transgressed, revolution may become necessary. The British Crown had imposed the tax on tea, but our revolutionary fathers struck for human rights and self-government. We recognize the unwritten law of right in control of this universe, and no one is free to transgress human rights and the righteousness of God. . . .

"What is freedom under Christ? First of all it is voluntary, motivated by love. The first limitation a Christian places on his freedom is the will of Christ. In every decision he asks, 'What would Jesus have me do?' Paul voiced it this way, 'Christ liveth in me.'

"The second limitation on Christian freedom is the effect our conduct will have upon others. We are so bound up together in the bundle of life that no man lives unto himself. All that we do affects others for good or evil. No man is free to do as he pleases unless he pleases to do right. No one is free to do wrong."

V. Write stories from the following notes:

A. Last week
Plans completed on campaign
To raise $100,000
For County Heart Association
Yesterday about 120 volunteers
Held luncheon at Ritz Hotel
Jarvis Armistead, local attorney who is campaign chairman
Gave pep talk
Today workers began soliciting
Business firms and homes of county
"We have one of the best records of any city our size, and we
    want to keep it," said Mr. Armistead
Fund will be used for research in heart disease
And assisting special cases of needy heart patients
    (Source: Hal Druid, executive secretary of association)

B. Suggest a suitable promotion picture for assignment A and write cutlines.

C. West Blankville Businessmen's Club
Has been active
In many civic projects
Takes on new project
To increase collection
Of Westside Library
Decided to conduct campaign soliciting books
And money to buy books
Leonard T. Bunch, club president
Authorized to appoint special committee

To carry out campaign
At club's meeting last night
Hope to get at least 5,000 books
For Westside Library
Used by school children
As well as adults of area
  (Source: Mr. Bunch)

D. Suggest a suitable promotion picture for assignment C and write cutlines.

E. Blankville has
A very good Symphony Orchestra
Whistler Hemington, famous conductor, is director
City's best musicians
Are members
Orchestra is an asset to the city
It has been artistically successful
But is struggling financially
Will begin annual campaign
Next Monday
Selling season tickets to concerts
Sales from these tickets
Constitute basic budget for orchestra
Telephone campaign planned
Volunteer workers will call for subscriptions
Tickets: $10 regular price; $25 for "contributors"; $100 for "patrons"
Chauncey Keating, president of Keating Industries
Is chairman of Blankville Symphony Board
In charge of campaign
"It has been hard going, financially speaking, for the orchestra," he said
"If Blankville wants good music, support of the orchestra is the way to show it," he added
  (Source: Mr. Keating)

F. Suggest a promotion picture for assignment E and write cutlines.

G. City's United Fund
Sponsors industrial firm
Which employs handicapped persons
Firm's name, Faithope Industries
Located at 103 Fifth Street
220 persons working there
Manufacture wide variety of novelties
Conditions of plant overcrowded

Special committee of United Fund
Today approved campaign
To raise $850,000 for expansion
Of Faithope Industries
To increase employment
To 400 persons
Campaign plan to be organized
To solicit contributions
   (Source: William H. Henley, chairman of United Fund)

H. Suggest a promotion picture for assignment G and write cutlines.

VI. Suppose you were appointed publicity chairman of a student campaign on your campus to raise a fund for new band uniforms. Outline publicity plans for the campaign, detailing your suggestions on possible promotional stories and pictures.

THE COMPLETE REPORTER
PART SEVEN

WRITING THE SPECIAL STORY TYPES

The following discussions concern more specialized types of writing than those examined previously. The sports page, the society page, the editorial page, and reviewing or criticism are usually considered to be newspaper departments with special problems of their own.

The principles of straight news reporting apply to all special types of writing when the news intention is paramount. Both the sports page and society are primarily news departments. Both go in for extracurricular activities, however, and develop certain devices of their own.

Editorials and criticism are largely beyond the news intention, but they are based upon the news, and the reporter will touch both sooner or later in his assignments.

Chapter 27

Society-Women's Section

DECIDING the title of this chapter was a problem. Virtually all newspapers used to have a page or section labeled "Society," which contained information on social activities of the community's elite—people who were Society-with-the-capital "S." Now most newspapers strive to make it more of a society-with-a-small "s" section for and about the entire community. However, while its scope has been broadened, this section still is designed to appeal primarily to women, the most faithful readers. The editor assumes and hopes, nevertheless, that men will also be interested in reading this section, since they too are involved in social functions.

The names now given this section by various newspapers reveal the transition from the capital to the small "s." "Society-Home," "Society and Women," "For and About Women," "Woman's World," and "Women" are some of the titles, but a number of newspapers have stuck with "Society" while changing the contents of the section. Besides devoting attention to the entire social life of the community instead of merely chronicling activities of a select few persons, the modern society section has taken on the responsibility of keeping women informed on all phases of home life, from a recipe for biscuits to a formula for a happy marriage. Moreover, with the blossoming out of women in the business and professional worlds during and after World War II, the society section is also concerned with women's activities in these fields.

Except on the smallest newspapers the society-women's section is under supervision of a special editor, and on the larger newspapers this editor has one or more assistants. The writers of this section usually operate independently of the city editor, and they may be responsible only for the gathering and writing of news or also for the editing—copyreading, rewriting, headlining, and makeup.

The society-women's staff of a newspaper is generally a "woman's world" both figuratively and literally. In a few cases, however, men serve as competent members of this staff.

News Values. Personal items occupy a large amount of space on the society page, and their reader appeal may be measured by the various news values in miniature (see Chapter 15), but the largest single value is eminence. The eminence of the persons involved measures the importance and therefore the length of society stories. Eminence in this sense must be understood as local and relative rather than national or absolute. The smallest and most unpretentious town or community will possess its relatively important social personages. It was to report the nonessential and purely social activities of these persons and groups that the society page was created. Since social importance is relative, the newspaper is usually liberal with its space and does not recognize too definitely a favored "society set." It bases its general policy on the principle that names, especially the well-known names, make news and that all names make news if they are involved in certain types of activities suitable for the society-women's section.

Types of Society-Women's News. All engagements and weddings are reported in greater or less detail as measured by the eminence of the contracting parties. Indeed, the wedding has more content and substance than most other social events. It is news in the sense of having economic and social consequences aside from highlighting a social "season." Most other material used in the society-women's section can be classified as follows:

1. Personals and brevities not carried elsewhere in the newspaper.
2. Births (if not published elsewhere).
3. Entertainments: receptions, teas, parties, dances, luncheons, dinners.
4. Women's clubs and organizations: routine meetings, programs, speeches, and special activities such as benefits, bazaars, recitals, and charities.
5. The society column of gossip and editorialized comment.
6. Stories and columns on fashions, recipes, child training, gardening, interior decorating, family relationships.
7. Stories and columns on local women in the business and professional worlds.

News Sources. The society editor generally becomes personally acquainted with the prominent women and others of the community who are the principal news sources. Weddings and many social events are planned with the cooperation of the society reporter and with adequate publicity arrangements. Clubs and organizations usually have publicity officials to cooperate in promoting society news. If tips are required, the country club, the hotel, the florist, the caterer, and others supply them with abundance. Far from having to seek news, the editor is generally under pressure for more and more space. However, to have a well-rounded section, the editor does have to seek timely stories and features that do not come in from regular sources.

Another valuable source of information for the society writer could be her own specialized knowledge in the broad field of home economics. Foods and nutrition, family relations, child development, textiles and clothing, interior decorating, and other subjects classified under home economics are vitally important to the modern society-women's section. The college student who is looking forward to the prospect of serving on a society page staff will do well to select courses that may be available in this field—or to fill this gap with independent reading if no such courses are offered at her institution. The society writer should be as familiar with the subject matter of her field as the political writer is with the field of government. Writers highly qualified in certain aspects of home economics (such as foods or clothing) often are called upon to write special byline columns.

Problems of Society-Women's Section   27a

The frequent lack of story substance—in events, formal speeches, business conducted, and real consequences of any sort—confronts the society reporter with definite problems. Society events not only are typed but tend to be stereotyped. Yet the reporter must strive for freshness and variety. She must avoid monotonous, stereotyped story forms. A second and very definite responsibility is that all names must be spelled correctly. To misspell a name or use the wrong initial of a person is to strike at the heart of the society section with the poisoned arrow of carelessness. Also, great care must be exercised by the society editor to check the source of announcements of engagements and weddings to assure validity. Many a practical joker has sent a phony engagement announcement to the newspaper "to get a laugh on a friend," and some of these announcements have unfortunately been printed.

Lead Features. One of the most critical problems for the society reporter, in avoiding stereotyped forms and writing   **27b** more effectively, is the selection of a proper feature or features for the lead. Any society function or "occasion" will afford the following subject matter, within which the feature may be sought:

1. The occasion itself may be defined. Perhaps it is an anniversary or perhaps the hundredth anniversary of an event. Perhaps it is devoted to a "cause," or it may have other special features.

2. The place itself may be significant. An ancestral home, a national shrine, or the newly decorated "Melodeon Hall" of the Blankville Hotel may suggest features.

3. In general, the persons present offer the most obvious feature. Host and guests, honorees, distinguished visitors, those in the receiving line, those who "poured," committee members, names—all are available features.

4. Decorations and color schemes may be featured—or costumes, or gowns, or jewelry.

5. Refreshments and music or other forms of entertainment may also be featured.

The following are typical examples of society-page leads:

> The golden wedding anniversary of Mr. and Mrs. R. A. Mayland of Westover was celebrated by a reunion of family and friends from 13 states at the Mayland country home, Westover Heights, yesterday.

> The dungeon of old Fort Willoughby was lighted by a thousand candles and festooned with trailing arbutus as Lt. James C. Dickerson and Mrs. Dickerson were feted by the local chapter of the Daughters of the American Revolution Friday afternoon, honoring Lt. Dickerson's great-grandfather.

> Mrs. Norman Kingman, author of "The Divide" and other fiction, and her sister, Mrs. Emily Stanton, were honored at a party given Thursday evening at the Westside Country Club.

> Colored autumn leaves and artificial white frost formed the luncheon motif for the Reviewer's Club at its monthly meeting Wednesday noon. Thornton Webster's "Winter's Diary" was reviewed by . . .

> Paul Wayman's orchestra will furnish the music for the Tri Kappa tea dance at the Kappa Kottage Saturday.

Writing Style. Not only must the society reporter overcome **27c** the stereotyped story form wherever this can be done without straining for effect, but also she should strive for variety and freshness of language. "Mr. and Mrs. L. B. Brooks of Tracy City announce the marriage . . ." may become monotonous except in standardized columns of announcements. In describing events of social importance, the society writer has the privilege of going into detail, including a measure of freedom in using adjectives. However, this freedom is limited by accuracy, and it does not permit the use of puffs or gushy language. Not all parties and entertainments can be "the biggest social event of the season." Superlatives should be used with great care, if at all. Such expressions as "everyone is cordially invited" and "the refreshments were delicious" are as out of place in the society section as in any other section of the newspaper. Accurate language, reporting the facts of the occasion with restraint and adequacy, will lend strength to the society page.

Engagements and Weddings

The wedding story of socially prominent persons is perhaps the most important assignment for the society staff. While the engagement is played up by means of pictures and stories about entertainments preceding the wedding, the society editor submits a "wedding report" to be filled out by the bride. Such a report is an elaborate questionnaire providing for all names and addresses of those participating, for descriptions of gowns, flowers, ribbons, type of ceremony, and for all other essential information about the bride and bridegroom and their families, backgrounds, and future plans. With such adequate preliminary information, the society reporter needs to take few notes on the actual occasion of the wedding.

The following illustrations will make clear the technique of these stories:

A Wedding Story Lead

Miss Nelle Mooney, daughter of Mr. and Mrs. C. D. Mooney of 1010 Yale Street, became the bride of Guy Robert King of Cookville, son of Mr. and Mrs. Guy King, Thursday at 5:30 p.m. at the Fifth Street Methodist Church, with the Rev. A. N. Galles, the pastor, officiating.

An Engagement Story Lead

Mr. and Mrs. Edward Orrick Monnel of Mill Neck, L.I., announce the engagement of their daughter, Elizabeth, to Lieut. Thomas Walker Dewey of the United States Army, son of Mr. and Mrs. Thomas Walker Dewey Jr., of Brentwood, Tenn.

A Complete Wedding Story

Wightman Chapel of Jameston College will be the scene this afternoon of the marriage of Miss Kathryn Miller, daughter of Mr. and

Mrs. William S. Miller, to James Phillip Hanley of Blankville. The marriage vows will be taken at 4 p.m. in the presence of a large assemblage of friends and relatives.

Dr. Thomas C. Borden, pastor of First Presbyterian Church, and Dr. Prentice Post, rector of the Church of the Advent, Episcopal, will officiate. Mrs. Pollard Parsons, organist, and Charles S. Ragland, vocalist, will give the program of nuptial music.

The altar will be banked with gardenia plants, centered with a fan-shaped arrangement of Ascension lilies and flanked on each side by single cathedral standards holding white tapers.

The chancel and choir loft will also be banked with greens, Woodwardia fern, and palms, intermingled with four seven-branched candelabra holding white tapers. Candelabra with burning tapers will also be used in the aisle.

The bride, who will be given in marriage by her father, will wear a gown of white ivory satin, the bodice being styled with long tight sleeves and a heart-shaped neckline and trimmed with Princesse lace; the skirt, following the vogue of the day, has the fullness at the back and terminates in a long train.

Her veil of ivory illusion will be adjusted to her coiffure with a coronet of lilies of the valley, and she will carry a shower bouquet of lilies of the valley and gardenias.

Mrs. Otto Bowles will be the matron of honor, and the bridesmaids will be Miss Sara Sellers, Miss Helen Trune, Miss Sara Grant, Miss Gale Bailey of Columbia, and Mrs. Kenneth Johnson and Miss Jane Hanley, both of St. Paul, Minn., and both sisters of the bridegroom.

Mrs. Bowles and the bridesmaids will wear gowns of faille taffeta fashioned along lines similar to that of the bridal gown and will wear small hats of alegane rose velvet. They will carry tailored bouquets of Rubrum lilies. Mrs. Bowles' gown is in a desert rose shade, and the bridesmaids' in the popular Spanish raisin shade.

Isaac Bell of Baltimore, Md., will be Mr. Hanley's best man. The groomsmen will be William Skeates of Washington, D.C., Bertram Haynes, Richard Lindley, Otto Bowles, and William Hanover of Florence, Ala., and William S. Miller Jr., a brother of the bride.

Mr. and Mrs. Miller, parents of the bride, will entertain following the ceremony at their home on Clairmont Drive with a reception for the bridal party, members of the two families, and out-of-town guests here for the wedding.

Miss Daisy Hanley of St. Paul, Minn., an aunt of the bridegroom, will receive with the hosts and Mr. Hanley and his bride.

Mrs. Miller will wear a gown of Groseille wine taffeta with a matching hat trimmed in wine and old blue velvet, and Miss Hanley will wear a gentian blue lace dress. Both will wear gardenias arranged in a shoulder bouquet.

Mr. Hanley and his bride will leave for a southern motor trip and will take the boat from Charleston to New York, where they will make their home. The bride will wear for traveling a costume suit consisting of a blue skirt, white blouse, and cerise jacket. Her hat and accessories will be dark blue and her flowers will be gardenias.

The bride was graduated from the junior college department of Belmont School and from Union University, where she was a member of the Delta Delta Delta sorority.

Mr. Hanley was graduated from Montgomery Wall Academy and State University, where he was a member of the Alpha Tau Omega fraternity. He was graduated from the Law School of Harvard University and is connected with the law firm of Role and Cheek in New York.

Miscellaneous Stories

The largest group of society stories is provided by entertainments. Receptions teas, parties, dances, luncheons, and dinners are all reported as fully as the eminence of the persons and the magnitude of the occasion require. Another large group includes the reports of church and club activities which may be largely social yet may also have significant program substance. They present no special difficulties or peculiar problems other than those already mentioned. Examples follow:

Entertainments

Miss Ruth C. Nobbins entertained today at the Wilson Hotel at a luncheon for Miss Mary Helen Franklin, whose marriage to Roy L. Felts will take place next Saturday.

The guests included the bride's attendants and a few close friends. Pink gladioli and asters were used in the decorations.

Clubs and Organizations

The Harding Garden Club will hold a flower show Oct. 4 at the home of Mrs. T. G. Murphy on Lynnwood Drive, it was decided by the club at its meeting yesterday at the home of Mrs. T. M. King of Shadow Hills.

In addition to making plans for the flower show, the club voted to enter an exhibit in the State Fair flower show.

Mrs. Ernest Hart, whose flower arrangements have won regional and state awards, spoke to the club. She was introduced by Mrs. R. B. Pace.

Trips

Announcements of the comings and goings of local people compose the most voluminous group of personals. Prominent within the group are vacation trips, sons and daughters going to and from college, and ordinary visits to friends and relatives. Following are common examples which perhaps could have been enriched with feature materials:

John Burton of 2200 Courtland Avenue will leave tomorrow for Chicago, where he will be with the General Construction Company as medical aide.

Leonard J. Trawick has returned from Philadelphia after a visit with his parents, Mr. and Mrs. W. L. Trawick.

Mrs. M. Biddle and daughter, Margaret, of 424 East Vine Avenue, left Thursday for Greenville, N. H., where they will visit Mrs. Biddle's daughter, Mrs. Horace Morton.

Mrs. C. G. Penegar of Rushville and her sister, Mrs. L. F. Dean of Plainville, will leave tomorrow to take Mrs. Penegar's son, Robert, to New York, where he will enter Columbia University.

Guests

Hosts and hostesses with out-of-town guests are prone to announce the fact not only to honor the visitors but also to inform other friends who might wish to entertain them. So numerous are personals about visits that they might well be labeled "Arrivals" and "Departures." Following are examples:

Charles Gross arrived yesterday by plane to be the weekend guest of Mr. and Mrs. Neil Wimberley and daughter, Betty Ann, 3426 Lake Street.

Mrs. Thomas Thorne of Milwaukee will arrive today to visit her sister, Mrs. Julian Ackers, of Laurel Boulevard. She will remain over the weekend.

Mrs. Mable Fowler is vacationing with her parents, Dr. and Mrs. W. E. Drinnen, Tazewell Road, between sessions of the Western School of Optometry in Denver.

Births

New York and Hollywood columnists elevated personals to a level of national interest. Their gossip columns concern persons so eminent that proximity is not a consideration. Prenatal announcements first became common in these columns, where mention of pregnancy was softened by such items as "anticipating," "blessed-eventing," "three-ing," "infanticipating." Locally, too, birth is an interesting subject for personal items, though the announcements are usually more conventional and postnatal. The birth notice will usually give the names and address of the parents, the time and place of birth, weight and sex of the infant, and the name, if it has been chosen. Examples are as follows:

A daughter, Mary Jean, was born at 11 p.m. yesterday to Mr. and Mrs. Henry Gillenwater, 709 Scott Drive, at the Protestant Hospital. Her weight was eight pounds.

Mr. and Mrs. Arthur Handley of Jonesboro have named their son, born Wednesday at 2 a.m. at St. Mary's Hospital, James Arthur Jr. Mr. Handley is superintendent of the Jonesboro public schools.

Exercises

I. Clip newspaper stories illustrating five types of society news and analyze them.

II. Write a routine wedding announcement from the following facts:

Miss Rose Mary Sanders to marry
She is a graduate of Salem University
Member of Chi Chi Chi sorority
Engagement announced by Mr. and Mrs. William J. Sanders, parents
Marriage on 28th of next month
To be at First Presbyterian Church
Miss Sanders lives at 2930 Cummings Drive
Mr. Leory M. Bridges will be groom
He is an attorney
Many parties for Miss Sanders planned by friends
Wedding trip to be to Miami, Florida
Mr. Bridges lives on Oakland Road
He graduated from University of Paris
Out-of-town guests for wedding: Mr. and Mrs. M. M. Sanders of New York City; Miss Grace Sanders of Pittsburgh; Miss Mary Roth of Atlanta; Mr. Paul D. Heath of Manchester, Conn.; and Mr. Sam F. Murrian of Albany

III. Adding the following facts to those above, rewrite the first two or three paragraphs of the story:

Miss Sanders is also an attorney
The two met six months ago
As opponents in divorce suit
Miss Sanders attorney for wife
Mr. Bridges attorney for husband
Through efforts of the two attorneys
The husband and wife in the case were reconciled

IV. Attend a wedding and write it up in news fashion.

V. Write a feature story on a woman who is successful in the business or professional world.

VI. Write stories using the following notes:

A. City Garden Club
To meet tomorrow afternoon at 3 p.m.
Home of Mrs. H. G. Tatum, 1017 Banks Road
Dr. B. E. Wayland
Horticulturist at university
To demonstrate and explain
How to prune, spray, and plant roses
Refreshments will be served
By Mrs. Tatum
Mrs. K. D. Lilly, club president, will introduce Dr. Wayland

B. Mrs. H. F. Bryley
Of Washington
Visiting Mr. and Mrs. Thomas Chapman, 740 Park Avenue
For 10 days
Mrs. Bryley was Miss June Freeman
Lived here when child
Mrs. Chapman plans
To give reception
In honor of guest
Will be announced later

C. Mrs. Clarence Post and husband, of Center Pike
And two children
James, five, and Evelyn, eight
Leave tomorrow
For California
Two-week vacation
To travel by automobile
Will visit many places
Both going and coming

D. Mrs. Charles D. Bingham
10 Circle Boulevard

Had guests yesterday
At tea
In honor of daughter, debutante
Miss Margaret Bingham
Home from Lannings College
For weekend
Those assisting in receiving at tea: Mrs. D. L. Hopkins,
Mrs. T. W. Temple, Mrs. B. W. Mitchell, Miss Grace
Champe, and Mrs. G. I. Phillips
Alternating at presiding at tea table: Mrs. W. J. Johnson,
Mrs. G. C. Nottingham, Mrs. F. F. Voit, Mrs. J. G. Barr
Members Debutante Club
Presided at punch bowl
Mrs. Bingham dressed
In flesh-colored lace gown
Over satin
Corsage orchids
Miss Bingham's gown
Imported pink brocaded lamé
Fashioned bouffant
Bodice with draped sleeves

E. Write a story using the following excerpts from a speech given
by Miss Gladys Korum, home demonstration agent, before the
Women's Cooking Club yesterday afternoon. The club met at
the home of Mrs. M. E. Liebeck, 1203 Lane Street. After Miss
Korum's speech, refreshments were served by Mrs. Liebeck.

"Cooking today is something more than the preparation of
a tasty dish attractively served. It also includes the conservation of food nutrients—vitamins, minerals, proteins, carbo-
hydrates, and fats.

"While certain losses are unavoidable, considerable quan-
tities of these valuable substances are needlessly thrown away
every day and the minerals and vitamins, which are most
apt to be low in the diet, are lost to the greatest extent.

"The oxygen of the air and certain light rays are destructive to vitamin content of foods. Therefore the fruits and
vegetables should be as fresh as possible. For this reason,
frozen foods may have a higher vitamin content than fresh
market vegetables since freezing does not appear to appre-
ciably affect the vitamin content. Frozen foods rapidly lose
vitamin C if allowed to stand after thawing, and it is
recommended that cooking be started while they are in the

frozen condition. Frozen fruits which are to be used un-
cooked should be served immediately after thawing.

"Perhaps the greatest loss, and the one most easily controlled in the home, occurs through the dissolution of nutrients into water which is then discarded. This loss can be
minimized by, first, not soaking the vegetables before cooking; second, using as small a quantity of water as possible;
third, having as short a period of cooking as possible; and
fourth, utilizing the cooking water. The cooking period can
be shortened by having the water boiling before the vegetable is put in and removing the vegetable as soon as it is
tender. Covering the cooking vessel also reduces the cooking time but green and strong-juiced vegetables have a
better appearance and flavor if cooked uncovered. Soda
should not be used in cooking any vegetables because it is
destructive to vitamins and tends to make vegetables soft
and slimy.

"The nutrient content of canned and dried foods depends
upon the method of preservation and the treatment before
use. Most vitamin losses in canning are due to oxidation and
the aim in canning methods should be to exclude as much
air as possible. Processing the foods directly in the jars helps
to keep down vitamin loss. Canned foods should be used as
soon as opened and, if heated, should be brought to the
boiling point as quickly as possible and served immediately
since they require no further cooking. The water from
canned foods should always be used since it contains valuable nutrients. Vitamin losses during the drying of foods
may be serious. However, sulphur dioxide, frequently used
in the commercial drying of fruits and vegetables, helps to
prevent vitamin destruction. Dried foods should be cooked
in the water in which they are soaked since this water also
contains valuable nutrients."

Chapter 28

Sports

THE sports reporter has a field of investigation more limited than the general staff reporter's. That very limitation prescribes a fixed zone of interest and a definite body of knowledge to challenge professional competence. The general reporter will be assigned to various beats, most of them being ill defined and heterogeneous in content. He is subject to call for miscellaneous assignments and should know at least a little about everything. All the advantages of being able to know much about little are with the sports reporter.

The sports reporter's field is broad enough, however, to challenge the finest talent. Every sport has both its rules and its records. It has its gallery of personalities and its hall of fame. Psychological factors deserve exploration, in the Grantland Rice fashion. Sports ethics and aesthetics and larger aspects of recreation and the social good are involved. There are abuses to be corrected, campaigns to be waged, promotion and education to be designed. Perhaps in no other field of reporting is the opportunity greater for mastery of background and for application of standards of judgment.

The World of Sports. The sports section is a world unto itself. Generally, on larger newspapers, it is operated by an independent department, with the sports editor and his staff responsible for all phases of gathering, writing, and editing. Having this freedom, the sports staff often leans toward a flamboyant display of its wares, producing pages that are heavy with large headlines and illustrations plus detailed treatment of sports developments. Some intellectuals may see a curious misconception of news values in a newspaper's having a three-paragraph story with a small headline telling about a $100,000 cancer-research grant on a page in the general news section, then a nine-paragraph article with a four-column headline and a photograph presenting the news about a baseball pitcher's sore arm on a sports page of the same newspaper. A journalistic truism that the sports pages constitute an isolated special section, its stories not to be weighed with the scales used for other news columns, has brought about the apparent anomaly. If anyone doubts this reasoning, the newspaper can support its contention by pointing to the high readership of the sports section.

News Values of Sports. The whole scale of news values characterizes sports news. Clustered around conflict as the pivotal appeal are eminence, progress, disaster, human interest, and in the sports sense, consequence. Moreover, the reader is a "fan," highly conditioned for ready response, at once appreciative and critical. The sports reporter—usually a byline writer—acquires "a public" which may become a valuable career asset. Thus, there is something over and beyond the news values—something of camaraderie and clan *esprit* which enhances reader interest in the sports page. Men particularly, but also women and children, look it over for news on their favorite teams.

Qualifications of the Sports Writer. The sports reporter has certain responsibilities in his work which are perhaps not different from, but merely more obvious than, those in less specialized reporting. Two of these have been mentioned—background and judgment.

28a A background can be acquired. Probably most sports reporters are "addicted" to one or more sports and have the invaluable "feel" of the game and an intimate knowledge of the fine points. Other sports they may have to master somewhat vicariously, but master them they must. The background should be historical as well as technical. A fire, an accident, or an occasion may be reported adequately from within the event. Too frequently, also, sports reporting confines itself in the same manner. But the richness of reporting from a full background outside the event is self-evident. The Kentucky Derby winner is related to Derby winners of all time, and of all tracks, and of the current season, and is the foal of sire and dam of distinguished ancestry with various records and winnings scattered along the way. Many or most readers will have a partial knowledge of this background. They not only want to be told what they already know but they want their knowledge expanded. They want the whole significance of the event, and they look to the sports reporter as interpreter and final authority. They demand that he have background.

To some extent also, the sports reporter can acquire good judgment, since it is aided by adequate knowledge. Familiarity and experience with the various sports will afford knowledge of the standards which measure the merits and demerits of plays and players. Ultimately, though, the reporter will succeed or fail because of the accuracy or inaccuracy of his independent judgment. In baseball, for example, sagacious qualities are sometimes required in distinguishing between a hit and an error. It is insight, too, and not background, that must detect the cause of weakness or the source of strength of a team or of an individual player. Nor can the sports reporter take comfort in the thought that, if he fails to detect and report an error or an achievement, no one will be the wiser. Unlike other reporters, he writes for a public which has observed the same events with highly critical eyes. A positive mandate for his success is sound judgment.

A third desirable qualification is perspective or detachment—which should be the result of sufficient knowledge plus good judgment. Thumping the drums for the local team with brass and bias is not detached reporting. The reporter's responsibility is to the public and not to the local team. Although the fans are quick to resent any slackening in defense of the local heroes, they will in the long run respect the sports policy of honesty, accuracy, and detachment. The sports reporter is not merely a reporter; he is a judge and must conduct himself accordingly. With his judgship privileges, he must avoid arrogancy, for this violates detachment and honesty. The sports writer cannot take over and run a team through the newspaper columns, and he is usurping the coach's authority when he attempts to do so.

Scope of Sports Writing. Sports writing ranges from straight news reporting through all degrees of interpretative and feature writing and the editorialized column. A sports event may be treated in any one of these degrees or in all of them combined. The general practice is to treat an important event as straight news (thus utilizing any of the lead and story forms already discussed) with sufficient interpretation to enrich the report with its background. Separate stories, features, and editorial columns then surround the event with all necessary sidelights. Moreover, many newspapers place few restrictions upon editorializing in the sports news, except the pressure of events and the consequent necessity of reporting first things first.

For important sports events, "build-up" stories and articles are used for days or weeks prior to the event, then the event is thoroughly covered when it occurs, and "postmortem" stories may be used for days following in commenting on what took place.

News Sources. Local and regional schools and colleges, recreation bureaus, professional teams of all types, sponsors of all kinds of sports leagues (such as Little League groups, bowling lanes, and country clubs), and other local organizations which promote or conduct events belonging in the sports world should be covered by the sports editor and his staff. The editor has, on the one hand, a problem to keep from overlooking some activities deserving space and, on the other, to avoid giving too much space to some teams and groups which have very active promotional agents. A sports staff could not begin to cover all events deserving space, but with the proper encouragement and instructions the sports writers can get valuable assistance in gathering news from many of the people engaged in the various sports. Every team of any type likes to be reported as a winner, and this appeal can be used as a lever in achieving wider coverage of events which the sports staff cannot find time to witness.

28b A word of warning is needed on sports news sources. Gambling on sporting events seems to be a national pastime, but the sports staff should cautiously avoid being put in league with illegal gamblers. Publicity given to gamblers or the gambling odds does just that.

28c **Style of Sports Writing.** Sports writing is expected to be vigorous, virile, audacious. But it should not be fantastic. Somewhere between standard English rhetoric and the bizarre patterns into which the language can be bent, the reporter must find his own style. This does not mean that he is relieved of the responsibilities of observing basic rules of English grammar. His object is to bring the sports event to the reader with all the impact the event has upon the spectators. He cannot achieve this effect through extraordinary strains and stresses and ornamentations of language. Nor can he obtain a quick passport to success by imitating a style that another reporter has made effective. Perhaps the only possible advice is "Be yourself, but be your best self through constant practice and self-criticism."

Sports copy smacks of informality, even raciness. The sports writer uses colloquialisms, metaphors, similes, and other figures of speech which other reporters avoid. He achieves both brevity and vividness with "He cracked the line for two yards" instead of "He gained two yards by going through the line." However, such expressions as "he pilfered the second sack" evince too much straining for effect, and such expressions as "banged the apple" and "smacked the pill" are definitely hackneyed. Since the sports reporter does have so much freedom, he should try to be original but must temper his language to sound judgment and good taste. By all means, he must remember that he is writing to the spectator rather than the athlete,

and his language must not be so technical that the general public
will not understand it.

Sports Story Leads 28d

The sports page contains stories of a wide variety of events. Most
space is devoted to football, baseball, basketball, golf, boxing, and
wrestling, but other sports include swimming, hunting, fishing, automobile and horse racing, tennis, track, volleyball, trapshooting,
bowling, and billiards. In certain sections of the nation, there are
stories on skiing, hockey, soccer, polo, rowing, rodeos, hiking, and
other local sports. The sports page may also handle horse shows,
dog shows, and other events of a more general sports nature.

The sports reporter usually reports these events in a news fashion.
Although allowed more freedom in the use of language, he usually
follows the regular news principles in building the story. The 5 W's
should be in the lead, and the features should be properly summarized at the beginning and elaborated in the body of the story.
The general principles of the single-feature and the several-feature
leads also apply to sports writing.

No matter what type of sports event he covers, the reporter may
look for one or more of the following elements to furnish him with
features for the story:

1. The score of the game or the outcome of the event (The final
   score should be in every lead, but frequently it is subordinate
   to other features.)
2. Spectacular plays
3. Scoring plays or sequences of plays
4. Individual stars
5. The significance of the game—championship or effect on
   record
6. General comparison of teams or opponents
7. Background of game—weather, crowd, special occasion.

The following leads illustrate the use of the various features available to the sports reporter:

The Score or Outcome

Piling up a 40-0 score, the Blankville High School Cats won an
easy victory over the Johnstown High School eleven yesterday afternoon.

Spectacular Plays

The gray-bearded "Statue of Liberty" play baffled Johnstown High School's eleven yesterday, enabling the Blankville High School Cats to scratch out a 7-0 win over the visitors.

Individual Stars

Five bullet passes shot by Quarterback Dick Melton carried Blankville High School 37 yards to a touchdown and a 7-0 victory over Johnstown High School yesterday.

Significance of the Game

Blankville High School's Cats kept one of the best records in the state intact by trouncing Johnstown High School 40-0 on B. H. S. field yesterday.

Comparison of Teams

Outclassing a weak but spirited Johnstown High School eleven, the Blankville High School championship-bound Cats toyed through a 40-0 win on B.H.S. field yesterday.

Background of Game

Before 10,000 rooting old grads who braved bitter cold and an occasional snowfall, Blankville High School's Cats pleased their guests with a 40-0 victory over Johnstown High School yesterday.

28e   *The Body of the Story*

The body of the sports story must, of course, complete the development of the lead. If the lead is a summary, the body may proceed in the 1, 2, 3, 4 development of the various features. If the lead is a salient feature, it must be followed by a summary of the other features and by the subsequent development of each feature. These are the general principles of lead and body development that have been observed from the beginning as applying to all types of stories.

In many sports stories, however (as in some stories of trials and lawsuits and meetings), two types of body development must be utilized: (*a*) the general interpretation, (*b*) the running story.

The general interpretation is essential. It is merely the development of the lead or lead block. The reporter must narrate and explain (interpret) the highlights (features) of the event. This is the logical body development which is used in other types of stories. The running (chronological) story (play-by-play, inning-by-inning, round-by-round account) is sometimes given, appearing after the general interpretation or printed separately under a heading of its own. Play-by-play or blow-by-blow accounts of sports events are used only infrequently by some newspapers and not at all by others, particularly when radio or television covers the major events.

Exercises

I. Clip from newspapers five to ten stories on different sports and analyze them.

II. Tabulations are used in some sports stories to summarize certain important facts and statistics (names of players, statistics on each player, and statistics on the whole team). The form of these tabulations varies from newspaper to newspaper. Study the newspapers and draw up sample tabulations used in stories on (1) a football game, (2) a baseball game, (3) a basketball game, (4) a track meet, (5) any other sports popular in your locality. Define all abbreviations used in these tabulations. (*Note:* Check back issues of the newspapers in the library to find sample tabulations on the seasonal sports.)

III. Clip from the newspaper a *long* sports story, paste it to blank sheets of paper, and make the following study:
  A. Underline all *interpretative* phrases—that is, every part of the story which is more than an objective account of a game.
  B. Make marginal notes on examples of achieving vividness and of hackneyed expressions (if any).

IV. Attend some current sports event and write it up in news fashion.

V. Write stories using the following notes:

  A. Basketball game
  Between Blankville High Bears
  And Centerville High Cats
  At B. H. S. gym last night
  Blankville High won
  Score 56-55
  Points made by Blankville players: Ward Randle, forward, 14; Mort Jones, forward 24; Frank Jones, center, 1; George Smith, guard, 16; Richard Webb, guard, 1.
  By Centerville: Daniel Evans, forward, 3; Peter Wells, forward, 16; Frank Downey, forward, 15; John Smith, center, 17; William Johnson, guard, 3; William Shaw, guard, 1.
  Score at half: B. H. S., 9; C. H. S., 17
  Blankville remains undefeated
  Crowd, 1100

B. Blankville baseball team
    Played game
    Against Centerville team
    Yesterday afternoon
    At Blankville Park
    Blankville lost, 4-1
    Johnny Donald pitched for Blankville
    Al Henry pitched for Centerville
    Hits: Blankville, 3; Centerville, 6
    Crowd 1000
    Blankville holds third place in league
    Centerville, second place
    Sixth straight win for Henry
    Homer by Tommy Thomas, catcher, Centerville
    Brought in Kyle Rolfe, centerfield
    In fifth inning
    Homer hit by Kelt Walker, right fielder, Blankville
    In fifth inning
    Centerville scored 1 in first
    Dick Sullins, first baseman
    Beat out bunt
    Gained second on sacrifice
    By Davy Mack, left fielder
    Came in on two-base hit
    By Alvin Yankee, third baseman
    Mack scored in third
    Made three-base hit
    Came in on single
    By Yankee
    Henry struck out eight; Donald, five

C. What type or types of sports story leads have you used for the
    assignments above? Illustrate every other type by rewriting one
    of those same leads.

D. Blankville High to play Central High
    In basketball next Friday
    Will be crucial game
    Blankville High undefeated, 10-0
    Central High lost one game to Lem's Corner High
    By one point
    County championship may hinge on next week's game
    Gamblers betting on Central High
    And will give one point
    Blankville beat Lem's Corner High

But star of LCHS (Frank Holt), best player in entire county, was
out of game with flu

VI. Write a story using the play-by-play account of the football game
that follows. The game is between the local University of Blankville
and its greatest rival, Aston State College. Your story is to appear the
day after the game.

Other facts needed to write the story: Colors and nickname of UB,
orange and white, Bearcats; of ASC, red and white, Bulldogs.
Weather, cloudy with light rain througout game and temperature
around 60 degrees. Crowd, about 30,000. UB's first defeat in six
games. UB had been favored to win by one touchdown. ASC had
lost two of five games. With this defeat, UB now ties University of
Centerville for first place in Big Twelve Conference. Last week UB
led the league.

ASC won the toss and elected to defend the south goal. UB lined
up to kick off from the north. (Hereafter, ASC is A and UB is B.)

FIRST QUARTER

Marm kicks off to Ruml at the goal line and Ruml returns to
A21, stopped by Deltos and Marm. Ford through right guard for
2, stopped by Alderman and Deltos. Ramsey stopped at line of
scrimmage by Voltz and Sully. Simms punts out of bounds at
B42. Fess tries right guard, stopped for no game by McNew. Fess,
around right end, is thrown for loss of 3 by Ford. Melvin
through right tackle for 2, stopped by Ramsey. Cutland punts to
Ruml, who takes fair catch at A32.

Simms, on option play around left end, keeps and makes 2,
stopped by Deltos and Toms. Simms, on option right, completes
pass to Ruml on A40, where Ruml is tackled by Melvin. Ford
through right guard for 2, stopped by Sully and Deltos. Ross
thrown by Hunning and fumbles, recovered by Fiddle at A45.
Fess through left tackle, stopped by Vellmer after 1. Fess' pass
intended for Pannella is incomplete. Wally's pass intended for
Pannella is incomplete. Cutland punts out of bounds at A22.

Simms, on option, throws to Ross but incomplete. Ross drops
hand off and ball recovered by Alderman. Melvin goes through
left guard for 5, stopped by Ford and Ramsey. Fess on a fake
spinner goes through left guard for 5, stopped by Ford. Fess
through right tackle for 3, stopped by Ramsey and Thomas.
Fess thrown by Ross and Ruml for 2 yard loss. Melvin through
right tackle for 3, stopped by McNew. Lane kicks field goal.
Score: B, 3; A, 0.

Marm kicks off to Ramsey in end zone, and Ramsey returns
to A23 where he is stopped by Toms and Voltz. Simms goes

through left end for 3, stopped by Hunning and Voltz. Simms fumbles and ball recovered by Sully on A26. Melvin through right tackle for 3, stopped by Koff and Gamey. Fess, around right end, goes over the goal because of great block by Hunning, but play is called back because B was holding and was penalized 15 yards. Fess completes pass to Fiddle at A32, tackled immediately by Ely. Fess completes pass to Toms at A8, and Toms goes over for touchdown. Extra point by Lane. Score: B, 10; A, 0.

Marm kicks off to Ruml, who touches ball as it goes out of bounds at A7. Simms goes through the center of line and stopped after 3 yards by Gay. Simms, on option, keeps and is stopped after 3 by Gay and Gomez. Simms punts to Walling on B45, and he is stopped on A48 by Welling and Allred. Cannus tried right guard but loses 3, stopped by Ross. End of first quarter.

SECOND QUARTER

Walling tries passing to Tombrass, but it is incomplete. Tombrass on a reverse to the right is stopped at the line of scrimmage but play is called back and A is penalized 5 yards for off sides. Fess goes through left tackle for 5, stopped by Ross and Ely. Cutland punts to Ruml, who takes a fair catch on the A14. Simms throws pass to Ross but it is incomplete, broken up by Tombrass. Ford hits right tackle for no gain, stopped by Walling and Tombrass. Then A is penalized 5 for off sides. Simms slips down in end zone, rushed by Elvis. Safety for UB. Score: B, 12; A, 0.

Koff punts from A20 to Fess on B25, and ball is returned to B39, the tackle by Ramsey and Bell. Walling thrown by Gamey for loss of 7 in attempting to pass. Walling attempts screen pass to Cannus, but it is incomplete. Cutland punts to Ely on the A30 and ball is returned to A34, tackle by Jackson and Gay. Simms on option throws to Lemons but pass is incomplete, broken up by Eman. Simms hits right guard .for 5, stopped by Gomez. Gamey goes through right tackle for 8, stopped by Gomez and Tomkins. Simms makes 2 through left guard, stopped by Deltos and Sully. Simms tries pass to Lemons but it is incomplete. Another Simms pass to Ramsey is incomplete. Koff punts out of bounds on the B1. Fess goes through right tackle for 2, tackled by Welmer. Fess fumbles when hit by Olms, then recovers in end zone to give ASC a safety. Score: B, 12; A, 2.

Marm kicks from B20 out of bounds on the A24 and B is penalized 5. Marm kicks again from the B15 to Ruml on the A38 and ball is returned to the B45. Ford on a right end run is knocked out of bounds by Pannella after a gain of 8. Ross stopped for no gain by Deltos. Ross gains one through right tackle, stopped by Deltos and Hunning. Simms on an option play around right end runs for 13, stopped by Voltz and Pannella. Simms completes a pass for 9 to Smith, who is tackled by Fess. Simms goes through right guard for 4, stopped by Toms. Ford up the middle gains 1, stopped by Deltos. Simms throws a pass to Ruml in the end zone for a touchdown. Extra point by Wendhill. Score: B, 12; A, 9.

Lemons kicks off to Fess at the goal line, and Fess returns to the B24, stopped by Lemons. Melvin gains 4 up the middle, stopped by Welmer. Melvin gains another 12 through the middle, stopped by Ely. Fess goes around right end for 3, but B was penalized 15 yards for clipping and ball ends on B28. Melvin goes through right guard for 11, stopped by Garney. A penalized 5 for delay of game. Melvin gains 3 through right guard, stopped by Ford and Vellmer. Fess picks up 3 through right tackle, stopped by Welling. Melvin goes around right end for 11, stopped by Ford. Fess thrown for loss of 7 by Koff. Fess' pass to Gay was incomplete. Fess makes 7 around left end, stopped by Iglehart and Ross. Cutland punts into end zone. Simms is stopped by Voltz after gain of 3. End of half.

THIRD QUARTER

Lemons kicks off to Pannella, who hands off to Fess on the B3, and Fess goes to B15, stopped by McNew. Fess tries right tackle, trips, no gain. Fess thrown for 2 yards by Welling. Fess completes a pass to Fiddle to B28, tackled by Ford. Fess gains 8 through right tackle, stopped by Parks and Ford. Melvin goes through right tackle, stopped by Parks and Ford. Melvin goes through right tackle for 2 stopped by Parks. Melvin goes through middle for 1, stopped by Koff and Ford. Cutland punts to Ruml on A12, and return is to A16, then A is penalized for clipping to A19.

Simms on an option to right keeps and makes 6, stopped by Fess. Ford makes 9 through left guard, stopped by Alderman. Simms on an option around right end makes 10, stopped by Deltos. Simms completes a pass to Smith on the A49, but play called back and A penalized 5 for off sides. Ross fumbles after hit by Eman and ball recovered by Melvin on B47.

Fess goes around right end for 1, stopped by Ross and Parks. Melvin goes through right tackle for 9, stopped by Parks. Olms jumps off sides and A is penalized 5. Fess tries left guard, stopped after 1 by Koff. Melvin goes through left tackle for 9, stopped by Ruml. Melvin makes 2 through left tackle, stopped by Ford. Fess goes up middle for 2, stopped by Holt and Thomas. Melvin makes 6 through left tackle, stopped by Ruml. Melvin tries middle of line for 1. Melvin again tries middle of line for no gain. Ball goes over to A. Simms on a pass attempt fumbles, recovered by Fiddle on A16. Fess completes pass to Gay, who is stopped at A2 by Ruml. Fess goes through left tackle for touchdown. Extra point by Lane. Score: B, 19; A, 9.

Marm kicks off to Ramsey on the A12, and return is to A23, stopped by Elvis. Lemons tries left tackle but stopped by Ferguson, then A penalized 5 for off sides. Simms completes a pass to Gamey, who goes out of bounds on the A30, then B is penalized 15 for personal foul. Gamey goes through right tackle for 2, stopped by Elvis and Ferguson. Simms laterals to Lemons, who goes around right end for 8, stopped by Walling. Quarter ends.

FOURTH QUARTER

Simms' pass intended for Ramsey is incomplete, but A penalized 15 for holding. Simms on an option passes to Ruml, who is stopped after 8 at the B48 by Melvin. Simms on an option passes to Ford, who is stopped on the B31 by Fess and Hunning. B jumps off sides and is penalized 5. Simms on an option around left end is run out of bounds at the B8. Simms completes a pass to Ruml for a touchdown. Extra point by Wendhill. Score: B, 19; A, 16.

Lemons kicks off to Pannella on B8, and return is to B22, stopped by Welling. Fess makes 6 through left tackle, stopped by Ruml. Fess makes 3 through left tackle, stopped by Koff. Melvin stopped for no gain in the middle. Cutland punts to Ruml, who takes fair catch at A35. Ross makes 5 through right tackle, stopped by Evers and Hunning. Ford makes 13 around left end, stopped by Melvin. Simms misses pass to Smith. Simms' pass to Smith intercepted by Toms, who is downed at the B41.

Fess tries left tackle, stopped by Vellmer, but B penalized 15 for holding. Fess is stopped for no gain on run through middle, but B penalized back to B12 for holding. Melvin makes 3 through left tackle, stopped by Ross and Vellmer. Melvin is stopped for no gain in the middle by Koff. Cutland punts to Ruml, who takes fair catch at B43.

Simms on an option goes around right end for 6, stopped by Melvin. Simms goes through left tackle for 9, stopped by Evers and Hunning. Ramsey goes through left tackle for 5, stopped by Ferguson, but A penalized 5 for off sides. Simms on an option completes pass to Smith, who is stopped on B22 by Fess. Simms misses pass intended for Ruml. Ford goes through the middle for 4, stopped by Deltos and Ferguson. Simms' pass to Ruml is incomplete, broken up by Eman. Simms on an option runs to

B2, stopped by Hunning. B jumps off sides and is penalized to B1. Simms goes through left guard for touchdown. Extra point by Wendhill. Score: A, 23; B, 19.

Lemons kicks off to Marm, whose fumble at the B31 is recovered by Holt of A. Simms is stopped in the middle by Falls, but A penalized 5 for off sides. Simms on an option makes 9 around left end, stopped by Gomez. Simms goes through right guard for 2, stopped by Elvis. Simms' pass for Ramsey is incomplete. Ford makes 2 through the middle, stopped by Mannings. Ball goes to B.

Walling makes 6 around right end, stopped by gang tackling. Cannus fails to gain through middle. Walling's pass for Page is incomplete. Walling's pass for Toms is incomplete. Ball goes to A. Simms makes 3 through the middle, Simms fails to gain in middle, and off sides penalties against both A and B cancel each other. Simms fails to gain in the middle. The game ends. Score: A, 23; B, 19.

THE LINEUPS:
UB
Left ends—Fred Toms, Lucius Gay, Lon Fanara, Dick Lane
Left tackles—Frank Voltz, Lennie Falls
Left guards—Welton Sully, Whiz Ferguson, Dave Phelps
Centers—Sun Alderman, Jack Manning, Eden Eman
Right guards—Dan Deltos, Jim Danl, Jim Elvis
Right tackles—Sam Evers, Joe Jackson, DeLong Long
Right ends—Bish Fiddle, Shu Marm
Wingbacks—Joe Pannella, Fix Tombrass, Don Page
Blocking backs—Chick Hunning, Joe Gomez, Jim Dunn
Fullbacks—Heck Melvin, Whip Cannus
Quarterbacks—Tom Fess, Hugh Walling, Cotton Cutland
ASC
Left ends—Hitch Smith, Jim Holt
Left tackles—Charlie Thomas, Hips Holms
Left guards—Zip Hent, Charles Olms
Centers—Alf Allred, Fred Masters, Pop Palling
Right guards—Hart Vellmer, Dick Welmer, Sam Pellmer
Right tackles—Fells McNew, Henry Bell
Right ends—Wimps Welling, Lou Iglehart
Quarterbacks—Hike Simms, Sam Koff, Windy Wendhill
Left halfbacks—Hal Ford, Switch Ely, John Lemons
Right halfbacks—General Ruml, Walt Ramsey, Slow Parks
Fullbacks—Neal Ross, Good Gamey, Al Cupps

GAME STATISTICS

	ASC	UB
Total first downs	15	9
Yards gained rushing	195	147
Yards lost rushing	11	26
Net gain rushing	184	121
Number pass attempts	17	11
Passes completed	8	4
Passes had intercepted	1	0
Net gain passing	83	66
Number punts	3	8
Punts blocked	0	0
Punting average	43	30.5
Number punts returned	6	2
Total yards punts returned	26	21
Number kickoff returns	5	3
Total yards kickoffs returned	72	51
Total yards penalized	70	83
Number own fumbles	5	2
Number own fumbles lost	5	1

Chapter 29

Literature, Fine Arts, Criticism

THE chief function of the newspaper is to report the news accurately, truthfully, and fully. At times the plain facts do not convey the significance of the news event, and the reporter goes beyond straight, objective reporting into more interpretative writing. Nevertheless, he restricts himself to reporting facts. He does not give expression to his own judgments. And the news intention is paramount.

In bringing to readers the world of literature and the fine arts, however, something more than interpretative reporting is required. The purpose of such writing is not mainly or solely to convey news and interpret cultural materials. The writer must also appraise and evaluate such materials for the public. Naturally the new book or play, the concert, the art show, or the performance of a Shakespearean drama will be the "news peg" upon which the story is hung. But the writer is no longer limited by the news intention. He is expected not only to present the subject but also to explain its inwardness of argument, or construction, and to evaluate its outwardness, or its significance to society.

Reviewing Versus Criticism. The difference between reviewing and criticism may be mainly one of definition, but a useful distinction can be made between the two in newspaper practice.   **29a**

A commercial pamphlet is subject to review; a work of art—which includes most books, paintings, music, plays—is subject to criticism. In reviewing, the reporter confines himself to announcing the publication (date, author, publisher, format), or the art show, the musical program, or the dance recital, and he writes a summary (review) of its contents. He does not pass judgment upon the work nor otherwise engage in editorializing. He remains behind the curtain of anonymity. Any material to be reviewed may be handed by the city editor to the most available staff reporter with the instruction, "Give us a story on this." No especial experience or background need be brought to bear upon this task. All the subject matter of the review is present in the materials. The reporter writes his review in the same manner that he reports a publication or speech (see Chapter 16).

Criticism is something else. Usually the newspaper will not engage in criticism unless it has a definite book, theatrical, or music column or department. At times, however, it may assign its most cultured reporter or employ an outside specialist (musician, artist, playwright) for special occasions. The critic is given a byline. He shares the limelight with the subject and stands forth as guide and commentator. Editorializing and pronouncing judgment, he draws from a background of knowledge of the subject matter. He knows the standards that should be achieved, and he measures the success and failure of the effort at hand. He compares the given work with others of its class and judges the ability of artists or performers. He not only evaluates the work within its genre but frequently attempts to stimulate the cultural impulses of the community and to extend its horizons.

Literature and the fine arts that would come under the purview of criticism (or critical review) include:

1. Books and articles
2. Dramatic performances
3. Concerts and other musical performances
4. Recordings
5. Motion pictures
6. Radio and television programs
7. Lectures
8. Art—painting, sculpture
9. Architecture
10. Professional dancing
11. Photography
12. Nightclub acts

29b **Principles of Criticism.** To achieve his purposes the critic will find common-sense generalizations useful. Following are important points deserving consideration:

1. It is important to give readers a view of the woods before pointing out the individual trees. The reader is interested in knowing what sort of experience he will encounter in the book, play, or painting. What is the general nature of the work? Is it sensational, intellectual, calm or boisterous? Is it worth while and in what particular way?

2. The work should be criticized in the light of its intentions and within its genre. A detective story or mystery play need not achieve the same standards as heavy drama. Amateurs have a right to compete with other amateurs and not to be judged by professional standards.

3. The contents of book or play should be outlined only to the extent needed for readers to determine whether they are interested, not so fully as to give away the plot. The purpose of the critic is to promote popular interest, not to discourage it.

4. The criticism should be interesting in itself. Readers will not read dull criticism any more readily than they will read dull news. Good criticism may rise to the heights of literature in itself.

5. The critic is addressing lay readers who do not possess technical vocabularies. They probably cannot be expected to know the difference between *crisis* and *climax, protagonist* and *antagonist,* and they are not familiar with Aristotle's theory of the dramatic purge. The critic should write in simple language. He should not attempt to be too erudite or to "show off" his literary prowess.

6. The significance of the work should be suggested. Is it extraordinary, distinguished, superior, mediocre, below standard? Does it have social or economic implications?

7. If the critic likes or dislikes what he is evaluating, he should explain why. It is not enough merely to praise or to condemn a literary or artistic production.

8. The critic must stay within ethical and legal bounds (see Chapter 5)..In using copyrighted material, he may quote a reasonable amount with no fear of violating the law. A reasonable amount may be interpreted as only a taste (but not a full swallow) of the quality of the material. In other words, the critic cannot steal the full impact of this quality under the guise of a critical review.

9. Above all, the critic must keep in mind that his major responsibility is to his readers—not to the authors, performers, painters. He must tell the readers whether the production is worth seeing or or hearing, and he must be honest with them. He should not be too harsh or too lenient. By all means he should not permit himself to become so involved with a production that he is nothing more than a publicity agent.

Writing Style of Criticism. Except for certain set forms which some newspapers use to give essential data at the beginning **29c** of a critical review, there is no pattern for critics to follow in writing their stories. If anything, these stories could be described as essays, a form which gives the writers all of the liberties in composition that they could expect. The first person is permitted and often used, because the critic is writing under his byline.

To those starting out in the field of criticism, the best advice is to read the works of other critics—particularly the good ones—and to analyze all of the devices and techniques employed by them. The beginning critic can strive for his own writing style, one that is characteristic and easily developed, but he should not try to go far afield from the best of essayism and journalism in doing so.

In the paragraphs which follow are special notes on different areas of criticism.

29d   *Subjects for Criticism*

Books and Articles. Most metropolitan dailies conduct book-review columns or departments. The public looks to the local critic not only to mold its taste but also to enable it to economize in reading time in the proper selection of books. The critic has an opportunity to promote the use of libraries and otherwise to stimulate cultural activities. The active critic will not, therefore, confine his attention to new books coming to his desk.

In judging a book, the critic must not lean too heavily upon the publisher's *blurb*, which is issued in publicizing the book. The blurb can be used as an aid, and the critic may find that he agrees with some of its claims, but it should not influence the critic's own appraisal. Sometimes the blurb will contain interesting, usable facts on the history of the book.

Movies, Radio, Television, Recordings. Many newspaper writers who report on motion pictures, radio, and television content themselves with simple reviewing, but there is opportunity for conscientious criticism. The critic has an opportunity to do more than promote audiences. He can exert upon these media as much influence as upon any other. With due consideration of the sensational genre of westerns and mysteries, he can throw his support into the struggle for a higher type of entertainment. In the final analysis the moviegoers and radio-television audiences will largely determine the fare which is offered them. The critic can do much to refine their tastes.

While there are similarities in motion picture and radio-television productions to the extent that their audiences do not see or hear the performers in person (and to the extent that movies are used on television), there are also differences. The audience must pay for the privilege of attending a motion picture house; radio-television audiences are "on the house" as guests of commercial sponsors. Movie audiences, therefore, can be more demanding of the quality of the productions. Radio-television audiences cannot claim that they did not receive their money's worth, but they still can exercise their dislikes by a simple twist of the dial. If all radio-television programs reach the unfortunate stage when twisting the dial brings no favorable results, the critic who contented himself with simple reviewing will have been remiss in his responsibilities.

Another type of mechanically made production subject to criticism is the recording—the type that is purchased by the public. Here is the popular substitute for radio-television programs. The critic, by keeping the public informed on the best in new recordings, can promote good taste and combat poor programming by influencing the number of persons that surveys show are listening to inferior broadcasts.

Live Performances—Music, Drama, Dancing, Lectures. The most sensitive job of the critic is his appraisals of the work **29f** of performers when he sees them in person. In other forms of the fine arts he views their work at long range, so to speak; in live performances he looks them in the eye—which may call for more fortitude on the part of the critic.

The critic of a live performance may have to make certain allowances for unpleasant conditions of the presentation that are the fault of local facilities (which the critic should point out). Certainly he should not pounce or dwell upon a minor defect if the performance as a whole is superior. Nor should he compare a famous star's performance with his appearance in a motion picture, which has been shorn of imperfections by the film editor.

On the other hand, a star should be expected to perform like a star, and the critic has full rights to give an honest appraisal of a local appearance.

If the presentation involves new music, a new play, or a new dance, the criticism should deal with the vehicle as well as the performers. If it is a performance of a well-known work, comparisons can be made with interpretations by other artists.

As was pointed out earlier, amateur performances are not compared with professional. The critic should encourage and promote amateur productions. This does not mean that he must praise every amateur production, nor should he "damn it with faint praise." He can be completely honest in favorable comments on performers worthy of applause (as amateurs) without violating his conscience as a critic. And he can (and should) be as encouraging as he is critical.

Art—Paintings, Sculptures, Photographs. The art critic must

29g be versatile in his knowledge not only of the different forms but also of the various interpretations of art. One who is prejudiced for or against any distinctive interpretation is obviously not a qualified judge. Before the critic ventures to assess the worth of a production, he should understand not only what the artist sought to do but also how well the artist succeeded in his efforts.

Exercises

   I. Clip from newspapers a review and a critical review. Underline the phrases in the critical review which put them in that category. Evaluate the critical review from the standpoint of the "principles" given in this chapter.
  II. Write a review of Chapter 29 of this book.
 III. Write a critical review of the same chapter.
  IV. Write a review or critical review, as assigned by your instructor, of the following:
   A. A motion picture
   B. A television program
   C. An art show
   D. A book
   E. A live musical performance
   F. A live dramatic performance
   G. The architecture of some building on the campus
   H. A collection of photographs

Chapter 30

Editorials and Columns

THE editorial page is essentially a page of news, though it is written from a different viewpoint. Here the editor and a corps of columnists, cartoonists, and specialists have their say, but quite generally they discuss the same subjects which are found on other pages of the newspaper. The reporter himself may be called upon to cooperate in editorial campaigns, and if he is the best informed staff member on a given subject, he may face the task of writing an occasional editorial.

The editorial page represents journalism as practiced in its early days, the days of "personal journalism" when the editor interpreted current events as he saw them and when readers were about as familiar with the name of the editor as with the name of the newspaper. The policies of the editor for or against a public issue or candidate were also well known by the readers, recognizable through the editor's interpretations of the news. As modern journalism evolved from these early personalized newspapers, the news was presented objectively (and, presumably, accurately) by anonymous reporters, but the editor retained his right to express his opinions and state his policies—on the editorial page. And the byline column is a specialized development of editorialized news which fits into the same category.

On the modern editorial page the readers also have a right to express their opinions, and they may "talk back" to the **30a** editors and columnists. This they do in the "letters to the editor" used in many newspapers. Only bona fide, signed letters are generally used, and the editor reserves the right to reject a letter or to reduce its length in order to meet space limitations or to abide by the journalistic code of ethics or the laws of libel. In a sense, each of these letters is an editorial, but it is an expression of the opinions of a reader instead of the editor.

Although editorials normally do not carry bylines, they are understood to be statements of the editor—whose name usually appears in the newspaper's *masthead*. The editor may use contributions of special editorial writers or of syndicates, but he still assumes responsibility for the views expressed in all editorials. The "editorial we" in the regular editorial section refers to the editor.

With byline columns, however, the situation is different. While these often appear on the editorial page (but also appear on the sports page, the society page, the front page, and elsewhere), the editor assumes no responsibility for the views expressed by the writer. Statements in regular editorials are sometimes quite contrary to statements in byline columns. In fact, publishers today assume that a newspaper has a social responsibility to seek out and publish the opinions of writers who effectively represent all points of view which citizens of a democracy deserve to know. Usually the byline writer uses the first person "I," but if he uses the "editorial we," he is still referring to himself alone.

Both the editorial and the byline column represent personal journalism and have some things in common (personal opinion), but other characteristics are different. Such differences are brought out in the sections which follow.

Editorials

While the reporter's duty is to explain the news from an objective point of view, the editorial writer is privileged to add his own interpretation and appraisal of those events. The attributes, purpose, value, and contents of editorials may be delineated as follows:

30b **Attributes of Editorials.** To comment on current events, editorials should be timely. Readers are more interested in news than in history. What happened today affects them today, and they are open to suggestions and opinions on such matters. This factor dovetails with the second essential attribute—consequence. Minor news stories rarely make interesting editorials. The editorial writer usually may choose from a large selection of important events—events which attract and affect a large number of readers. The current issues and problems arising from events, rather than events themselves, form the subject matter for editorials.

Value of Editorials. The editorial is valuable to both the newspaper and the reader. It gives the newspaper a chance to present its policies and beliefs without coloring the regular news stories with biased statements. If the newspaper believes taxes are high, it can carry on a long-time campaign for lower taxes, using every timely opportunity that arises to present its arguments. The newspaper's appraisal of local, state, national, and world-wide events can be offered effectively in this manner. On the other hand, readers benefit by the expert interpretations and opinions on current events offered by the informed thinkers who write the editorials. Needless to say, the editorial writer must be a trained thinker, a keen student of society, a skilled interpreter. His work requires knowledge in many fields as well as patience and aptitude for careful research. The average reader does not have the ability or the time to unravel the complexities of day-by-day events. He relies to a large extent upon editorial writers to do this for him.

Types of Editorials. The ultimate purpose of the editorial is to convince, whether or not the writer hopes to rouse his readers to immediate action. When the editorial writer comments on a current event, he is an attorney speaking to a jury. "Here is the evidence," he declares. "With these facts before you, the verdict should be as I have indicated." Just how far he goes in his effort to influence opinion varies from editorial to editorial, and from his purpose arise three principal "types" of editorials.

In one editorial the writer may merely *interpret* an event, offering no specific action but simply explaining and appraising something to inform the reader. In another, he may **30c** *suggest* (outright or subtly) one or more satisfactory courses of action. In a third, he may *exhort* the readers to take immediate action, pointing out the gravity of the matter. Of course, the writer who shouts "Wolf!" too often without sufficient cause is soon unheeded. Yet another "type" of editorial is a short, humorous one intended to lighten the seriousness of the editorial section and to inject an element of entertainment, although it also can be a humorous jab on a serious subject.

Contents of Editorials. An editorial is usually composed of two parts: (*a*) a brief explanation of a current event and **30d** (*b*) the writer's interpretation and appraisal of that event. The reader must understand the question before he can understand comments upon it. The editorial writer often **30e** must assume that the reader knows little or nothing about the current event under consideration. He first serves as a reporter by briefly reporting the news which has prompted his editorial, and this part of the editorial is similar to the tie back in the follow-up story. Then the editorial writer is free to add his own (the "editorial we") interpretation. No standardized form or style, except that of effective newspaper English, is used in writing editorials. The writer is free to use whatever form best conveys his idea—essay,

news, narrative, verse, or what not. In style, however, the editorial
should be as well polished as anything in the newspaper. Editorial
effectiveness is a blend of sound thinking and good writing,

30f and the two are often indistinguishable. A catchy headline
and opening will be helpful for any editorial, no matter
what subject is discussed. The concluding paragraph also

30g deserves special care in the writing, for it is the last chance
the writer has to impress the reader on the points that he
is making in the editorial.

Columns

Displaying the byline of the writer, the column is a vehicle that
thrives only on "box office" appeal of the writer's name. The columnist seeks to develop such rapport with readers that they will turn
regularly to the page on which the column regularly appears to
"see what Joe Blow (the columnist) has to say." If he cannot recruit
a sufficient following to do just that, he will not remain for long in
the vocation of column writing.

Essential Qualities of Columns. How does the column writer

30h cultivate box office appeal? First and foremost, he must
have something to say. He must have both an extensity and
an intensity of knowledge to possess the resources that

30i qualify him as a commentator on the subjects that he covers.
Next, the columnist must say his part interestingly. The
most erudite individual fails as a columnist if he cannot convey his
knowledge in a readable, interesting style.

Having something to say and saying it interestingly are absolute
requirements for a successful columnist. If, in addition, he can say
it entertainingly, he has a greater chance for success. Many readers
will take pills of knowledge that are attractively packaged and
offered in doses not distasteful, but many more persons will gulp
down pills offered in the form of sugar-coated, colorful delicacies.
That is the difference between "interestingly" and "entertainingly."

The acid test of a columnist is his durability. If he can maintain
high quality day after day and week after week, he has a chance.
As soon as he runs out of something to say (interestingly and,
possibly, entertainingly) he will run out of box-office appeal.

Types of Columns. There are four broad types of byline columns.
The largest group, the one that includes a wide variety of offshoots,
is the "straight editorial" (or the commentary or the analysis-of-the-

news) type which editorializes on current events. This is the type of
most columns that appear on the editorial page. The sports column
also fits into this category. Two other types are the humor column
and the gossip column—and both of these also deal with current
events. Humor columns appear sometimes on the editorial page,
sometimes on the front page, and sometimes in the Sunday edition
only. The gossip column is a type used in the society-women's
section to give interesting news notes on local citizens, and it is also
a syndicated type giving intimate facts and rumors about famous
and infamous people. The fourth type of column is the "how to
do it" or "what to do" series. This could be one on golfing, appearing on the sports page; on fashions, appearing on the society page;
or on health, dancing, or any other subject of current interest,
appearing anywhere in the newspaper.

Writing Style of Columnists. The writing style of a columnist
is one that he himself must develop. He does not want to   **30j**
mimic other columnists, nor does he want to be so "different" that he is not understood by readers. Whatever his style, he
must write interestingly and, if possible, entertainingly.

Exercises

  I. Clip from newspapers five editorials and editorial columns plus the
     news stories on which the editorials and columns are based. Paste the
     "pairs" on sheets of paper and analyze the difference between each
     pair.
 II. Clip from newspapers three editorials, one merely interpretative, one
     suggestive of a certain course of action, and one exhorting readers to
     action. Paste these on sheets of paper and analyze their contents and
     style.
III. Clip from newspapers three editorial columns which obviously have
     different points of view regarding current events. Paste the clippings
     on sheets of paper and write your own opinion of the logic, form,
     and style of each.
 IV. Clip from newspapers three news stories which you believe contain
     subjects calling for editorial comment. Paste the clippings to sheets
     of paper and write an editorial on each of them. Make one inter-
     pretative; the second, suggestive; the third, exhortative. Then write
     an editorial column in which you give your comments on all three
     of these news stories, using any form and style you desire.
  V. Write a "Letter to the Editor," the length assigned by your instructor,
     on some subject of current interest. The instructor may assign the
     subject or he may permit you to write on any subject you choose.

THE COMPLETE REPORTER
PART EIGHT

EDITING THE NEWS

With this section the discussion turns from news writing to news editing. All previous theory and exercises have dealt with the gathering and writing of news. Now the reporter needs to learn what happens to the story after it passes from his hands, for he frequently must "follow through" the entire editorial process.

After the story is written and before it appears in print, the news copy is handled by several persons. It moves through the following stages:

1. It may need rewriting.
2. It must be copyread.
3. It must be headlined.
4. It must be set in type.
5. It must be proofread.
6. It must be given a place in the newspaper by the make-up editor.
7. It must be printed.
8. It must be circulated (delivered, mailed, and sold on streets).

The editorial department performs only the first, second, third, and sixth steps, and these will have the closest attention.

The reporter has frequent opportunities to serve in an editorial capacity. It is his duty to turn in clean copy requiring minimum alterations, and in this respect he should be his own copyreader. In addition, he may be called upon— if he is properly equipped—to serve at editorial desks. Of most importance, the editorial perspective will strengthen the reporter's grasp of his work as a writer.

Chapter 31

Rewriting Faulty Stories

THREE different types of stories are called rewrites in newspaper offices. One type was considered in the discussion of stories which have appeared in competitive papers (see Chapter 11, Rewrites and Follow-Ups). The second type includes stories written by "desk men" from facts given them over the telephone by "leg men." As the names indicate, desk men are reporters who remain in the office, and leg men are reporters who go out to gather news. The third type of rewrite—the type discussed here—is the story that is rewritten because of its flaws.

Serious Errors

The reporter seeking reasons why stories need to be rewritten should glance over all preceding discussions. There he will find many "do's" and "do not's" to observe in writing news stories. Many of the errors mentioned can be corrected by the copyreader, but some are so serious as to require the work of a rewriter, who is generally one of the newspaper's most experienced staff members. What are those "serious" errors?

The Main Feature May Not Be Stressed in the Lead. As pointed out, choice of the main feature may be a matter of opinion. **31a** The reporter's sense of values is usually an excellent guide in selecting the lead feature if there are several to choose from. However, the reporter sometimes does overlook what is undoubtedly the outstanding feature, burying it deep in the story. To illustrate, suppose a reporter wrote his lead about an automobile accident, using three or four paragraphs to describe the accident and mentioning in the fifth paragraph that five persons were killed. The story, or at least the lead, would have to be rewritten.

The Story May Be Badly Organized. Though the main feature may be handled properly in the lead, the body of the **31b** story may be a rambling puzzle. Or the reporter may jump too quickly into a chronological account of the event, forgetting to summarize all features before he relates details. Sometimes the rewriter needs only to change a few paragraphs of the story. Sometimes he is fortunate to salvage one paragraph.

The Story May Be the Wrong Type. The reporter may have

31c tried to write a feature story about an event which was definitely straight news. Unless the facts of an event justify this type of story, the reporter should avoid straining to achieve a feature angle, for the strain will be evident in his copy. On the other hand, the reporter may overlook an excellent feature story in writing up an event as straight news. When he converts a feature into a straight news story or a straight news story into a feature, the rewriter usually must revise the entire story.

Exercises

I. The following story has, among other errors, a lead which does not play up the proper feature. Rewrite the story.

A Lakeville salesman was found early this morning tied to a tree near a back road atop Hogback Mountain where he had been left by two kidnappers who stole his car.

John Daniels, who sells vacuum cleaners, was apparently unharmed following his ordeal at the hands of two armed and dangerous brothers, Jay and Curtis Smith, both ex-convicts.

The brothers, Capital City natives who served prison terms for armed robbery, were captured two hours after Daniels was found.

They surrendered after Curtis Smith, 48, had been shot in the leg by state police at a roadblock on Highway 44 outside Timber City.

State Police Captain A. T. Totter said the kidnappers tried to crash the roadblock in Daniels' stolen car. Jay Smith, 32, exchanged shots with the police as the car, driven by his brother, roared up to the barricade.

The vehicle went out of control when the driver was hit and plunged down a roadside ravine.

Daniels said he gave the brothers a ride when he came upon them hitchhiking near Lakeville. He said the younger brother pulled a gun and ordered him to drive to the lonely mountain road.

"They probably were on their way to rob a bank or commit some other crime when we caught them," Captain Totter said.

The brothers were to be charged with kidnapping and armed robbery upon their release from City Hospital.

II. The following story has flaws in its organizations. Rewrite it.

A five-passenger airplane with stuck landing gear made a safe belly landing at City Airport yesterday without injury to the pilot or his single passenger and with little damage to the plane.

Barney Richards, 42, of Gladeville, Florida, and his business partner, Kenneth Maxey, 38, also of Gladeville, were returning home from New York where they had been on business.

They planned to stop at City Airport to refuel, but discovered the landing gear on the twin-engine plane would not lower.

The two men are partners in the Rixey Corporation, operators of a motel chain headquartered in Gladeville. Richards is a veteran pilot with some 2,500 hours of flying time.

After taking all emergency measures in an effort to lower the wheels, Richards circled the airport for almost two hours, making a dozen test runs at the field.

The plane touched down on the asphalt strip at about 80 miles per hour, leaving a cloud of smoke and flying sparks. It skidded on its belly approximately 500 feet before stopping.

Airport Manager Joseph McKinley advised the pilot of runway conditions by radio. Another plane took off from the airport and flew beneath the crippled plane in a vain effort to locate the trouble.

Meanwhile, fire trucks and ambulances were rushed to the field.

About 2:56 p.m., Richards radioed McKinley: "I'm coming down."

Maxey was advised to get into the rear seat to balance the craft when it landed.

After the crash landing, the only visible signs of damage to the plane were crumpled propellers and a badly scratched fuselage.

When the plane stopped, many spectators who had assembled let out a cheer and ran out to meet the two men, who scampered from the plane to safety, fearing the craft might catch fire.

The two men were to continue their trip home by commercial airlines today. They said the plane would remain at the field here until it can be repaired.

III. Convert the following straight news story into a human-interest story.

Police arrested Leroy (Jughead) Phillips, an ex-convict, on a charge of robbing a filling station operator of $500 at gunpoint.

Arnold Hinton, operator of the station on Wilson Street, identified Phillips as the unmasked gunman who robbed him about 11:30 p.m. yesterday.

Police arrested Phillips at a downtown bar where he was trying to pass one of the stolen bills minutes after the hold-up.

"I became suspicious when I saw the denomination of the bill," Earl Arpessos, bartender, told police. "A customer as poorly dressed as Phillips was doesn't go around flashing hundred dollar bills."

Police found a revolver in Phillips' coat. All of the money was recovered.

IV. Rewrite the following stories.

A.

A proposed one-cent sales tax is the city's only alternative to a tax increase next year, Comptroller Paul Y. Woodson said today. Much higher taxes are in prospect for Lakevillians unless city and county voters approve the sales tax in the November 3 election, Woodson warned.

Woodson declined to estimate the increase which might be forthcoming next year "until our budget figures are complete," but said: "We have been talking about a sales tax for many years. I think this is the year in which we must have one. It is either a sales tax or much higher real estate tax rates next year."

The city tax rate now is $2.10 per $100 of assessed valuation, or $105 on a home assessed at $5,000.

Each penny of the tax rate brings the city $113,000 in revenue, and a 57-cent rate increase would be necessary to raise the $6,400,000 additional funds which preliminary estimates show the city will need next year.

A 57-cent increase would raise the tax rate to $2.67 per $100 of assessed valuation, and increase the tax bill of the owner of a $5,000 home from $105 to $133.50.

The proposed one-cent sales tax would bring an estimated $9,000,000 a year for the city and county, Woodson explained. Of this amount, $7,000,000 would go to the city, enough to provide additional funds required for operations next year and still leave a surplus equivalent to a six-cent tax levy.

The surplus could be used to reduce the present $2.10 tax rate, or to stabilize the existing rate for several years, the comptroller said.

"The sales tax is urgent," Woodson said. "Costs of city government will continue to rise, due to expanding population. Additional revenue sources must be found, and the sales tax would be the most productive I can think of."

Woodson emphasized that there is "no easy way to ease the property tax."

"One way is to cut costs, and the other way is to find a substitute revenue source," he said.

The comptroller said the City Council has been cutting costs everywhere possible, and still more taxes are needed.

B.

A cold-drink machine in City Hall released 25 bottles of pop when Miss Lucille Freeman, stenographer in the finance office, dropped in her nickel. Something stuck in the machine, which delivered its entire supply in rapid-fire order.

Miss Freeman called the company, whose agent put the 24 extras back into the machine. Her only comment, "It happened too early in the morning to drink all 25."

C.

W. E. Dale, attorney of Salem, was the speaker at the Rotary Club at its regular weekly meeting yesterday.

Mr. Dale spoke on "American Citizenship" and brought a wonderful message. Mr. Dale said in part, "let us keep America for Americans. We can do that by teaching our children what it means to live in a country that is not always fearing an invasion or preparing to invade another country. It has been about a half century since we fought a war to end all wars but unfortunately we have found that was not true. But let us through our public schools teach our young that the privileges they enjoy, with their parents and homes, is not true of most children in many countries of Europe."

Mr. Dale was presented by W. J. Kind, who was chairman of the program.

D.

It was roundup time in the north end of town last night after police headquarters received a report that three hogs—not steers —were on the loose. Wary police officers rode herd on the stubborn and formidable beasts, the largest weighing about 350 pounds.

While several policemen were cautiously scouting the range in the 1200 block of East 12th Street in search of the hogs, Sgt. Clyde Baker and Patrolman Tony Spivak came upon the porkers in the 1400 block of Cabot Boulevard. The animals presented a distinct traffic hazard as they wandered about the busy street, poking their snouts into garbage cans.

The two officers shooed the hogs into an alley and stood guard as they awaited the arrival of a Humane Society truck. They intended to load the wayward critters into the truck and take them to the city pound. It was a good idea but it took some doing.

The situation was deceptively quiet until the truck arrived. With a crowd of onlookers gathered, the roundup began. Two of the hogs were caught in traditional roundup fashion—by throwing ropes over their heads. This turned out to be a mistake, for it left their feet free.

Patrolman L. J. Kelly met head-on with one of those feet and was taken to General Hospital where the doctors repaired the damage to his head.

The third hog was roped by his hind legs, which proved more satisfactory.

Capt. Charles Logan said it was not learned how the hogs happened to be out on the town. It is suspected they escaped from a stockyard or a meat-packing plant. They are being held —without bail—in the pound until someone claims them.

E.

City officers today were searching for a burglar who looted the West Avenue Barber Shop of merchandise valued at $85 last night.

Included in the loot were six large bottles of hair tonic, a quantity of powder and soap, and several combs, hair clippers, and razors, according to F. C. Snell, manager.

The burglar left evidence that he had used part of the loot before taking it with him. One of the wash basins showed signs that someone had shaved during the night, said Mr. Snell.

The shop was entered through a rear window.

F.

In his quarterly report to the County School Board today, Superintendent John Finney named a number of improvements.

New school rooms have been completed at Dole's, Five Points, Lynn Station Schools. Steel lockers have been installed at East Hill, Craiton, and James Park Schools, and new science equipment added at Gibson's.

One thousand new chair desks have been distributed among county schools and many loads of tables and cabinets built by Industrial Art Department students have been distributed to the schools.

By employing bigger school buses on a mileage basis Superintendent Finney believes a material transportation saving will be effected.

G.

Twice in the past week the manager of a Lakeville service station has stared down the barrel of a bandit's gun.

"They say lightning never strikes twice, but—" said John Watson, manager of the Hi-Power Gas Station at Ninth Street and Hoover Avenue.

At 1:30 a.m. Nov. 10, Watson was attacked by two men when he was getting a package of cigarettes for one of them from a vending machine.

Watson grappled with the men, tried to grab the gun, and was shot at three times. All the bullets went wild.

"When the men walked up, I was almost ready to close for the night," Watson said. "One of them asked for a pack of cigarettes, so I turned my back on him to get the cigarettes. That was my mistake."

He said the hold-up man stuck a gun in his back and ordered him into the station.

"I whirled and grabbed at the gun," Watson said. "He began pulling the trigger, and shooting into the air. The noise must have scared them, because they ran."

The second robbery attempt came last night at about 10 p.m. when Watson was preparing to write up the day's sales.

"I saw this man come in the side door of the office," Watson explained to police. "He flashed a gun and told me to put my hands behind my neck."

Watson said he had to watch helplessly while the man raked up the day's sales and dumped the money into a paper bag. The bandit went out the same side door, carrying $420 in cash.

Watson described all three unmasked bandits to police, who are confident arrests will be made soon.

V. Study the papers for examples of stories which should be rewritten. Rewrite the stories, handing in both clippings and rewrites.

Chapter 32

Copyreading

COMPARATIVELY few stories are completely rewritten before being sent to typesetting machine operators. So long as the organization of the story approaches the standard form, only the needed changes are usually made on the reporter's copy by the copyreader, who reads the story carefully to eliminate mistakes, to improve the language, and to write headlines.

One broad statement can cover the work of the copyreader in checking a story: He should right everything that is wrong. The last person to check the copy before it goes to the printer, he is the watchdog of the newspaper and the guardian of the reporters. This statement is broad, indeed, for the number of possible "wrongs" in newspaper copy is very great. Many of the most common errors which he might correct are violations of the "do's" and "do not's" of past exercises.

Copyreader's Duties

32a
1. *The copyreader checks the story for accuracy.* A careful reader of the newspaper, he knows the background of all events. He has the habit of checking doubtful statements. He usually is familiar with the city—its streets, buildings, leading citizens, officials. He is armed with the city directory, dictionary, atlas, encyclopedia, clippings, and other reference material. With his background and references, the copyreader is able to correct many errors, but he is helpless when the reporter makes an erroneous statement that can be verified only on the scene, or at the source of the story.

32b
2. *The copyreader makes corrections of grammar.* Standards of good English must be observed in writing all newspaper stories.

32c
3. *The copyreader eliminates verbosity in newspaper copy.* Whether it is one word or a complete paragraph, he "kills" all unnecessary copy.

4. *The copyreader eliminates libelous statements.* He tones down "dangerous" statements and makes sure that defamatory reports are justified. He can catch some libelous statements but not those resulting from erroneous reporting.

32d

5. *The copyreader simplifies the story.* He eliminates all confusing or ambiguous statements and all words which will not be understood by the layman. He replaces or defines all technical terms.

32e

6. *The copyreader eliminates editorialized matter in news stories.* If a story is bylined, however, a certain amount of editorial expression is permitted.

32f

7. *The copyreader checks all stories for adequacy.* If the reporter evidently has omitted certain essential facts, the copyreader returns the story to the reporter or gives it to the rewrite man for completion.

32g

8. *The copyreader sometimes must trim or shorten a story.* If the story is longer than the city editor or news editor desires, the copyreader is instructed to "cut it down" to a certain length. He eliminates the least essential paragraphs as he copyreads the story.

32h

9. *The copyreader makes the story conform to the newspaper's "style."* Each newspaper has certain rules covering optional forms of punctuation, abbreviation, capitalization, and spelling, and the copyreader sees that every story observes those rules.

32i

10. *In general, the copyreader attempts to polish and improve the story.* He tries to give the copy more vividness and smoothness by changing certain phrases, by inserting or deleting certain words, or by rearranging paragraphs or sentences. Nevertheless, he restrains himself from being too critical and attempts to preserve the reporter's original story as far as possible.

32j

11. *The copyreader writes identifying labels and instructional notes.* He does this for each story or portion of a story to expedite processing in the mechanical department. Such labels and notes include:

32k

(*a*) *Sluglines* of one to three words, written at the top left of each page of copy. The sluglines are set in type to accompany the story until it is matched with the proper headline, which ordinarily is set on a separate machine because it is larger type. Many newspapers use a system of slugging each story with the first word or two of the headline; others use a story label, such as "storm" or "fire," which may be the same as the guideline used by the reporter.

(b) Identifications for materials to be combined with stories already sent to the composing room. These identifying terms are:

(1) *Add*—to be added to the end of the story.

(2) *Insert*—to be inserted within the story, as new material or as a substitute for material deleted or "killed."

(3) *New Lead*—to replace the lead.

(4) *Precede*—to precede the lead of the story.

32| *Copyreader's Symbols*

To expedite their work, copyreaders have a set of symbols which they use in making pencil corrections. The reporter has already studied some of the symbols in the exercise on "preparing copy." Following is a more complete list:

Symbol	Definition	Example
⊘ or ⊙	Period mark	He was there⊗ He was there⊙
⌄	Comma	Therefore⌄he will . . .
⌄	Apostrophe	Ill let you know . . .
⌄⌄	Quotation marks	I'll let you know . . .
≡ or ⌣	Make capital letter	later that monday . . .
/	Make lowercase letter	Later in the day . . .

Symbol	Definition	Example
◯	Abbreviate or spell out word or number	(Doctor) Smith said . . . Dr. (Wm.) Smith said . . . The (2) men were . . . The (twelve) men were . . .
L or ⅃ or ⌗	Start new paragraph	⌊The end of the . . . ⌋The end of the . . . ⌗ The end of the . . .
no ⌗	Do not make this a new paragraph	no ⌗ The end of . . .
⌋ or ⌊	Indent on left or right	This symbol may be used on either side of the page or on both sides. If used on both sides, it indicates that the material should be centered.
/	Separate letters	Some of our students . . .
⌢	Bring letters together or close space	So͡me of the students . . . Some͡ of the students . . .
Line from one word to the beginning of the following word.	Bring copy together or join paragraphs	Four men, ~~who were~~ ~~found~~ were found adrift near . . .
⩸	Delete letter, word, or phrase	Sa͡ailing on . . . Sailing on ~~an~~ toward . . .

Symbol	Definition	Example
$\wedge$ or $\vee$	Insert letter, word, or phrase	Saíling on . . . Sailing on the . . .
$\sim$	Transpose letters, words, or phrases	Sailiing on . . . Sailing to on the . . .
Stet	Restore original text	*stet* Four ~~of the~~ men . . .
~~	Set in boldface type	**New residents here** . . .
_____	Set in italics	The *habeas corpus* case

In polishing or correcting a story, the copyreader frequently must write whole words or phrases between the typewritten lines, and he uses still another symbol to clarify such corrections. The handwritten *a* looks much like the *o*, the *u* like the *n*, and the *m* like the *w*. To clarify these for the compositor, the copyreader draws a short line beneath a handwritten *a*, *u*, or *w* and above the *o*, *n*, or *m* if there is danger that a letter may be misread (for example, "bay" in handwriting may look like "boy").

Another custom of copyreaders to prevent possible errors is the use of the paragraph symbol (illustrated above) to indicate the beginning of every paragraph, whether or not the paragraph is indented. This custom serves two purposes, first making paragraph indentation readily apparent, then offering an easy method of determining whether the story has been copyread in part or in whole.

Telegraph News. Most of the copy coming into the news-
32m paper office via teletype or telegraph requires treatment that is different from that given copy prepared locally. Teletype and telegraph news comes in all capital letters, as illustrated:

BILOXI, MISS., MARCH 22-YOUNG TOM MORGAN,

ROOKIE INFIELDER, IS THE TALK OF THE

BLANKVILLE BEARS' TRAINING CAMP BECAUSE HIS

HUSTLE AND DETERMINATION PUT HIM AT SECOND

BASE AHEAD OF VETERAN SWATTS WHITE.

If the proper symbol were used to mark down all letters to be set in lowercase, the copy would be covered with pencil marks. By agreement with composing room men, the desk man indicates only the letters which are to be capitalized, and all unmarked letters are set in lower case. A few lines of marked telegraph or teletype copy:

CENTERVILLE, JAN. 7-GOVERNOR LYNN SMITH

TODAY DISCLAIMED ANY INTENTION OF TAKING

ACTION AGAINST THE STATE CITIZENS LEAGUE

BECAUSE OF . . .

Exercises

I. Copyread the following stories. (Note to instructor: To avoid mutilating the text, these exercises can be duplicated for student use, or the student can be instructed to copy the stories before copyreading them.)

A. Hodges—Wade speech

The newspaper has xxxx ha d many headlines which warn that there may be foreign country xxxxxx spies in america plotting to overthrow the government, but thier is another type foreign en emy who activiteis type of foreign enemy whose activities seldom are Recognized in newspaper. Fully fifty per cent of the destructive insects that are doing their bit toward internal strife are univted "guests from forEign countries, said to Dr. R. L. Wade, state entomologist, in a speech before the Lions c,ub yesterday.

Dr. Ward spoke on Man's wa Against Insects', explaining what his department has been doing to eliminate these terrible destrubtive inspects. The present-day method of agriculture and of farming and planting make ideal conditions for them to level happily in our land he revealed.

"They ar xxx mulplying as they would not have done had not man given them a cnance, providing them with enormous equ ntities of food and Placing it before them in the most inviting manner," he said.

There are in all the states of amoerica about two hundred major insects damaging and eating and living off of crops, trees, stored products, timber, household goods, and other goods, causing approximately two and a hlaf billion dollars worth of damage each of the years, he continued More than half of the distroyers was introduced from China, japan, India Afirca, France, xxxxxxx nd the shores of the Meditteranan Sea.

"To prevent foreign introductions of dangerous ins ct pests, all parts of entry have inspection Officials who examine all fruts and vegatables and all types of nursery stock which might insects harbor."

B. Ford—robbery

James L. Macey, eighteen year old youth of Big Springs, was arrested for highway robberty last night after police found him near the scene of his crime. He help up Mrs. D. M. Felts, 45, 1013 Tillman Street, and robb ed her to ten dollars in cash and a wed ding ring.

Macey strongly denied his innocence at plice Station last night, though Mrs. Felts has identified him for sure as the outrageous thief. A ton dolar bill were found on his perons but, knowint that he was to be captured, he had cleverly did aw ay with the rung.

Mrs. Fells, housefife of Mr. D. M. Felts, 1013 Traman Street, was up held near her home. It was about 7 P.M. at night, and she was walking from the store, when Maccey steped out of an ally and demanded that she dive over her muney and jewelry, which she did, of course.

Macey was picked up by police walking down the West Street, seven blocks frum the crime, about a half of an hour after the cirme. Policement Railey and Edwards made the arrest.

"I ain't guilty," cried Macey. "I just got in town from Big Springs, and I was looking for a room forthe night when they got me. They can't probe nothin no me cause I ain't guilty."

It is xxxxx pa thetic that such a oung man should hvar to be arrested on sich chargs, but he will have to subber, believe t ose atthopolice station. The streets must be made safe for women and children to walk on, xx and hex police will prosecute Mace to the fullest extent.

C. Lewis—grand jury

A new Grand Jury, sowrn into offic yesterday, was directed by Judge Thomas C. Crockett to continue "the investigation of the corruption in public office in Blank County."

Although the judge did not refer directly to the recent investigation which resulted in "ture bills" agianst 6 Constabals on bribery charges and against eight other persons on conspiracy charges, we have no doubt whatsoever that he had reference to that probe. Something should be done to eradicate public officials.

The grand jury was orderedxxxxxxxxxxxxxxxxxxxxxxxxxxxxxxx xxxxxxxxxxx to report back today to start its work on the rpesent term, P. F. Noll who became foreman at the last session of the Criminal Court of the County of Blank and will continue in that capacity.

"Certain officials are elected by the people to enforce the statures of this state in Blank County," Judge Crockett's charge said in one of its parts. "All laws should be enforced justly as long as they exist. If some law enforcing agencies are diligent in the enforcement of the criminal laws and other agencies are not, then a question arises as to why some officers are lax in performance of their duties.

"The Grand Jury as inquisitorial power to look their into conduct, to investigate such matters and if suficient eividence of improper conduct is heard by your body you should return indictments for such offense as the facts warrant.

"It is common knowledge that the Grand Jury for the last term of courtmade a good beginning by the investigation of the corruption in public office in Blank County. That good work must be continued. . . ."

Judge Crocket touched all the common law violations in his charge to the Grand Jury, and emphasized laws against gaming, xxxxxxxxxxxxxxx drunken driving and the "uncontrolled roadhouse" conditions, such as those that we know exist at the Riley Dance Hall on Centerville Pike.

"Gaming is an evil that exists in connection with roadhouses," the judge said, pointing out that gaming also may be carried on elsewhere. Among the forms we mentioned were slot machines, the "numbers" game and "butter-and-egg" racket.

"The uncontrolled roadhouse is a place where serious crimes are planned and ofttimes committed. One who protects crime is a bad citizen because the criminal class will come in increasing numbers and commit crime in that place or county where it knows it will have a hide-out and protection."

The judge pointed out the well-known fact that it "take a skilled person to drive an automobile when he is sober, if he is intoxicated, it is criminal and he should be indicted. Our Laws are such that a man can buy an automobile for $100 or $200, get a drivers permit and get out on the highways without previous diving experience."

D. Gordon—Jones trial

During a bitterly-fought trial in which Attorney Andrew Fiske charged that the city Health Department is trying to run.xxxxxx xxxxxxxxxxxxlittle dairy operators out of business to the benefit of major concerns, Fred Jones of Jones Bros. dairy, Plainview Pk., was fined $25 in city court yesterday.

The charge was that the Jones' twenty-four cow diary was retailing milk after the grade of the milk had been reduced and after their permit to retail the sale of milk had been revoked by law.

"Isn't it a fact," barked Attorney Fisk, "that the city is trying to run the small dairyman out of business"?

Prosecutor Marvin Ragsdale jumped to his feet protesting in a fit of passion and Judge John Turney sustained him.

Later Fiske charged that the city sanitation department was persecuting the little dairyman to the advantage of such firms as City Wide and Blankville dairies.

"I don't see where you find prosecution," replied Inspector Joseph Ray, "when the average size of the dairy herds with city selling permits has remained at 13 cows for seven years."

He testified that the Fred's milk was reduced because equipment was not always found properly clean and that barn improvements were needed. If this is true, the grade certainly should have been reduced.

"I didn't write the ordinance and Mr. Jones has admitted that he has violated it,", said the judge.

"I'll have to fine you $35."

Attorney Fisk immediately took an appeal.

E.

```
        CENTERVILLE, MARCH 21--THE DETERMINA-

    TION OF A HOUSE ANTI-ADMINISTRATION

    BLOCK TO BRING ALL GENERAL BILLS TO THE
```

FLOOR FOR A VOTE POINTED TO A STORMY
WEEK IN THE STATE LEGISLATURE, WITH
PARLIAMENTARY MANUEVERS DECIDING THE
FATE OF MANY MEASURES AS THE ASSEMBLY
HEADS TOWARD ADJOURN SATURDAY.

REP. JAMES H. CAREY (R., SMITHVILLE),
LEADER OF THE BLOC AND RECOGNIZED AS ONE
OF THE KEENEST PARLIAMENTARIANS IN THE
LEGISLATURE, SAID HE WOULD FORCE A
VOTE TODAY ON HIS RESOLUTION TO BRING
ALL GENERAL BILLS OUT OF COMMITTEE AND
TO THE HOUSE FLOOR FOR A VOTE.

THE RESOLUTION WAS OFFERED FRIDAY
BY THE GOOD-NATURED BUT FIERY LITTLE
REPRESENTATIVE AFTER HE WAS BEATEN IN
AN ATTEMPT TO STOP PASSAGE OF A RESO-
LUTION ADJOURNING THE SESSION NEXT
SATURDAY. THE HOUSE DEFEATED A MOTION
TO TABLE CAREY'S PROPOSAL BUT BEFORE A
VOTE ON THE MEASURE ITSELF COULD BE TAKEN
SPEAKER JOHN E. HEITS RUSHED THROUGH

A MOTION FOR A WEEK END RECESS UNTIL

10 A.M. TODAY.

ADMINISTRATIVE FORCES WERE EXPECTED

TO MEET THE THREAT TO AN ORDERLY AD-

JOURNMENT BY SEEKING APPOINTMENT OF A

STEERING COMMITTEE TO KEEP A RUSH OF

BILLS FOR FINAL PASSAGE FROM LEAVING

THE LEGISLATIVE CALENDAR CLOGGED WITH

IMPORTANT UNFINISHED BUSINESS.

CAREY DECLARED HE WOULD GET A VOTE

ON EVERY BILL "I WANT A RECORD ON"

REGARDLESS OF THE VOTE OF HIS

RESOLUTION.

"IN THE LAST SESSION BILLS DISAP-

PEARED IN COMMITTEES AND PEOPLE NEVER

KNEW WHAT HAPPENED TO THEM OR WHY THEY

NEVER WERE VOTED ON," HE SAID. "IF

NECESSARY I'LL MOVE ON EACH BILL THAT

A VOTE IS NEEDED ON TO HAVE IT BROUGHT

UP, EVEN IF A TWO-THIRDS VOTE WILL BE

REQUIRED. AT LEAST ANY KIND OF VOTE

ON A MEASURE WILL SHOW HOW EACH

MEMBER STANDS."

A CALENDAR OF THE HOUSE'S ACTION ON

ALL OF ITS GENERAL LEGISLATION THROUGH

LAST WEEK WAS PUBLISHED OVER THE

WEEKEND, IN COMPLIANCE WITH A RESOLUTION

INTRODUCED BY CAREY AND PASSED BY THE

HOUSE.

IT SHOWED 253 HOUSE BILLS YET TO BE

FINALLY ACTED ON OF THESE, 202 ARE

READY FOR FINAL PASSAGE, BUT ONLY 55

HAVE BEEN REPORTED OUT OF COMMITTEE,

FIFTY-ONE OTHERS HAVE NOT BEEN

ASSIGNED TO COMMITTEES.

II. Study the newspapers for examples of corrections which copyreaders failed to make. Hand in the clippings, along with an explanation of each correction needed.

Chapter 33

Proofreading

33a AFTER a news story has been set in type, it must be proofread to eliminate any errors made by the compositor. Proofreading is not copyreading. That is, the proofreader does not attempt to improve the story. His sole job is to see that the proof follows the original typewritten story. However, the proofreader is free to correct misspelled words, incorrect English, and other such blunders which have escaped the eyes of reporters and copyreaders.

Using Proofreader's Symbols

The proofreader also has a set of symbols, many of them like the copyreader's symbols. But there is an important difference in the use of these symbols. The copyreader employs his symbols within a story at the places where they are needed. The proofreader **33b** must place all of his symbols in the margin of the galley proof, indicating at what point changes are needed in the story. Two methods are employed in making this indication.

1. The correction is noted in the margin directly to the right or the left of the line in which the error appears, with an additional symbol within the line pointing out the error. The correction should appear in the margin closest to the error. For example:

Three men rode|in the rear of   #

If a line contains several errors, the correction symbols in the sequence are placed as needed and are separated by slanting lines:

three men rode|in the ⱦear ⸤ſo⸣   #/l.c./tr.

2. The correction is noted in the margin with a line drawn from the symbol to the error. This method is satisfactory if there are few errors. Example:

three men rode⌃in the rear of   #

The proofreader will find that his symbols enable him to abbreviate instructions on all corrections except those which require the writing out of words, phrases, or sentences. Words and short phrases usually can be handled as marginal corrections by either of the two methods illustrated above, but a rather long sentence can be manipulated more effectively by the second method. If the compositor has omitted, or jumbled, a large portion of a   **33c** story, the proofreader may mark "See copy" in the margin, returning the original copy to the compositor with the corrected proof. For all such corrections as those mentioned in this paragraph, the proofreader must indicate exactly where words or phrases must be changed or added. Note the example:

the rear

three men rode in ~~there~~ of   **33d**

If the error is only a single letter, the correction can be   **33e** made as follows:

_n_

three men rode in the ɳear of

As an additional duty, the proofreader must check the typesetter's method of splitting words between lines. He must   **33f** correct the words which are not split between syllables according to accepted usage. A dictionary is usually his guide for this purpose. Split-word corrections are made as follows:

next door and had failed to rep-

_ρ_ ∧lace rocks and gravel which were

The more common proofreader's symbols are shown on pages 426–427.

Exercises

I. Following are newspaper stories in manuscript form, and below each story is a galley proof of that story. Proofread each galley proof. (Note to instructor: These galley proofs can be duplicated to avoid defacing this text. Or the students can be instructed to copy the lines containing errors and to indicate the proper method of correcting the errors.)

A.

Blankville's annual Clean-up, Paint-up,
Fix-up Campaign will be observed during the
week of April 20, it was decided this morning at a meeting of the arrangements committee at City Hall.

Elaborate plans including the annual "tin
can parade," speakers in schools, poster
contests, and other features, were made by
the committee, which is predicting that the
campaign this year will top all previous efforts.

Attractive and colorful posters, window
displays, banners, buttons, and stickers will
be used to advertise the week, being sponsored
by the Blankville Boy Scouts with the cooperation of the executive committee named
at the meeting today.

At the meeting next Tuesday the committee
will complete the daily program for the seven-
day period. Tentative plans call for the fea-

turing of one phase of the drive on each day

of the week.

> Blankville's annual Clean-up, Paint-up, Fix-up Campaign will be observed during the week of April 20, itt was decided this morning at a meeting of the arraugements committee at CityHall.
>
> Elaborate plans, including the annual "tin can parade," speakers in schools, contests, and other features were made by the committee, which is predicting that the Campaign this year will top all previous efforts. Attractive and colorful posters, window dis plays, banners, buttons, and stickers will be used to advertise the week being sponsored by the blankville Boy Scouts, with the cooperation of the executive committee named at the meeting today
>
> At a meeting next Tuesday the committee will compete the daily porgram for the 7-day period. Tentative plans call for the featuring of one phase of the drive on each day of the week

B.

W. Earl Sample, an attorney here for 14

years, today announced announced he will be a

candidate in the April 11 primary for the

Republican nomination for judge of the First

Division of General Sessions Court.

Mr. Sample is seeking the post now held by

Judge Richard Holmes. N. A. Bales, attorney,

also has announced as a candidate for the

Republican nomination for this judgeship.

"I feel that I am fully qualified to hold
this office, as my 14 years in the practice of
law have amply acquainted me with the problems that arise in a court of this nature, both
from the standpoint of the plaintiff and
defendant," Mr. Sample said.

"I have never before held public office, nor
am I the candidate of any political group or
faction, but am depending upon the recommendation of those who know me to nominate and
elect me.

"It is my desire to assure all my friends
that, if elected, my administration of the
affairs of this office will be such as will
reflect credit on the party whose nomination
I seek."

> W. Earl Sample, an attorney here for
> 14 years, today announced he will be a
> candidate in the April 11 primary for
> the Republican nomination for judge of
> the First Di vision of General sessions
> Court

Mr. Saml is seeking the post now held by Judge Richard Holmes. Atty., N. A. Bales also has announced as candidate for the Republican nomina-ion for this judgeship. ████

"I feel that I am fully qualified to hold this office as my 14 years xxx in the practice of law have amply ac-quainted with the me problems that arise in a court of this nature, both from the standpoint of the *plaintiff* and defendant," Atty. Sample said.

"I have never before held public office, not am I the candidate of any political group or faction, but am de-pending upon the recommendation of those who know me to nomi ate and elect me.

"It is my desire to a ssure all my friends that if elected, m^y administra-tion of the affairs of this office willbe this office will be such as will reflect credit on the ;arty whose nomination I seek

C.

A third alleged member of a juvenile theft ring was jailed last night, and Blank county officers said their "solved" list of recent housebreakings was increasing rapidly.

The third youth jailed, J. B. Nichols, 22, of 1932 Magnolia avenue, admitted partici-pating in seven break-ins, Detective J. B.

Austin said.

Previously the other suspects, James Lane, 142 Mitchell street, and W. H. Coster, 2600 Washington avenue, both 21, confessed committing at least eight other burglaries.

Detective Cate has been working on the burglaries, centered about the Indian Hills residential district for several weeks.

The officer said last night the seven burglaries admitted by young Nichols would be "checked" today.

A large quantity of jewelry, guns, and small articles taken from the homes was recovered, officers said.

The detective said a total of about 15 housebreakings had been admitted. Hearings for the suspects will be held at 4 p.m. Monday.

A third alleged member of a juvenile theft ring was jailed lat night and Blank county officers said their "solved list of recent housebreakings was increasing Rapidly.

The third youth jailed, J. B. Nichols, 15, of 1932 Magnolia avenue, admitted participating in seven break-ins Detective J. B. Austin said.

Previously other the suspects, James Lane, 412 Mitchell Street. and W. H. Coster, 2600 Wash. A enue, both 21, confessed committing at least 8 other burglaries.

the burglaries, centered about the Detective Cate has been working on Indian Hills residential district for several weeks

The officer said last night the seven burglaries admitted by young Nichols would by be "checked" today.

A large quantity of jewelry, guns, and small articles taken f₁om thehomes was recovered, officers said.

The detective said a total of about 15 housebreakings had been admitted. hearings for the suspects would be held at 4 p.m. Mon.

II. Check the newspapers for errors which have escaped the eyes of proofreaders. Paste clippings of such errors to a blank sheet of paper and make corrections as a proofreader would do it.

Symbol	Definition	Example of Use
✗	A defective letter	Civil liberty is freedom from restraint by ✗ any law, save t/at which conduces in a greater or ℘ less degr/ee to the general welfare.
℘	Delete material	
ℭ	Letter is inverted	To do what I will is ℭ nat/ral liberty. To do what I will, consistently
#	Insert space	# with equal|rights of others, is civil liberty, the only liberty possible
w.f.	Wrong font	w.f. in / state of civilized society.
stet....	Do not make change. Let copy stand as it is.	If I wish to act, in every instance, in accordance w̶i̶t̶h̶ my own unrestrained will, I am made to reflect that all
ⓙ	Insert semicolon	others may do the same‿in which case I shall meet
⌒	Close up space	with⌒ so many checks and obstructions to my
tr.⌒	Transpose	tr. own will\my/that\ liberty tr. and hap/ȶ\piness will be far less than if I, with the
⋀	Insert comma	⋀ rest of the community⋀ were subject to the restraints of reasonable
⊙	Insert period	⊙ laws applying to all⋀
¶	New paragraph	¶ ⌊So it is, that proper and adequate laws are essential to the well-being and good order of
cap ≡	Capital letter	cap. civil society. b̲ut legal restraint, for n̲o other
l.c. /	Lowercase letter	l.c. /Reason than mere restraint, is certainly unphilosophical, and in-inherently wrong, be-

Symbol	Definition	Example of Use
Rom⁓⁓⁓	Use Roman type	cause it amounts to a Rom deprivation of <u>natural</u> liberty without any
Ital —	Use italics	Ital <u>compensating</u> benefits to the public at large.
⊙ (:)	Insert colon	James C. Carter, in his "Origin and Function (:) of Law," says∧
] or [	Move to right or left, as indicated	] ["It is the function] [of government to de- fine the limits or sphere
⌐ or ⌙	Move down or up, as indicated	in which the individual <u>may</u> act ⌐as a member of the social state, without at the same time encroach-
eg.#ˇˇ	Equalize spacing	eg.# ing upon✓the✓freedom ˇˇ of others.∧
ˇˇ	Insert quotation marks	It follows, there- fore, that to live under
spell out ◯	Spell out circled word	spell civil(gov.) is to surrender out a portion of our natural
ˇ	Insert apostrophe	ˇ liberty for the publics good, in order that that which remains to us may be the better safeguarded by the strong arm of the
⌣	Push down slug that prints	⌣ law. But liberty■may be destroyed by law. The
!/	Insert exclamation mark	Romans furnish a con- !/ crete example∧The pre- vailing ethos or national
b.f. ⁓⁓⁓	Use boldface type	spirit of the Romans b.f. was <u>law</u>. Did not law
?/	Insert question mark	?/ regulate everything∧A citizen could not fix a price upon his own goods.
=/	Insert hyphen	It was the oppression of =/ law which cheap∧ ened the desire for life.

427

Chapter 34

Headlining

AFTER the copyreader reaches the end mark of a story, the editing process is still incomplete. Then he or some other member of the desk staff must write the headlines—a job sometimes as difficult as writing the entire story. What the reporter says in 50 or more words, the headline writer may have to say in five or six words. Moreover, the reader appeal of the story itself usually depends upon the headline. In other words, the headline is, like the lead, the showcase of the story.

The purpose of the headline is twofold: to attract attention to the story and to tell the story as completely as possible so that hurried readers may obtain the news at a glance. Since the lead summarizes the whole story, the headline is drawn largely from the lead. It is, in fact, the lead translated into vivid phrases, though long headlines (containing several *decks*) may go below the lead into the body of the story for additional material.

Since the headline is an abbreviated lead, the headline writer will encounter problems similar to those of the reporter in packing a great deal of information into a few words. If the reporter can briefly summarize the whole event in the lead, he does so. If multiple features would result in a very long lead, the reporter begins with one feature and summarizes others later. The headliner follows exactly the same rules, either summarizing the entire lead or selecting only the main feature or features of the lead.

34b *Types of Headlines*

One glance at a newspaper will give the impression that it contains dozens of types of headlines. True, the different sizes and styles of type afford an almost unlimited number of typographical combinations, but there are only five basic headline forms. All newspapers build their headlines from some combination of these forms. They are illustrated below.

Name	*Diagram*	*Example*

Crossline or Barline—a single line, centered

X X X X X X X **Rain Forecast Tonight**

Inverted pyramid—two or three lines, each shorter than the line above it, all centered

X X X X X X X **Lawyers Fight Effort**
X X X X X **To Eliminate Bar**
X X X X **Examinations**

Drop or stepped lines—two or three lines, each approximately the same length. The first line is flush at left, the last line flush at right, intermediate line (if any) centered.

X X X X X **Attorneys Oppose**
X X X X X **Effort to Abolish**
X X X X X **Bar Examinations**

Hanging indention—two, three, or four lines, the first line longer than other lines and not indented. Other lines are equal in length, and are indented equally at left.

X X X X X X X **Lawyers Protesting**
X X X X X **Efforts to Repeal**
X X X X X **Bar Examinations**

Flush-Left—two or three lines, each set flush at left. Lines can be different lengths, so no diagram is standard.

X X X X X **Lawyers Oppose**
X X X X X X X **Effort to Eliminate**
X X X X X **Bar Examinations**

The headline of one story may combine two or three of the forms above, called *decks* or *banks* (the latter term generally applies only to subordinate decks). If a one-deck head is used, it is usually the crossline, flush-left, or dropline variety. If a combination, the dropline or flush-left form usually tops the combination, and the flush-left, inverted-pyramid, hanging-indention, and crossline forms are used as subordinate decks (or banks). However, the flush-left form is not combined with such centered styles as the dropline and inverted pyramid; it usually takes a flush-left bank which is slightly indented from the left. Pleasing multideck combinations are obtained by alternating the inverted-pyramid or hanging-indention banks with crossline banks. Note the following diagram:

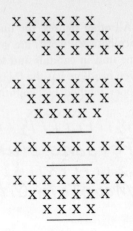

The size (type size as well as number of decks) of the headline is naturally determined by the news value of the story. In order of importance, headlines range upward from a one-column crossline, through all the one-column heads of one or more decks, through two-column, three-column, four-column heads, up to the *streamer* or *banner*, which is an eight-column head (usually one line but it can be more) set in large type. The copyreader or headliner does not have an unlimited choice of headlines, however. Most newspapers limit the number of headline combinations used day after day to those prescribed in a *headline schedule*.

The flush-left style of headline is the most popular form used by newspapers. The flexibility offered by this style makes headline writing easier and quicker, and it permits the writer more freedom in using the precise word to add punch to a headline.

34c "Counting In." Any line of type will contain a definite number of letters and spaces, and additional letters cannot be squeezed in. The headliner is able to make each line the right length by "counting in" the number of units (letters and spaces) which the given size of type permits in the line. For headlines composed of all capital letters, he generally counts one unit for each letter, except the M, W, and I. The M and W are equal to one and one-half units, and the I equals only half a unit. If the head is set in both capitals and lowercase letters, the l and i are counted as a half unit, the m and w and each capital letter are counted as one and one-half units (the capitals M and W as two), and all other lowercase letters and the I as one unit. The figure 1 and all punctuation marks except the question mark and dash are counted as half units. All other figures, the question mark, and the dash are full units. Space between words are generally one-half unit in capital heads and one unit in capitals and lowercase.

If, for example, a given headline has the following form in capitals and lowercase, the proper method of "counting in" is illustrated:

$$\tfrac{1}{2} \; \tfrac{1}{2} \; 1 \; 1 \; \tfrac{1}{2} \; 1 \; 1 \; 1 \; 1 \; 1 \; 1 \; \tfrac{1}{2} \; 1 \; 1 \; 1 \quad = 18$$

Two Persons Hurt

$$\tfrac{1}{2} \; 1 \; 1 \; 1 \; 1 \; 2 \; 1 \; 1 \; 1 \; 1 \; \tfrac{1}{2} \; 1 \; 1 \; \tfrac{1}{2}\tfrac{1}{2} \; 1 \; 1 \quad = 19$$

Near Mountain City

The unit count system is based upon the comparative width of each letter in each style and size of type. One unit is the "average letter," since most letters of a given type style and size will—comparatively speaking—be about the same width. M, W, I, i, l (and the capital letters in heads containing both capitals and lowercase) are the common exceptions, being either wider or narrower than the average. In some type styles other letters ($t, f, j,$ and perhaps others) vary too much to be included among the average, but for purposes of study these exceptions can be overlooked. Note the following table:

Units	Using Capital and Lowercase Letters	Using All-Capital Letters	Applies to Both Styles Headlines
½ unit	Lowercase i and l	The letter I Spaces	Punctuation marks except question mark and dash The figure 1
1 unit	Spaces All lowercase letters except $i,$ $l, m,$ and w capital I	All other letters except M and W	Question mark and dash All figures except 1
1½ units	All other capital letters except M and W Lowercase m and w	M and W	
2 units	Capital M and W		

This is the accepted method of counting in headlines, but headliners on some staffs do not follow the system carefully. Writing the headlines on a typewriter, they count each letter and space as one unit, depending upon the compositors to space the lines correctly. In most cases such headlines will fit the space, but frequently they must be rewritten.

34d   *Selection of the Headline*

Though every reporter must be a good judge of reader interest in news events, the responsibility for evaluating news stories rests largely upon the key desk men. The city editor, the telegraph editor, the state editor, or the makeup editor must decide which headline combination shall be written for every story at the time it is copyread. As mentioned, a newspaper has a number of different headline combinations which are used day after day. Each head differs from others in size or in the kind of type used. How does an editor determine which headline should go above each story?

In general, the importance of local interest of a news story dictates the size of the headline for the story. Since reader interest of a news event dictates the length of the story, one can conclude that the larger headlines are generally found on the longer stories. This is true generally, but there are exceptions. Even if a long story looks "overgrown" beneath a small headline, and a short story looks "topheavy" beneath a large headline, it is nevertheless not length but reader interest of the story that determines the headline display.

Another factor must be considered in deciding the size of a headline. One story must be weighed against other stories available that day to determine the relative value of each story. In other words, the stories must compete with each other. A fairly good story may get a rather large headline on a day when good stories are scarce. If several good stories are available, not all can be given equal space in the headlines. And even the best story of the day is not always given a front-page streamer. The importance of the story still should dictate the approximate size of the headline, and stories should not be greatly overplayed or underplayed to meet space requirements.

Besides selecting the proper size of headline which each story justifies, the editor also strives for variety. Most of the leading stories may be equally important, but the editor cannot use the same type of headline for all of them. In such a case he would attempt to make all of them approximately equal in size but would seek a variety of type faces. For the large majority of stories not among the "leading" class, a newspaper uses only a few headline combinations. Even so, variety is possible—if selections are well distributed among the often-used combinations and if other heads are carefully chosen.

In selecting heads, it is advantageous to remember that (1) nearly every page will need a few large heads; (2) double-column and other multicolumn heads improve the appearance of pages; and (3) both roman and italic type faces are available. Italic type is preferred for features or change-of-pace heads.

Fundamentals of Type

A brief consideration of the fundamentals of typography is appropriate at this point. The editorial worker does not propose to be a specialist in printing, but he must know enough about the subject to determine the potentialities and the limitations of the various styles of type at his command. Most printers (composing room men) do not think it is their responsibility to exercise their creative abilities; they will follow instructions in setting the type, but they are sparing in their suggestions of pleasing type combinations. Because he must select the type combinations and work closely with printers, the editorial worker should know the rudiments of typography.

To begin with, the editorial worker must learn and remember that type can be neither compressed nor expanded (except photographically) and that enough space must be provided to accommodate the size and style of type desired. That statement may have a sarcastic ring but it should be taken seriously because it reveals a principal source of irritation between editorial workers and printers.

Type Sizes. In the accompanying diagram are shown the three principal parts of metal type: the *face,* the *shoulder,* and the *body.* The face is the letter itself—the part of the type which actually does the printing. The shoulder is the part of the type upon which the typeface rests. The body, slightly less than one inch in depth, supports the typeface (with the top of the body being the shoulder). Type size is determined by the shoulder measurement and not actual typeface measurement.

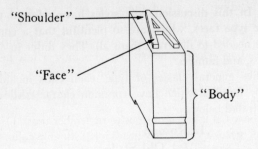

Metal type is used in the *letterpress* printing process. In the *offset* process metal type may also be used, but in this case proofs of the type are made and pasted into place, then a negative is made, and from that a plate is burned for printing on an offset press. Other typesetting machines, ranging from an ordinary typewriter to highly complicated equipment, are also used to eliminate the need for metal type in the offset printing process.

Measurement of type is designated according to "points," each point equal to about $\frac{1}{72}$ of an inch. Eight-point type, therefore, would be $\frac{8}{72}$ or $\frac{1}{9}$ of an inch, 12-point $\frac{12}{72}$ or $\frac{1}{6}$ of an inch, and so on. Before this point system was adopted, the different sizes were given specific names, which are still common in printing offices. Examples follow:

This is 4½-point, Diamond.

This is 5-point, Pearl.

This is 5½-point, Agate.

This is 6-point, Nonpareil.

This is 7-point, Minion.

This is 8-point, Brevier.

This is 9-point, Bourgeois.

This is 10-point, Long Primer.

This is 11-point, Small Pica.

This is 12-point, Pica.

This is 14-point, English.

This is 16-point, Columbian.

This is 18-point, Great Primer.

Type Styles. In this discussion type styles have referred to the varieties in the type faces, which are so plentiful that a complete book would be needed to illustrate them all. They differ in classes, width, heaviness, and families.

There are five general classes of type, each class including a number of type families which have common characteristics. The classes are illustrated below:

1. Roman
   (a) Old Style
   (b) Modern
2. *Italic.*
3. *Script*
4. Gothic
5. 𝕿ext

Only the roman, italic, and gothic classes of type are used by the editorial department of most newspapers. The other classes are considered too ornate for news columns.

In designating the type he desires, an editorial worker refers to the family instead of, or in addition to, the class. A family of type is a specific design of type—including a whole series of sizes. The families differ in the width and uniformity of strokes, the structure of the letters, and other such details. Many of the families will include two type classes: roman and italic. In these families roman type is designated merely by naming the family (for example, "14-point Caslon"); italics, by special notation ("14-point Caslon italics").

Some of the type families are named after the designers, whereas others are given descriptive titles. Following are some of the common families, with the name of each family set in appropriate type face:

Caslon	Bodoni	Garamond
Bruce	Scotch Roman	Modern
Bookman	Gothic	Goudy
Cheltenham	Tempo	Cooper

The width of letters in a given family may be:

1. **Standard**   3. **Condensed**

2. **Extended**   4. **Extra-Condensed**

The heaviness of this same type could be:

1. Standard   3. **Boldface**

2. Lightface   4. **Extrabold**

The same type could be set in:

Capitals and Small Capitals

Since one newspaper uses only a few type families, the editor need not become expert in this field. Many editors work mostly with only two or three families, yet it is possible for them to compile a great variety of heads.

Principles of Headlining

From a study of headlines, good and bad, a few general principles may be established for headline writing.

34e   1. The headline should tell the whole story (or the outstanding feature) as fully as possible and tell it accurately.

It should give as many of the 5 *W*'s as necessary, playing up the proper *W*. Each head should be a complete sentence, in telegraphic English (omitting unnecessary words):

Wrong   *Better*

Man Sustains   **Bellhop Killed**
A Fatal Injury   **In Hotel Fight**

34f   2. The symmetry of line-length and deck-wordage required by the style of the particular headline should be achieved. The lines must not appear crowded with type nor too empty:

Wrong   *Better*

South High Captures   **South High Wins**
State Grid Cup   **State Grid Crown**

Crowded

| Crowds Attend Opening
Of New Empire Theatre |

Better

| Many View Opening
Of Empire Theatre |

Empty

| Rainfall Sets
New Record |

Better

| Rainfall Establishes
New Month's Record |

| Rainfall Sets
New Record |

| Rainfall Establishes
New Month's Record |

3. If a headline is made up of several different forms, each **34g**
part should be a full statement and should stand alone:

Wrong

Janitor Falls Out
Of Broken Window

To Instant Death, While
Installing New Pane

Better

Janitor Killed
In 31-Foot Fall

Crashes Through Window
In Repairing Pane

4. A thought should not be repeated. Each deck or bank **34h**
should advance the story with additional information:

Poor

Mediation Board Ends
Steelworkers Strike

Conference Results in
Closing Steel Strike

Better

Mediation Board Ends
Steelworkers Strike

Four-Day Conference
Produces New Pact

5. Involved, confusing, or ambiguous heads should be **34i**
avoided:

Poor

Aged Fight Pension
Plans for Future

Better

Aged Group Fights
New Pension Plans

34j   6. Feature stories should have feature headlines:

Poor   *Better*
Blythe City Boy   ### Police Help Jimmy
Lost Down Town   ### Find 'Losted Mamma'

34k   7. The headline should suggest newness and action and should, therefore, contain a verb in order not to appear as a mere label. It should not start with a verb or an infinitive unless absolutely necessary, but it should have the verb in the first line if possible.

Wrong   *Better*
Civitan Club   ### Civitan Club Meets

Poor   *Better*
Urge Milk Fund   ### Milk Fund Urged
For City's Needy   ### For City's Needy

34l   8. The active verb is preferred over the passive, but the passive is often necessary:

Poor   *Better*
Bonds Rejected   ### Council Rejects
By City Council   ### Bond Issue Plan

Poor   *Better*
Rotarian Elect   ### Dr. Smith Elected
Smith President   ### Rotary President

34m   9. The present or future tense of the verb should be used. The historical present takes the place of the past tense. "Policeman Shoots Bandit" has much more immediacy than "Policeman Shot Bandit":

Poor   *Better*
Mayor Has Returned   ### Mayor Returns Home

Poor   *Better*

City Has Decided   **City To Construct**
    To Build Viaduct   **Railway Viaduct**

10. The headline should use vivid, fresh language; avoid   **34n**
the dull and the trite:

Wrong   *Better*

Gay Old Blade   **70-Year Veteran**
Cuts Pretty Figure   **Shows Zippy Stunts**
In Dancing Contest   **In Dancing Contest**

11. Words should not be repeated in the headline: **34o**

Poor   *Better*

Strike Conference Ends   **Mediation Board Ends**
Steelworkers Strike   **Steelworkers Strike**

12. Try to find the exact word to convey a thought: **34p**

Poor   *Better*

Youth Damaged   **Youth Slashed**
    In Knife Battle   **In Knife Battle**

13. Avoid provincial slang expressions: **34q**

Poor   *Better*

Bearcats Sock Away   **Bearcats Victorious**
Victory Over Center   **In Clash With Center**

14. The headliner cannot use simplified spelling (such as   **34r**
"tho") unless it is the style of the newspaper:

Wrong   *Better*

Rain To Continue   **Rain To Continue**
Thru Another Day   **Through Tomorrow**

34s   15. Use the single and not the double quotation mark. Divide thoughts with a semicolon. No period is necessary at the end of a head.

Wrong   *Better*

"Hot" Election Forecast.   ### 'Hot' Election Forecast;
90,000 Voters Ready   ### 90,000 Voters Ready

34t   16. Abbreviations should not be used unless standard, conventional, and generally understood, such as U. S., FBI.

Poor   *Better*

Eng. Club Holds   ### Engineers Hold
Annual Convention   ### Annual Convention

34u   17. Words, phrases consisting of nouns and adjective modifiers, prepositional phrases, and verb phrases should not be split between lines:

Wrong   *Better*

Three Men Es-   ### Three Escape
cape in Flood   ### Flooded River

Poor   *Better*

Council Passes Ice   ### Ice Tax Law Passes
Tax Despite Protest   ### Despite Opposition

34v   18. Headlines should not editorialize:

Poor   *Better*

Visitors Acclaim   ### Visitors Acclaim
Our Hospitality   ### City's Hospitality

Wrong   *Better*

Rent Too High   ### Rent Too High,
In City Suburbs   ### Say Suburbanites

19. Articles and other unnecessary words should not be used, except with names of books and other proper titles. **34w**

Wrong	*Better*
Fireman Saves A Little Puppy	**Fireman Saves Dog From Blaze**

20. "Half truths" must be avoided. Sometimes such heads can be libelous: **34x**

Wrong	*Better*
Pastor Sought In Larceny Case	**Pastor Sought As Eyewitness**

Subheads. Subheads are used within the news story, but they follow the general principles of headlining. They are cross-line heads, usually capital and lowercase letters in boldface **34y**
type of the same size used for the body of the story. They are placed between every three or four paragraphs in longer stories, and they serve both to "break up" the story and to play up minor highlights in the body of the story. The general rule is that no subhead is used unless the story is long enough for two subheads.

Headline Symbols

In order that the typesetter may clearly understand which type of headline is intended, the copyreader can use a certain symbol flanking each headline. The symbols are: **34z**

Type of Headline *Example*

Crossline ⌐ Thief Robs Pastor ⌐

Inverted pyramid \ Masked Bandit Robs /
\ Aged Pastor in /
\ Parsonage /

Hanging indention Aged Pastor Robbed
⌐ By Masked Bandit

Drop or stepped lines   Bandit Robs
                                                         Aged Pastor

Flush   Masked Bandit
                                                         Robs Aged Pastor
                                                         In Parsonage

Exercises

I. Clip from a daily newspaper a sample of each type of headline used. Arrange in order of importance from largest to smallest. Paste in notebook and "count in" the number of units in each head. Indicate the number of units in the margin opposite each line.

II. Do the same for another newspaper which uses a different style of headlines.

III. Following is a list of local stories available for one edition of a newspaper. Estimate as nearly as the given facts permit the news value of each story, and clip from a newspaper an example of the size and type of headline you would recommend for the story.

A. Mayor to attend meeting of State Association of Mayors. Length, two inches.

B. State Supreme Court judge dies. A native of this city and a leading lawyer here before elected 20 years ago. Length, 20 inches.

C. Professor to speak to Parent-Teacher Association. Speech to be on child psychology. Three inches.

D. City's leading night club goes bankrupt. Established 10 years ago. City ordinances against gambling, enacted last year, led to bankruptcy. Fifteen inches.

E. One hundred students from Sweden visit city. On tour of United States. Seven inches.

F. Two persons killed in automobile accident. A head-on collision just outside city limits. Twelve inches.

G. Three local high school seniors awarded scholarships at state university. Will receive $500 each as freshmen. Five inches.

H. Man sentenced for holdup of jewelry store. Had been arrested three months ago trying to escape with $2,000 in cash and $48,000 in jewelry. Ten inches.

I. Showers expected tomorrow. Little change predicted in weather. Two inches.

J. Chamber of Commerce Board of Directors asks for reorganization of city's Industrial Development Department. Head of this department recently criticized by Chamber of Commerce. Twenty inches.

IV. Write each of the following leads as briefly as possible in telegraphic English, using either the same words or synonyms, but select only the important words and ignore every word which a headline writer might ignore.

A.

J. T. Young, 12, 1701 Tenth Street, suffered a fractured skull in a fall down a stairway at his home yesterday. He was admitted in General Hospital, in critical condition.

B.

Richard Brooks of Chicago, president of the National Association, will speak here May 5, at the annual banquet of the City Retail Credit Association.

C.

A blanket 10 percent increase in the salaries of all city employees was announced today by Mayor T. R. Franks. The increase, which becomes effective next month, is "a restoration of part of the salary reduction of two years ago," said Mayor Franks.

D.

Eighty-year-old Y. O. Conner, former railroad engineer, fatally shot himself in the head here last night, after telephoning a friend that he was "tired of living." He died a short time after being taken to General Hospital, where he pleaded with attendants to let him die.

E.

Property owners should "organize and revolt" against the recent increase in property assessments, declared John F. Kale, prominent realtor, in a speech to the City Property Owners League last night. He suggested that the league petition the City Equalization Board for an immediate investigation of the increase.

V. Write a two-line drop headline for each of the stories in Exercise IV above. Use capitals and lowercase with 14 or 15 units in each line. Make use of the telegraphic sentences already prepared in completing this exercise.

VI. Following are defective headlines. Explain what is wrong with each one and then rewrite it within the maximum unit count of the original head. It may be necessary to add imaginary facts in rewriting some of them.

A. **Taxi Involved in
Serious Accident**

B. **Mayor Asks
Tax Increase**

C. **CLUB MEETS TODAY**

D. **Smith Has Filed
Suit For Divorce**

E. Principal Is Ousted
   By City School Board

F. Retail Credit Men
   Attend State Conv.

G. Our City Gets
   Safety Citation

H. 14 Suffered Injury
   In Bridge Collapse

I. Williams Given
   Sentence, Fine

J. Council Changes Tax
   Law To Aid Retailers

K. Church Board Splits
   In a Stormy Session

L. Robber Arrested
   In Robbery Try

VII. Study the newspapers for defective headlines. Hand in clippings,
along with an explanation of the faults of each head.

Chapter 35

Makeup

THE last step in editing the news is the arrangement of headlined stories so that each is displayed properly and attractively when it appears in the newspaper. The arrangement of stories—the physical makeup—contributes much to the paper's "personality." The importance of this phase of editing cannot be overemphasized, for the impression given to the reader by the newspaper's typographical appearance may prejudice him for or against the actual content.

Displaying the news is the job of the makeup editor (who on the average daily is the news or managing editor). Every story sent to compositors goes through his hands. He keeps a "schedule" (or list) of the stories, noting also the size of the headline and the approximate length of each story. He confers often with the desk editors, seeking a consensus on the most important stories of the day and determining the proper size and style of headlines for certain outstanding stories. Much of his time, however, is spent in the composing room, where he instructs compositors on the placement of stories.

Procedure for Makeup. In making up the newspaper, the editor gives his attention first to the most important stories available. Other stories must be arranged to suit the major stories. Though the editor does not complete making up the all-important first page until last, holding it open for last-minute news, he fills the inside pages with stories which he feels are not worth front-page display. Determining which page a story deserves is only the beginning. Next, he must decide which place on a specified page a certain story should have. Each page offers its own makeup problem.

Whether it is the front or an inside page, the editor first designates places for the major stories he wants on that page. **35a** He builds from the top down, putting the most important stories in the most conspicuous columns of the page. The eighth column (the last one at the right) is considered the most conspicuous on the front page. The first column is next in importance. Columns seven and two are reduced somewhat in importance by their immediate proximity to columns eight and one.

The conspicuousness of columns on an inside page is determined by the amount and position of advertisements and by the size of headlines used over the main story on the page. Big type, whether in an advertisement or in a headline, will diminish the importance of the adjoining column. Ordinarily, the first column is the most prominent one on an inside page.

As the makeup editor builds from the top down, he generally places the largest headlines above the half-fold of the newspaper. And, again, the large heads should occupy the most conspicuous columns above the fold. The main story of the day is usually found at the right-hand top of page one. The story of second importance appears at the top left. The largest pictures are usually placed at or near the top (but not in the eighth column).

Rule of Contrasts. After placing the main story, the makeup
35b editor must study the page carefully to give the best play
to other major stories, which also carry rather large black headlines. Putting two such headlines together will kill the effect of both. The reader first sees the whole page at once; then his eyes travel from one "black spot" to another. These black spots are large headlines and pictures. If they are separated by lighter type, the whole page is easier to read. Hence, the editor arranges the largest or blackest headlines on the page first; then he fills in other columns with stories carrying smaller or lightface headlines. This principle is called the rule of contrasts.

This principle does not apply merely to the proper spacing of "black spots." It is observed also in selecting headlines that must go side by side in adjoining columns. Two or three one-column headlines of the identical size and style of type may appear, at first glance, like one two-column or three-column head, if placed together side by side. This sort of error, commonly called a "tombstone," is avoided by using headlines of different sizes, styles, or faces of type. Some newspapers permit two identical heads in adjoining columns, if enough white space separates the heads, but
two are the limit. Proper separation of identical heads can
35c often be accomplished by use of pictures or by "staggering"
the headlines—that is, placing them so that every headline begins below or above a headline in either adjoining column.

Another problem the makeup editor must face is the proper
35d display of long stories. The use of subheads or boxed short
stories is useful for "breaking up" purposes, but the makeup

editor can break up the story further by cutting it in the middle (planting another story at the break) and continuing it in another column. A front-page story may be continued in the right-hand adjoining column, if it remains directly beneath the story's own head; otherwise, it must be "jumped" to an inside page. An inside-page story may be continued in the right-hand adjoining column, whether or not it remains beneath the headline.

Jumping Stories. The makeup editor usually observes a few general practices in jumping stories. They are: **35e**

(1) Do not jump short stories. A story of a few paragraphs can be fitted into a page without being continued to another page. If necessary, some paragraphs may be deleted to avoid a jump.

(2) Avoid jumping a story within the first few paragraphs. Enough paragraphs should be placed beneath the headline to balance the size of the headline (preventing the story from appearing top heavy). Jumping a story within the lead block is also undesirable.

(3) Avoid too many jump stories. This practice is followed because of the average reader's dislike of turning pages to read continued stories. A few newspapers have a policy of continuing no story from the front to an inside page.

(4) Do not jump stories from one inside page to another. Unless there is enough space on an inside page to accommodate the entire story, it should not be placed in that position.

Related Stories. Sometimes the makeup editor finds that he has several stories relating to one event. For example, he   **35f** may have reports from several cities on the effects of a storm. He groups such stories in making up the newspaper. The most common method is to use one large headline and a short roundup story to cover the whole event, placing the report from each city under a separate, minor headline beneath the general roundup.

Types of Front-Page Makeup   **35g**

The general designs used by makeup editors in arranging the front page may be classified in four different groups. These schemes have been established by custom, not by rule.

Types of front-page makeup are shown in the accompanying charts.

1. *Balanced Makeup*

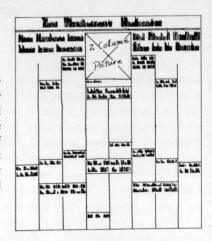

The editor strives for symmetry by balancing one side of the paper with the other. The same size and type of headlines are used above stories on corresponding sides of the page. The diagram at the right is carried to the extreme. Rarely is a page as perfectly balanced as this "dummy."

2. *Contrast and Balance*

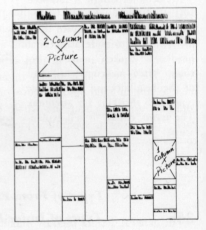

This type of makeup observes balance but not by symmetry. The object of the editor is to balance the focal points, or "black spots," on one side of the page with those on the other. In the diagram the two-column picture is placed at the left to balance the large three-column headline on the right. The two-column headline on the left at the bottom of the page would be in black type to balance the one-column picture. Altogether, one side of the page is about as "heavy" as the other.

3. Brace Makeup

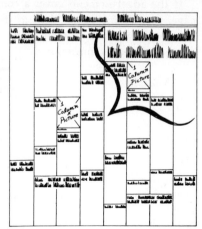

Using this type of makeup, the editor devotes his attention to the right-hand top corner of the page. One or more big stories are placed where their headlines may be seen if only that corner shows when the paper is displayed on the newsstand. In this case, the first four columns are diminished in importance, and the bottom half of the page usually contains no major stories.

4. Broken Makeup

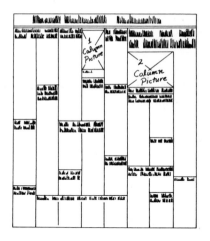

No definite pattern is followed by the editor in using the broken makeup. He tries to avoid symmetry, using a wide variety of headlines. Broken makeup becomes "circus makeup" when most of the headlines are in boldface type, each shrieking for attention. The term "circus" is self-explanatory.

35h   *Types of Inside-Page Makeup*

Since inside pages contain advertisements, the makeup editor is influenced to a large degree by the arrangement of the advertisements on each page. Obviously, he is also influenced by the material available to fill each of the pages. Hence, the following general schemes of inside-page makeup are qualified by "if's."

If the advertisements cover a comparatively small portion of the page, pyramiding to the right as they usually do, and if the editor has a wide selection of main stories carrying rather large heads, he can use a balanced makeup:

1. *Balanced*

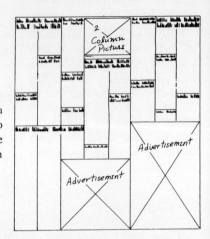

The objective here, just as in balanced front-page makeup, is to balance one side of the page against the other in building from the top down.

If the advertisements cover half the page, more or less, and if the makeup editor plans to use few stories carrying blacker-than-average heads, he could lay out a descending makeup:

2. *Descending*

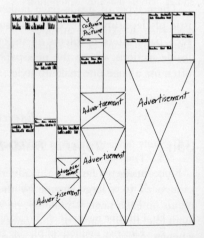

This pattern builds from the left to the right. The strongest head or a picture is placed at the left, and other heads are arranged in descending prominence toward the right.

If the advertisements cover a very large portion of the page, the makeup editor will do the best he can to "plug" the remaining space.

3. *Plugging*

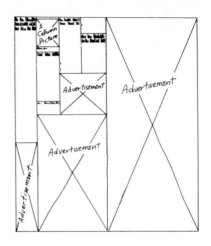

An attempt is made here to fill the little remaining space in such a manner that news can compete with advertisements in attracting the reader's eyes. Caution must be taken to avoid use of heads which are too large for the small space. On the other hand, the space should not be plugged with filler stories only.

These three types of inside-page makeup illustrate widely different problems and practices of makeup editors. The types can be combined or shuffled to result in a number of hybrids. The descending makeup is frequently used effectively on a page containing few advertisements. And certain features of both the balanced and the descending types of makeup are often combined. No stringent rules tie the hands of the makeup editor.

These types of inside-page makeup are frequently not characteristic of departmentalized pages (such as sports and society). Each such page offers problems all its own. Pages which begin separate inside sections, where the newspaper's nameplate may be repeated, often use a page-one makeup style.

Exercises

I. Study the newspapers to find examples of:
  A. Tombstoned heads.
  B. Staggered heads.
  C. Two or more large headlines which are placed so close together, that they clash with each other.
  D. Effective methods of "breaking up" long stories.
  E. Effective methods of placing several related stories.

II. Study the newspapers to find examples of different types of front-page and inside-page makeup.

III. Adding the following list of stories to the 10 in Exercise III of Chapter 34, select the stories you would place on the front page (use as many as needed) and diagram the front-page makeup you would suggest.

A. From Centerville—Governor says he will not run for reelection. Length, 10 inches.

B. From Washington—Senate enacts bill, previously enacted by House of Representatives, giving college students an additional $600 exemption on their income taxes. Length, seven inches.

C. James City (located 40 miles away)—Four men hold up city's leading bank and escape with $65,000 in cash. Thirty inches.

D. Charleston, W. Va.—Man freezes to death in ice factory. Three inches.

E. Hollywood, Calif.—Famous director announces he will retire. Three inches.

F. Washington—Government plans to build 10 new post offices, one of which will be in nearby Spring City. Ten inches.

G. Austin, Tex.—Divorced wife shoots former husband for refusing to pay alimony. Ten inches.

H. Cleveland, O.—Gangster kills two detectives. Ten inches.

I. New York—Four thousand meet to protest cut in budget for public schools. Fifteen inches.

J. Lincoln, Neb.—New traffic officer arrests city judge on speeding charge. Five inches.

General Exercises in Headlining and Makeup

On the following pages are two general exercises on editing, including selecting and writing headlines, and makeup. Each exercise contains all the stories and pictures available for use in making up one front page. Instructions for handling stories in each exercise are as follows:

1. Using the headline schedule (samples of different headlines) which follows, determine what size head each story deserves. This headline schedule includes all sizes and types of heads you may use. Each head has been given an arbitrary number (to expedite these assignments), and the maximum unit count per line is designated. Keep in mind that all of these (and only these) stories are available for the first page of a newspaper.

2. Write all headlines.

3. Make up a dummy first page using the headlines you have written. Page-sized dummies, marked off in two-inch columns, are usually available at nearby newspapers, or they may be made of wrapping paper. (Or, if

the instructor so chooses, it will be satisfactory to line off an unruled 8½ x 11-inch sheet of writing paper, which will be half-scale, every inch equal to two inches on the page-size dummy.) The page should be made up as follows:

a. Clip a flag, or nameplate, from a newspaper, and paste it in the proper place on the dummy.

b. Select the stories and pictures one by one, in the order of importance, and determine the appropriate place on the page for each. It will assist in arranging the stories to have newspaper clippings of heads similar to those in the headline schedule of this exercise, because these clippings can be laid on the dummy and will give a clear picture of the effect of the page.

c. When a final decision is reached on the position of a story, print the story's headline (which you have written) on the dummy in the space reserved for the head. The size and style of the hand-printed letters should resemble as much as possible the size and style of letters in the head schedule for this exercise.

d. In the column or columns below each head (where the story would appear if printed), measure and mark the amount of space necessary to provide for the story. If a story is continued to another page, mark the length of the portion jumped at the end of the story on page one (e.g., "5 inches jumped"). In the column space reserved for the story, write the story's guideline lengthwise of the page.

Headline Schedule: The Blankville News

Note: The schedule offers the instructor a flexible plan which can be used either for the dropline or the flush-left form of heads. It is suggested that the instructor assign the flush-left form of head for the first exercise and the dropline form for the second. Students are free to combine these heads in any series to give ample play to a story. For example, a combination of heads 1 and 3 could be used to play up the main story on the page.

Number of Head	Sample Letters and Description of Head	Size of Type	Maximum Count Per Line
1	**C** Streamer—one line deep. Roman type, all capitals. Six, seven, or eight columns wide	84 pt.	Six columns, 16 units; seven columns, 18½ units; eight columns, 22 units

Number of Head	Sample Letters and Description of Head	Size of Type	Maximum Count Per Line
1a	**_Th_** Streamer—one line deep. Italic type, capitals and lower case. Five, six, seven, or eight columns. Also can be scheduled two lines deep.	72 pt.	Five columns, 23 units; six columns, 27 units; seven columns, 32 units; eight columns, 36 units
2	**LE** Streamer—one line deep. Roman type, all caps. Five, six, seven, or eight columns.	60 pt.	Five columns, 20 units; six columns, 24 units; seven columns, 28 units; eight columns, 32 units
3	Eq Two-column head, three lines deep. Roman type, caps and lowercase	48 pt.	15 units
3a	Ze Three-column head, two lines deep. Italic type, caps and lowercase	48 pt.	22 units
4	Ch Two-column head, two lines deep. Roman type, caps and lowercase	48 pt.	15 units
4a	So Two-column head, two lines deep. Italic type, caps and lowercase	48 pt.	15 units
5	Kn One-column head, three lines deep. Roman type, caps and lowercase	36 pt.	11 units

Number of Head		Sample Letters and Description of Head	Size of Type	Maximum Count Per Line
6	**Ez**	One-column head, three lines deep. Roman type, caps and lowercase	30 pt.	14 units
6a	*Ra*	Two-column head, two lines deep. Italic type, caps and lowercase	24 pt.	31 units
7	**Lo**	One-column head, two lines deep. Roman type, caps and lowercase	24 pt.	16 units
7a	*Th*	Two-column head, two lines deep. Italic type, caps and lowercase	18 pt.	38 units
8	**FU**	One-column head, two lines deep. Roman type, all caps	18 pt.	19 units
8a	*Ba*	One-column head, two lines deep. Italic type, caps and lowercase	18 pt.	19 units
9	**T**	One-column head, one line deep. Roman type, all caps	12 pt.	23 units
10	o	One-column head, one line deep. Roman type, all caps	8 pt.	31 units

Exercises

I. Story notes appearing at the end of each preceding chapter of *The Complete Reporter* will be considered as stories in this and the second editing exercises. Since copyreading and rewriting are not involved in these exercises, it is not necessary to have the stories written as they would appear in the newspaper. And since the student's study of previous chapters has familiarized him with these story notes, he should be able to select and write suitable headlines after a quick review of each set of notes. However, if the student has retained the stories he has written from these notes, he will find them helpful.

Twenty stories have been chosen as those "available" for the front page of one edition. They are listed below by chapter and exercise number and by page number. A guideline is designated for each story. The length of the story is also listed.

Chapter and Exercise Number	Page Number	Guideline	Length in Column Inches
Ch. 17, Ex. III	227	Highway meet	3
Ch. 18, Ex. IIB	244	Mrs. Wells	1½
Ch. 19, Ex. IIA	249	Truck wreck	2½
Ch. 20, Ex. IIIB	259	Weather	2
Ch. 9, Ex. VII	141	Fairmont fire	35
Ch. 11, Ex. I	166	Termite eradicators	3
Ch. 22, Ex. IIIA	288	Circuit court	4½
Ch. 25, Ex. III	336	Riverside college	2½
Ch. 10, Ex. VI	159	Jewelry feature	5½
Ch. 23, Ex. V	310	Troll candidacy	12
Ch. 22, Ex. V	290	Murder case	18
Ch. 26, Ex. VA	353	Heart association	4
Ch. 14, Ex. IA	193	City council	15
Ch. 15, Ex. IIIB	204	Court visit	2
Ch. 19, Ex. IIC	249	Bus accident	16
Ch. 9, Ex. IXA	143	City court	5
Ch. 21, Ex. IIIC	271	Shoplifters	3
Ch. 16, Ex. III	216	Patt speech	6½
Ch. 24, Ex. IIIF	323	Sterling expansion	12
Ch. 21, Ex. IIIB	271	Body found	4

Pictures available for use if desired with stories above:
1. One-half column, 1½ inches deep, of Mrs. Wells.
2. Three column, 4¼ inches deep, of Fairmont fire.
3. One-half column, 1½ inches deep, of Sally Sewell.
4. One-half column, 1½ inches deep, of Valerie Collins.
5. One-half column, 1½ inches deep, of Mr. Troll.
6. Two column, 2½ inches deep, of murder hearing.
7. Two column, 3 inches deep, of bus accident.
8. One-half column, 1½ inches deep, of Mr. Patt.

Instructions: Indicate placement of pictures on the dummy by shading out the space which would be covered by each picture.

Note: It will, of course, be unnecessary and perhaps impossible to use all of these pictures and stories on one page. The least important will be left over when the page has been filled.

II. Follow the same instructions as for Exercise I.

Chapter and Exercise Number	Page Number	Guideline	Length in Column Inches
Ch. 10, Ex. VIIB	160	Police help	2½
Ch. 18, Ex. IIA	243	Roberts faints	1½
Ch. 21, Ex. IIIG	273	Counterfeiter	4
Ch. 25, Ex. IIID	337	Dean	3
Ch. 10, Ex. VIIC	160	Newsvendor	6
Ch. 24, Ex. IIID	322	Insurance company	3
Ch. 23, Ex. VIII	312	City election	30
Ch. 22, Ex. IIIB	288	Grand jury	5
Ch. 14, Ex. IB	194	City council	12
Ch. 21, Ex. III I	274	Suicide couple	7½
Ch. 22, Ex. VI	292	Murder case	13½
Ch. 16, Ex. V	217	Legislative committee	9½
Ch. 19, Ex. IIF	250	Church fire	15
Ch. 9, Ex. VIII	142	Tax assessor	12
Ch. 11, Ex. II	166	Termite eradicators	3½
Ch. 9, Ex. IXB	144	Plane crash	22
Ch. 19, Ex. IID	250	Salesman shot	2½
Ch. 15, Ex. IIID	205	Library books	2
Ch. 17, Ex. V	228	Press meet	9
Ch. 26, Ex. VG	354	United fund	6

Available pictures for use if desired:
1. One-half column, 1½ inches deep, of Mr. Roberts.
2. One column, 3 inches deep, of "Maggie."
3. Two column, 3 inches deep, of Mr. Miller
4. One-half column, 1½ inches deep, of Mr. Walker.
5. Two column, 3¼ inches deep, of murder hearing.
6. One-half column, 1½ inches deep, of tax assessor.
7. Two column, 3 inches deep, of plane crash.
8. One-half column, 1½ inches deep, of Mr. Cobb.

Appendix: Journalistic Terms

Ad   Advertisement.

Add   Copy to be added to a story already written.

Advance   A preliminary story concerning a future event.

Agate   Type 5½ points in depth (72 points to the inch).

A.M.   Morning paper.

Angle   The aspect of or phase emphasized in a story.

A.P. or **AP**   Associated Press, press service.

Art   All newspaper illustrations.

Assignment   Reporter's task.

Bank   (1) Part of headline (also called *deck*); (2) table upon which type is set.

Banner   A page-wide headline (also called *streamer*).

Barline   A one-line headline.

Beat   (1) The reporter's regular run; (2) an exclusive story.

Ben Day   Mechanical process used in shading engravings.

B.F. or **bf**   Boldface or black type.

Blind interview   Interview which does not give name of person interviewed.

Blurb (**Publisher's**)   A short statement issued by a publisher to promote the sale of a book.

Body type   Small type in which most of paper is set (usually 8 point).

Boil down   Reduce in size.

Boiler plate   Stereotyped or metal-plate material ready for print.

Border   Metal strips of type used to box stories, ads, etc.

Box   An enclosure of line rules or borders.

Break   (1) The point at which a story is continued to another column or page; (2) as a verb, the word refers to the time a story is available for publication.

Bromide   A trite expression.

Bulldog   The early edition of a paper.

Bulletin   A brief, last-minute news item on an important event.

Byline   The author's name at the start of a story: "By John Smith."

C. and **L.C.** or **clc**   Capital and lowercase letters.

Canned copy   Publicity material.

Caps   Capital letters.

Caption   Headline for picture or illustration.

458

Clip Newspaper clipping.

Col. Column.

Condensed type Type that is narrower than regular width.

Copy All written material.

Copypaper Paper used by newspapermen in writing stories; usually made of newsprint.

Copyreader One who edits and headlines news stories.

Correspondent Out-of-town reporter.

Cover To get the facts of a story.

Credit line Line acknowledging source of a story or picture.

Crusade Campaign of a newspaper for a certain reform.

Cub A beginning reporter.

Cut (1) A newspaper engraving; (2) to reduce the length of a story.

Cutlines Explanatory lines with a picture or illustration.

Dateline Line at the beginning of a story which includes both date and place of origin of story: "NEW YORK, Jan. 1—."

Deadline The time all copy must be completed in order to make an edition.

Deck Part of a headline.

Desk The copy desk.

Dope Advance information, sometimes rumor.

Dope story Story based on rumor or opinions.

Double truck Two adjoining pages made as one.

DPR and **NPR** "Day press rates" and "night press rates," in cost of sending telegrams.

Dummy Diagram of a page for use in making up a page.

Ear Small box in the upper corner of a page.

Edition Issue for one press run, as mail edition, home edition, extra edition.

Editorialize To include opinion of the writer in copy.

Em Unit of measuring column widths. The pica em is approximately one-sixth of an inch.

Embargo A restriction, such as the precise date and time, placed upon the release of news.

En One-half em.

Filler Short news or informational items used to fill small spaces in a page.

Flag Title of paper appearing on first page.

Flash A short message briefly summarizing a news event.

Fold Place where paper is folded.

Follow or **Follow-up** Story giving later developments of an event already written up.

Follow copy Instructions on copy to set story or word exactly as written, used often to indicate that word is purposely misspelled or that spelling is unorthodox.

Folio   Page or page number.

Folo   Short for *follow*.

Font   An assortment of type of one size and style.

Form   Page of type locked in a chase.

Fotog   Short for photographer.

Future   Memo of future event.

FYI   For your information.

Galley   Metal tray for holding type.

Galley proof   Proof made of a galley of type.

Green proof   Uncorrected proof.

Guideline   A slug line, giving title of the story for convenience of makeup editor and compositors.

Half stick   Type set a half-column in width.

Halftone   A cut taken from a photograph.

Head   Short for headline.

Headline schedule   All of the headline combinations used by a newspaper.

Hold for release   Instructions to hold copy until editor orders it printed.

HTK or **HTC**   Instructions on copy of a "head to come."

Insert   Copy that is to be inserted in a story already sent to the compositor.

Itals.   Italics.

Jump   To continue a story from one page to another.

Jump head   Headline above a continued story.

Jump lines   Lines such as "Continued on page 6" or "Continued from page 1" to identify a continued story.

Kill   To delete or exclude copy.

Layout   (1) Diagram of page (see dummy), showing where stories and ads are to be placed; (2) arrangement of pictures in order to make a cut.

L.C. or **lc**   Lowercase type.

Lead (*lĕd*)   (1) As noun, metal pieces placed between lines of type for spacing; (2) as verb, to space out page with these metal pieces.

Lead (*lēd*)   The first paragraph of a news story.

Leg man   Reporter who gathers news, phoning it in instead of going in to write it.

Letterpress printing   Process of printing which uses metal type or other raised surfaces that make a direct impression on paper.

Library   Newspaper morgue or files of clippings, photographs, prepared obituaries, biographies, etc.

Lobster shift   Working hours after a paper is sent to press. Also called the "dog watch."

Localize   To emphasize the local angle in a story.

Log   City editor's assignment book.

Make-over   Rearrangement of stories on page to provide for new copy or to change the position of stories.

Makeup   Arranging stories, pictures, ads, etc., on a page.

Masthead Editorial page heading, giving information about the newspaper.

Matrix or **Mat** A matrix or papier-mâché impression of a cut or of type.

Mill Slang for typewriter.

Minion Seven-point type.

More Used at end of a page of copy to indicate story is continued on another page.

Morgue Files for depositing clippings, pictures, etc. (also called *library*).

Mug shot Head-and-shoulders photograph of an individual.

Must Instructions that story must be used on that day without fail.

Nameplate Name of paper on page one (also called *flag*).

Newsprint The inexpensive grade of paper used in printing most newspapers.

Nonpareil Six-point type.

Obit Obituary.

Offset printing Process of printing which uses a rubber roller that takes the impression from a metal plate and transfers it to the paper.

Overline Caption above a *cut*.

Overset Type in addition to that needed to fill a paper.

Pad To make longer.

Page Opp. Page opposite the editorial page.

Pi Jumbled type.

Pica Twelve-point type; also unit of measurement, one-sixth of an inch.

Pick up Instructions to use material already set in type.

Pix Picture.

Plate A stereotyped page of type, ready to lock in the press.

Play up To emphasize.

P.M. Afternoon paper.

Point A depth measurement of type, $1/72$ inch.

Policy story A story showing directly or indirectly the newspaper's stand on an issue.

Pork Material which can be held for use as needed.

Precede Material to precede the copy already set in type.

Proof An imprint of set type used in correcting errors.

Proofreader Person who reads proof to correct errors.

Puff Editorialized, complimentary statements in a news story.

Q and A Question-and-answer copy, printed verbatim.

Quad A type character or space equal in width and height.

Query Question on an event sent by a correspondent to a paper or by a paper to a correspondent.

Quote Quotation.

Railroad To rush copy through to the compositor without careful editing.

Release Instructions on the time to publish a story, as "Release after 3 P.M. Feb. 6."

Revise Proof made after type is corrected.

Rewrite (1) To write a story again to improve; (2) to write a story which has already been written up in an opposing paper; (3) to write a story from facts given by another reporter (sometimes a leg man over the telephone).

Rim The outside edge of the copy desk (usually in horseshoe shape).

Roto Rotogravure.

Rule Metal strip used in separating columns, making borders, etc.

Run Reporter's territory or beat.

Run in Instructions to make a series of sentences, names, etc., into one paragraph, if each one of the series has been set up as a separate short paragraph or line.

Running story Story sent to compositors in sections.

Runover That part of a story which is continued on another page.

Sacred cow News or promotional material which the publisher or editor demands printed in a special manner.

Schedule List of assignments.

Scoop An exclusive story.

Second front The first page of a second section.

Sectional story A story sent to compositors in sections (also *running story*).

Sheet Slang for newspaper.

Shorts Brief stories.

Sked Schedule.

Slant To emphasize a certain phase of a news event.

Slot The place occupied by the head of the copy desk (on the inside of horseshoe-shaped desks).

Slug (1) The guideline at the beginning of the story, to make it easy to identify (see "guideline"); (2) a strip of metal, less than type high and used to space between lines; (3) a line of type cast by the typesetting machine.

Soc Society.

Squib A brief story.

Stet Restore text of copy which has been marked out. (This is a copyreader's and proofreader's sign.)

Stick (1) A measuring unit for type—about two inches; (2) a small amount of type, about 100 words.

Stone A table, sometimes stone-topped, upon which a page of type is assembled.

Streamer Eight-column headline (*also banner*).

String Newspaper clippings pasted together.

Subhead Small, one-line headline used in the body of a story.

Take A section of a running story.

Thirty The end of a story (numeral usually used).

Tie back or **Tie in** That part of the story which reiterates past events in order to refresh the reader's mind in giving latest developments.

Time copy   Copy which might be held over and used when needed.

Top heads   Headline at top of a column.

Tr.   Transpose or change the position of.

Trim   Reduce length of story.

Turn rule   Instruction for printer to turn a column-wide rule or slug upside down to indicate the need of an insert, correction, etc.

U.C. and L.C.   Uppercase and lowercase type.

U.P.I. or UPI   United Press International, press service.

Wrong font or W.F.   Wrong style or size of type.

Selected Bibliography

The Journalistic Profession

(History of Journalism; Biographies of Famous Journalists, Journalistic
Vocations)

Barrett, J. W. *Joseph Pulitzer and His World*. New York: Vanguard, 1941.

Berger, M. *The Story of the New York Times*. New York: Simon and
Schuster, 1951.

Bleyer, W. G. *Main Currents in the History of American Journalism*.
Boston: Houghton, 1927.

Brucker, H. *Eyewitness to History*. New York: Macmillan, 1962.

Buranelli, V., (ed.). *The Trial of Peter Zenger*. New York University
Press. 1957.

Canham, E. D. *Commitment to Freedom: The Story of the Christian
Science Monitor*. Boston: Houghton, 1958.

Carlson, O. *The Man Who Made News: James Gordon Bennett*. New
York: Duell, Sloan & Pearce, 1942.

Cochran, N. D. *E. W. Scripps*. New York: Harcourt, 1933.

Emery, E. *The Press and America*. Englewood Cliffs, N.J.: Prentice-Hall,
1962.

Gramling, O. *AP: The Story of News*. New York: Farrar, 1940.

Johnson, G. W. *An Honorable Titan: A Biographical Study of Adolph S.
Ochs*. New York: Harper, 1946.

Johnson, I. F. *William Rockhill Nelson and the Kansas City Star*. Kansas
City: Burton, 1935.

Kaltenborn, H. V. *Fifty Fabulous Years, 1900–1950*. New York: Putnam.
1950.

Lee, A. M. *The Daily Newsaper in America*. New York: Macmillan. 1937.

Morris, J. A. *Deadline Every Minute*. Garden City, N.Y.: Doubleday, 1957.

Mott, F. L. *American Journalism: A History of Newspapers in the United
States through 270 Years, 1690–1960*. New York: Macmillan, 1962.

Nixon, R. B. *Henry W. Grady: Spokesman of the New South*. New York:
Knopf, 1943.

Peterson, T. *Magazines in the Twentieth Century*. Evanston: University
of Illinois Press, 1956.

Ross, I. *Ladies of the Press*. New York: Harper, 1936.

Ryan, L. E., and Bernard. *So You Want To Go Into Journalism*. New
York; Harper & Row, 1963.

Schaleben, A. *Your Future in Journalism.* New York: Richard Rosen Press, 1961.

Shuler, M. B., R. A. Knight, and M. Fuller. *Lady Editor: Careers for Women in Journalism.* New York: Dutton, 1941.

Starr, L. M. *Bohemian Brigade: Civil War Newsmen in Action.* New York: Knopf, 1954.

Stone, C. *Dana and the Sun.* New York: Dodd, Mead, 1938.

Tebbel, J. *The Life and Good Times of William Randolph Hearst.* New York: Dutton. 1952.

Van Deusen, G. G. *Horace Greeley: Nineteenth Century Crusader.* Philadelphia: University of Pennsylvania Press, 1953.

Van Doren, C. *Benjamin Franklin.* New York: Viking, 1938.

White, W. A. *The Autobiography of William Allen White.* New York: Macmillan, 1946.

Williamson, S. T. *Imprint of a Publisher: The Story of Frank Gannett and His Independent Newspapers.* New York: McBride, 1948.

Wolseley, R. E., and L. R. Campbell, *Exploring Journalism.* Englewood Cliffs, N.J.: Prentice-Hall, 1957.

Journalism and Society

(Freedom of the Press, Journalistic Ethics, Legal Aspects of Journalism, Public Opinion and Propaganda)

Albig, W. *Modern Public Opinion.* New York: McGraw-Hill, 1956.

Ashley, P. P. *Say It Safely.* Seattle: University of Washington Press, 1956.

Bird, G. L. and F. E. Merwin (eds.). *The Press and Society.* Englewood Cliffs, N.J.: Prentice-Hall, 1951.

Bogart, L. *The Age of Television.* New York: Ungar, 1956.

Brucker, H. *Freedom of Information.* New York: Macmillan, 1949.

Commission on Freedom of the Press. *A Free and Responsible Press.* Chicago: University of Chicago Press, 1947.

Cross, H. L. *The People's Right to Know: Legal Access to Public Records and Proceedings.* New York: Columbia University Press, 1953.

Gerald, J. E. *The Social Responsibilities of the Press.* Minneapolis: University of Minnesota Press, 1963.

Katz, E., and P. F. Lazarsfeld. *Personal Influence: The Part Played by People in the Flow of Mass Communications.* New York: Free Press, 1955.

Lee, A. W. *How to Understand Propaganda.* New York: Holt, 1952.

MacDougall, C. D. *Understanding Public Opinion.* New York: Macmillan, 1952.

Mott, F. L. *The News in America.* Cambridge, Mass.: Harvard University Press, 1952.

Nafziger, R. O., and D. M. White (eds.). *Introduction to Mass Communications Research.* Baton Rouge: Louisiana State University Press, 1958.

Powell, N. *Anatomy of Public Opinion*. Englewood Cliffs, N.J.: Prentice-Hall, 1951.

Schramm, W. *Responsibility in Mass Communication*. New York: Harper, 1957.

Siepmann, C. A. *Radio, Television, and Society*. New York: Oxford University Press, 1950.

Spring, S. *Risks and Rights in Publishing, Television, Radio, Motion Pictures, Advertising, and the Theatre*. New York: Norton, 1956.

Thayer, F. *Legal Control of the Press*. Brooklyn, N.Y.: Foundation Press, 1962.

General References on Journalistic Writing

Abbott, W., and R. L. Rider. *Handbook of Broadcasting*. New York: McGraw-Hill, 1957.

Bernstein, T. W. *Watch Your Language*. Manhasset, N.Y.: Channel Press, 1958.

Bush, C. R. *The Art of News Communication*. New York: Appleton, 1954.

Callihan, E. I. *Grammar for Journalists*. New York: Ronald, 1957.

Flesch, R. *The Art of Readable Writing*. New York: Harper, 1949.

Hyde, G. M. *Newspaper Handbook*. New York: Appleton, 1941.

MacDougall, C. D. *Interpretative Reporting*. New York: Macmillan, 1957.

Mott, G. F. (ed.). *New Survey of Journalism*. New York: Barnes & Noble, 1959.

Public Relations Handbook. Englewood Cliffs, N.J.: Prentice-Hall, 1950.

References on Special Types of Journalistic Writing

Bailey, R. *Techniques in Article Writing*. New York: Appleton, 1947.

Baird, R. N., and A. T. Turnbull. *Industrial and Business Journalism*. Philadelphia: Chilton, 1961.

Bird, G. L. *Article Writing and Marketing*. New York: Holt, 1956.

Byerly, K. *Community Journalism*. Philadelphia: Chilton, 1961.

Columbia Broadcasting System Staff. *Television News Reporting*. New York: McGraw-Hill, 1958.

Charnley, M. V. *News by Radio*. New York: Macmillan, 1948.

Chester, G., and G. R. Garrison. *Radio and Television: An Introduction*. New York: Appleton. 1956.

Costa, J., (ed.). *Complete Book of Press Photography*. New York: National Press Photographers Association. 1950.

Cutlip, S. M., and A. H. Center. *Effective Public Relations*. Englewood Cliffs, N.J.: Prentice-Hall, 1958.

Danilov, V. J. *Public Affairs Reporting*. New York: Macmillan, 1955.

Davis, H. W. *The Column*. New York: Knopf, 1926.

Fine, B. *Educational Publicity*. New York: Harper, 1951.

Foster, J. *Science Writer's Guide.* New York: Columbia University Press, 1963.

Fox, R. *Agricultural and Technical Journalism.* Englewood Cliffs, N.J.: Prentice-Hall, 1952.

Heath, H. and L. Gelfand. *How to Cover, Write, and Edit Sports.* Ames: Iowa State University Press, 1957.

Hicks, W. *Words and Pictures: An Introduction to Photo-Journalism.* New York: Harper, 1952.

Hilliard, R. L. *Writing for. Television and Radio.* New York: Hastings House, 1962.

Jones, L. *How To Criticize Books.* New York: Norton. 1928.

MacDougall, C. D. *Covering the Courts.* Englewood Cliffs, N.J.: Prentice-Hall. 1946.

Patterson, H. M. *Writing and Selling Feature Articles.* Englewood Cliffs, N.J.: Prentice-Hall, 1956.

Reddick, D. C., and A. A. Crowell. *Industrial Editing.* New York: Bender, 1962.

Stabler, N. C. *How To Read the Financial News.* New York: Harper, 1951.

Waldrop, A. G. *Editor and Editorial Writer.* New York: Holt, 1955.

Weil, B. H., (ed.). *Technical Editing.* New York: Reinhold, 1958.

Wolseley, R. E. *Interpreting the Church through Press and Radio.* Philadelphia: Muhlenberg, 1951.

————. *The Magazine World: An Introduction to Magazine Journalism.* Englewood Cliffs, N.J.: Prentice-Hall, 1951.

References on Editing the News

Allen, J. E. *Newspaper Designing.* New York: Harper, 1947.

Arnold, E. C. *Functional Newspaper Design.* New York: Harper. 1956.

Bastain, G. C., L. D. Case, and F. K. Baskette. *Editing the Day's News.* New York: Macmillan, 1956.

Kalish, S. E., and C. C. Edom. *Picture Editing.* New York: Rinehart, 1951.

Sutton, A. A. *Design and Makeup of the Newspaper.* Englewood Cliff, N.J.: Prentice-Hall, 1948.

Taylor, H. B., and J. Scher. *Copy Reading and News Editing.* Englewood Cliffs, N.J.: Prentice-Hall, 1951.

Index

SIMPLE STORY TYPES

(Note: in many cases "story" has been abbreviated as "Sy." on this page.)

Illness, Deaths, Funerals	18a Contents, Illness, Sy.	18b Illness Features	18c Obituary	18d Death Story	18e Contents, Death Sy.	18f Objectiveness
	18g Contents, Funeral Sy.					
Fires, Accidents	19a Story Contents	19b Features F. & A.	19c Story Forms	19d Fact Reporting		
Seasons, Weather	20a Writing Seasonal Sy.	20b Contents, Seasonal Sy.	20c Routine Weather Sy.	20d Writing Weather Sy.	20e Contents, Weather Sy.	
Crime	21a Stating Charges	21b Contents, Crime Sy.	21c Features, Crime Sy.	21d Policies, Suicides	21e Contents, Suicide Sy.	21f Suicide Features

COMPLEX STORY TYPES

Courts, Trials	22a Trial Features	22b Body of Trial Sy.	22c Q. & A. Forms	22d Interpreting Trials		
Government, Politics	23a Interpreting Government	23b Reporting Government	23c Covering Election	23d Interpreting Politics		
Business, Industry, Agriculture, Labor	24a Free Advertising	24b Story Forms	24c Simplifying Statistics	24d Technical Terms	24e Covering Business	24f Covering Industry
	24g Covering Agriculture	24h Covering Labor	24i Interpreting Economics			
Education, Research	25a Covering Education	25b Education Sy. Forms	25c Covering Research	25d Interpreting Research	25e Research Sy. Forms	
Religion, Philanthropy	26a Religion Section	26b Interpreting Religion	26c Promoting Philanthropy			

SPECIAL STORY TYPES

Women's Section	27a Stereotyped Stories	27b Lead Features	27c Writing Style			
Sports	28a Interpreting Sports	28b Gambling in Sports	28c Sports Language	28d Sports Leads	28e Body of Sports Sy.	
Literature, Fine Arts, Criticism	29a Reviewing vs. Criticism	29b Criticism Principles	29c Writing Style	29d Books & Articles	29e Movies, Radio, TV	29f Live Performances
	29g Art					
Editorials and Columns	30a Letters to Editor	30b Timeliness of Editorials	30c Types of Editorials	30d Explaining Events	30e Appraising Events	30f Editorial Headlines
	30g Concluding Paragraph	30h Substance of Columns	30i Writing Interestingly	30j Style of Columnists		